D0242897

EDUCATION AND SOCIAL CHANGE

Also available from Continuum

Children and Social Change, Dorothy Moss

Education and Community, Dianne Gereluk

Educational Attainment and Society, Nigel Kettley

Education, Democracy and Discourse, Knud Jensen & Stephen Walker

Education, Policy and Social Justice, James Avis

Educational Practice and Society, Nigel Kettley

Higher Education and the Public Good, Jon Nixon

Values in Education, Graham Haydon

Education and Social Change

Connecting local and global perspectives

Edited by

Geoffrey Elliott, Chahid Fourali and Sally Issler

LIS LIBRARY

Date	Fund
06/12/12	

Order No

University of Chester

continuum

Continuum International Publishing Group
The Tower Building, 11 York Road, London SE1 7NX
80 Maiden Lane, Suite 704, New York NY 10038

www.continuumbooks.com

© Geoffrey Elliott, Chahid Fourali, Sally Issler and Contributors 2010

First published 2010
Paperback edition first published 2012

All rights reserved. No part of this publication may be reproduced or
transmitted in any form or by any means, electronic or mechanical,
including photocopying, recording, or any information storage or retrieval
system, without prior permission in writing from the publishers.

Geoffrey Elliott, Chahid Fourali and Sally Issler have asserted their rights
under the Copyright, Designs and Patents Act, 1988, to be identified as
Authors of this work.

British Library Cataloguing-in-Publication Data
A catalogue record for this book is available from the British Library.

ISBN: 978-0-8264-4409-7 (hardcover)
      978-1-4411-3698-5 (paperback)

Library of Congress Cataloging-in-Publication Data
Education and social change: connecting local and
global perspectives / edited by Geoffrey Elliott, Chahid Fourali and
Sally Issler.
      p. cm.
  Includes bibliographical references and index.
  ISBN 978-1-4411-3698-5 – ISBN 978-0-8264-4409-7 –
ISBN 978-1-4411-7202-0 – ISBN 978-1-4411-5796-6 1. Education–Social
aspects–Cross-cultural studies. 2. Social change–Cross-cultural studies.
3. Education and globalization–Cross-cultural studies. I. Elliott,
Geoffrey, Dr. II. Fourali, Chahid. III. Issler, Sally.

  LC192.E38 2012
  306.43'2–dc23   2011048170

Typeset by Pindar NZ, Auckland, New Zealand
Printed and bound in Great Britain

Contents

Tables and Figures

Tables

Figures

Photo

From Geoffrey, for Joe, Sam and students worldwide.

From Chahid, for Samih, Nour and the wider family (local and global).

From Sally, for family and friends and in addition fellow community workers and researchers who make this kind of work possible.

Acknowledgements

The authors would like to acknowledge and thank the following for their contributions to this book:

Sam Elliott, for his expert and timely assistance with proofreading.

Elizabeth Pelka, for her expert advice and suport on social marketing issues.

Alison Williamson of Burgess Pre-Publishing, for her expertise and excellence in text preparation and indexing.

Notes on the contributors

Kwame Akyeampong is a senior lecturer and Deputy Director at the Centre for International Education (CIE) at the School of Education and Social Work (ESW), University of Sussex. Prior to joining Sussex, he was Director of the Institute of Education, University of Cape Coast in Ghana. His research has focused on basic and post-basic education provision and teacher education in sub-Saharan Africa (SSA). His most recent publications have been on educational access issues in Ghana, teacher education policy and practice, vocationalization of secondary education, and issues on multimedia technologies in education reform in Africa. He is a co-author of the book, *Key Issues in Teacher Education: A Sourcebook for Teacher Educators* (2009). He has recently won, with two colleagues at the CIE, a recent grant from the William and Flora Hewlett Foundation, USA, to research Teacher Preparation and Continuing Professional Development in six African countries.

Vanessa Andreotti is a senior lecturer at the School of Maori, Social and Cultural Studies in Education at the University of Canterbury, New Zealand. Her research focuses on building bridges between contemporary debates in cultural and postcolonial studies and pedagogical practices. She is involved in various research-based international collaborative projects related to the creation of theory-informed strategies and methodologies for the introduction of global issues and perspectives in multiple educational contexts.

John Annette is Professor of Citizenship and Lifelong Learning, Pro Vice-Master for Lifelong Learning and Engagement at Birkbeck College, University of London, UK, and Chair of the International Centre for Education for Democratic Citizenship, which is a joint research centre with the Institute of Education. With Dr Dina Kiwan, he recently secured an ESRC Research Seminar on diversity, nationality and citizenship education. He is an advisor to the Department for Children, Families and Schools on youth volunteering and citizenship education, also the Department for Communities and Local Government on capacity-building for citizenship and community development. John has written a number of books and articles on citizenship, community involvement and diversity. A special issue of his work was published in 2008 by the London Review of Education, *Diversity and Citizenship Education* (2008).

After a chemistry degree, **David Bainton** taught high school science in state schools in Zimbabwe, Bhutan and England. These experiences have framed his core research agenda – the challenge to understand the interface between Western models of schooling and indigenous knowledge as they articulate within shifting social and economic practices associated with development and globalization. His doctoral thesis from the University of Bristol, UK, 'Suffering development: Western education and indigenous knowledge in Ladakh', took a critical narrative approach to explore an indigenous perspective on educational practices. After carrying out postdoctoral work at the University of Bristol, he is currently a research fellow at the European University Institute in Florence, Italy.

Douglas Bourn is Director of the Development Education Research Centre at the Institute of Education, University of London, UK. The Centre acts as the knowledge hub for development education and related themes and is responsible for a range of research and consultancy projects on themes such as students as global citizens, global learning for global colleges and global dimension to education. He is editor of the *International Journal of Development Education and Global Learning*. His most recent publications are *Development Education: Debates and dialogues* (2008) and *Global Skills* (2008). He has also had numerous articles published on themes such as global citizenship, sustainable development education and building understanding of international development. From 1993 to 2006 he was Director of the Development Education Association and has been an advisor to the UK Government on development awareness, global citizenship and sustainable development education. He is also Chair of Earth Charter UK.

Val Chapman is Director of the Centre for Inclusive Learning Support at the University of Worcester, UK. In 2004 she was awarded a National Teaching Fellowship for her work on Disability and Inclusion in Higher Education and the following year the Centre was accepted as a partner in the LearnHigher Centre for Excellence in Teaching and Learning. From 2006 to 2007 she held a UNESCO funded Chair in Special Education at Qatar University. Dr Chapman has published widely, and has presented at conferences in South Africa, Australia, Qatar, Israel, Canada, Greece, West Germany, Belgium, Spain and Poland.

Michael Crossley is Professor of Comparative and International Education, Joint Director of the Research Centre for International and Comparative Studies at the Graduate School of Education, and Director of the Education in Small States Research Group (www.smallstates.net), University of Bristol, UK. He has been the editor of the journal *Comparative Education* since 2004, and was Chair of the British Association for International and Comparative

Education (BAICE) from 2002 to 2004. Professor Crossley has published widely in the field and undertaken teaching, research and consultancy work in numerous countries worldwide. Major research interests relate to: theoretical and methodological scholarship on the future of comparative and international education; research and evaluation capacity and international development co-operation; and educational development in small states. He is an Academician (AcSS) of the British Academy for the Social Sciences.

Máiréad Dunne's research interests are in social and cultural studies of education focused on identities, equity, institutional processes and educational mobility with respect to gender, sexuality, ethnicity and social class/poverty. She has contributed to scholarship around educational policy and practice in a wide range of national contexts. Her writing has attracted several excellence awards and she won a teaching award at the University of Sussex, UK, where she founded the International Professional Doctorate in Education. Her most recent publication is *Gender as an Entry Point for Addressing Social Exclusion and Multiple Disparities in Education* (2009), available at www.ungei. org/ny2009/docs.

Geoffrey Elliott is Professor of Lifelong Learning and Director of Regional Engagement at the University of Worcester, UK. He has taught in schools, further and adult education, and has previously taught at the University of East London and the Open University. He has published widely in post-compulsory education, and since 1999 has been Chair of the Further Education Research Association (FERA). He is founding Editor of the international peer refereed journal *Research in Post-Compulsory Education* published by Taylor & Francis, and has recently authored a textbook (with Carol Costley and Paul Gibbs): *Doing Work Based Research: Approaches to enquiry for insider-researchers* (2010). He is married with two grown-up sons, and lives in Bewdley, Worcestershire.

Lynn Fee works in a large health and social care Trust within Northern Ireland, with responsibility for post-registration education for registered nurses and midwives and the development of unregistered nursing support workers. She completed a Post-Graduate Certificate in Professional Education before undertaking a Masters degree in work-based learning through the School of Education at Queen's University Belfast, UK. Her primary areas of interest are work-based learning, inter-professional learning and continuing professional development. When not at work, she spends time with her three teenage boys, and enjoys watching football and swimming.

Siobhán Fitzpatrick, Chief Executive of Early Years – the Organization for Young Children, has been in post since 1989, having worked previously for the statutory sector within Health and Social Services in Northern Ireland. Early Years is the largest group-based early years organization working in Northern Ireland, currently with a thousand member groups including playgroups, parent and toddler groups, day care groups and after school provision. She is the European representative on the World Forum Foundation for Early Years Care and Education and President Elect of ISSA, the International Step by Step Association for Eastern Europe and the former CIS countries. She acts as Chief Executive of High/Scope Ireland and chairs an all-Ireland Cross Border Project Management Group with the Border Counties Childcare Network which is implementing a Cross Border Early Years Management and Leadership programme, a Special Needs programme for early years staff and a Respecting Difference Programme. She is married with three grown-up daughters.

Chahid Fourali has been Head of the UK Marketing and Sales Standards Setting Body for the past eight years. He previously headed the quality assurance and curriculum development division at the Chartered Institute of Marketing and, before that, was Senior Research Officer at the City and Guilds of London Institute. He is a trustee or non-executive director to several organizations in the UK and abroad including his native Algeria. He has published many works on education, psychology and marketing and presented his work both in the UK and abroad. Dr Fourali is a Fellow of the Royal Society of Arts, Manufactures and Commerce, a Fellow of the Chartered Institute of Marketing and is an approved psychotherapist of the British Association of Behavioural and Cognitive Psychotherapy.

Peter Hubert is Head of the Faculty of Art, IT and Media at Highlands College in Jersey. His MBA in educational management kindled an interest in leadership research which he has pursued through a series of practitioner research projects in collaboration with Professor Edward Sallis. Their project for the Learning and Skills Improvement Service on the impact of solutions-focused coaching on the culture of colleges was Highly Commended in the 2008 Association of Colleges' Beacon Awards and with it they jointly won the 2009 LSIS Research Prize. During his time at Highlands College he has led the development of a Foundation Degree in Art and Design and been instrumental in establishing a research culture in the College.

Sally Issler is an independent education research consultant specializing in development and community education. She is an adviser to the DEA (Development Education Association) and Sustainability and Environmental Education (SEEd). She is a member of the Further Education Research Association (FERA) and a member of the editorial advisory board of its journal, *Research in Post-Compulsory Education*. Originally a secondary education teacher, Dr Issler worked on cultural exchange programmes for the United States Information Service and then as a Senior Research Officer at the City and Guilds of London Institute.

Gary Jones is Deputy Principal at Highlands College, Jersey. He has as background in educational management, having gained an EdD at the University of Bristol where his doctoral thesis focused on school development planning in the primary schools of a small state. He has also undertaken work on the development of a solutions focused performance management system which is now being used across many Jersey primary and secondary schools. In 2000 Dr Jones received the National Information and Learning Technologies Association Award for his outstanding leadership contribution to information and learning technologies in further education in the UK.

Alireza Kiamanesh is a retired Professor of Research Methods and Evaluation at Tarbiyat Moallem University of Tehran, Iran. His areas of interest are educational evaluation, student assessment and mathematics and science education. He has taught at different levels of education from elementary school to PhD level. He has worked with the International Association for the Evaluation of Educational Achievement (IEA) as the national research coordinator of Iran from 1994 to -2001. He has worked with UNICEF and UNFPA offices in Iran for evaluating different projects and is now teaching in the Islamic Azad University, Science and Research Branch in Tehran.

Simone Kirpal is an economist and social scientist. Her research interests include international comparisons of labour markets and training systems; skills development and learning; and careers and work identity. As senior research fellow of the Institute of Technology and Education of the University of Bremen, Germany, she has been managing European research and development projects for the past eight years with a recent focus on teachers and trainers in vocational education and training. Recently she moved to the Centre of Social Policy Research of the University of Bremen as senior lecturer and research fellow, shifting her focus to international labour studies, gender issues and the welfare state. Before joining the University of Bremen in 2001 she worked for two years as Education Specialist for the Human Development Network of the World Bank.

Ning Rong Liu is Associate Professor at the University of Hong Kong. He is also Associate Head of College of Humanities and Law in the School of Professional and Continuing Education at the University of Hong Kong. He received his Bachelor's degree from Nankai University, China, his Master's degree from Indiana University, USA, and his doctorate degree from the University of Bristol, UK. Before joining HKU SPACE, he served as Assistant

Director at HKU's Centre for Journalism and Media Studies. He has strong interest in marketization and decentralization of higher education and has published in the field of marketization of adult and continuing education in China, in international journals such as *International Journal of Educational Development, Journal of Further and Higher Education,* and *Research in Post-Compulsory Education.*

A native of South Wales, **Francis Murphy** is a lecturer in Mechanical Engineering at Cork Institute of Technology in Ireland. He is a graduate of the Institution of Mechanical Engineers and is a Chartered Engineer (Institution of Gas Engineers, 1972). His research interest in engineering education led him to complete a postgraduate diploma in Engineering Management (Institution of Mechanical Engineers, 1992), a Master of Science degree in Training (University of Leicester, 1996) and a Doctorate in Education (Open University 2005). Dr Murphy lives with his wife of twenty-one years in County Cork, continuing to teach engineering at Cork Institute of Technology and occasionally publishing the results of his research into course effectiveness.

Elda Nikolou-Walker was born and raised in Athens, Greece. She graduated from Birkbeck College, University of London in 1993, and obtained her Masters in Education at Queen's University Belfast in 1997. Elda has held the post of Tutor Organizer for BELB in the Workers' Educational Association, and currently is a senior teaching Fellow and Head of Work-Based Learning in the School of Education at Queen's University Belfast, Northern Ireland. She has published extensively on work-based learning and her latest publication is *The Expanded University; Work-Based Learning and the Economy* (2008).

Edward Sallis is Principal and Chief Executive of Highlands College in Jersey. He is the author of six books, including *Total Quality Management in Education* (2003) and, with Gary Jones, *Knowledge Management in Education* (2002), as well as a large number of articles and conference papers. In 2004 he was awarded a British Academy research grant to map higher education developments in small states, which led to the establishment of a University Centre at Highlands College. He has undertaken a number of practitioner research projects, including one with the Learning and Skills Improvement Service on the impact of solutions-focused coaching on the culture of colleges which was Highly Commended in the 2008 Association of Colleges' Beacon Awards and with which he and Peter Hubert jointly won the 2009 LSIS Research Prize. Professor Sallis is a former Trustee of the Centre for Excellence in Leadership and a Visiting Professor in the Partner College Faculty of the University of Plymouth. He was awarded the OBE for services to Education in the 2010 New Years Honours List.

Carla Solvason's interest in the concepts of inclusion and educational equality emerges from a background of teaching in schools in socially deprived areas. During a decade of teaching neglected children who struggled to overcome deficiencies in their upbringing, she began to question whether it was ever possible to provide an equal education for all. Other areas of interest have included concepts of gender (the focus of her Masters) and changing cultures (the focus of her PhD). After a period of time as a consultant supporting schools in providing for children with communication difficulties, Dr Solvason now lectures in the Centre for Early Childhood at the University of Worcester.

Andy Smith is Professor of Management and Pro Vice-Chancellor (Schools and Programs) at the University of Ballarat, Victoria, Australia. He was formerly Head of the School of Commerce at Charles Sturt University in New South Wales and from 1999 to 2002 General Manager, Research and Evaluation at the National Centre for Vocational Education Research (NCVER). His particular area of expertise is employer and enterprise training in Australia and he has conducted a large number of national research projects in this area over the last fifteen years. He also has substantial experience as a training and human resource manager in industry. Before embarking on an academic career, he held a number of positions in the area of human resource development and organizational change in the UK aerospace and automotive industries. He is the author of numerous articles on aspects of employer training and of *Training and Development in Australia (1998)*.

Erica Smith is Dean of Graduate Studies and Professor of Education at the University of Ballarat, Victoria, Australia. She has published widely, mainly in the areas of competency-based training, apprenticeships, workplace training, training policy and vocational education and training (VET) teachers. She has also undertaken extensive research and publication on part-time working by school and university students. Dr Smith has a particular interest in undertaking research that challenges traditional notions of the nature of skill. Before becoming an academic in 1993, she was a personnel manager in the retail industry, a further education teacher and community worker. In periods of leave without pay and secondment, she has had recent experience in the VET sector as Executive Director of a State Sector Skills Council and as a training provider manager. She is currently President of the Australian Vocational Education and Training Research Association (AVETRA) and Co-Chair of the international research network on apprenticeships (INAP).

Manuel Souto-Otero is Lecturer in Education Policy at the University of Bath. Before this, he acted as a policy consultant, directing a framework contract for the evaluation of the European Commission programmes in education and training. He has published in the areas of education policy, policy evaluation and internationalization in education. He obtained his DPhil. in Social Policy from the University of Oxford.

James Stanfield is based at the E.G. West Centre, School of Education, University of Newcastle, UK, a research centre which is dedicated to developing a better understanding of the role of choice, competition and entrepreneurship in helping to achieve education for all. He has recently completed his PhD on the subject of the right to education and the growth of private schools for the poor in Kenya.

Maryam Danaye Tousi is an Assistant Professor of Linguistics at the University of Guilan (Iran). Her research interests include cognitive aspects of reading behaviour and policy making in national language education. She has worked with the Research Institution of Curriculum Development and Educational Innovations, Ministry of Education, since 2001. She now teaches research methods and reading in the English Department at the University of Guilan.

George K. Zarifis is a lecturer in Continuing Education in the Department of Education (School of Philosophy and Education, Faculty of Philosophy) of the Aristotle University of Thessaloniki in Greece. His area of expertise is continuing education, with a specific interest in the development of educational methodologies for accommodating adult learning. His research focuses on the study of adult participation in organized educational and training activities, and the comparative examination of NVAE, VET and CPD policies and practices in Europe. He is the convener of the ESREA Research Network on Adult Educators, Trainers and their Professional Development (ReNAdET).

Introduction

This book was conceived through informal discussions between the editors, who are connected through friendship, shared academic and political interests, and joint membership of the Management Board of the UK Further Education Research Association (www.fera.uk.net). We share an abiding care and concern regarding the effectiveness of current educational theory and practice in inducing changes to promote a healthier, more responsible and inclusive society. We have all been involved in educational initiatives with the aim of effecting change in society. In particular we have either been involved in work to enable disenfranchised learners to gain support from more effective programmes of education or have been working on programmes to support widening participation and help create the conditions for developing education into a real tool for change.

As argued by many educationists, education can either be part of the solution or the problem to world issues. If it wants to be part of the solution, education has to find ways of addressing real social issues and help the learner face new and future challenges with an attitude that values inclusiveness and sustainability and, ultimately, values the individual, society, humanity and the environment at large. Many researchers have argued in the past that Western society, despite its advances, has yet to address the undue focus on individual benefits at the exclusion of local or global community. The approach adopted here is to help re-establish the balance and adopt a global perspective that is at the same time sensitive to local needs.

Our early discussions soon crystallized into a programme for a book and, as they say, the rest is history. In the next pages we will outline the importance of this project, and the themes by which we have structured this book, as well as taking into account our reservations and issues that are yet to be addressed.

Why the topic is important

Education policy and practice has always been developed within the context of the nation state (the local). However, the interconnections made available by globalization, including pressures imposed on policy makers by the World Bank and the IMF, the entry of students from a variety of cultural backgrounds, media globalization, and the availability of the internet, have prompted educationalists to review their practice in the light of international influences (the global).

The increasing importance of global issues such as global warming, national and international conflicts and depletion of earth resources have also contributed to an increase in awareness of the role of education in playing its part in helping resolve these issues.

This book takes this one step further by investigating the potential for the creation of a transnational value system in education and focusing the attention of policymakers on some key human rights issues, both at home and overseas. We claim that it does this by setting up a genuine dialogue between practitioners, with the ultimate objective of using mutual learning to enrich the quality of discourse through better knowledge of and respect for 'the other'.

The text is problem-based and focuses on 'how' education can bring about social change, since application is an important consideration for the book's principal readership of policy makers, NGOs, support volunteers, students, researchers, teachers and lecturers. The book will connect with theory at the level of cultural impact and policy implications.

The work is not only truly international in scope, but also directly addresses restrictions on freedom of communication experienced by academics and practitioners in developing countries. There are a number of books that recognize the importance of globalization on learning and educational institutions (e.g. Lauder et al., 2006, pp.i–xxvii, 1182; Gundara, 2000). However, this book goes one stage further by providing the opportunity for educational research practitioners to engage in active dialogue to develop transnational values in relation to knowledge production and educational reform, particularly in connection with the promotion of human rights in education in a global age. The book also brings together and adopts a 'hands on' approach to several key challenges in education that require procedural as well as theoretical understanding. In this way the book should benefit both practitioners as well as academics.

Connecting the local with the global has become of paramount interest in a number of fields such as the environment and the economy. In education, both policy makers and practitioners seek solutions from educational researchers to problems arising from globalization. We anticipate this book will resonate with those who are beginning to realize the contribution to social change that could be made by this developing field of educational research. By the very nature of the problems addressed in the book, its perspective is also multidisciplinary as the authors tend to capitalize on any findings that contribute to inducing social change. This makes it a fresh way of addressing educational challenges as it is global, multidisciplinary and practically orientated at the same time.

Aims and values of education

Clearly, the issue of values and ethics is a complex one (see LaFollette, 2007; Frey and Wellman, 2005) and there is an argument that could be made along the lines of: 'if we are going to half bake this issue then we may as well not address it at all'.

From a psychological perspective, part of the reason why it is never easy to discuss values is that they are the very foundation of our ways of acting, feeling and seeing the world. A more social dimension is that any view we may venture to advance could constitute a de facto self-categorization in a world where there is a strong tendency to understand primarily through categories of inclusion or exclusion. One of the authors realized long ago that in many cases there is no right or wrong answer or, in many cases, it is both 'right and wrong' (Fourali, 1997). One of the authors has extensively critiqued many UK Government reforms in post-compulsory education which, no matter how well intentioned, 'have been misguided in intention and contradictory in outcome' (Elliott, 1996, p. 1). This is what encourages us to strive harder to get a consensus that perceives the nuances, to help us move closer to a fairer world. There are several views on what constitutes 'right and wrong', all clamouring for attention and, as some writers put it in this book, 'hegemony'. The position in this book is that all views can aid insight and understanding. 'How can I learn from this?' is a question to which there is no final answer, according to many of our contributors who have an underpinning lifelong learning perspective on education and social change.

Our working assumption in compiling this book is that there is a universal right of access to education (Howe, 1999; UNESCO/UNICEF, 2007; Stanfield, this volume) which is usually associated closely with the value of 'fairness'. This issue is closely linked to the global versus local dimension and tackling it, even very briefly, gives a clue to the complexity of issues addressed in this book. The principle for equality of educational opportunity has traditionally been addressed in terms of the question: 'how much equality of provision is enough for a responsible society?' One view argues that, as long as individuals are afforded equal opportunities to obtain an education, inequalities in educational results are morally acceptable (Howe, 1999). A non-interventionist perspective would see this statement as perfectly acceptable, whereas a more proactive, positive interpretation would require direct intervention to eliminate disadvantages (e.g. social factors) that result in persistent inequality. However, there are continual debates about what constitutes a fair source of advantage and what does not. For instance, while it is widely unacceptable to discriminate on the basis of race, there are different opinions about whether it is morally acceptable to discriminate on the basis of natural talent or hard work. Such differences of opinion are usually expressed or justified in terms of broader views about social justice (Fine, 1992, on Social Marketing; Howe,

1999). Fourali (2000) has summarized the three broad perspectives on equality of educational opportunity based on the predominating three theories of social justice (Howe, 1999) in Table 0.1.

Table 0.1 Three perspectives on justice

	Libertarianism	*Utilitarianism*	*Liberal egalitarianism*
Position	States should refrain from exercising power.	An action is right if it maximizes the total good.	The principle of equality is paramount and any inequality must be justified.
Consequence	Hence should not intervene and redistribute resources to achieve equality among its citizens.	Interventions to support disadvantaged groups are welcome.	Interventions are primarily for removing disadvantages and prior to maximizing the good.
Negative effect	Educational achievement may be largely dependent on the lottery of conditions that the learner has access (or no access) to.	If programmes prove to be less effective in helping disadvantaged groups these may be replaced by programmes that may benefit less disadvantaged groups.	May affect liberty and also criticized for not having an overarching principle and having to balance competing principles.

Despite criticism against liberal egalitarians, they seem to be least prone to injustice since:
1. Liberty is hollow unless supported by equality.
2. Flexibility in terms of having to balance principles, while criticized as a negative aspect, can be seen as a strength since it does not hold itself hostage to a rigid principle.

It is worth noting that Rawls (1972), one of the strongest proponents of liberal egalitarianism, has come up with a strong procedural argument for justice. Rawls sought to understand justice through the justifiability and fairness of the social institutions. He introduced the idea of an original position to prevent bias towards our own condition. This is demonstrated by encouraging thinkers about justice to reason from behind a veil of ignorance about basic principles for social institutions. He argues that if we reason from a position of ignorance about our wealth, beliefs, abilities or social position then we exclude the possibility of favouring anybody. Govier (2002) used this approach following the blind persecution that followed the 9/11 event and to criticize knee-jerk reactions, whether from people, institutions or governments.

The place of education

Sen (2009) makes a distinction between the 'ideal' state as presented by Rawls, which has dominated philosophical thought since the Enlightenment, and a theory of justice which enables comparative merits of different societies to be taken into consideration. As he put it:

> What is important to note here, as central to the idea of justice, is that we have a strong sense of injustice on many different grounds, and yet not agree on any particular ground as being *the* dominant reason for the diagnosis of injustice.
>
> (Sen, 2009, p. 2, original emphasis)

The argument here is that this theory of justice, based on practical reasoning, will allow for diversity and support different societies in their interaction with other social groups who adhere to different principles. The contention is that education is designed to enable individuals to understand what is socially valued in their own societies. However, in a globalized world there is a pressing need to build individual capacity to understand and interrelate with others from a wide variety of backgrounds.

Taking a broader perspective on the aims of education, John White (1990) argues that the aim of education is to 'shape the tendencies and propensities with which children are born into settled dispositions of certain sorts' (p. 23). He also argues that 'children are brought up in conformity with certain reasons for action . . . to have certain desires rather than others' (p. 24). He identifies these desires with values and lists among these the following physical pleasures: avoidance of harm to themselves, personal relations, protecting and promoting the well-being of people universally, engaging in activities primarily for intrinsic reasons, and higher order values to avoid abuse of natural or normal needs. Hence education is perceived as instrumental in developing interests and desires that serve learners, their community and the environment.

In line with this thinking, according to Elkington (1997) a more responsible world will need to have its citizens adopt a triple bottom line approach to their entrepreneurial pursuits. This concept was developed primarily in order to encourage responsible businesses to weigh up the three dimensions of economic, social and environmental interests.

Bearing in mind both the value of the model and the importance of education (whatever its sources) in influencing our attitudes towards ourselves, others and the world, Fourali (2009) argues for the need to adapt educational aims to match the aims of the triple bottom line, as shown in Figure 0.1.

Many educationists would be happy to support these broad aims of education. However there are views that argue that as we are becoming a multifaceted society the move towards a global perspective can be damaging as a result of both process and outcomes.

Towards a consensus in education
The above approach to the issue of aims of education has been criticized for being restrictive and heavily influenced by the European Enlightenment which favoured the primacy of reason in human affairs and helped create a moral order based on individualism and atomism (Bracken and Thomas, 2009). This view is also tacit in a number of chapters in this book.

Foucault (1967) argued that social institutions, as well as research and practice, developed in a cultural framework heavily influenced by Enlightenment and post-Enlightenment preoccupations. Gould (1981) provided an example about how such a cultural environment could help develop institutions that not only favour an 'elite' group, but lead to the excesses of the Eugenics movement.

More recently, voices started being heard about the dangers of universalism in education. For instance, Bainton and Crossley in this volume, supported by progressive educationists since the 1960s, argue that school is not the only source of education (let alone the most effective). To illustrate the consequences of a unilateral perspective, some of the dangers are associated with developing an industrialized, modernized world that could lead to social fracture and unsustainable living. However, there is a clear awareness that not all global tendencies are negative (e.g. Andreotti; Bainton and Crossley, this

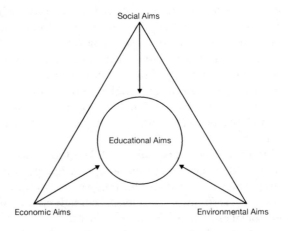

Figure 0.1 Education and the aims of the triple bottom line

volume). After all, we all live in the same world and have to learn to maximize co-operation and minimize destruction to sustain our different communities and our common environment. So there is the dilemma reflected in the sub-title of the book: To be (local or global), or not to be; that is the question, to borrow a Shakespearian phrase.

In fact, part of the problem reflected in the question is the human mind's tendency to simplify its world and avoid complexity and uncertainties by resolving to present manufactured clear-cut answers that avoid natural over-laps or fuzziness (Fourali, 1997). This tendency in fact spreads itself to even the most so-called 'objective' enterprises such as science, IT developments and mathematical thinking. The origins of such an approach have been linked as far back as Aristotelian 'either/or' thinking. Although this thinking may have its benefits, in the long term and when dealing with large-scale issues the results can be not only unrealistic, but even dangerous (Fourali, 1997).

Another associated problem is the language issue. There are huge differences in understanding of concepts between individuals within one culture, let alone a number of cultures. What shades of understanding can be associated with concepts such as globalism or, say, democracy? Does the first one allow within its understanding schema 'localism' as well, or does democracy allow for what may be termed 'objective/non-exclusive result-focused consultation'? Hence the usual question, 'whose democracy?' Now, these differences in understanding may be multiplied when we deal with several cultures in conjunction with one concept.

Our suggested way forward is through genuine, sensitive negotiated discourse that respects the other. This way forward needs to acknowledge care, difference and uncertainty and, dare we say, encourage humility to recognize the possibility that one may have got it wrong. After all, we have a whole history of fashionable ideas which were soon replaced by other, more fashionable, ideas. In other words, the more inclusive the perspective is, the more chances it has to survive, since it maximizes the possibilities of reflecting the complex reality. This reality must take into account both a multifaceted environment and multitude of multilevel modes of understanding (metaphysical, experiential, logical, practical, etc.) to minimize direct or indirect exclusions.

The structure of this book

The themes addressed in this book are organized according to the following categories:
- global policy context;
- community integration and inclusion;
- curriculum reform;
- learning and pedagogy.

Please note that the selected categories of themes are not mutually exclusive, but represent broad thematic pigeonholes that may be helpful in drawing common threads across diverse perspectives and contexts. We acknowledge that one chapter could relate easily to all categories of themes.

The book offers a much-needed global perspective on education, tackling a multitude of issues ranging from vocational education and training (VET), to critical theory, to practical considerations associated with dealing with large changes in educational demand, whether as a result of economic or social challenges. The authors present and clarify the challenges, but also suggest solutions based on their experiences. However, the authors and editors are under no illusion that the book either provides an exhaustive coverage of the key global educational issues or offers a 'one-fix-all' answer. In particular, by the very nature of the subject, it is very hard to address all associated topics with the global education challenge. Accordingly, there could be accusations of bias or exclusions – bias towards a certain perspective (the Western perspective?) or exclusions for not including more representatives from continents such as South America, Africa, Asia or the Middle East compared to the representatives from the Western perspective.

Clearly, any bias may be intentionally or inadvertently reflected in the arguments of the authors. To refer, for instance, to Enlightenment as though it was the sole influence on modern-day education or philosophy may already brand the author as Western/Eurocentric. Its origins, and the origins of any enterprise 'seeking scientific truths', lie beyond the West; for example, among the influences of Enlightenment in Europe are several Moorish philosophers such as Ibn Tufayl and Ibn Rushd (Averoes).

If we are to adopt a global perspective, we may as well identify the dimensions of 'globalism' and its sources and then try to pinpoint which of these are problematic for which community. We may, for instance, include among these problematic dimensions the atomistic and individualistic tendencies which neglect the broader environmental, economic and cultural dimensions. Such atomistic perspectives, explained away by the continuous need for more accuracy, may divert our attention from the bigger picture. For instance, in our attempt to find the most effective and efficient ways of preparing trainees for the world of work, we take the risk of neglecting other important aspects of education that not only may be key to the learner, but to national and international integration as a whole. There is a common accusation by members of our societies who feel 'education has failed us' when faced, for example, with excesses of behaviours such as 'it is cool to drink too much' or 'to have an ASBO (anti-social behaviour order)'.

At the moment, several of current societies' problems are routinely addressed *after* the problem occurs. It is possible to argue that a responsible society ought to address such issues in a pre-emptive manner to maximize results and prevent some of the misery associated with excesses of behaviour.

Such a perspective can, of course, lead to accusations of authoritarianism. However, such authoritarianism would be greatly minimized if the pre-requisites of genuine dialogue and mutual respect have been established before any discussions take place on what is to be done. This seems to be the general consensus of the work presented by our contributors. It is always helpful to be cautious, however, as long as the caution does not prevent us from trying new ways and being ever ready to recognize when it is time to change direction.

In this respect it is important to encourage a debate about values which, although tacit in many works, are not clearly specified. We hope that this and other topics could be added to a future subsequent publication that could lead to a series of works on global education issues. We believe that there are enough topics to be addressed at this level to warrant such an initiative.

Surely, if financiers can find a corporate logo supported with the strapline 'the world's local bank', educationists could do it as well. That is, promoting a global perspective that also takes into account local needs.

Finally, after considering everything, we feel that this has been a worthwhile initiative that has highlighted many good works that are already bearing fruit in several countries. We are hoping that readers will benefit from this work by helping them develop their thinking and supporting them in their practical educational initiatives. Eventually we hope that readers would also like to share their experience by contacting us at g.elliott@worc.ac.uk, to be taken into consideration for a forthcoming sequel to this book.

References

Bracken, P. and Thomas, P. (2009), 'Cognitive therapy, cartesianism, and the moral order', in R. House and D. Loewenthal, *Against and For CBT: Towards a Constructive Dialogue.* Herefordshire: PCCS Books.

Elkington, J. (1997), *Cannibals with Forks: The Triple Bottom Line of 21st Century Business.* Oxford: Capstone Publishing.

Elliott, G. (1996), *Crisis and Change in Vocational Education and Training.* London: Jessica Kingsley.

Fine, S. H. (1992), *Marketing the Public Sector.* New Brunswick, New Jersey: Library of Congress.

Foucault, M. (1967), *Madness and Civilisation: A History of Insanity in the Age of Reason.* Trans. R. Howard. London: Tavistock.

Fourali, C. (1997), 'Using fuzzy logic in educational measurement', *Evaluation and Research in Education,* 11(3), 129–48.

—— (2000), Unpublished paper. 'Educational Rights: A discussion paper for the Research Group', London: City & Guilds of London Institute.

—— (2009), *Education, Business and the Triple Bottom Line.* Briefing paper. Cookham. Berkshire, Marketing and Sales Standards Setting Body (MSSSB).

Frey, R. G. and Wellman, C. H. (2005), *A Companion to Applied Ethics.* Oxford: Blackwell.

Gould, S. J. (1981), *The Mismeasure of Man.* New York: W. W. Norton & Company.

Govier, T. (2002), *A Delicate Balance: What Philosophy Can Tell Us About Terrorism.* Oxford: Perseus Book Group.

Gundara, J. S. (2000), *Interculturalism, Education and Inclusion.* London: SAGE.

Howe, K. R. (1999), 'Equality of educational opportunity: philosophical issues', in P. Keeves and G. Lakomski (eds), *Issues in Educational Research.* Oxford: Pergamon.

LaFollette, H. (ed.) (2007), *Ethics in Practice: An Anthology* (3rd edn). Oxford: Blackwell.

Lauder, H., Brown, P., Dillabough, J. A. and Halsey, A.H. (eds) (2006), *Education, Globalization and Social Change.* Oxford: Oxford University Press.

Rawls, J. (1972), *A Theory of Justice.* Oxford: Clarendon Press.

Sen, A. (2009), *The Idea of Justice.* London: Allen Lane: Penguin Books.

UNESCO/UNICEF (2007), *Approach to Education For All: A Human Rights-Based Approach to Education.* Paris, France: United Nations Educational, Scientific and Cultural Organization (UNESCO). Website: http://unesdoc.unesco.org/images/0015/001548/154861e.pdf

White, J. (1990), 'The aims of education', in N. Entwistle (ed.), *Handbook of Educational Ideas and Practices.* London: Routledge.

PART I

The Global Policy Context

Overview

This opening global context-forming section of the book focuses on policies adopted by national governments and multi-nation groupings on how to address economic and social challenges they face through mutually agreed policies. This section gives a perspective from several continents on educational access, inclusion and impact.

David Bainton and Michael Crossley's chapter, which opens our first section, is set against the backdrop of an arid and mountainous landscape in which two young children of Tibetan nomads living in Ladakh receive their schooling. The authors' focus is the lines of power that both bring these children's lived reality into being and reveal the hegemonic influence of global assumptions about education and schooling, the sedentary and nomadic, the central and the marginal, the traditional and progressive. In their discussion of what we might call 'the politics of consensus', the authors rightly warn against the uncritical transfer of educational models and ideas across cultures and contexts and call for a reconceptualization of education – not necessarily to resolve tensions between the local and the global, but to reconceptualize what the global might be, and in particular to seek an ethic of respect for different local experiences in ways that afford alternative ways of knowing and thinking.

James Stanfield helps to shed light on the recent growth of private schools for the poor in developing countries, a grassroots movement which has the potential to transform the way we think about increasing access to education in developing countries. He demonstrates that a growing number of people and organizations are now prepared to take seriously the idea that private schools can cater for low-income families, a concept which was still being dismissed a decade ago. In response to the increasing awareness of the growth of private schools serving low-income families, a number of different organizations have responded to help stimulate growth in the sector. The impact of these developments on the concept of the right to education and the rights-based approach are critically examined and an alternative freedom-based approach is recommended.

The international agreements such as Education for All (EFA) and World Millennium Goals (MDGs) and the United Nation (UN) policies promoting human rights have influenced the formation of the Ghanaian constitution and education policymaking, particularly in relation to access to quality education for women. Quantitative research for international monitoring purposes by the UN and World Bank has revealed that in Ghana progress with entry rates for both boys and girls at primary school level are higher than in other sub-Saharan countries, but more boys complete than girls. This difference has consequences for further education and occupational opportunities for girls. Máiréad Dunne's contribution recommends the use of complementary qualitative research, which focuses on gender as a social construct and concentrates on the school as a location for constructing identities and a place that reinforces discriminatory practices such as favouring of boys and where the sexual harassment and bullying of girls is more likely.

Gary Jones, Edward Sallis and Peter Hubert offer a critique of policymaking models imported from large states and applied to small states, such as to the Island of Jersey where their case study of college self-assessment is located. Such policy models rely on the notion of separation of the spheres of influence of national stakeholders, the policy text itself, and implementation, whereas the authors argue that, in the context of small states, the same individuals who are involved in trying to shape and influence policy will invariably also be involved in both production of policy documents and their subsequent implementation. This therefore raises the question as to what extent it is possible to separate the three contexts in a small state. This question is explored through a specific example, presented as a case study of how policy and approaches to college improvement have been imported from a large state and then subsequently amended to meet the local needs of the importing small state. As well as providing guidance for small states on policy importation, the authors point out that small states provide opportunities for large stage policymakers to examine what policies and innovations might look like if implemented within a different setting.

Against the Lisbon Strategy and European policies of lifelong learning, VET teachers and trainers have become a key target group. Good-quality services provided by teachers and trainers is regarded as an immediate contribution to fostering the quality, attractiveness and accessibility of opportunities for lifelong learning, and also to enhancing social integration and economic competitiveness of the European member states. Consequently, VET practitioners as a target group have received considerable attention in

European policy papers over the past ten years. However, little is known about the work, qualification and professional development of VET practitioners, particularly at the European level. As a response, the European Commission and other European bodies have launched and supported different research and development initiatives targeted at VET teachers and trainers in past years. Interestingly, those 'top-down' approaches were concurrently complemented by several 'bottom-up' approaches in form of project proposals and initiatives developed by researchers or other stakeholders. Simone Kirpal explores how those different initiatives interlink and what implications they have for modernization and social change.

Chapter 1

Lessons from comparative and international education

David Bainton and Michael Crossley

Introduction

Context lies at the heart of research in the multidisciplinary field of comparative and international education. In this chapter we draw upon many of the qualitative principles and perspectives that have done much to advance context sensitivity in recent comparative studies relating to education and social change (Crossley, 2009). In doing so, we argue that in times of intensified globalization – when international policy prescriptions are becoming increasingly powerful – concerted efforts must be made to ensure that the voices of local actors – community members, parents, school children – are included in genuine dialogue by development partners, ' who not only talk but also listen and hear' (Samoff, 1998, p. 24). The chapter, therefore, presents a critical, locally grounded and forward-looking analysis of the impact of globally inspired educational development agendas with particular reference to the context of Tibetan nomads of Ladakh, in northern India. Building bridges between the social sciences and the arts and humanities, the analysis is informed by postcolonial theoretical positionings, detailed fieldwork and revealing personal narratives.

Photo 1.1 Ladakh: narrative research in context

Spaces of experience 1

At the age of five, Stanzin was one of the oldest children in the boarding school. She was just starting her third year here, and she was well used to the routines of the school. Soon it would be time to go down to the river to take a quick wash and clean her teeth before the sun went down. It was midsummer, yet the wind sweeping down off the higher mountain plateau was still cold. She faced into the wind, trying to imagine where, amid the mountains, her family might be now.

Last week she had been playing with her elder brother and baby sister at the summer huts. Not far away – a day's walk past the hot springs, where the grazing was good for their Pashmina goats that her family lived off; but the memories of the two-week summer holiday had faded together with her father's retreating figure back into the landscape.

Stanzin looked down at Tashi next to her, playing with stones like the other little ones. He looked up and then turned his face away as she distractedly wiped his runny nose on her sleeve. She looked more closely at him. 'And don't forget to wash your eyes, you're starting to get redeye', she said. Stanzin tried to look out for him – she remembered her own first year here. It was tough for some of them, not understanding why their parents had left them here in this windy place, having to wash and look after themselves. They soon learnt, soon made friends, as she had, had begun to understand why their families thought that education was so important, had begun to learn to read and write. She knew the Tibetan letters now, and could sing plenty of the Tibetan songs that made her family laugh so much.

She smiled to herself, took Tashi's hand in hers, and headed down to the river.

Education and social change

Next year, most likely, Stanzin will no longer be here, at the point of this camera. For this boarding school, with its forty or so children and three teachers, with its single dormitory, with its nearby river, testament as it is to the human capacity to bring into being schools in the most unlikely places, teaches only preschool-age children, Montessori years 1–3, typically children aged three to six. If Stanzin is to continue her education, she must travel, not up the valley to her family, but away, down the valley into those warmer lands where the soil is rich enough, even in this arid landscape, to enable you, if you are skilled enough, to grow crops. Down even further for high school, where the valley floor is wide enough for a town to have grown up over the years, with its taxis and shops and airport.

Stanzin speaks the first words, and locates us, for now, here in this windy place, in the lived reality of her young life, that Gramsci reminds us is necessary for any meaningful consideration of the dynamic between education and social change (Gramsci, 1985; see Crehan, 2002, for a cultural reading of his work). For Gramsci, these lived realities are less an expression of culture, reified as some form of idealized pre-industrial state, but rather understood as an expression of culture that has been formed out of inequality and power. How do Stanzin and Tashi, young children of Tibetan nomads, end up just here? What are the lines of power that bring their particular lived reality into being?

Comparative and international education has a long history of analysis of educational practices that are particularly sensitive to the uncritical transfer of educational models and ideas across cultures and contexts (Crossley, 2004, 2008; Crossley and Watson, 2003) and, as such, seeks to trace the lines of influence that materialize a global hegemony through the enaction of particular local educational practices. And yet, standing here at 5,000m, even with the help of postcolonial critiques that seek to de-centre an understanding of this particular reality as remote or marginal (Ashcroft et al., 1995; Loomba, 2005), it is difficult to shake off the feeling that this place – a place that must stand, if any place ever could, as the epitome of the 'local' – is somehow far away from inscription by the 'global'.

And yet her story is offered here as a testament to the ever-complex relations between these spheres of influence and the mechanisms of hegemony through which global educational discourses operate. A hegemony that starts by understanding schooling as the only legitimate form of education – the dominance, even here, of the sedentary over the nomadic. A hegemony, too, of the uncritical transfer of progressive Montessori methods – an approach that, in the urban centres of the Tibetan diaspora, stands against didactic methods and for the possibility of the development of a particularly Tibetan education, while here in the mountains it makes boarding school the lived reality for three-year-old children. A hegemony that is materialized through the financing of Tibetan education by NGOs and individual supporters.

Stanzin's lived reality, inscribed by discourses of progress, of possibility, of action – discourses, one might say of modernity, of development. The winds of change are flowing off the mountain, winds that bring with them schools and knowledge from other places, bring perhaps a better life, bring with them hope. Crapanzano, in an anthropological essay on hope, quotes Minkowski as noting that 'We are charmed by hope, because it opens the future broadly before us' (Minkowski, in Crapanzano, 2004, p. 103). The nomad hopes for a better life for her children; the Westerner hopes for a better outcome for the Tibetan community;the Tibetan authorities hope for educational success; and Stanzin hopes for her family's laughter.

Hope, the softer side of hegemony. Hope inevitably implicates the global, implicates that which is beyond the individual for, as Crapanzano goes on to say, 'while desire presumes a psychology, hope presupposes a metaphysics. Both require an ethics – of expectation, constraint, and resignation' (Crapanzano, 2004, p. 100). Social change, development, globalization – the world is made anew, and we respond to it (for how else might we do so) with hope. But this is not a blind hope. We are ambivalent, aware of our powerlessness in the face of global change. We do what we can; and Stanzin stares into the wind.

The hegemony of the global

The Millennium Development Goals (MDGs) and the Education For All agenda (EFA) are testament to the possibilities of coherent global action. At the same time, while these initiatives have clearly made progress in mobilizing support for educational development and have made steps towards achieving their goals (Packer, 2008), they have been criticized for failing to address issues of educational inequality (EFA Global Monitoring Report Team, 2009), and for failing to offer quality education for marginalized groups (Bainton, 2007).

It is perhaps unsurprising that there has been a turn to such concerted global action as the MDGs and EFA agenda as a means of addressing issues of global concern, based as they are on the universality of education as a human right (Bainton, 2009). Nevertheless, the dominance of a discourse that privileges not only the global, but an understanding of it as a space of 'global consensus' and 'concerted global action', must be understood in the context both of Václav Havel's struggle, noted above, and in the context of the danger of hegemony that such a global consensus necessarily creates. Stanzin reminds us that the apparent demand for global coherence that an era of globalization fetishizes must be cautioned by listening to the entropic voices of the particular. She reminds us that we must trouble the assumption that what the world – what Stanzin – needs is a new global consensus as the principal solution.

Context matters

'Context matters' (Crossley, 2008), and the discussion of Stanzin's story serves to offer such a context within which we can engage in discussions on the inter-relationship between education, globalization and social and environmental change. For Stanzin's family, social change is a reality and it is important to understand the dynamics of the relationships between educational and social changes for families such as hers – to understand not only how schools might offer the possibility of sensitively responding to global concerns, but the critical ways that schools already act as agents of social change, often unwittingly and with unintended consequences. This is not to say that the social changes that are taking place within this nomadic community are only a consequence of educational provision, but that, for Stanzin's family and indeed for herself, the act of going to school has repercussions – in dislocating her from her family, from the knowledge of how to live in this landscape. A dislocation that will, most likely, lead her to an urban, modern livelihood.

In the context of the main theme of this book – the possibility of a trans-national educational response to global concerns – such repercussions are not simply social in their nature. Here, in the arid, high-altitude Himalayan desert, where life is only maintained by the replenishment of glaciers through winter snowfall, concerns of global warming are less global than immediate. Stanzin's story highlights the critical role of schooling in the articulation of a broader development discourse that, in its hegemonic industrialized, mod-ernized, globalized forms, is often complicit with a shift to the unsustainable forms of livelihood that we might wish, through it, to challenge. There is an irony to the realization that, just as we might wish education to contribute toward the development of sustainable values, through its complicity with a Western modernity its structural effects can lead to social fracture and modern livelihoods.

As such, what we are arguing for in the possible development of transna-tional educational values is that such debates take a broad and radical canvas to understand how diverse, non-modern livelihoods, knowledge and attitudes might contribute to the reconceptualization of educational provision and practices. For this to take place we must find ways to open up dialogic spaces where conversations about educational and social change across cultures and contexts take place that do not privilege the global, and this is where we now turn.

Transnational dialogues within the pluri-verse

Comparative and international education foregrounds the importance of contextualized understandings of educational practices and possibilities. From this perspective, any discussion of the likelihood of transnational educa-tional values to respond to global concerns inevitably raises the question of how diverse local contexts might be considered, during attempts to formulate a set of transnational values.

Such a tension is not between the local and the global as such, but a call to reconceptualize what the global might be, and to reframe how the emergence of global spaces might function in ways that offer a different articulation, and a different directionality, between them. The acknowledgement of the global issues that face the planet offers a critical moment to reconceptualize education in a way that meets these challenges. At the same time, if this is done uncritically, it shall be a moment where certain educational practices will become hegemonic, and unsustainable educational provision will be further embedded in the name of global consensus.

   Inevitably, this reframing of the global is both critical and plural; critical in the sense that it must stand against, and overcome, an industrial modernity that has led us to a global environmental crisis. As the sociologist of globalization, De Sousa Santos, puts it:

> The critical analysis of what exists lies in the assumption that existence does not exhaust the possibilities of existence, and that there are, therefore, alternatives capable of overcoming what is criticizable in what exists. The discomfit, non-conformism, or indignation vis-à-vis what exists inspires the impulse to theorise its overcoming.
>
> (Santos, 1998, p. 122)

It is plural insofar as it acknowledges that, while global warming is a challenge that faces us all, this challenge must necessarily be faced in the particular circumstances wherein the 'local' encounters the global, where Stanzin meets modernity.

> Stanzin would have a lot to say
> if anyone asked her the right question.
> She knows how to light a dung fire in a way that would stay alight.
> She knows how to herd the Pashmina goats in a way that does not scare them.
> She knows how to tell if a storm is coming.
> She knows how to find her way home from the valley in the dark.
> She knows how to mend her clothes when they get torn.
> One day, her teacher asked, 'What is sustainable development?'
>   Stanzin did not say anything.

In contrast to the dominant understanding of the global as a space of global consensus and concerted action, for the Argentinian theorist, Walter Mignolo, what is needed is a fundamental shift away from the hegemony of a singular universality towards a pluri-versality as a universal project (Mignolo, 2007). Such a pluri-verse offers a reframing of the global as a site of dialogue between different locals that, while sharing commonality of experience in relation to modernity, retains respect for individual spaces of experience. As Mignolo puts it:

> The 'space of experience' and the 'horizon of expectations' are di-verse, or rather, pluri-verse – what each diverse local history has in common with others is the fact that they all have to deal with the unavoidable presence of the modern/colonial world and its power differentials, which start with racial

classification and end up ranking the planet (e.g., First, Second and Third World was a racialization of politics, economy, cultures and knowledge).

(Mignolo, 2000, p. 70)

What Mignolo and de Sousa Santos share is the call for dialogue between different local experiences in ways that afford alternative ways of knowing and thinking. Such alternatives, precisely because they are based in diverse experiences and precisely because they seek a critical understanding of social experience, offer the possibility of creating new forms of educational practice.

What is critical in any such space is to find ways to resist the prospect that one local 'is more successful in its translocal articulation' (Raffles, 2002, p. 327) and so becomes hegemonic. We suggest that such a prospect is best resisted through maintaining the contextual, narrated, experiential nature of such local understandings. Such narratives, in remaining rooted in context, have no imperial ambitions and so it is here, within the alternative global of the pluri-verse, that transnational values might form.

Spaces of experience 2

Within the pluri-verse the directionality is different.

The teacher sits and listens.

'What do you know, Stanzin?' he asks.

'I know that the glaciers are melting,' she says, 'and I know, a little, how to live in this landscape.'

'What shall we do, Stanzin?'

'I do not know, but my father and mother and grandfathers and grand-mothers have crossed the glaciers since they were children, perhaps they will know.'

'What will they tell us, Stanzin?'

'They will tell you how to live in this landscape.'

The path strikes its way up the valley to the high plateaux beyond, the path that has been drawn by generations, connecting the winter pastures to the spaces 'beyond'. For Dorji and his young son Sonam, the path constitutes their experiences that day. There is a comfort to be found, up here, on this path, where in tracing the lines that others have walked safely they cannot but inscribe it further for others to follow.

This path has heard many stories of wealth or desolation, of love and of the everyday. But that day, as Sonam and his father walked, the stories were of the goats, of the place where the grass that would heal grows, of the best way to move them safely across the mountains, of how to care for them in those uncertain first days of life. There is knowledge here, knowledge of livelihoods, of how to live in this landscape, intimate knowledge both enacted and narrated this day in this place.

Fragile knowledge for sustainable development

These two narratives say something about the dynamic between social, educational and environmental change in the Himalayas – two narratives that also emphasize the fragility of local 'intimate knowledge' of how to live in this landscape. Raffles uses the term 'intimate knowledge' to emphasize:

> how people enter into relationships among themselves and with nature through embodied practice; how it is through these relationships that they come to know nature and each other and have relationships, the knowledge and the practice are always mediated not only by power and discourse but by affect.
>
> (Raffles, 2002, p. 326)

There is a fragility to Dorji's intimate knowledge – fragile flowers in this desert landscape. Fragile knowledge that perhaps only emerges, is possible to be revealed and passed on in these moments. For the father, this is knowledge to live by; for the son, perhaps, too – his future is not yet decided. Today this knowledge is told, but this is not a certain transmission – the merest shifting of the path takes us elsewhere; takes us away from these fragile places, away from this landscape where knowledge lies dormant waiting for their moments to be narrated.

Subordinated knowledges (Foucault, 1980) such as these should not be thought of as sitting in a repository of old people's heads or bodies, like a library or an archive. There are only moments of experience where knowledge is enacted or it is not. It is easy to talk hypothetically about such knowledge being preserved; easy to see that there are still people who have this knowledge; easy to say that there is no reason why young people are not able to listen. But the life dries out from them as the stories are untold, as some knowledge simply gets left behind, forgotten about, passed over, unrecognized, unspoken.

Such intimate knowledge is, for now at least, available to be used in the fight against global warming, but perhaps not for long, Today, Dorji's son walks with him. Perhaps next year he will be, like Stanzin, in the boarding school, where other stories and the knowledge that they maintain cannot reach him.

An emergent critique

These two narratives, offered as 'spaces of experience' to debates around transnational values for sustainable development are left here, left deliberately unabstracted from their context. And yet such a desire to retain the contextual does not mean that there is a rejection of the search for clarity that looking at the whole can bring. Rather, this distancing is less a search for deeper structural elements, and more towards what Deleuze helpfully calls the transversal, allowing us to redefine the relationship between that which emerges from local articulations along less structural lines. As Schrag describes it, the transversal is a conceptual tool that allows us to consider broader emergent conceptualizations that offer 'convergence without coincidence, conjuncture without concordance, overlapping without assimilation, and union without absorption.' (Schrag, 1997, p. 128).

It is hoped that these two narratives offer a critique, in de Sousa Santos's use of the term, of education in the context of a global environmental crises. The social and knowledge landscapes that have been shown through these two narratives act as examples of locally meaningful educational critiques that remain rooted in the context. Taken together, they suggest: that we should pay more attention to the ways that schooling, through its dislocatory effects, moves children away from more sustainable livelihoods, and into modernist biographies; and that we might try to find ways to educate that do not disrupt the possibilities of utilizing local knowledge to challenge the global environmental crisis.

Such emergent critiques, like the narratives that help to formulate them, are at their best, it would seem coherent to argue, when they too are located in culture and context. So, rather than ending this chapter with an outline of what an alternative education for these particular nomadic goatherders might look like – for that next step is surely something that Stanzin, Tashi, Dorji and Sonam are better placed to say than we are – we end with a final narrative.

Although taking a more explicitly critical tone, this narrative, like the first two, is located in the Tibetan culture of the Himalayas. However, its starting point is humorous critique of Drukpa Kunley, the sixteenth-century Tibetan 'divine madman' who wandered the villages of Tibet and Bhutan 'deconstructing' the taken-for-granted notions of people (Dowman, 2000). The ambition of such narratives, then as now, was to offer an analysis of how people's actions affected them, and so we have adapted the style of the original tales for our purpose. In the spirit of the possibility of local knowledge and local critique that this chapter has been offering, we shall end this chapter in Drukpa Kunley's capable hands.

Drukpa Kunley visits school: on the emptiness of being

On his return from Lhasa, the lama entered a dry region. On his way across the valley, through a small village he met a group of goatherders and, with their children, were packing food and clothes in a bag.

'Oh fair ladies and hardworking gents, where are you all going on such a day, when there are goats to be tended to and songs to be sung?' asked the lama.

'We are going to town to take our children to school,' one replied.

The others nodded in agreement.

The lama then turned to the children.

'Children, where are you going on such a day, when there are places to explore and games to be played?' he asked again.

'We are going to school so that we can know all of the important things in the world. Knowledge is power,' said one.

Drukpa Kunley went on his way, until a little further down the road, he came across a group of men in a field taking a break from their ploughing. So Drukpa Kunley asked the men about the school.

'It's a magnificent new school,' one man said to Drukpa Kunley.

'It was the vision of a great lama,' said another.

'Our children will learn things we were never able to learn,' said the fourth. The others all nodded in agreement.

'Well,' said Drukpa Kunley, 'I must go and see this wondrous place of learning.'

So Drukpa Kunley, hiding his real identity, went down to the school and met with the head teacher.

'Oh wise one, master of truth, I am a poor acolyte from across the mountains. I have heard that your lore is great. May I come and learn at your feet?'

'Go away, old man. Can't you see that this is place for children,' the head teacher replied. 'There is no place for you here.'

'But I am like a child, next to your own great self. Let me stay!' Drukpa Kunley said, bowing low before him.

The head teacher looked troubled, but could not very well turn away this old man. Finally he said:

'Very well, but you will need a uniform. Come back tomorrow, dressed properly.'

The next day Drukpa Kunley returned dressed from head to feet in a goat fur.

'What are you doing here like this, I said to come in uniform,' the head teacher said angrily, waving his stick in the air.

'But I came in uniform. I saw that the children here move together like goats from place to place, so I came as one.'

The children in class were singing songs.

'Do you know any children's songs?' the head teacher asked Drukpa Kunley. He was sure that the old man would feel foolish and go away.

'I know the song of the ten steps to the perfect realization of the ultimate emptiness of existence. Let me sing it for you,' Drukpa Kunley said.

'In step one you learn not to pee in your pants for one hour at a time.

In step two you learn the art of staying for the whole day in a small box without talking.

In step three you learn how to sit cross-legged on the floor.

In step four you learn that if you carry a pile of books between home and school you become strong.

In step five you learn that if you cook for the teachers you will pass automatically to the sixth step.

In step six you become master of the chalkboard duster.

In step seven you learn the art of copying things you do not understand from one paper to another.

In step eight you learn how to remember things you do not understand so you can copy them directly onto a paper.

In step nine you learn the illusory nature of true knowledge.

In step ten, you have realized the full meaning of emptiness and become enlightened, and get a certificate to show to everyone else just how empty your head is.'

At this, Drukpa Kunley got up and went on his way, laughing.

References

Ashcroft, B., Griffiths, G. and Tiffin, H. (1995), *The Post-Colonial Studies Reader*. London: Routledge.

Bainton, D. (2007), 'Suffering development: indigenous knowledge and western education in Ladakh', unpublished PhD thesis. Bristol: University of Bristol.

—— (2009), *Realising Children's Right to Education: Priorities, Strategies, Policies and Trends in International NGOs*. Bristol: GES.

Crapanzano, V. (2004), *Imaginative Horizons: An Essay in Literary-Philosophical Anthropology*. London: University of Chicago Press.

Crehan, K. (2002), *Gramsci, Culture and Anthropology*. London: Pluto Press.

Crossley, M. (2004), 'Dialogue, multidisciplinarity and comparative and international research', *Comparative Education*, 41(1), 1–4.

—— (2008), 'Bridging cultures and traditions in comparative research in education: dialogue, difference and context', *International Review of Education*, 54(3): 319–36.

—— (2009), 'Rethinking context in comparative education', in R. Cowen and A. M. Kazamias (eds) *International Handbook of Comparative Education* (Part Two). Dordrecht: Springer.

—— and Watson, K. (2003), *Comparative and International Research in Education: Globalisation, Context and Difference*. London: Routledge.

Dowman, K. (ed.) (2000), *Divine Madman: The Sublime Life and Songs of Drukpa Kunley*. Ilford: Wisdom Books.

EFA Global Monitoring Report Team (2009), *Overcoming Inequality: Why Governance Matters*. Paris and Oxford: UNESCO and Oxford University Press.

Foucault, M. (1980), *Power/Knowledge: Selected Interviews and Other Writings 1972–77*. Brighton: Harvester.

Gramsci, A. (1985), *Selections from Cultural Writings*, ed. D. Forgacs and G. Nowell-Smith. London: Lawrence & Wishart.

Jones, Phillip W. (2007), 'Education and world order', *Comparative Education*, 43(3), 325–37.

Loomba, A. (2005), *Colonialism/Postcolonialism* (2nd edn). Abingdon: Routledge.

Mignolo, W. (2000), *Local Histories/Global Designs*. Princeton: Princeton University Press.

—— (2007), 'Delinking: the rhetoric of modernity, the logic of coloniality, and the grammar of decoloniality', *Cultural Studies*, 21(2), 449–514.

Ochs, E. and Capps, L. (2001), *Living Narrative: Creating Lives in Everyday Storytelling*. Cambridge, MA: Harvard University Press.

Packer, S. (2008), *Making Education Work for All: A Report from the International Working Group on Education*. Paris: UNESCO.

Raffles, H. (2002), 'Intimate knowledge', *International Social Science Journal*, 173, 325–33.

Samoff, J. (1998), 'Education sector analysis in Africa: limited national control and even less national ownership', paper presented to the 10th World Congress of Comparative Education Societies, Cape Town, South Africa, July.

Santos, B. de Sousa (1998), 'Oppositional postmodernism and globalizations', *Law and Social Inquiry*, 23(1), 121–39.

Schrag, C. (1997), *The Self after Postmodernity*. New Haven: Yale University Press.

Chapter 2

Education for all: a freedom-based approach

James Stanfield

The rights-based approach

The prevailing consensus within the international community on how to achieve education for all, or universal access to education, is based upon what is commonly referred to as the rights-based approach. According to UNESCO/UNICEF (2007), the goal of a human rights-based approach to education is 'to assure every child a quality education that respects and promotes her or his right to dignity and optimum development' (UNESCO/UNICEF, 2007, p. 1). A conceptual framework for this approach is also provided which includes the following three interlinked and interdependent dimensions:

The right of access to education – the right of every child to education on the basis of equality of opportunity and without discrimination on any grounds. To achieve this goal, education must be available for, accessible to, and inclusive of all children.

The right to quality education – the right of every child to a quality education that enables him or her to fulfil his or her potential, realize opportunities for employment and develop life skills. To achieve this goal, education needs to be child-centred, relevant and embrace a broad curriculum, and be appropriately resourced and monitored.

The right to respect within the learning environment – the right of every child to respect for her or his inherent dignity and to have her or his universal human rights respected within the education system. To achieve this goal, education must be provided in a way that is consistent with human rights, including equal respect for every child, opportunities for meaningful participation, freedom from all forms of violence, and respect for language, culture and religion (UNESCO/UNICEF, 2007, p. 4).

For the right to education to be guaranteed, according to UNESCO/UNICEF, each of these three dimensions must be addressed simultaneously. Organized attempts at promoting the concept of the right to education have been made since 1948, and they have been directed and controlled by UNESCO, UNICEF, the World Bank and an increasing number of government agencies, NGOs and charities. International aid has been at the heart of these developments and it has been used to build new schools, train new teachers and provide educational technology and equipment. A major initiative over recent decades has been the United Nation's School Fee Abolition Initiative (SFAI), where international aid has been used to abolish school fees at all government primary schools, predominantly in African countries. This has been the general approach over the previous half-century and important progress has been made in increasing access to education across the developing world. This is the context in which the following developments have taken place.

The rise of private schools for the poor

For the majority of development experts, as private education is concerned only with serving the privileged, it is irrelevant to interests about extending access to the poor. However, the existence of a burgeoning private education sector serving the poor is now acknowledged in the development literature. For example, the Oxfam Education Report states, '. . . the notion that private schools are servicing the needs of a small minority of wealthy parents is misplaced . . . a lower cost private sector has emerged to meet the demands of poor households' (Watkins, 2000, pp. 229–30). In India, the Probe Team (1999) examined villages in four north Indian states and found that 'even among poor families and disadvantaged communities, one finds parents who make great sacrifices to send some or all of their children to private schools, so disillusioned are they with government schools' (p. 103). Reporting on evidence from Haryana, Uttar Pradesh and Rajasthan, De et al. (2002) have noted that 'private schools have been expanding rapidly in recent years' and that these 'now include a large number of primary schools which charge low fees' (p. 148). For the poor in Kolkata there has also been a 'mushrooming of privately managed unregulated . . . primary schools' (Nambissan, 2003, p. 52), and research in Haryana, India, has concluded that private schools are now operating practically 'in every locality of the urban centres as well as in rural areas' (Aggarwal, 2000, p. 20). These findings are reinforced by the EFA (2009) *Global Monitoring Report*, which confirms that private provision in some developing countries is no longer the sole preserve of the rich and that '[p]rivate primary schools charging modest fees and operating as small businesses, often with neither regulation nor support from government, are changing the education landscape' (EFA, 2009, p. 162).

Tooley and Dixon (2007) have carried out more detailed research in Hyderabad, Andhra Pradesh, and of the 918 schools they found located in low-income areas, 320 (34.9 per cent) were government, 49 (5.3 per cent) were private aided, and 549 (59.8 per cent) were private unaided. Of these, the largest number are unrecognized (335 schools, or 36.5 per cent of the total), while 214 private unaided schools were recognized (23.3 per cent of the total) (Tooley and Dixon, 2007, p. 21). Not only were government schools in an overall minority, but there were more unrecognized unaided schools than government schools. The total number of children in all 918 schools was 262,075, and 65 per cent of school children attended private unaided schools. Therefore, a large majority of the children in the low-income areas of Hyderabad are reported to be attending private unaided schools (ibid., p. 22). Tooley and Dixon also carried out extensive testing on children in both private and government schools in Hyderabad and found both that mean scores in mathematics were about 22 per cent and 25 per cent higher in private unrecognized schools and recognized schools than in government schools, and that this advantage was even more pronounced in English. While the majority of parents with children attending private schools in Hyderabad paid school fees, approximately 18 per cent of children in Hyderabad were provided with a free school place. Salaries in government schools were also nearly four times the reported salaries in private schools.

Based upon their research, Tooley and Dixon (2005) make the following conclusions. First, the majority of children in the poor areas of Hyderabad which they studied were attending private unaided schools. Second, this meant that the official number of school enrolments was widely underestimated. Third, children were getting better results in private unaided schools and, finally, the teacher costs in private unaided schools were significantly less than government schools. It is fair to suggest that Tooley and Dixon (2005) had stumbled across a 'notable education revolution' currently taking place in Hyderabad and their research also found similar developments occurring in China, Kenya, Ghana and Nigeria.

Based on his research findings over the previous five years, Professor Tooley's 2006 essay, *Educating Amaretch: Private Schools for the Poor and the New Frontier for Investors*, won the first prize in the International Finance Corporation and *Financial Times*' first annual essay competition, 'Business and Development: Private Path to Prosperity', and on 17 February 2007, the *Financial Times* also referred to the subject in its editorial under the heading 'Educating the Poorest':

Without literacy and numeracy, people are doomed to a life of poverty. Development experts know that. So, too, do parents. Disgusted by corrupt and incompetent public sector provision, many of the world's poorest people are turning to private sector alternatives. This is a fascinating development, on which the world should now build . . . Almost everybody knows that governments cannot run factories, farms or shops. But many people still expect them to do a first-rate job of delivering education. They are deluded. Poor parents have realised this already. They have also done something about it . . . Education is not, as has long been believed, too important to be left to the private sector. It is, instead, too important to be left to failing public monopolies. The private-sector revolution empowers the one group of people that cares about the education of children: their parents. Outsiders – both official and private – must build on the initiative the poor have shown.

(Educating the Poorest, 2007)

While views to the contrary may well be found in other national newspapers, these are still significant developments as it suggests that an increasing number of people and organizations are now prepared to take seriously the idea that private schools can cater for low-income families, a concept which was still being dismissed a decade ago.

In response to the increasing awareness of the growth of private schools serving low-income families, a number of different organizations have responded to help stimulate growth in the sector. For example, Scholarships for Kids is a UK charity set up in 2008 to provide the first scholarship programme dedicated to helping children in some of the world's poorest slum areas attend a new generation of budget private schools. With a scholarship costing only £75 per year, the programme is already giving access to education to hundreds of children living in the Kibera slums on the outskirts of Nairobi.

Opportunity International is the UK's largest microfinance charity seeking to empower people in developing countries with microfinance so that they can work their own way out of poverty. In 2008, Opportunity International started its new Microschools programme, which provides loans to 'edupreneurs' to help set up new private schools serving low-income communities. Microschools are now operating in fifty locations in Ghana and nine in Malawi and they now intend to expand this pilot into several other countries across Africa and Asia.

According to the Indian School Finance Company (ISFC), the low-cost private school market in India is now booming, with an estimated 75,000 private schools in low-income areas across the country. As a result, in January 2009 the ISFC began to provide medium-term loans at market rates to low-cost private schools across India for computer laboratories, teacher training, furniture and building more classrooms. By September 2009 they had already financed 119 schools and impacted the lives of 90,882 children. The ISFC's goal is to identify the most capable school entrepreneurs in local communities and help them improve the academic quality of their programmes for more children. Starting in Hyderabad, Andhra Pradesh, they now intend to expand their operations to four more cities by the end of 2010.

In September 2008 a joint venture between the Deutsche Bank Americas

Foundation, NewGlobe Schools, Gray Ghost Ventures and the Kellogg Foundation announced an $8 million commitment to finance emerging affordable private schools across Kenya and India. Gary Hattem, President of the Deutsche Bank Americas Foundation, stated that '[w]e recognize the important role that low-cost private schools play in educating poor children in the developing world and are excited to be a part of those initiatives, which strive to achieve scalable models for high quality low cost schools' (Hattem, 2008). The project will aim to develop scalable systems that will use new capital to strengthen local expertise to extend the reach of low-cost private schools to poor children in India and Kenya. This commitment is expected to help develop the capacity of teachers, principals and school leaders; improve the management of resources; and work towards creating a standardized, high-quality delivery model. During the first two years, it will hope to directly impact 100,000 poor children in India and Kenya, and potentially benefit millions more in the future. According to Steve Hardgrave, Managing Director at Gray Ghost Ventures, the aim will be to build upon the success of the use of microfinance in other sectors of the economy to help 'dramatically expand access to quality education for poor children in the developing world, and this will have a game-changing effect on poverty alleviation'.

Understanding the right to education

The recent growth of private schools for the poor in developing countries has raised a number of important questions concerning the concept of the right to education and its relevance in the twenty-first century. The original definition of the right to education agreed and sanctioned by the United Nations and the wider international community can be found in Article 26 of the 1948 Universal Declaration of Human Rights:

Article 26, Universal Declaration of Human Rights

(1) Everyone has the right to education. Education shall be free, at least in the elementary and fundamental stages. Elementary education shall be compulsory. Technical and professional education shall be made generally available and higher education shall be equally accessible to all on the basis of merit;

(2) Education shall be directed to the full development of the human personality and to the strengthening of respect for human rights and fundamental freedoms. It shall promote understanding, tolerance and friendship among all nations, racial or religious groups, and shall further the activities of the United Nations for the maintenance of peace;

(3) Parents have a prior right to choose the kind of education that shall be given to their children (UN, 1948).

While readers may be familiar with the contents of the first two paragraphs, the inclusion of Paragraph 3 raises further difficult questions. For example, what is meant by the right to choose in education for parents living in developing countries? And how does this right relate to the right to free and compulsory education outlined in Paragraph 1?

The answers to these questions can be found in the historical documents which recorded the debates and discussions that took place during the process of drafting Article 26 in 1947 and 1948. Until the final stage of the drafting process, Article 26 still only included the first two paragraphs. However, there remained serious concerns about the inclusion of the word compulsory in Paragraph 1, after a previous vote to remove it had been narrowly defeated by eight votes to seven. The fear was that free and compulsory education might be misinterpreted to mean that the control of education should be left entirely to the discretion of the state, or that the state should have unrestricted authority over education. It was important to exclude the possibility of situations in which governments had the power to prevent parents from educating their children as they wished. There were also concerns that the first two paragraphs had completely failed to acknowledge the importance of the people who were ultimately responsible for children's education – their parents.

For many of those involved in the drafting of Article 26, free and compulsory education was no longer sufficient to guarantee the right to education in the post-war period. The abuse of education in Nazi Germany was still too fresh in their minds. Free and compulsory education did not mean that education should be controlled by the government, or that a government monopoly should be allowed to develop, as this would clearly undermine the right of parents to choose. The purpose of Paragraph 3 was to safeguard this right by stating it explicitly. Paragraph 3 was therefore included in Article 26 to help ensure that free and compulsory education was not misinterpreted to mean that the state was free to develop a monopoly in the delivery of education and deprive parents of the right to choose, and also to recognize that, while the state can guarantee education, the primary responsibility and the right to determine education rests with parents.

The UN records also provide a unique insight into the relationship between each of the three paragraphs of Article 26 and help to shed new light on the purpose and meaning of the right to education, as defined by the international community in 1948. While the three paragraphs are numbered one to three, this merely reflects the order in which they were drafted and does not reflect a particular hierarchy of importance. The records also suggest that it was not the original intention of those who drafted Article 26 for each of three paragraphs to be addressed separately, or that any single paragraph should take priority over the others. In particular, it was not their intention for Paragraph 1 to be addressed in isolation to the others. Instead, while each paragraph addresses a different component of the right to education, all three components are interconnected and dependent upon each other. The right to education, therefore, can only be guaranteed when a careful balance between the three components is achieved. Figure 2.1 shows the interconnected paragraphs of Article 26.

In Figure 2.1 the right to education is represented by three interrelated components which interact not only with each other, but also with the surrounding environment. It is only when all three components interact together that the right to education is guaranteed – the whole (the right to education) is therefore greater than the sum of its parts.

The fact that Paragraph 3 was included specifically to prevent a government monopoly in the delivery of education implies that the right to education cannot be guaranteed unless there is a large and healthy private sector in education. This suggests that the recent growth of private schools serving low-income communities in developing countries is entirely consistent with the original concept of the right to education as defined in Article 26 in 1948. It simply represents an example of parents exercising their basic right to choose in education and, contrary to popular belief, this basic human right is not only relevant to middle and high-income families but it is important to all parents, irrespective of income.

However, when comparing the current rights-based approach to education for all, discussed earlier, with the above interpretation of the right to education, it immediately becomes clear that the basic right of parents to choose

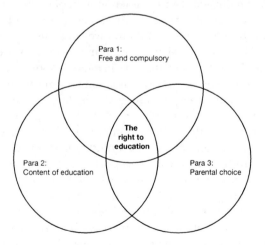

Figure 2.1 Article 26 and the right to education

and control the kind of education their children receive has completely disappeared. Instead, it is the rights of children which now appear to dominate the discussion. This point has previously been discussed by Willmore (2002), who suggested that while the failure to educate all children has received much attention, 'failure to allow freedom of choice, in contrast, has received little attention in international fora, even though this human right, without question, is violated more frequently than the right to free education'. Willmore (2002) concludes that this violation of a basic human right is so widespread that many development experts no longer question its wisdom or its morality.

A freedom-based approach

If the international community is to reverse this ongoing neglect of the rights and responsibilities of parents, and if it is to embrace the growth of private schools for the poor, then a new freedom-based approach may now be required.

A useful insight into what the freedom-based approach to education for all will look like is provided by the way the United Nations approaches the task of guaranteeing the right to food, and food for all. While there are obvious differences between food and education, both can be defined as basic human needs, with food clearly ranking as the most important.

The UN's Food and Agricultural Organization (FAO) was established in 1945 with a mandate to raise levels of nutrition and to improve agricultural productivity. Food was recognized as a basic human right in Article 25 of the 1948 Universal Declaration of Human Rights, and at the World Food Summit in 1996 the UN reaffirmed the fundamental right of everyone to be free from hunger and the right of everyone to have access to safe and nutritious food. Member states therefore pledged themselves to achieve Food for All, with an immediate objective of halving the number of undernourished people by 2015. While the FAO states that the primary responsibility for ensuring the right to adequate food and the fundamental right to the freedom from hunger rests with national governments, this does not mean that governments have a duty to distribute food to all their citizens. Instead, they have an obligation to respect the right to food by not interfering with individuals' efforts to provide for themselves, and should help those who do not already enjoy the right to food by creating opportunities for them to provide for themselves. It is only after these safeguards fail to secure food for all that a government has a responsibility to provide food, especially to those unable to help themselves. However, while the FAO refers to a government's obligation to provide for the vulnerable by the direct distribution of food, an alternative is also recommended; governments may also issue food vouchers, which may be much more cost-effective.

The government's obligation to fulfil the right to food comprises an obligation to facilitate, which means that it should create and maintain an 'enabling environment' within which people are able to meet their food needs. Therefore, facilitating the enjoyment of the right to food does not necessarily mean direct government intervention, but that government can take steps to ensure private markets are allowed to perform well. National governments can therefore take a number of measures to promote private food markets without resorting to direct food assistance, including reducing barriers to obtaining trade licences, making it easier for companies to enter the market, reducing value-added taxes to keep food prices affordable and by introducing legislation to prohibit monopolies.

The question of how a freedom-based approach will operate within the existing human rights framework has also previously been outlined by the Special Rapporteur on the Realization of Economic, Social and Cultural Rights, Danilo Türk. In a 1992 report, Türk reflects on the need for new approaches in implementing social and economic rights and, under the sub-heading 'Creating standards or creating space?' he raised the question of whether the United Nations should perhaps focus more on the creation of space than on creating standards:

> Creating political, legal, social and economic space, implying the expansion of access to space, to decision-making, to individual, family and community choices and to *de facto* opportunity to assert, demand and claim economic, social and cultural rights are processes at least as critical to the attainment of these rights as is the creation of new legal or quasi-legal standards.
>
> (Türk, 1992, para. 188)

As Türk suggests, creating space recognizes the fact that a significant proportion of the obligations associated with economic, social and cultural rights are negative in nature, implying that government has a duty not to intervene in certain areas of people's lives. The creation of space therefore does not require substantial government expenditure, but instead requires a government to create the conditions necessary for the eventual fulfilment of these rights, and so '[t]he creation of space by Governments can, in fact, lead to improvements in the livelihood of citizens by simply allowing people to create their own solutions to their own problems' (Türk, 1992, para. 192). According to Türk, this approach also recognizes the frequent inability of governments to intervene sufficiently or provide the necessary resources for these rights to be widely enjoyed. The government should allow these processes to flourish, while simultaneously acting in full accordance with any international obligations concerning these rights. He concludes that '[i]t is in these areas that the relevance of "freedom" enters the domain of economic, social and cultural rights' (Türk, 1992, para. 193).

Therefore, when the freedom-based approach is applied to education, governments will have an obligation to create and maintain an 'enabling environment' within which parents are free to exercise their right to choose how their children should be educated. This places a further obligation on governments to respect the rights and responsibilities of parents by not interfering with their efforts to help themselves. Creating space for education to develop will therefore allow parents to create their own solutions to their own problems. A critical role of government in the freedom-based approach to education will be to ensure that private education markets are allowed to perform well by: establishing and maintaining a fair and level playing field; promoting competition; reducing barriers to entry and making it easier for new schools to enter the market; restricting monopolies; reducing all forms of taxation on schools; and removing all unnecessary and bureaucratic regulations. The role of government will be to positively encourage choice, competition and entrepreneurship in education.

Finally, the freedom-based approach in education is also based on the clear recognition that national governments do not have access to the knowledge or resources that would enable them to guarantee education for all, while also respecting the rights and responsibilities of parents. In circumstances where parents are unable to help themselves, governments can address this problem through the issue of school vouchers, which parents are free to use at the school of their choice. This is the only way of guaranteeing universal access to education without undermining the right of parents to choose.

Conclusion

In his 2008 publication *The Power of Freedom – Uniting Development and Human Rights,* Jean-Pierre Chauffour is heavily critical of development experts who often promote top-down poverty-reduction and growth strategies, supported by international aid and aid agencies, while completely neglecting the fundamental role of freedom in development. Chauffour concludes that 'the debilitating outcomes of traditional development policies in many low-income countries are often the direct, albeit unintended, result of a disregard for freedom in development' (p. 131). These same arguments can equally be applied to the international community's efforts to assist in the growth and development of education in developing countries over the previous half-century. While the focus of attention has been on state intervention and control, top-down central planning and international aid, there has been less attention paid to respecting the rights and responsibilities of parents and restricting government intervention in order to allow the natural growth of education to flourish.

A government monopoly of free and compulsory state schools and a rights-based approach to education for all is not the only approach which national governments across the developing world can choose to embrace. For those governments prepared to reject the prevailing consensus and blaze new trials, the freedom-based approach to education for all may soon become an increasingly attractive alternative.

References

Aggarwal, Y. (2000), *Public and Private Partnership in Primary Education in India.* New Delhi: National Institute of Educational Planning and Administration.

Chauffour, Jean-Pierre (2008), *The Power of Freedom: Uniting Development and Human Rights.* Washington DC: Cato Institute.

De, A., Majumdar, M., Samson, M. and Noronha, C. (2002), 'Private schools and universal elementary education', in R. Govinda (ed.), *India Education Report. A Profile of Basic Education.* New Delhi: Oxford University Press, pp. 131–50.

Educating the Poorest (17 February 2007), *Financial Times.* London.

EFA (2009), *Global Monitoring Report – Overcoming Inequality: Why Governance Matters.* Oxford: Oxford University Press.

Hattem, G. (24 September 2008), Deutsche Bank press release.

Nambissan, G. B. (2003), *Educational Deprivation and Primary School Provision.* IDS Working Paper 187, Institute of Development Studies, Sussex.

The Probe Team (1999), *Public Report on Basic Education in India.* Oxford and New Delhi: Oxford University Press.

Tooley, J. and Dixon, D. (2005), *Private Education is Good for the Poor: A Study of Private Schools Serving the Poor in Low-income Countries,* Washington DC: Cato Institute.

—— (2007), 'Private education for low income families: results from a global research project', in P. Srivastava and G. Walford (eds), *Private Schooling in Less Economically Developed Countries.* Oxford Studies in Comparative Education. Didcot: Symposium Books, pp. 15–40.

Türk, D. (1992), *The Realisation of Economic, Social and Cultural Rights.* United Nations, Economic and Social Research Council. E/CN.4/Sub.2/1992/16.

UNESCO/UNICEF (2007), *A Human Rights Based Approach to Education For All.* New York: UNESCO/UNICEF.

United Nations (1948), *Universal Declaration of Human Rights.* New York: UN.

Watkins, K. (2000), *The Oxfam Education Report.* Oxford: Oxfam in Great Britain.

Willmore, L. (2002), *Education by the State.* United Nations, DISA Discussion paper No. 27.

Chapter 3

Women's education in the developing world
Máiréad Dunne

Introduction

Education and gender equality hold key positions in the development agenda, with an international consensus articulated in the Education for All (EFA) goals and Millennium Development Goals (MDGs). In this context, this paper provides an overview of basic education in Ghana since around the turn of the century with specific reference to gender. It starts with a brief review of the international agreements relevant to schooling and gender. Then the specific case of Ghana is discussed using the available statistical descriptions about basic education. Many positive changes at the macro level over the last ten years or so are noted. Following this, qualitative, micro-level research within schools is used to provide deeper and sociologically nuanced accounts of educational quality and gender equality in Ghana. These provide insights into the local, everyday experiences that lie behind the numbers.

The concluding section discusses the contrasting scenarios provided at the macro and micro level. Given the significance of schools for the production of identities and patterns of social relations, the argument points to the evident need for more contextually located research to explore how the progress towards educational (and social) goals impacts on schools, classroom environments and the conditions for learning. Notwithstanding the significant gains in educational development recorded by Ghana, such contextually rich research would help to breach the discursive hegemony of quantification, its concomitant narrow definitions of development and truncated conceptualizations of gender. Greater synthesis of quantitative and qualitative data in monitoring progress and in research studies would allow the processes and outcomes of development policy and practice to be more fully understood and addressed.

The international context

An international focus on education was signalled in the EFA initiative launched in 1990 at the World Conference on Education for All in Jomtien,

Thailand. Importantly, this initiative highlighted an integrated focus on education and gender for development. Gender remains a key variable in promoting and monitoring access, equity and quality improvements in education. In 2000, the World Education Forum in Dakar, Senegal, restated the international commitment to gender and education in the establishment of the Dakar Framework for Action and six EFA Goals. These were echoed in the MDGs that linked gender equality and formal education through a target for the attainment of gender parity in primary and secondary schools. This was the only target specified for the achievement of Millennium Development Goal 3: to promote gender equality and empower women (Humphreys et al., 2008). These international education goals have permeated national policy in Ghana and elsewhere across the globe and they have provided a focus for statistical data collection used to measure and compare development outcomes in Ghana and internationally. These data are available in the annual global monitoring reports (GMR) produced by UNESCO and reports from other international agencies.

Notwithstanding the importance of these outcome measures in shaping and gauging development progress, there is also a more generalized international focus on the social processes of development which, although more difficult to measure, refer to the conditions of everyday life within any given context. These derive from a human rights approach that highlights the importance of social processes as well as outcomes of development efforts. This approach is manifest in the Convention on the Rights of the Child (United Nations, 1989), Health-promoting Schools (WHO, 2003), and the EFA goals as well as in multi-agency advocacy for child-friendly schooling. All have direct significance for education. Alongside these, there are further international declarations that refer directly to gender, many of which have been taken up at national levels. For example, under the Ghana Constitution such commitments include the Convention on the Elimination of All Forms of Discrimination against Women (CEDAW), the Declaration on the Elimination of Violence against Women (DEVAW), the Protocol to the African Charter on Human and Peoples' Rights on the Rights of Women in Africa and, most recently, the Domestic Violence Act of 2007. This public acknowledgement is highly commendable and relevant to the achievement of gender and educational equality in Ghana; however, in practice the realization of these commitments remains an enormous challenge (Amankwah, 2008).

Educational progress in Ghana[1]

Turning specifically to progress in basic education, recent reports show that gross primary enrolment in Ghana (98 per cent) was higher than that in both sub-Saharan Africa as a whole (94 per cent) and all low-income countries (94 per cent). In Ghana this comprised almost equal proportions of females (97 per cent) and males (98 per cent) that again compare favourably with statistics for females across sub-Saharan Africa (88 per cent) and low-income countries (89 per cent) (World Bank, 2007). As expected, net primary enrolment is lower, and in Ghana currently it is reported at 71 per cent, which represents a positive increase from 63 per cent in 2000. Over the same period, the ratio of female to male enrolment has also increased from 93:100 to 99:100. Similarly, in both secondary and tertiary education, gender ratios have all shown increases over the last decade, but they are much lower than for primary schooling, at 88:100 and 54:100 respectively (World Bank, 2007).

The wider gap between female and male enrolments through successive stages of education is also apparent in Table 3.1. In pre-primary and primary education the Gender Parity Index (GPI) has been 0.93 and above since 2003 (Republic of Ghana, 2008). At junior high school (JHS) level both the GPI and gross enrolment rates are lower.

Table 3.1 Gross Enrolment Rates (%) and GPI by education sector in 2007/8.

	Female	*Male*	*GPI*
Pre-school	89	91	0.98
Primary School	93	97.3	0.96
Junior High School	75.3	82.2	0.92

Source: Republic of Ghana (2008).

More detailed analysis adds to the generally positive picture for Ghana. Gross admission to Primary One has increased from 89.4 per cent in 2004/5 to 107 per cent in 2007/8.[2] Over the same period, net admissions show a massive growth from 26 per cent to 74 per cent. Increases have also been experienced in JHS admissions although these have been less dramatic and more variable from year to year. Currently the GER and NER at JHS are recorded as 78.8 per cent and 53 per cent respectively (Republic of Ghana, 2008).

The statistics show Ghana's positive response to the MDGs and EFA goals in terms of access and gender. This, however, is only part of the story as the goals stipulate gender equality and access to *quality* education. In this vein, there has been increasing statistical emphasis on outcomes as an indicator of quality. For example, the Ghana National Education Report (Republic of Ghana, 2008) presents school completion rates. It calculates current average primary completion rates of 88 per cent and JHS completion rates of 67.7 per cent. As noted elsewhere, in both cases the completion rates are worse for girls than for boys (Dunne et al., 2005; Republic of Ghana, 2008). For Ghana, the completion rates show smaller and more fluctuating increases than described by the access data. This raises significant questions about quality and gender equality after admission to school.

In addition to completion rates, the Basic Education Certificate Examination (BECE) results, taken at the end of the basic education cycle in JHS3, have been monitored in Ghana. The pass rate, which has remained at just over 60 per cent since the beginning of the decade, is currently recorded at 63 per cent. A disaggregation by region and gender shows that girls record lower results than boys in all regions except Greater Accra. At the national level, the data show 62.08 per cent of boys and 37.92 per cent of girls achieving a pass (Republic of Ghana, 2008). These pass scores do not guarantee entry to Senior Secondary School (SSS). At this point, between the end of basic education and the start of senior secondary schooling, there is a sharp dropout from education. The gross enrolment rate at SSS has been decreasing over recent years and stands at 32.2 per cent, comprised of 44 per cent females (Republic of Ghana, 2008).

Poor progression to SSS has implications for access to further educational and occupational opportunities which continue the gendered trend observed in Table 3.1. In a period of increased third-level entry in Ghana, the proportion of females enrolled in state universities has remained around one-third since the beginning of the decade. Private universities have shown massive growth in student numbers over the decade, but with stable although slightly higher proportions (40 per cent) of female enrolments. In addition, studies have indicated that subject specialisms remain stereotypically gendered. For example, there is a strong dominance of females in Home Economics and males in Engineering (Dunne et al., 2007; Morley and Lussier 2009). The gender inequalities evident in the educational data are further marked in the broader social picture, in which only around 36 per cent of women are in non-agricultural employment. Women have only 18 per cent representation in the national parliament. These data have shown minimal change over the last decade and indicate deepening inequalities, even for those who have successfully navigated education to graduate level (UNESCO, 2008; World Bank, 2009).

Low completion rates and poor progression through the levels of education indicate problems with educational quality that are clearly gendered. This throws a shadow on the positive picture provided by the statistical evidence, and raises concerns about the school experiences, especially of girls, and thereby with the achievement of the EFA goals that stipulate 'access to quality education'. To some extent, a dominant focus on access has made issues of quality a secondary concern. Also, in a field dominated by quantitative data, the main indicators of quality are outcome measures. This is exemplified in the recent education report in Ghana in which discussions of quality refer to BECE results, national tests on basic pupil competencies in mathematics and English and the Trends in International Mathematics and Science Study (TIMSS) data for science and mathematics performance outcomes (Republic of Ghana, 2008). Since 2006, however, school numeracy and literacy tests have been made available as diagnostic tools, a development that highlights classroom processes as integral to educational quality.

A number of in-school factors were used in the GMR on Quality (UNESCO, 2004) in acknowledgement that examination results, while important, are not sufficient to capture school quality. Accordingly, in Ghana the data on access and outcomes are supplemented by data on teachers and the school environment. These include proportions of trained teachers, teacher education enrolment, teacher attendance, pupil time on task, pupil teacher ratio, textbooks per pupil, toilet facilities, availability of water, classroom building conditions and child health. This represents a wider capacity to gather data relevant to deeper understandings of the conditions for teaching and learning in Ghanaian schools.

Another important effort for improved quality has been articulated in the widespread advocacy for learner-centred pedagogies. In some cases this has been interwoven with a gender equality advocacy message (FAWE, 2005; Oxfam, 2007). The focus on pedagogy is clearly significant to the learning environment and therefore to quality. Linking quality to this specific pedagogical ideology, however, while justifiable in educational, democratic and human rights terms, highlights considerable difficulties and tensions (Mokgosi, 2009). First, for many in Ghana and elsewhere, it represents a challenging shift in perspective about educational and social practices (Tabulawa, 1997; Aikman and Unterhalter 2005). Second, the relationship between learner-centred pedagogy and the key quality indicators of examination outcomes is weak. Third, the link to learner-centred pedagogies emphasizes the problems in capturing quality in quantitative terms. Despite the centrality of quality to educational (and social) goals, quantification still dominates to effectively marginalize key aspects of school quality that do not lend themselves to the definitive categorization that typifies mainstream development discourse (UNESCO, 2004).

Qualitative insights

The dominant emphasis on targets and statistics has reflected a policy concern with the macro level and a rather instrumental perspective on schooling which has obscured knowledge and understanding about the quality of the school environment. As discussed above, issues of quality are not only integral to the educational goals of the EFA and MDGs, but have relevance for the other international commitments (e.g. CRC, CEDAW). The school environment as the social context of formal schooling has significance not only for examination and occupational outcomes, but for the experience of schooling and the production of citizenship identities of pupils (Humphreys et al., 2008). This section reviews predominantly qualitative research evidence on the quality of the school environment with specific reference to gender in Ghana. This research is not directly connected to the quantitative data presented earlier and neither can local level studies be generalized in the same way. Nevertheless, these studies open avenues to explore quality and provide valuable, complementary evidence on social and educational development.

It is important to note that numerous small-scale studies across sub-Saharan Africa have also added to our knowledge about access. Many studies on gender and access refer to out of school factors including cost, cultural and religious practices, distance and domestic labour or income generation responsibilities (see for example, Stephens, 1998; Avotri et al., 2000; Academy for Educational Development, 2002). Although these factors militate against the access for girls, in certain contexts they have also been found to affect access for boys. Research on access in Ghana has directly connected access to the quality and relevance of schooling, which were cited as the main reasons for school dropout (Pryor and Ghartey Ampiah 2003; Akyeampong et al., 2007).

Focusing inside schools, studies from a range of countries across the continent have explored the school environment from a gender perspective, reporting poor quality and highly gender-differentiated contexts for learning. They refer to the lower classroom participation of girls, more verbal interaction between boys and teachers (although often in a disciplinary context) and teacher assumptions about the higher intellectual abilities of boys (see, for example, Odaga and Heneveld, 1995; Colclough et al., 2003; Pattman and Chege, 2003; Humphreys, 2005). Other studies indicate that being in school has often placed young girls and boys in difficult, uncomfortable and even vulnerable circumstances (Longwe, 1998; Mirembe and Davies, 2001; Aikman and Unterhalter, 2005).

Close ethnographic work in six Ghanaian JHSs has produced detailed observations of how gender structures play out through the everyday routines of schools. The study shows how gender is (re-)produced in the organization and management of staff and pupils; the distribution of formal and informal school responsibilities; the use of space; discipline and in the formal and informal relations between teachers and pupils (Kutor et al., 2005; Dunne, 2007). It was evident in this research that physical space for pupils and teachers was highly gendered within and outside the classroom. This was typified by gender segregation in classroom seating patterns, the use of the playground and within the staffroom or staff area. Being in the proper gender space was so important for pupils that teachers were able to use this as a disciplinary sanction, in which they moved boys to sit among girls. The boys also commanded the verbal space of the classroom by speaking out to claim and gain more teacher attention. Attempts by girls to participate were actively discouraged through ridicule and other forms of harassment. Teachers demonstrated their complicity with the gender regime, irrespective of their own gender, by taking these conditions as the normal run of things. Some teachers, in efforts to motivate boys further, degraded girls through negative comparison to the expected low standards of their work (e.g. 'even the girls can do it better than that'). These insights indicate informal practices that regulate gender identities and provide gender differentiated opportunities for learning.

Formal regulations in schools were more explicitly gendered. These include gender-specific uniforms as well as tasks allocated to male and female pupils and teachers. In broad terms, these tasks reflected the domestic division of labour in which males did physically intensive jobs and females cleaned and serviced males and visitors. Examples include male teachers' customary responsibility for corporal punishment and boys' occasional tasks around the school compound, including digging. Female pupils, on the other hand, were responsible for cleaning the classrooms daily and female teachers took care of hospitality in welcoming school visitors. Gender stereotypes extended to teacher subject specialisms and a male-dominant hierarchy was expressed by all teachers in their views in favour of school leadership by male principals. The gender hierarchy was manifest in the appointment of male pupils as head prefect, with a female as deputy. This pattern was repeated at the class prefect level and the prestigious post of bell-ringer was always a male pupil. These aspects of the gender regime structured the school environment to regulate gender identities and constrain the possibilities for female and male pupils' agency in schools with important implications for how they experienced all aspects of their education (Dunne et al., 2005).

The institutional organization of schooling clearly does more than prepare pupils for examinations and a focus only on these, or dropout or access, obscures the connections between educational quality, gender and social development. Despite the positive quantitative indicators on access, the paucity of research and understanding about the quality of the school experience and environment leaves doubt about the possibilities of achieving the EFA goals and MDGs. Research evidence in schools suggests that other commitments by the Ghanaian Government, including the Rights of the Child, Convention on the Elimination of All Forms of Discrimination against Women (CEDAW) and the Declaration on the Elimination of Violence against Women (DEVAW) are also in jeopardy (Leach et al., 2003; Dunne, et al., 2005).

The ethnographic study referred to earlier (Kutor et al., 2005) clearly showed gender as a major structure of the social world in schools. Multiple forms of coercion and control were normalized within the institution as 'natural' aspects of everyday school life that provided gender-differentiated experiences and outcomes. In this and other studies across the region (see, for example, Human Rights Watch, 2001; Shumba, 2001; Leach and Mitchell 2006) more severe manifestations of the gender regime were found in acts of physical, symbolic and sexual violence.

Caning, for instance, despite specific policy regulation, was an everyday feature of school life widely used or threatened by teachers as a disciplinary sanction. In all schools boys received more corporal punishment than girls. Random or excessive corporal punishment was cited by boys as a major factor in truancy and absconding. For many pupils the use of verbal abuse, another common disciplinary strategy, was more personally damaging than the physical violence of corporal punishment. Boys, in explaining the extent of the corporal punishment they were subjected to, accused male teachers of favouring girls because they wanted sexual favours. Observations provided evidence that some male teachers engaged with female students in personal and even sexually suggestive ways. Reactions to this from girl pupils ranged from a visible shrinking from public attention to those who boasted privately of this special attention. As discussed earlier, girls' attempts at public verbal participation left them open to routine intimidation by the boys, a process through which they were silenced and marginalized. As these and earlier examples indicate, teachers often exacerbated the hostile learning environment for girls (for more detail see Dunne et al., 2005).

Between pupils, too, there was widespread bullying in many schools in which older boys intimidated or took money and property from girls and younger boys. Girls were subject to sexual harassment through inappropriate or violent physical contact and there were some cases of sexual assault and rape by male teachers, as well as pupils. Sanctions against such teachers were rarely implemented, although they are delineated in national education policy, and in many cases may be classified as defilement and subject to criminal prosecution. By contrast, pregnant schoolgirls were forced to drop out and in many cases did not return to school (Kutor et al., 2005). Beyond the educational consequences, a study in Ghana shows the enormous personal damage, especially in relationships within their families, suffered by young women who are victims of sexual abuse (Forde and Hope, 2008).

The above-cited research on the quality of the school environment in Ghana reveals the important part played by schools in the production of learner identities. In particular, institutional life in schools is structured by gender and socially regulates and reinscribes polarized and antagonistic gender identities. In taken for granted, everyday practices and sometimes in explicitly violent and sexual ways, a male-dominant gender hierarchy produces differentiated experiences of school. It is against this background that the statistical descriptions need to be re-read. We can begin to think in broader gender terms about issues of retention, examination performance and progression in the educational and occupational spheres. In short, the qualitative insights offered by this research are critical for deepening the understandings of educational and social development provided by statistical data. Importantly they indicate some key spaces for action in the accomplishment of the human rights and equity commitments made by the Government of Ghana.

LIBRARY, UNIVERSITY OF CHESTER

Conclusions

In the almost two decades since Jomtein, the focus on gender and education has been reflected in positive changes in Ghana. Nevertheless, the achievement of universal access to quality schooling remains elusive, especially in gender terms. The above discussion provided two views of educational access, quality and gender equality in Ghana. The picture produced by the macro-level quantitative data shows important steps towards gender parity in access and a few points where the gradient has moved in favour of girls (Akyeampong et al., 2007). This perspective is moderated through a consideration of micro-level case studies that provide contextual and relational detail about the social arena. The gender picture is much less positive. This methodological fracture, however, provides a point for reflexive engagement that offers productive potential in conceptual and practical terms.

Starting with gender, it is clear that the different approaches to research offer different conceptualizations. The fixed, static and binary categories of the macro data define gender as an outcome or status in which sex and gender are not differentiated. While this has its uses for monitoring purposes, it militates against understanding the complex social processes of becoming a gendered individual. Rather than being accomplished in an active process of social signification through continuous performances of femininity and masculinity, the statistical data assumes gender identities are given and refer back to sex at birth. Explanation of poor educational progression and low female representation in government and business can only be referred to as the consequences of biology. Understandings of educational and social development are thus seriously limited by the conceptual restrictions imposed by the categorical gender binary (Oyĕwùmí, 2002). More complex and heterogeneous conceptualizations of gender and sexuality (masculine and feminine) identities used in recent research illustrate how it can strengthen understandings of what is going on in learning environments (Morrell, 2001; Leach, 2003; Pattman and Chege 2003; Dunne et al., 2005; Humphreys, 2005).

In the same vein, it is clear that attempts to capture educational quality in statistical terms is limited, offering restricted insights into the conditions for, and experience of, learning. Further, given the insights provided in the case study research discussed above, different indicators might be more important for gauging school quality. A convincing case might be made to suggest that gender disaggregated data on incidents of violence might be a higher priority than data on the pupil–teacher ratio. Such data on gender discrimination, harassment and violence might also be useful in a range of social institutions including the workplace.

A further strength of small-scale, qualitative approaches to research lies in the capacity to capture and articulate local insights and perspectives. This contrasts with the quantitative data sets that focus on outcome measures produced in response to international priorities and parameters. While this might be useful for various comparisons and rankings, the indicators are temporally and socially frozen, affording no access to the dynamics of the social in which teacher and pupil agency is actively engaged, for example the production of gender and sexual identities and hierarchies. This obscures the very relations through which quality and gender equality are produced and veils the spaces for positive productive intervention. On the other hand, contextually located research with a relational and contingent theorization of gender has provided understandings of heterogeneous masculinities and femininities and their intersections with other identities (Dunne, 2009). Importantly, this kind of sociologically nuanced research has contributed to the deconstruction of the images of the universally dominant 'bad' male and subordinated 'good' female (see, for example, Morrell, 1998; Wood and Jewkes 2001). It is research of this genre that has given rise to richer theorizations that offer more space and scope for successful, contextually relevant intervention towards gender equality.

Finally, any grasp of social and educational development in Ghana, or elsewhere, requires contextually located and rich accounts of social process. These are needed to act as a foil to the discursive hegemony of quantification within development discourse. That is to say, we should be informed by the trends and differences that quantitative research can offer as long as we keep its limitations in constant view. The case of gender in Ghana discussed here provides examples of those multiple limitations. There is much to be said for keeping the methodologies and substantive findings in creative tension, and with this the range of global and local positions and perspectives. In practical terms, this means that there is a need for more systematic qualitative research in specified policy or practice contexts that is theoretically reflexive. It should be clear that this description moves far beyond the illustrative anecdote. Whether such studies are carried out in their own right or combined with quantitative data and analysis, it is important that the conceptual and theoretical framing is held under constant critical review. Such knowledge practices would render dominant assumptions more fragile, avoid theoretical imposition and thereby allow improved understandings of local contexts and perspectives. The interplay of such reflexive engagement offers space and scope for emergent, locally informed theorizations, priorities and strategies for educational and social development especially related to gender.

Notes

1. The statistical data in this section comes from a number of different sources which means that the data collection and statistical processes have not been uniform. Similar trends are evident in the data despite these variations. Refer to the source documents for details of the specific data collection and analysis.

2. Gross enrolment includes over-age children, and this means that the numbers enrolled in a class or school can exceed the number of children of the correct cohort age, thus more than 100 per cent is possible, and not uncommon.

References

Academy for Educational Development (2002), *A Transnational View of Basic Education: Issues of Access, Quality, and Community Participation in West and Central Africa*. Washington, DC: Academy for Educational Development.

Aikman, S. and Unterhalter, E. (2005), 'Conclusion: policy and practice change for gender equality', in S. Aikman and E. Unterhalter (eds), *Beyond Access: Transforming Policy and Practice for Gender Equality in Education*. Oxford: Oxfam.

Akyeampong, K., Djangmah, J. Oduro, A., Seidu, A. and Hunt, F. (2007), *Access to Basic Education in Ghana: The Evidence and the Issues*. CREATE Country Analytic Report. Winneba and Brighton: University of Winneba/Centre for International Education, University of Sussex.

Amankwah, A. A. (16 June 2008), *Ghana: Violence against Women Still Common in Country*, from http://allafrica.com/stories/ 200806161363.html (accessed 24 September 2009).

Avotri, R., Owusu-Darko, L., Eghan, H. and Ocansey, S. (2000), *Gender and Primary Schooling in Ghana*. Research Report No. 37. Brighton: IDS/FAWE.

Colclough, C., Al-Samarrai, S., Rose, P. and Tembon, M. (2003), *Achieving Schooling for All in Africa: Costs, Commitment and Gender*. Aldershot: Ashgate.

Dunne, M. (2007), 'Gender, sexuality and schooling: everyday life in junior secondary schools in Botswana and Ghana', *International Journal of Educational Development*. 27(5), 499–511.

—— (2009), *Gender as an Entry Point for Addressing Social Exclusion and Multiple Disparities in Education*, www.ungei.org/ ny2009/docs/Gender%20as%20an%20 Entry%20Point%20for%20Addressing%20Social%20Exclusion%20and%20 Multiple%20Disparities%20in%20Education.pdf (accessed 13 May 2009).

——, Akyeampong, A. and Humphreys, S. (2007), *School Processes, Local Governance and Community Participation: Understanding Access*. CREATE Pathways to Access Research Monograph No. 6. Brighton, UK: Centre for International Education, University of Sussex. See www.create-rpc.org/publications/ pathwaystoaccesspapers.shtml (accessed 20 December 2007).

——, Leach, F., Chilisa, B., Maundeni, T., Tabulawa, R., Kutor, N., Forde, L. and Asamoah, A. (2005), *Gendered School Experiences: The Impact on Retention and Achievement in Botswana and Ghana*. DFID Education Research Report No. 56. London: Department for International Development.

—— and Sayed, Y. (2007), 'Access to what? Gender and higher education in Africa', in K. April and M. Shockley (eds), *Diversity in Africa: The Coming of Age of a Continent*. London: Palgrave, pp. 223–37.

FAWE (2005), *Gender Responsive Pedagogy: A Teacher's Handbook*. Nairobi: FAWE.

Forde, L. D. and Hope, W. (2008), 'The impact of sexual abuse on Ghanaian schoolgirls' family relationships', in M. Dunne (ed.), *Gender, Sexuality and Development: Education and Society in Sub-Saharan Africa*. Rotterdam: Sense Publishers, pp. 133–46.

Human Rights Watch (2001), '*Scared at School: Sexual Violence against Girls in South African Schools.* New York: Human Rights Watch.

Humphreys, S., Undie, C. and Dunne, M. (2008), 'Gender, sexuality and development: key issues in education and society in sub-Saharan Africa', in M. Dunne (ed.), *Gender, Sexuality and Development: Education and Society in Sub-Saharan Africa.* Rotterdam: Sense Publishers. ch. 1, pp. 7–38.

Humphreys, S. (2005), 'Schooling identity: gender relations and classroom discourse in selected junior secondary schools in Botswana', unpublished DPhil thesis, University of Sussex.

Kutor, N., Forde, L. D., Asamoah, A., Dunne, M. and Leach, F. (2005), *Life in Schools: Gendered Experiences in Junior Secondary Schools in Ghana.* Takoradi, Ghana: St Nicholas Press.

Leach, F. (2003), 'Learning to be violent: the role of the school in developing adolescent gendered behaviour', *Compare*, 33(3), 385–400.

——, Fiscian, V., Kadzamira, E., Lemani, E. and Machakanja, P. (2003), *An Investigative Study of the Abuse of Girls in African Schools.* DFID Education Research Report No. 54. London: Department for International Development.

—— and Mitchell, C. (eds) (2006), *Combating Gender Violence In and Around Schools.* Stoke-on-Trent, UK: Trentham.

Longwe, S. H. (1998), 'Education for women's empowerment or schooling for women's subordination?' *Gender and Development*, 6(2), 19–26.

Mirembe, R. and Davies, L. (2001), 'Is schooling a risk? Gender, power relations and school culture in Uganda', *Gender and Education*, 13(4), 401–16.

Mokgosi, L. (2009), 'Quality in Botswana schools', unpublished DPhil thesis, University of Sussex.

Morley, L. and Lussier, K. (2009), 'Intersecting poverty and participation in higher education in Ghana and Tanzania', *International Studies in the Sociology of Education*, 19(2), 71–85.

Morrell, R. (1998), 'Of boys and men: masculinity and gender in Southern African studies', *Journal of Southern African Studies*, 24(4), 605–30.

—— (2001), 'Corporal punishment and masculinity in South African schools', *Men and Masculinities*, 4(2), 140–57.

Odaga, A. and Heneveld, W. (1995), *Girls and Schools in Sub-Saharan Africa, from Analysis to Action.* World Bank Technical Paper No. 298. Washington DC: World Bank.

Oxfam (2007), *Practising Gender Equality in Education.* Oxford: Oxfam.

Oyĕwùmí, O. (2002), 'Conceptualizing gender: the Eurocentric foundations of feminist concepts and the challenge of African epistemologies', *JENDA: A Journal of Culture and African Women's Studies*, 2(1), www.jendajournal.com (accessed 20 July 2007).

Pattman, R. and Chege, F. (2003), *Finding Our Voices: Gendered and Sexual Identities and HIV/AIDS in Education.* Nairobi: UNICEF ESARO.

Pryor, J. and Ghartey Ampiah, J. (2003), *Understandings of Education in an African Village: The Impact of ICTs.* Education Series Research Report No. 52. London: Department for International Development.

Republic of Ghana (2008), *Education Sector Performance Report 2008.* Accra, Ministry of Education, Science and Sports.

Shumba, A. (2001), 'Who guards the guards in schools? A study of reported cases of child abuse by teachers in Zimbabwean secondary schools', *Sex Education*, 1(1), 77–86.

Stephens, D, (1998), *Girls and Basic Education: A Cultural Inquiry.* Education Research Paper No. 23, Brighton, University of Sussex.

Tabulawa, R. (1997), 'Pedagogical classroom practice and the social context: the case of Botswana', *International Journal of Educational Development*, 17(2), 189–204.

United Nations (1989), Convention on the Rights of the Child, www.unhcr.ch/ html (accessed 12 September 2009).

UNESCO (2004), *Education for All: the Quality Imperative.* EFA Global Monitoring Report 2005. Paris: UNESCO.

—— (2008), *Overcoming Equality: Why Governance Matters.* EFA Global Monitoring Report 2009. Paris: UNESCO.

WHO (2003), *Creating an Environment for Emotional and Social Well Being: An Important Responsibility of a Health-promoting and Child-friendly School,* www.who. int/school youth health/media/en/sch childfriendly_03_v2.pdf (accessed 24 September 2009).

Wood, K. and Jewkes, R. (2001), '"Dangerous" love: reflections on violence among Xhosa township youth', in R. Morrell (ed.), *Changing Men in Southern Africa.* Scottville and University of Natal: Zed Books.

World Bank (2007), *Ghana at a Glance,* devdata.worldbank.org/AAG/gha_aag.pdf (accessed 12 September 2009).

—— (2009), *Ghana and the Millennium Development Goals,* http://ddp-ext. worldbank.org/ext/ddpreports/ViewSharedReport? &CF=&REPORT_ ID=1305&REQUEST_TYPE=VIEWADVANCED (accessed 12 September 2009).

Chapter 4

Self-assessment in the further education college of a small state

Gary Jones, Edward Sallis and Peter Hubert

Introduction

Education systems around the world, and particularly those based in small states, are faced with having to respond to the accelerating demands of economic, political, technological, environmental and social change. One way in which education systems in small states have sought to bring about improvement is through the importation of 'best practice' from larger states. This chapter provides a case study of the importation of policy and practice into a small state. It looks at the particular example of how a small further education college has imported policy on self-assessment and adapted it in order to increase its ability to improve the quality of its provision. As such, it generates a critique of large state policymaking models. In doing so, it also directs attention to the role of research capacity and capability in the initiation, implementation and institutionalization of policy and practice. Furthermore, it identifies the possibilities that individuals have in small states to contribute to their organization's future.

This chapter uses the work of Hubert et al. (2009) which is an *ex post facto* case study that describes the self-assessment and self-improvement journey undertaken by Highlands College in Jersey. Evidence for this narrative was gathered using interviews with internal participants on that journey, and from focus groups of internal and external participants, e.g., college inspectors, governors and representatives of Jersey's education service. The interviews were conducted by a research associate who also acted as the facilitator for focus groups to elicit what they considered to be the factors that have contributed to making the journey possible. This information was analysed to establish which factors may have been critical to the success of the quality processes and the importance participants attached to those factors.

Self-assessment

The fundamental premise behind self-assessment is that if an educational organization wishes to bring about improvement it needs to have an accurate self-assessment or evaluation of the quality of its provision. Underpinning this view is that the responsibility for bringing about improvement lies with the organization itself. Nevertheless, within this process it is necessary for there to be a significant degree of external validation of that self-assessment. Indeed, self-assessment can no longer be described as 'fashionable' as it has been part of the process of managing English further education colleges since the mid-1990s. Indeed, ever since the publication of the FEFC Circulars 97/12 and 97/13, further education colleges have been producing annual evidence-based self-assessment reports, which have been a critical part of any external accountability processes. The continued relevance of self-assessment is reflected in the Learning and Skills Improvement Service's (LSIS) 2009 handbook: *A User Guide to Self-Assessment and Improvement Planning* (Learning and Skills Improvement Service, 2009), which is the most recent of many such publications. In addition, OFSTED (2009) *Handbook for the Inspection of Further Education and Skills from September 2009* states that self-assessment 'should be an integral part of an organization's quality improvement arrangements' (p. 27).

Conceptual framework

A conceptual framework we can use to gain some critical purchase on this case study is through the use of the model developed by Fullan (2007) in seeking to understand educational reform. Fullan argues there are two ways of looking at the factors associated with educational reform: one, to look at the factors that affect success, which is described as an innovation focused approach; and, two, to look at how organizational capacity and capability to engage in continuous improvements is developed, which is described as the capacity building focus. Fullan states that these are not separate processes, as there can be high levels of interaction between the two.

Fullan argues that most educational researchers now regard the change process as consisting of three interacting phases:

- initiation/adoption – which consists of the process leading up to the decision to proceed with implementation;
- implementation and initial use – the attempt to put change into effect, lasting up to three years;
- continuation or institutionalization – where the reform becomes an integral part of the system, otherwise a decision is made to discontinue the reform.

The intimacy of small states makes it difficult to distinguish between change agents responsible for adopting and initiating an innovation and those charged with the innovation's implementation and continuation. This may require the amendment of theoretical models based on research in small states. An example of a large-state model is provided by Bowe et al. (1992) which was developed from the school reforms in the England of the late 1980s. Bowe et al. (1992) state that policy formulation and implementation is a cycle of mutual influence between the context of influence, the context of text production and the context of practice. The context of influence is primarily outside the public domain, and this is where interested parties develop ideas and objectives, often at national level. The context of text production involves the development of official texts representing policy, which may diverge from policy initiators' intentions, and again this is something that occurs at national level. The evaluation of policy at this level may lead to pressure within the context of influence to reformulate policy.

In the context of small states, there is the question of to what extent local text production is policy documents taken 'off the shelf' from other educational institutions. However, an oversimplistic approach of policy importation from one political, economic and social environment to another is not without its risks. Crossley and Watson (2003) cite Sir John Sadler's lecture, delivered at the beginning of the twentieth century:

> We cannot wander at pleasure among the educational systems of the world, like a child strolling through a garden, and picking off a flower from one bush and some leaves from another and then expect that if we stick what we have gathered into the soil at home, we shall have a living plant . . .
>
> (Crossley and Watson, p. 6)

However, in small states it is likely that the same individuals will be involved in both the importation of policy and the practice of implementation. Individuals who are involved in trying to shape and influence policy will also be connected with both production of policy documents and their subsequent implementation. Accordingly, it is necessary to ask the question as to what extent is it possible to separate the three contexts in a small state. Jones (1995) in a study of school development planning in Jersey primary schools analyses the overlapping of the three differing contexts and highlights the impact of a particular individual in each of the three contexts. This overlapping of contexts highlights the importance of personal impact upon the operations of an education department. John Rodhouse, former Director of Education in Jersey states: '. . . another feature of the culture of a small Department concerns the extent to which individuals can have a personal impact' (Rodhouse, 1991, p. 24).

Of particular interest is the possibility that the 'smallness' provides positive advantages to both policymakers and practitioners. Brock (1985) cites Cammish (1985) in viewing small states as providing laboratory-like conditions for educational experimentation. Indeed, this is a case study of how tertiary education in Jersey has become a laboratory for experimentation relative to England. It explores lessons that may have resonance for others who believe that a less regimented and bureaucratic approach is the prerequisite of the move from 'good to great' in public services (Learning and Skills Improvement Service, 2009, Cabinet Office, 2008).

The rest of this paper will consider a specific example of how policy and approaches to college improvement have been imported from a large state and then subsequently amended to meet the local needs of the importing small state.

The Jersey context

The Bailiwick of Jersey is completely independent in domestic affairs from the UK. It has its own legislative assembly, the States of Jersey. Despite this independence, the education system is essentially English in curriculum and organization. As such, Jersey is the importer of educational policy, although rarely are these policies adopted without significant change and adaptation to meet the needs of local circumstances. Moreover, when viewed closely it is an English education system with a peculiarly Jersey feel. A local history sums this sense of difference up in its title *Jersey: Not Quite British* (Le Feuvre, 1993). The island has customized its education service, imbuing it with its own distinct Jersey values and policies, including the teaching of the island's Norman French indigenous language, *Jerriais*.

The island has a further education college, Highlands College, which largely follows an English curriculum but which has found its own solutions to quality assurance and quality improvement. The college has been given the freedom to follow its own solutions and to match these to the challenges of operating in an insular context (Hubert et al., 2009). Focus will now turn to the specific policy and practice, which was imported, i.e. self-assessment and its role in bringing about quality improvement.

Validated self-assessment in action

The following section is based on Hubert et al. (2009), which provides a fuller account of validated self-assessment in action. Until the incorporation of colleges in the UK, Her Majesty's Inspectorate had a role in inspection in the Channel Islands, and Highlands College had last been inspected in 1991. Formed in 1992, the Further Education Funding Council's new inspectorate only had responsibility for English colleges so Jersey was left without an inspection regime. However, the publication of FEFC Circular 97/12 *Validating Self Assessment* and FEFC Circular 97/13 *Self-assessment and Inspection* prompted some early development work in the college on the development of self-assessment reporting. This development work was also encouraged by the education service's own innovation of validated school self-evaluation, launched in 1995.

In 1997 a new principal was appointed and he, in consultation with the governing body and the Director of Education, agreed to an inspection of the college in order to benchmark it against English performance. The full inspection was led by Dr Terry Melia CBE, the former FEFC Chief Inspector, and took place in April 1998. The use of self-assessment reporting was a key element of the inspection, as was the inclusion of a Jersey education department nominee on the inspection team. The combination of the initial work on self-assessment and the principal's initiating of a full inspection marks the start of the process by which Highlands College has taken ownership and responsibility for its performance.

After the inspection the governing body appointed a college inspector who would advise them on quality issues and, importantly, carry out development work with staff to improve quality. The first inspector was Dr Melia and he was succeeded by Dr Maureen Banbury OBE, a former senior inspector in England's Office for Standards in Education (OFSTED). From 1999 a process of annual visits by Dr Melia was instigated. During his visits he met with the team leaders for each of the curriculum areas, senior managers and those with college-wide responsibility for quality. In those meetings he received reports on progress against previous quality and performance action plans. This formed the basis of an annual report to the governing body.

In 2000, the governors strengthened their ability to work with Dr Melia by forming a Standards Committee. This gave the governing body the underpinning for what is now called self-regulation. Jersey's education service is represented on that committee.

In 2002 it was decided to adopt a different approach from England, but to use the same framework to make judgements (ALI and OFSTED, 2001). The intention was that the process would be far more developmental. Curriculum teams were grouped into six categories, of which two would be inspected each year for the next three years. One innovation was to involve Curriculum Team Leaders, working alongside inspectors, so that knowledge of standards in the college could be enhanced. Team Leaders conducted joint lesson observations with inspectors and contributed to the judgements. Colleagues from Guernsey College also formed part of the inspection teams.

Overlapping with the rolling self-assessment cycle was the introduction in 2003 of visits by critical friends to support curriculum areas prior to inspection. Dr Maureen Banbury led these visits with a brief to review the strengths

and weaknesses statements in self-assessment reports and data about retention, completion, success, progression, and so on. She and her team also
spoke with staff and students, scrutinized students' work and observed lessons.

The outcome was a discussion with the curriculum team and a report con-
firming strengths and suggesting areas where a change in practice would lead
to an improvement in performance and the students' experience. These visits
were designed to be supportive and bring about significant improvement.

In 2004 Dr Banbury took over as college inspector and the governing body
decided not to repeat the inspection procedure, but to develop a process that
emphasized self-improvement. This had been one of Dr Melia's recommendations following the publication of his inspection report. The use of external
experts was seen as valuable in an island community, to provide context and
benchmarks, so their use was incorporated into Supported Self-Improvement
(SSI), a process devised in collaboration with Dr Banbury. Her report for
OFSTED, *Why Colleges Succeed* (2004), was used to inform a 'future perfect'
for Highlands College towards which staff would work. SSI was not inspection
in another guise, but a beneficial and supportive process designed to help
the curriculum area improve. To obtain the most benefit it was necessary for
staff to be completely open about their work and treat the external reviewer/
inspector as a facilitator for improvement and critical friend, rather than as
an external auditor.

The format of SSI encouraged a speedy response by the curriculum
teams involved. This is largely because of the review's two-part structure: an
initial three-day visit by the critical friend to set the scene and put forward
a number of hypotheses to be tested out at the four-day second visit, some
three months later. Each visit included observations of teaching and learning,
discussion with learners and employers, scrutiny of student work and analysis
of performance data. The period between the two visits became, in almost all
cases, a period of rapid development and quality improvement. During the
second visit the critical friend would determine the extent of progress and
present a final report aligned to the Common Inspection Framework (ALI
and OFSTED, 2005). The extent of progress was taken as a direct measure
of capacity to improve.

Moreover, those areas which were to be subject to the SSI process the
following year invariably felt the positive pressure from the findings of critical
friends and endeavoured to make those improvements in their own provision.
Those that had had Supported Self-Improvement the previous year were
expected to do likewise. Consequently, improvement across the whole college
ratcheted up, year on year. Table 4.1 summarizes the key developments in the
history of self-assessment at Highlands College.

Table 4.1 Key developments in the history of self-assessment at Highlands College.

Year	Development
1991	Inspection of Highlands College by Her Majesty's Inspectorate.
1995	Jersey education service launch validated school self-evaluation initiative.
1997	Publication of FEFC 97/12 and 97/13 and resulting development work on self-assessment and appointment of new principal.
1998	Whole college inspection led by Dr Terry Melia.
1999–2001	Annual report by college inspector.
2002–4	Rolling programme of self-assessment and inspection.
2003	Introduction of critical friends process.
2005	Publication of revised Common Inspection Framework (OFSTED, 2005). Appointment of Dr Maureen Banbury as college inspector.
2005–9	Programme of supported self-improvement reviews.

Self-assessment and the change process

It is now necessary to try to locate the development of self-assessment within our conceptual framework; this will allow the identification of key messages for each of policymakers, practitioners and researchers. Attention will now focus on the process of initiation, implementation and continuation.

First, there are clearly a number of factors that were associated with the initiation phase. There was the existence of external innovation through the development of self-assessment by the Further Education Funding Council, and this innovation was easily accessible via FEFC Circulars 97/12 and 97/13 (FEFC, 1997a, 1997b). There was teacher advocacy in that some preliminary work had already taken place in developing a local self-assessment framework. Furthermore, this work was consistent with another local innovation, i.e. validated school self-evaluation. Finally, there is evidence of the problem-solving and bureaucratic orientation by the newly appointed Principal in that the 1997 inspection allowed for an external assessment of the strengths and weaknesses of the college.

Second, we turn to the ongoing implementation of self-assessment as a vehicle for improvement. In a world where there are continuing demands for ever-increasing levels of performance, there was a clear need for innovation that would contribute to ongoing college improvement. Indeed, this need to respond to continued demands for ongoing college improvement helped provide clarity to the purposes of the innovation. However, the innovation in itself was relatively complex in that self-assessment and its subsequent validation sought to capture all aspects of the college's performance. In addition, it involved working with external change agents, i.e. the college inspector to ensure the process remained manageable. The innovation also had the benefit of being of high quality in that there were substantial external materials available to inform the work being undertaken. At the same time, it remained practicable in the context of the relative autonomy given to the college by the Jersey education service, thus enabling it to shape whatever was done to meet the local requirements of the college.

Third, the innovation has now been embedded within the college for over ten years and we need to look at a number of key factors which have contributed to the institutionalization of the innovation. The senior leadership team of the college has been relatively stable, with both the Principal and Deputy Principal being in post for over ten years. There has been a joint commitment by both senior managers to bring about continued improvement in the college's performance. The Principal focused on outward-facing public relations efforts, while the Deputy Principal concentrated on internal improvement. Furthermore, continuation has in large part been facilitated by the progressing redesign and development of the process, with particular emphasis being placed on ensuring the authority and legitimacy of the process by involving high-quality external change agents whose background, experience and expertise enhance the credibility of the outcomes.

If we now shift to the capacity and capability orientation, we can observe a number of factors which have contributed to the ongoing development of the innovation. One, there has been a continued emphasis on sharing practice within the college, ensuring the lessons learnt in one part of the process are transferred to other parts of the college. As such, the process has contributed to the ongoing development of a professional learning community. Two, resources have continually been made available to support the validation of self-assessment. Lecturing staff at the college have been encouraged to visit other colleges so that they can see what is happening elsewhere, which could be used as a source of ideas or a provisional external benchmark. The way in which the process has unfolded, particularly in the supported self-improvement phase of the innovation, has involved a continued focus on working with external partners to ensure that staff within the college are able to make informed judgements about the quality of the provision for which they are responsible. As such, this helps create the conditions for accurate self-assessment.

Additionally, the college has invested in research and development capability to support self-assessment. It has used 'practitioner research' as the vehicle to assess and refine its middle-management capability and to build new skills, particularly in the area of performance management. This has sharpened the awareness of the extent to which the college is meeting its goals and has provided it with the tools to move forward. In recognition of this work the college was awarded the Learning and Skills Improvement Service 2009 Prize for Research, which contributed to developing the college's local community.

It is now necessary to ask the question, how does this account relate to Bowe et al.'s model of policy formulation? This case study provides clear evidence within a small state that there is overlap between contexts of influence, text production and of practice. The individuals involved in developing the policy and practice of ongoing self-assessment and subsequent implementation have been the Principal, Deputy Principal and the governing body of Highlands College. To some extent the contact of text-production has been bypassed, as policy texts have been imported from large states, i.e. the UK, and then been subject to high levels of adaptation through a process of ongoing experimentation and development.

Implications for small states, policy and research

The paper suggests that practitioners in small states have the ability to make significant changes to externally developed educational innovations. Individuals are in a strong position to make significant contribution to the education system to which they belong. In particular, it provides further evidence for Cammish (1985), in that small states can provide the opportunity to experiment and develop solutions to issues and problems through the thoughtful adaptation of large-state reforms. However, with this opportunity comes significant responsibility that the adoption of such reforms are undertaken for the right reasons and does not involve the importation of policies and innovation as 'fashion-accessories' which are legitimated through their adoption in other larger settings.

Jones (1996) argues that policymakers in small states will need to reflect on the degree to which they should introduce reforms that have led to the intensification and restructuring of other larger educational systems. Policymakers and practitioners will need to exercise significant professional judgement in determining the appropriate policies to adopt and how they should be reshaped to meet the specific requirements of local conditions. In addition, Jones argues that policymakers in large states may wish to look to small states for the source of educational reform and innovation. Rather than just being an importer of educational reforms, small states become re-exporters of policy and innovations. Small states provide opportunities for large-state policymakers to examine what policies and innovations could look like if implemented within a different setting. Indeed, the incorporation of Hubert et al. (2009) within the Learning and Skills Improvement Service's *Volume 12 Researching Self-Regulation in FE Colleges* provides evidence for how this process is occurring in the context of self-regulation.

As Crossley and Holmes (1999) argue elsewhere, further research is required into how small states can build the capacity to evaluate large-state educational reforms in order to bring about thoughtful local adaptation and implementation. In particular, this case study is a product of seeking to build research capacity, and as such further research is required in how to make 'practitioner research' more effective in supporting local adaptation and implementation. In addition, further research is required to find other examples of large-state policies, practices and innovations which have been adopted in small-state settings to see how these have been adapted to meet the requirements of such contexts. Finally, research is also required to look at the long-term impact of individuals within small states in order to understand what are the characteristics of effective practitioners within such intimate environments.

Acknowledgements

The report on Highlands College's development of its self-improvement processes, *Developing Self-Regulation at Highlands College*, which underpins this work, was funded by the Learning and Skills Improvement Services as part of their practitioner research programme into leadership in the further education sector.

References

ALI and OFSTED (2001), *The Common Inspection Framework for Inspecting Post-16 Education and Training*. London: OFSTED.

ALI and OFSTED (2005), *The Common Inspection Framework for Education and Training from 2005*. London: OFSTED.

Bowe, R., Ball, S. and Gold, A. (1992), *Reforming Education and Changing Schools: Case Studies in Policy Sociology*. London: Routledge.

Brock, C. (Ed.), (1985), *Educational Issues in Small Countries: Proceedings of a One Day Conference of the British Comparative and International Education Society*. Hull: BICES, University of Hull International Education Unit, pp. 22–9.

Cabinet Office (2008), *Excellence and Fairness: Achieving World Class Public Services*, www.cabinetoffice.gov.uk (accessed 17 March 2010).

Cammish, N. (1985), 'Educational issues in small countries: the case of the Seychelles', in C. Brock (ed.), *Educational Issues in Small Countries: Proceedings of a One Day Conference of the British Comparative and International Education Society*. Hull: BICES, University of Hull International Education Unit, pp. 22–9.

Crossley, M. and Holmes, K. (1999), *Educational Development in the Small States of the Commonwealth: Retrospect and Prospect*. London: Commonwealth Secretariat.

—— and Watson, K. (2003), *Comparative and International Research in Education: Globalisation, Context and Difference*. London: Routledge.

FEFC (1997a), *Validating Self Assessment*, Circular 97/12. Coventry: FEFC.

FEFC (1997b), *Self-assessment and Inspection*, Circular 97/13. Coventry: FEFC.

Fullan, M. (2007), *The New Meaning of Educational Change*, 4th edn. London: Routledge.

Hubert, P., Sallis, E. and Jones, G. (2009), 'Developing self-regulation at Highlands College', in D. Collinson (ed.), *Researching Self-Regulation in FE Colleges, vol 12*, Learning and Skills Improvement Service, pp. 27–44.

Jones, G. (1995), 'School development planning in the primary schools of a small state: an interpretive multi-site case study of an innovation', unpublished EdD thesis, University of Bristol.

—— (1996), 'School development planning in Jersey primary schools: a contingency analysis', *School Organization*, 16(3), 281–95.

Learning and Skills Improvement Service (2009), *A User Guide to Self-assessment and Improvement Planning*, www.excellencegateway.org.uk (accessed 17 October 2009).

Le Feuvre, D. (1993), *Jersey: Not Quite British*. St Helier: Seaflower Books.

OFSTED (2004), *Why Colleges Succeed*. HMI 2409.

—— (2005), *The Common Inspection Framework for Inspecting Education and Training*. London: OFSTED.

—— (2009), *Handbook for the Inspection of Further Education and Skills from September 2009*, www.ofsted.gov.uk (accessed 17 October 2009).

Rodhouse, J. (1991), 'Jersey', in M. Bray (ed.), *Ministries of Education in Small States: Case Studies of Organization and Management*. London: Commonwealth Secretariat.

Chapter 5

The contribution of European programmes to social change

Simone Kirpal

Introduction

With the adoption of the Lisbon strategy in the year 2000, the European Union set concrete targets to become the most competitive and dynamic economic area in the world. In this context, general education and vocational training were not only defined as key factors for attaining the targeted social and economic benchmarks, but they were recognized as essential foundations for innovation and enhancing the competitiveness of all European countries. Ultimately, realizing the Lisbon strategy does not only require extensive changes to the European economy, but also an equally ambitious modernization programme for the social welfare and education systems, with the enhancement of the quality, attractiveness and accessibility of opportunities for lifelong learning being a major goal.

Taking account of the close connection between economic competitiveness and human resource development, the training and preparation of teachers and trainers in vocational education and training were identified as central to the improvement of the educational systems in the future (Commission of the European Communities, 2001, pp. 6–7). Thereby it is assumed that in a knowledge-based economy the role of trainers and teachers is fundamentally changing, which requires that the way in which trainers and teachers are being prepared for their responsibilities and supported in their roles also needs to be adjusted. Dimensions that were considered to be subject to major changes in this context include: the promotion of new learning outcomes such as citizenship; accounting for social, cultural and ethnic diversity in teaching and training practice; the integration of ICT in learning situations; and taking responsibility for one's own professional development, among others (Commission of the European Communities, 2003, p. 22).

The role of teachers and trainers in VET as 'key actors to make lifelong learning a reality in Europe' was further emphasized in the work programme *Education and Training in Europe: Diverse Systems, Shared Goals for 2010* (European Commission/Directorate-General for Education and Culture,

2002). This work programme addresses three main areas of concern: the skilling needs of the target group; provision of adequate support structures; and solving recruitment problems that are anticipated for the future. That the continuing competence development of teachers and trainers should reflect their specific learning needs was further identified as a priority in the Maastricht Communiqué of 2004, which underlined the role of VET teachers and trainers as facilitators and innovators in the learning environment. Finally, a more embedded approach to support VET teachers and trainers was concluded with the Bordeaux Communiqué in 2008 that laid down new priorities of co-operation in vocational education and training for the future.

In line with those programmatic proclamations, the European Commission launched and supported different research and development initiatives targeted at VET teachers and trainers in the past years. Interestingly, those 'top-down' approaches initiated by the European Commission or other relevant European agencies were concurrently complemented by several 'bottom-up' approaches in the form of project proposals and initiatives developed by researchers or other stakeholders. How those different initiatives interlink and what implications they have for modernization and social change will be discussed in this chapter. Thereby I will seek to address both the structural impact of European projects as well as the content aspects that the different initiatives had and have, as some are still ongoing.

European initiatives targeted at VET teachers and trainers

While it seemed relatively easy to agree that VET teachers and trainers should be better supported, the development of concrete supporting measures for this target group turned out to be a difficult undertaking. One problem encountered relates to the different characteristics and needs of VET teachers on the one hand, and trainers on the other hand. While some measures for teachers in the general education system were already formulated in 2001, for example in terms of job descriptions and common European principles for teachers' competences and qualifications (Commission of the European Communities, 2003, pp. 21–2), the transferability of those principles to teachers and trainers in VET was found to be problematic, mainly because a teacher was defined as a person acknowledged to having the 'status' of a teacher (or equivalent) according to the legislation and regulations of a given country. For teachers in continuing training and trainers, however, we find that their status is not as clearly defined. This is particularly true for trainers involved in company-based training or external training services, who typically assume teaching and training responsibilities on a more informal basis and who are not designated as a particular occupational or status group (Kirpal and Tutschner 2008; EUROTRAINER Consortium, 2008).

Another problem encountered related to the limited information available on the situation, work, qualification and status of the target group that could give evidence of appropriate measures to undertake. As concerns trainers, research and basic data hardly exist and they are scarce with regard to the situation of VET teachers. Furthermore, a 'trainer' in most European countries is not a clearly defined occupational category and in some contexts considerable overlap between the functions and roles of VET teachers and trainers can be found. Thus, in response to the gap of research and information on VET practitioners in Europe, the first European studies and activities specifically sought to gather basic information on the situation and professional development of VET teachers and trainers to inform European policies in the area.

One of the first initiatives to enhance the visibility of the target group was supported by the European Centre for the Development of Vocational Training (CEDEFOP). Starting in 1998, the Training of Trainers Network (TT-Net) was set up as a pan-European forum for key players and decision-makers in the training and professional development of vocational teachers and trainers. Composed of national networks with representatives from the public and the private sector, TT-Net was funded to operate at the national level and at the international level to contribute to the development of European policy in the field. In 2005 TT-Net was given a study to explore job profiles of VET teachers and trainers and identify tasks, responsibilities and competence requirements for the different VET profiles defined. The description of these profiles was thus linked to the development of a European competence framework for teaching and training professions. In the implementation of the study, those were divided into practitioners working in initial vocational education and training (Lot 1) and continuing vocational education and training (Lot 2). Methodologically the study involved semi-structured interviews with representatives of each of the defined professional profiles across a range of European countries. The project deliverables covered: a Competence Framework; recommendations for the initial and further training of trainers; recommendations for policies targeted at VET teachers and trainers; and suggestions for the use of the framework.

As a parallel initiative, in 2005 the European Commission launched the European Focus Group on Teachers and Trainers in VET within the work programme 2010. This group based its activities on regular consultation activities (so-called 'Peer Learning Activities' – PLA), each of which would focus on a specific topic. Like the TT-Net, the Focus Group comprised national mainly government representatives or representatives from relevant stakeholders such as the social partners. The activities resulted in two commissioned studies on trainers in 2006. Lot 1 – Studies on Trainers in Enterprises (EUROTRAINER) – was to provide an analysis of the situation of trainers in companies. Lot 2 was to address the situation of trainers in private and public institutions and to provide an analysis of the respective training markets. Both studies covered the thirty-two European countries and combined quantitative and qualitative methods as well as country reports. They were the first Europe-wide studies on trainers geared towards providing an overview to inform European policies in the field.

Concurrently, another project on the continuing professional development of trainers (www.ttplus.org) was funded in 2006 under the Leonardo da Vinci Lifelong Learning Programme. (This is a European funding scheme for vocational education and training commonly geared towards training practice, transfer of knowledge and the development of practical tools. Currently it comprises several strands, a three-year, more research-oriented programme, a three-year network strand and the classical two-year transfer of innovation projects oriented towards training practice.) This two-year project was based on a proposal coming from six European countries that sought to develop a commitment-oriented professional development framework for trainers as an alternative approach to defining competence profiles of VET practitioners in relation to the European Qualification Framework. The second bottom-up initiative was a direct result of the co-operation among partners in the two studies on trainers commissioned in 2006. It resulted in the 'Network to Support Trainers in Europe', equally funded under the Leonardo da Vinci Programme in 2007 for a duration of three years. The key objective of the network was to provide a platform (www.trainersineurope.org) that could link the different European initiatives and facilitate an ongoing exchange between practitioners and stakeholders at the national and European level. The network further provided support to facilitate a community building process at the international level, on the one hand, and to establish national networks to develop the field for VET practitioners on the other hand. It involves about twenty European partners that support the development of the network and its activities in various ways.

The network initiative points to the idea that three elements need to be combined in order to effectively support VET practitioners in practice: generating more information on this so far under-researched target group; making available practical tools for the work and professional development of VET teachers and trainers; and enhancing the communication, exchange and community building among stakeholders and VET practitioners. The described initiatives to date have had two major impacts: they helped to establish a community interested in the field, and they raised the awareness of the key role that VET practitioners play in the education system and in society. However, a major shortfall had been that the different initiatives were largely uncoordinated. Against this shortfall the European Commission sanctioned another project in 2008 that implemented seven regional consultation seminars in order to bring the outcomes of the different studies and initiatives together and validate their main results in a regional and national perspective (www.consultationseminars.org). Finally, CEDEFOP in 2008 commissioned another study to investigate the 'Changing Roles and Competences of VET Teachers and Trainers' in nine European countries, seeking to develop a more in-depth international comparative perspective on the topic.

Some major trends

Several trends suggest that the teaching and training practice in companies and institutional contexts is changing, resulting in new competence requirements for VET practitioners both in terms of their basic qualification as well as their continuing professional development. In particular four major trends impact upon the changing education and training environment in which VET practitioners operate:

1 **Demographic shifts**
   There is demographic change in European societies, and the number of young people is decreasing. This affects the training market insofar as training providers increasingly compete for students, trainees and adult learners, who become more demanding in terms of expecting tailor-made training offers. A trend can be observed that clients expect training to be shorter, faster and more targeted. On the other hand, the demographic shift entails the risk of a shortage of skilled training professionals in the near future.

2 **Integration of VET into more comprehensive lifelong learning systems**
   The provision of vocational education and training is increasingly becoming integrated into more comprehensive learning and education systems. This raises issues concerning the modularization of programmes and the transferability between VET and other educational pathways. It can also be expected that this development will gradually undermine the distinction between the professional roles of VET teachers and trainers in terms of their work tasks, responsibilities and competence requirements.

3 **Decentralization of education and training systems**
   In many European countries a tendency towards decentralizing national education and training systems can be observed, leading to a greater degree of autonomy of training providers. This, on the one hand, increases the opportunities for training practitioners to influence training practice. On the other hand, it also induces new demands on the planning, implementation and coordination of training provisions, which may result in more pressure and higher competition for training practitioners. The increase in local or institutional autonomy also means that various stakeholders such as enterprises and professional organizations are becoming directly involved in the activities of VET institutions. This increases the networking and coordination

requirements for institutions, organizations and companies and their training staff.

4   **Enhanced standardization and professionalism of VET teachers across Europe**
Supported by the Bologna Process, European member states have established frameworks of national standards for VET teachers, for example for curriculum development, tutorial support, skills assessment, management of learning environments and teachers' continuing professional development. Those standards tend to be linked to competence frameworks which, however, are mandatory or legally anchored to different degrees depending on the respective national context. Also the formal qualification requirements for VET teachers are fairly standardized across Europe and are typically related to a certified teaching qualification. For permanent teacher positions a pedagogical qualification is increasingly becoming a legal requirement. One key objective of introducing higher levels of standardization for VET teachers is to enhance their professional status, which tends to be lower compared to the status of teachers of academic subjects or general schooling. The status issue results in problems of recruitment and retention of VET teachers in many countries. In addition, ongoing strategies to improve the quality of vocational teaching and learning through national standards are a key driver to the emerging professionalism among VET teachers.

5   **Persistent and growing diversity in training practice**
Contrasting with the situation of VET teachers, we find notable differences in the degree of regulation of training contexts and standards of qualification and professional development for trainers. Great differences exist between the European countries. For example, regulation is relatively high in Germany and relatively low in Denmark or the Netherlands. But this is also the case between work contexts, sectors or areas of training, where there is great variation in the level of standardization and regulation. While across Europe training provision and competence requirements for trainers working in health care are fairly strongly regulated, they are mostly unregulated in the ICT sector. They are more standardized for trainers working in public institutions than for those employed by private companies. Among companies, large companies usually have a clearly defined and advanced system of training, using specialized training departments and employing professional trainers, at least to some degree. In small- and medium-size companies (SMEs) by contrast, training provision is often provided by part-time trainers who assume training functions in addition to their regular work tasks as skilled workers. In some countries, those in-company trainers may have a craftsman qualification and some

further technical or commercial qualification as well as some years of work experience, the latter being a precondition in almost all countries in Europe. Their training activities take place alongside their general workload. A key issue here is that those skilled workers may not immediately identify as trainers, which makes it difficult to reach them for inclusion into programmes specifically targeted at trainers.

As concerns the different areas of training, initial vocational education and training (IVET) in some countries like Germany or Denmark is more regulated and standardized than continuing vocational training (CVET) or adult education. However, in other countries it is the reverse: Spain, Romania and the Baltic countries, for example, have introduced standards for CVET and adult education and certification for 'adult educators', while IVET remains largely unregulated. In countries where the IVET tradition is strong, such as in Germany, standards for trainers also apply in terms of providing evidence of their capacity to work with young people, and pedagogical competences are a requirement to train apprentices. However, in most countries pedagogical competences are not required to assume training functions. Moreover, in some countries like the UK and the Netherlands, IVET and CVET are not strictly identified as two separate domains, but are integrated into a common framework of lifelong learning.

Skilling needs and social change

Trainers' emerging skilling needs are closely related to social change and new learning pathways in modern society. There is a growing demand that trainers and teachers in vocational education and training possess well-developed pedagogical, social and communication skills, particularly as mentoring, coaching and facilitating the learning process are gaining significance and learner groups are becoming increasingly diverse. The diversification of the target groups of teaching and training refer to more heterogeneous youth cohorts in terms of their ethnical, social and educational background but also to the increasing numbers of adult learners coming from all age groups and social backgrounds.

On the other hand, skilling needs closely relate to the changing role of trainers, which essentially refers to two aspects: one concerns an *internal role redefinition* of the training practitioner from 'instructor' to 'coach' or 'facilitator', questioning the former authoritarian position of the trainer or teacher and requiring new forms of communicative and social competences to engage in team working, mentoring and facilitating innovative forms of learning. The other aspect addresses the *changing responsibilities* of VET teachers and trainers as the nature of the training practice itself is changing with more elements of project-oriented learning, new aspects of quality assessment in the learning processes and more complex coordination with other training facilities and educational institutions. The stronger focus on work-based learning, in-company training and the business processes, which can be observed across Europe, increases the amount of management and coordinating functions VET practitioners are expected to assume. This latter aspect points to reinforcing the development of management competences to be able effectively to support training-related processes such as quality monitoring, project management and the co-operation with other institutions, colleagues and stakeholders. Management competences are gaining significance against the above-mentioned trends: the decentralization of education and training processes; the integration of VET into broader lifelong learning arrangements; and the decreasing numbers of trainees which require combined training efforts and offers across companies and institutions.

Pedagogical and social competences are needed to facilitate didactic processes and working with young people and adults, in particular fostering the integration function of training, mentoring, corporate learning and effectively passing on knowledge to others. Didactical skills are required with regard to the combination of work and learning, the identification of learning opportunities in the workplace and the ability to motivate and guide the learner towards autonomy and independent learning. The latter becomes particularly important against the shift from simply passing on knowledge to self-directed learning, which requires the active participation of the learner and adequate support from the trainer, to motivating and facilitating learners' self-learning capacities. Greater emphasis is also being placed on the provision of situated learning, encouraging learning by doing, and on guiding and facilitating the process of reflection. Social competences include interpersonal, communication and team-working skills and the ability to convey social values and manage training relationships.

Very broadly it can be said that, while trainers have well-developed vocational and technical competences in combination with significant practical work experience, in all European countries they tend to lack substantive and even fundamental pedagogical and social competences. In the case of VET teachers it is the reverse: the focus of teacher preparation is typically placed on the development of pedagogical and social competences while their knowledge of up-to-date technical processes of the workplace is insufficient, in most contexts. Not surprisingly, many efforts are geared towards balancing this mismatch by emphasizing the development of pedagogical and social skills in the continuing training of trainers, and making periodic workplace practice obligatory for VET teacher preparation, at least in some countries. However, in reality the training and professionalization of trainers is altogether underdeveloped, as are work practice requirements for VET teachers. Moreover, the development of coordinating or management competences can only rarely be found in the training agendas for any of the two groups. To some degree it still remains unclear which types of VET practitioners actually need to dispose of management skills and, if they do, to what extent. There is some good evidence that training practice in many contexts has changed relatively little: that, despite the rhetoric about lifelong learning and innovations in training and teaching, the dominant job profile and tasks of trainers are still very much centred around the assessment of learning outcomes and the core delivery of training; that the training methods trainers apply remain fairly standard; and that tasks related to quality monitoring, recruitment or the co-operation with other institutions play a relatively minor role or no role at all in trainers' everyday work practice. Ultimately, it seems that the performance of networking and organizational tasks related to training are only relevant for a minority of VET practitioners.

While there are intensive ongoing debates about the usefulness of developing common frameworks for the competence and professional development of VET practitioners, research has shown that personal interest, more than any kind of formal or legal requirement, drives the work motivation and engagement with continuing learning to develop the necessary skills and competences required of the job (Kirpal and Wittig 2009). Ultimately, it is the lack of incentives and benefits or adequate training opportunities that prevent VET practitioners from engaging in continuing learning, rather than lack of legal enforcement. Intrinsic motivation such as becoming a better trainer, or personal development objectives, by contrast, are the most important drivers. In the network survey conducted with over 700 VET practitioners across Europe, self-employed trainers, who are probably the least regulated category of all possible trainer types, had the highest rating on self-initiative and engagement in continuing learning and demonstrated the most positive attitude towards their profession. This links up with another key competence required of VET practitioners: personal development competences related to demonstrating the willingness and having the capacities to foster one's own personal and professional growth over time.

Conclusions and perspectives for the future

Many European countries seek to establish some kinds of standards for trainers – and the companies that offer training placements – and strive to enhance the professionalism of both VET teachers and trainers. Thus, introducing standards for the work and qualification of trainers is not only geared towards trainers' professional development, but they are regarded as instrumental in raising the status and recognition of the training and teaching profession and the quality of the education and training systems. Particularly in countries where the training sector and training provision remain largely unregulated, the quality of the respective national VET system, the (low) status of training practitioners and the lack of recognition of trainers' competences, are major issues of concern. Here we often find that a national competence or qualification framework for VET practitioners is regarded as a stepping stone to improve the quality of training and teaching in the medium and longer term. It is also seen as an important tool to make the training profession more attractive and to strengthen the vocational route, both of which are prerequisites for the prevention of problems in recruiting VET practitioners in the future. These are some reasons why many of the transition countries, but also Spain or Turkey, have enhanced their efforts to develop a national qualification framework that can be applied to VET practitioners. At the European level it is assumed that such frameworks promote access to training between different pathways, facilitate mobility and acknowledge competences at least in an *ex post* manner. Yet it is not clear how qualification or competence frameworks can provide access to learning, and how they can acknowledge prior informal and work-based learning and work experience. Thus, those countries in question also tend to work along an alternative route towards trainers' recognition of prior learning.

National educational traditions further impact on the roles and status of VET teachers and trainers. Countries such as Spain, Finland, Denmark, or the Netherlands, with a school-based VET system – the predominant model in Europe – have strengthened their practice-based components for students and trainees during the past decade. This gives trainers in enterprises a new and more prominent role and calls upon a stronger and better coordination between VET schools and enterprises. Thus, in all European countries we have trainers or workplace instructors in companies that have to deal with trainees or apprentices in one way or another. The role of those trainers tends to be more important, the more time students are required to spend at the workplace. Currently this amount of time varies from about 15 per cent in Spain to over 80 per cent in Germany. Where workplace training forms a major part of the vocational programme, the status of in-company trainers tends to be higher and collaboration between the vocational school and the workplace tends to be more strongly and better developed.

Overall, approaches to the training of VET teachers are much more standardized across Europe, while the training of trainers remains highly diversified and unregulated. Here, each country pursues its own strategy in terms of how the training is being organized; the institutions and people that provide training; the contents and objectives of the training programmes; and for which target groups trainings are being offered and supported. While the training for VET teachers is consistently provided by universities or other institutions of higher education, there seems to be a trend that the training of trainers is increasingly organized (but not necessarily delivered) by sectoral committees or chambers. In some countries like Finland, VET schools are organizing and providing the training of trainers. Thereby, the training of trainers is not being linked to the formal education system in most cases.

It is common in all countries that it is particularly difficult for trainers working in small- and medium-size enterprises (SMEs) to benefit from the training opportunities provided. This issue can be identified as a major challenge across Europe. It addresses the issue of identity (or non-identity) as training practitioner and having access to training and resources. Some countries are piloting innovative approaches to reach those trainers by bringing the training to them, rather then seeking to attract them to attend courses. The systematic disadvantageous position of trainers in SMEs as compared to trainers in large companies is a recurrent theme that emerged in all European studies on VET teachers and trainers.

The changing role of VET teachers and trainers in the education and learning process has been chosen to illustrate how targeted projects and initiatives seek to respond to, but also impact on social change in society. For the target group chosen, the process of professionalization and acknowledging their key role in society as change agents is only at the beginning. In order to underline VET practitioners' key role in the educational system, some countries such as Germany, Romania and Spain are in the process of establishing training as a self-standing profession by defining professional profiles and corresponding competence requirements for 'professional trainers' at all levels, but also against growing and diversifying training markets across Europe; professionalization is important in order to enhance the mobility and recognition of VET practitioners. What this diversification means for the future tasks and responsibilities of VET practitioners, and whether teacher and trainer profiles will be coming closer together or becoming more divergent, still remain open questions. While in some countries the responsibilities and areas of operation of VET teachers and trainers are strictly divided, like in Germany, in other countries they are not. In Spain, Finland or Lithuania teachers and trainers may assume the same tasks, depending on the specific training context. In those countries the professional profiles of VET teachers and trainers are not strictly divided – and it is an interesting question whether a combined profile could not turn into a European model for the future.

References

The Bordeaux Communiqué on enhanced European cooperation in vocational education and training. Communiqué of the European Ministers for vocational education and training, the European social partners and the European Commission, meeting in Bordeaux on 26 November 2008 to review the priorities and strategies of the Copenhagen process. Available at http:// ec.europa.eu/education/lifelong-learning-policy/doc/bordeaux_en.pdf

Commission of the European Communities (2001), Report from the Commission: The concrete future objectives of educational systems, COM (2001) 59 final,

Brussels. Available at http://ec.europa.eu/education/policies/2010/doc/concrete-future-objectives_en.pdf

Commission of the European Communities (2003), Commission Staff Working Document: Implementation of the 'Education & Training 2010' programme. Supporting document for the draft joint interim report on the implementation of the detailed work programme on the follow-up of the objectives of education and training systems in Europe, COM (2003), 685 final. Available at http://ec.europa.eu/education/policies/ 2010/doc/staff-work_en.pdf

Commission of the European Communities (2007), Communication from the Commission to the Council and the European Parliament 'Improving the Quality of Teacher Education', COM (2007), 392 final. Available at http://ec.europa.eu/ education/com392_en.pdf

European Commission/Directorate-General for Education and Culture (2002), Education and Training in Europe: diverse systems, shared goals for 2010. The work programme on the future objectives of education and training systems. Luxembourg: Office for Official Publications of the European Communities. Available at www.esib.org/documents/external_documents/0206_DG-CULT_diverse-systems-shared-goals.pdf

EUROTRAINER Consortium (2008), *Studies on Trainers in Enterprises. Key Actors to Make Lifelong Learning a Reality in Europe.* Bremen: University of Bremen/Institute Technology and Education.

Kirpal, S. and Tutschner, R. (2008), *Betriebliches Bildungspersonal. Schlüsselakteure des lebenslangen Lernens.* ITB Research Paper Series No. 33/2008. Bremen: University of Bremen/Institute Technology and Education. Available at http://elib.suub.uni-bremen.de/ip/docs/00010388.pdf

—— and Wittig, W. (2009), *Training Practitioners in Europe: Perspectives on their Work, Qualification and Continuing Learning.* ITB Research Paper Series No. 41/2009. Bremen: University of Bremen/Institute Technology and Education. Available at http://elib.suub.uni-bremen.de/ip/docs/00010607.pdf

Maastricht Communiqué on the Future Priorities of Enhanced European Cooperation in Vocational Education and Training (VET), http://ec.europa.eu/education/news/ip/docs/maastricht_com_en.pdf (accessed 14 December 2004).

PART II

Community Integration and Inclusion

Overview

This section of the book focuses on innovations in addressing community integration and inclusion. The opening chapter introduces the new action-orientated, multidisciplinary, methodology of social marketing. Chahid Fourali presents social marketing as a promising approach to help address social ills and disadvantage. He introduces the concept and techniques which borrow from marketing and social sciences. He presents social marketing, supported with examples, as a powerful tool that has demonstrated its effectiveness in helping make social changes affecting large populations. He believes that there are yet many areas of conflict resolution and educational development that could still benefit from its capacity to:

- stimulate the debate on what constitutes worthwhile educational aims;
- relate local cultures to ethical and educational objectives;
- develop strategies that maximize results and minimize costs;
- reach and affect the behaviour of large sectors of the population; and
- adapt its practice according to existing best advice, thereby encouraging the use of latest effective approaches.

Maryam Danaye Tousi and Alireza Kiamanesh evaluate the basic education status, defined as reading, spelling and mathematics ability, of 793 Afghan male and female fifth-grade refugees who participated in a Department for International Development (DFID) project in different provinces of Iran at the end of the 2002–3 academic year. They show that the DFID project was successful in attaining its goals in providing its beneficiaries with basic education in reading and spelling, but not in mathematics. In reading tests and subtests the males outperformed the females. In spelling tests, 10–19-year-old females outperformed the peer males; however, older males outperformed the peer females. In mathematics tests, the 10–14-year-old females outperformed the peer males; however, again, older males outperformed the females. There was not a significant difference in participants' performance in reading subtests as their age increased, except for comprehension. The authors explore how these findings could play an important role in influencing education policy and thinking about the basic education of Afghan refugees in Iran and other countries.

Siobhán Fitzpatrick describes the development and progress of early childhood services in Northern Ireland, characterized as a deeply divided society where most educational services are segregated across religious divisions. In contrast, however, groups in the informal early education system have managed to maintain a cross-community, anti-sectarian focus and often provide the only opportunity for young parents and children from different backgrounds to get to know each other before entering a divided school system. As a result of this history, Early Years – the Organization for Young Children, was recognized by the European Union as a vital player in helping build the peace. The organization's position moved from a neutral non-sectarian and non-political stance to one that was more explicitly anti-sectarian, that encouraged respect for, and celebration of, difference. Building on local research into the development of, and influences upon, the values of young children and through adopting a partnership approach to its work, Early Years began to explore ways to deal more explicitly with difference and exclusion. The chapter highlights lessons learnt from the ensuing programme of work and its achievements in changing children's attitudes and behaviours. Implications for developments in early childhood in other countries and regions affected by conflict are presented, drawing upon the work of an International Network on Peace Building with Young Children led by Early Years.

Carla Solvason, writing in the context of sports specialism in secondary education in the UK, notes that there has been a subtle but significant policy shift away from inclusion and towards elitism within sports, which has run parallel to the marketization of education – a trend that she observes has also taken place in other countries. Through a case study of a specialist sports college, she tracks the impact and implications of specialization within an already fiercely selective educational climate, arguing that introducing yet another level of elitism (in terms of expertise within one particular skill area) may have a negative effect on some students within schools. Solvason rejects the increasingly myopic focus on economic outcomes, rooted in a view of the child as a social unit of production, and argues that a re-balancing of physical education (and the wider educational context) is required towards the health and happiness of the individual and the fulfilment of personal potential.

John Annette examines the nature of UK higher education's participation in community engagement programmes in the context of the concepts of citizenship and citizenship education upon which these are based. Noting that significant public engagement programmes remain at the margins of UK higher education, Annette argues for greater efforts to build capacity that enables deliberative democratic engagement, while acknowledging that we need to know more about how citizens can develop the civic skills necessary for such engagement. He raises some critical questions concerning the exact relationship between human capacity building, HE participation, active citizenship and civic engagement in a globalized world.

Chapter 6

Social marketing

Chahid Fourali[1]

There are many great products, services and ideas about how to make the world a better place but, as many marketing gurus would advocate, bad marketing usually leads to failed business enterprises.[2] The reverse is also true: how many 'unnecessary' (or even destructive) products affect huge sections of societies because of clever marketing (fatty food, alcoholic drinks, cigarettes, and so on)?

The aim of this chapter is to introduce the concept of social marketing as a potent force for social change and demonstrate its approach and results. I argue the case for raising awareness of this approach among educationists in order to promote the global aims of a humanistic and transformative education.

Introducing the concept

Social marketing (SM) is a relatively recent concept derived in the 1970s, following the development of the marketing concept, hence it will be useful to look at the broader concept of marketing before trying to understand SM.

According to the Chartered Institute of Marketing (CIM), 'Marketing is the management process responsible for identifying, anticipating and satisfying customer requirements profitably.'

The above definition, widely used during the last thirty years, is now considered to be restrictive due to its focus on profitable and commercial initiatives. In doing so, it overlooks long-term, sustainability-associated issues.

A more functional approach to marketing was produced by the Marketing and Sales Standards Setting Body[3] (MSSSB) in 2006 after extensive consultation with marketing professionals inside and outside the UK (MSSSB, 2006). The argument is that marketing's key purpose is 'to advance the aims of organizations, whether private, public or voluntary, by providing direction, gaining commitment and achieving sustainable results and value through identifying, anticipating and satisfying stakeholder requirements' (MSSB 2007, p. 6).

There are many examples of the effectiveness of marketing, explored by both the media and academics, in which persuasive methods create a situation in which the citizen is only on the receiving end of messages that

unconsciously guide them towards a belief and actions. At times, this is associated with a Second World War type of propaganda. However, irrespective
of the problems, when differentiating between myths and the realities of
marketing effectiveness it is clear that marketing's purpose is to develop and
test methods that work to help organizations determine the parameters for
success and then to apply them. At the heart of this success is understanding,
creating and satisfying customers' wants and needs. A broad definition of
'customers' does not just see them as direct consumers of a product or service,
but may include all influential people (stakeholders) in the organization's
business. Having said this, marketers do not always stop to ponder on whether
those wants and 'needs' are truly for the best and long-term interest of the
customer. The SM concept developed almost in parallel with the marketing
discipline, as a growing number of environmental and community advocates
became aware of the relevance of the marketing concepts, tools and practices
(Kotler and Zaltman, 1971). As a result, marketers started looking more
closely at the social side of marketing, to which I will turn in the next section.

Coming of age: a multidisciplinary approach for bettering the human plight

Social marketing seems to have appeared as an afterthought following the
realization by its early proponents, Kotler and his colleagues, Levy and
Zaltman.[4] In 1971 another article by Kotler and Zaltman developed the
concept further: that the marketing concept is inclusive and does not simply
apply to producing toothpaste and cars. It became apparent that this concept
was fairly conspicuous in several initiatives performed by organizations whose
primary concern was not profit in the usual sense. SM is one of the latest
marketing disciplines that appears to offer plenty of promise. Although we
say it is a marketing discipline, it is also many other things. This is precisely
what makes it a potent method for healthy social change, but before going
any further I will try and define what it is. This definition is based on consulta-
tions associated with a national programme for developing social marketing
standards, which is addressed later: it is the application of marketing alongside other social sciences concepts and techniques in order to influence
individuals, organizations and policymakers to adopt and sustain behaviour
which improves people's lives (MSSSB, 2008).

    The following is another, shorter, way of putting it: it is a tool box for
inducing healthy, sustainable changes for the benefit of human communities.

    In other words, its aim is to try to promote a healthier – in its largest
sense – society by making use of the powerful techniques of marketing and
other social sciences. One key word that is regularly finding its way into
marketing endeavour is 'sustainable'. This tends to be linked to a tripartite

interpretation: social benefit, environmental benefit and business benefit. The three facets are mutually supportive.

A recent study carried out by MSSSB (Boutall, 2008) showed that social marketing was pretty pervasive in terms of its influence. Its scope is shown in Table 6.1.

Table 6.1 Issues addressed by social marketing

blinding trachoma	physical activity
community involvement	racism
diabetes	reducing prison numbers
doping in sport	safe driving
energy and water conservation	smoking cessation
environmental protection	smoking in pregnancy
HIV/AIDS prevention	social enterprise
injury prevention	social exclusion
junk-food advertising	sugar-free medicine
mental health	suicide and domestic violence
obesity	transportation
oral and bowel cancer prevention	fighting abuse and inequality
waste prevention and recycling	

It is worth stating that, despite the multiplicity of contexts within which SM has been successfully applied, it seems that one global issue remains that, if addressed, could significantly improve the human plight. The issue is the pervasive and destructive wars (civil or otherwise) that take place throughout the world. The principles that could apply to 'fighting abuse and inequality' as well as 'domestic violence', as shown in Table 6.1, can easily and with great effect be extended to large-scale human conflict.

Too many times we hear politicians talking about legal or illegal justifications when, on a daily basis, we see and hear about gross abuse of power, in many cases perpetrated by so-called civilized societies. In this way social marketing has the potential to become an instrument that promotes social conscience, thereby offering a process that is inclusive in its valuing of human beings and seeking a solution that applies to all. As shown below, one of the important lessons of SM is also the adoption of a long-term and pre-emptive approach that focuses on prevention rather than cure.

Why social marketing?

For too long policymakers have known that the ills of society need a more effective approach that can reach many people. As an example, addiction problems can be dealt with in several contexts: on a one-to-one basis (through counselling) or through group counselling. However, given the costs and limited reach of these approaches, there is a need for a more effective method that can apply to wider populations. As an example, Nairn in Lannon (2008) quotes an example combating smoking in Scotland which, according to evidence, led to a reduction by 1.4 per cent of smoking for the whole of Scotland compared to a natural decay rate of 0.8 per cent. This difference was estimated to represent savings of £333 million to the NHS and to Scottish industry, not counting the health benefits. Finally, there is also the irresistible argument that 'prevention is better than cure'.

Researchers soon came to the view that marketing has been effective at developing products and services and communicating them to the public. They began adopting these techniques to help reach large groups of the population, in many cases scattered throughout wide geographical areas. However, this did not mean that they went without the informative knowledge and techniques gathered over decades by social scientists, and in particular psychologists. They adopted and integrated both tools. They endorsed marketing to ensure that approaches were client-oriented, and embraced a strategic perspective to address their challenges: appraising the situation, defining the problem, assessing the competing forces, and developing solutions that linked directly to the needs of the targeted groups, thereby maximizing the chances of success. Additionally, they made use of the social sciences to learn about what tends to be effective. What is interesting is that both marketing and social sciences tend to agree on what works. This is not surprising, as what generally tends to work at the individual level inclines also to function at group level. For instance, recent work by Robert Cialdini (2007) showed that people are likely to take certain messages more seriously (e.g. about protecting the environment) if certain communication principles are taken into account (principles of reciprocity, scarcity, use of expert/authority views, consistency and consensus). In practice, as described above, social marketing has been used successfully in many situations across the world. In this sense, social marketing has already demonstrated its effectiveness.

Philosophical/ethical underpinnings

The issue of ethics and values is of key importance, particularly since SM addresses a multitude of people who may have different views about what constitutes values such as justice, equality and freedom.

Another reason is that the central concept of marketing – exchange – should be based on fairness. According to Degeorge (1986), this can be met if both parties are free to enter, or not; if there are mutual benefits; and, finally, if there is satisfactory information accessible to make the decision. Fine (1992) argues that social marketers should be more ethical than commercial marketers, as more harm can come to both consumers and society from unethical practice.

Doug McKenzie-Mohr (2008) refers to the American Marketing Association's (AMA) Ethical Norms and Values for Marketers and feels they apply equally to social marketers. These ethical values include honesty, responsibility, fairness, respect, openness and citizenship.

Several ethical principles – see, for instance, Hastings, 2007 – have been proposed that underpin more specifically social marketing. These can be broadly summarized as:

- do into others as you wish to be done to you (known as the deontological argument);
- aim to maximize benefits and minimize harm (known as the teleological argument);
- ensure human rights (known as the rights argument).

One argument would favour adopting the human rights approach over the others. Despite the attractiveness of this argument, it may not be appropriate in some rare situations in which a person's or group background or values may not match exactly the list and ranking of the human rights. Modern psychology also tells us about many instances that may lead people to adopt different values, based on their different experiences. In my view this is another case of encouraging an 'either/or' perspective. Hence, I would favour a combination of all three. This approach takes into account background and intentions and with the view to minimizing harm in the long term.

However, there is also the principle of inclusivity. This principle's main contention is that, when decisions about welfare of people are being taken, there is a need to consult all those concerned and not refer to the views of a thinker who may be totally detached from the views on the ground. Inclusivity also refers to the need to address local and global issues and thinking both short and long term.

Ultimately, the above principles are linked to the principle of fairness and the need to think about conditions that lead people to act in certain ways rather than others, even if the outcome may be very bitter to swallow for the social marketers. This is, after all, the only way they can begin to understand the perspective of the people they are trying to help, dealing with questions along the lines of: What is (has caused) the current situation? Why is this person or group of people destroying themselves and others? What can be done to find solutions that show concern for others' welfare?

In this sense, social marketing may offer alternatives to many current unhelpful 'solutions' currently proposed by politicians whose main concern is quick political expediency.

Beliefs and values as key drivers of change

Much work on the psychology of change has highlighted the importance of personal values (Rose et al., 2007) and beliefs in driving behaviour (Rose et al., 2007; Prochaska et al., 1992; Andreassen, 2007; Fourali, 2009). As a result, motivational models of change are part and parcel of SM methodology. Beliefs have been identified in Cognitive Behavioural Therapy (CBT), which is one of the most potent counselling and psychotherapy theories, and of key importance to understanding and treating human emotional problems (Roth et al., 2006). More recently Fourali (2009) put forward a five-step theory of behavioural change (see Figure 6.1). This theory makes use of and develops Prochaska and DiClemente's approach to understanding the level of readiness for change at which individuals may be.

In contrast to Prochaska and DiClemente's model (e.g. see Prochaska et al., 1992), which does not systematically link the stage of change to beliefs, the

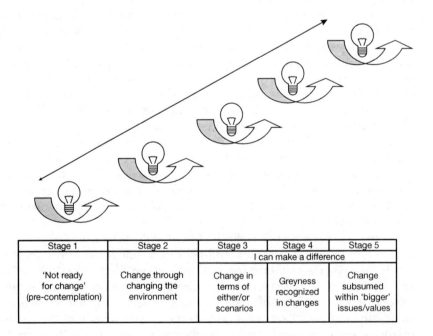

Stage 1	Stage 2	Stage 3	Stage 4	Stage 5
		I can make a difference		
'Not ready for change' (pre-contemplation)	Change through changing the environment	Change in terms of either/or scenarios	Greyness recognized in changes	Change subsumed within 'bigger' issues/values

Figure 6.1 Stages of readiness for change

above model identifies the attitude associated with each stage of readiness. These attitudes range from:

- 'not ready for change';
- making conditional change based on change of the environment;
- assuming responsibility for change 'as long as I can make a big difference';
- recognizing the complexity and greyness areas of change and committing to making change even small ones; and
- maintaining the new attitude because this is subsumed within a compatible higher value.

The above model for understanding the stages of readiness for change was inspired by work on both addiction and marketing. This is a good example of how SM encourages the cross-breeding of ideas between disciplines.

The best practice issues

Given that there is arguably a steadily growing social marketing industry (Kotler and Roberto, 1989; Fine, 1992; Lee et al., 2008) there is a growing need for advice on what constitutes best practice for this discipline. Clearly there is no lack of good intentions for improving the human condition. What is missing is standards of best practice that inspire credibility to practitioners and their clients. I have illustrated this point elsewhere (Fourali, 2009). Figure 6.2 shows the importance of both motivation (attitude and good intentions) and wisdom (knowledge and understanding that informs decisions) in maximizing the chance of successful professional practice. If we maximize either of these components and exclude the other, professional practice is inevitably affected.

The issue of motivation and values will be addressed later. The next point will focus on the issue of best practice.

| | | Motivation | |
		No	Yes
Wisdom	No	No basis for learning	Enthusiasm but no direction
	Yes	Knowledge but no effective action	Best of both world

Figure 6.2 Motivation and wisdom: two necessary ingredients for professional practice

Developing the best practice standards for social marketing: the process

In the light of the above and the comments gathered from many studies on best practice standards, there appear to be many reasons for the need to develop best practice standards (see Mansfield and Mitchell, 1996), including:

- performance management;
- assurance of product and service delivery;
- recruitment and selection;
- job design and evaluation;
- identifying learning needs;
- delivering and evaluating learning programmes;
- public recognition certification of competence; and
- regulating professional and occupational qualifications and institutions.

The first stage in this work was agreeing a description of the key purpose of the standards. After many discussions and incremental approximation, the key purpose adopted for social marketing was to apply marketing alongside other concepts and techniques in order to influence individuals, organizations, policymakers and decision-makers to adopt and sustain behaviour which improves people's lives.

After the key purpose was identified, five key areas were identified for social marketing, as follows:

1. Carry out social marketing research.
2. Establish and evaluate social marketing strategies.
3. Manage social marketing activities.
4. Deliver social marketing interventions.
5. Promote and continually improve social marketing.

This helped develop the further stages representing the functions associated with each of these key areas as shown in Figure 6.3:

The above key functions were further specified in terms of lower-level clarifications of the skills and knowledge components that represent each responsibility associated with SM. This led to many pages of best practice advice.

A speedier and meaningful summary description of the SM approach, following the general marketing planning steps, can be gleaned from Table 6.2.

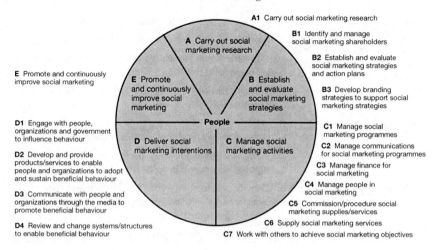

Figure 6.3 Five key functions of social marketing

Table 6.2 Marketing planning steps and their SM translation (adapted from Kotler and Lee, 2008)

Marketing Planning Steps	Translation into SM Context
Purpose/mission	What is the social problem to be addressed?
Situation analysis	What is the current situation *vis-à-vis* the problem at hand?
	How was it dealt with before and how successfully?
Objectives	What attitudes, knowledge and behaviour can we realistically target and change?
Target groups and obstacles	What variables should be used to segment the population to identify meaningful groups to target?
	What benefits and obstacles need to be considered?
	What competitors and alternative behaviours will work against us?
The customer proposition	What is the offer we are putting forward to our target groups?
	Is it attractive compared to the competing alternatives?
The marketing mix (4 Ps)	What products and/or services may be needed to support the targeted behaviour?

Most marketers extend the mix to 7 Ps (product, price, promotion, place, people, processes, physical evidence)	Is there a need for a financial incentive?
	How accessible are the required facilities?
	What message/mediums should we design that will be most effective?
	Which credible messenger/sponsor needs to be employed?
Implementation (the campaign)	What aspects of the environment do we need to influence to affect and sustain changes?
Resources	What resources (money, people, sponsors) are needed to get the results aimed for?
Monitoring and evaluation	How do we measure the outcomes using clear benchmarks to confirm impact of campaign or make adjustments?
	What lessons do we have for the future?

Clearly, the above shows several differences between commercial marketing and SM. In particular it can be argued that SM is much more difficult to implement, because the resources needed to change behaviour can be substantial. Consider the financial, social, physical and emotional challenges associated with changing beliefs and habits in circumstances such as addressing addictive behaviour, adopting environmentally friendly lifestyles, giving blood and becoming sexually abstinent.

The effectiveness of social marketing: from marketing education to education for all

When carried out properly, SM can be highly effective in inducing change in society. Its success is also partly enabled by the scale of its reach. An example of a well-known successful initiative (Fine, 1992) is that of the Save the Children Federation of America (SCF). This organization's objectives, targets and procedures (as specified in Table 6.2) were clearly defined and systematically implemented. The result is a credible organization that has been growing strongly since 1932 and has offices in many countries around the world. However, there were also several initiatives that failed. After analysis, such organizations had always key weaknesses, associated with a weaker marketing plan. As an example of a failed initiative, Fine (1992) refers to the failure of the US Government to introduce a one-dollar coin into circulation in 1979. Several reasons have been put forward to explain this failure: one primary reason was the fact that this was the marketer's goal, rather than the goal of the customer. Additionally, there were issues of trust about the initiative, as it was marketed by the government. Again, these are issues that could have been ironed out with a well-structured marketing plan.

SM has been applied to several educative initiatives (e.g. educating society about the benefits of seeking mental health support) (Lannon, 2008). One particular example associated with encouraging social change through education is the DfES Aimhigher initiative, to encourage working-class teenagers to pursue higher education. The initiative identified the financial incentives of going to HE, offering a greater likelihood of a job and, on average, a 35 per cent higher salary. It also identified the social benefits of better education, such as a reduction in crime and improved health.

The initiative attempted to understand the mindset of the subculture. It capitalized on this understanding by developing a brand and a communication strategy that reached 79 per cent of the targeted population and led to a large proportion taking initiative to find out more. It was estimated that if only one in every thousand of the pupils exposed to the Aimhigher initiative went on to attend higher education, an extra £80 million would be generated for the UK economy, more than offsetting the modest cost of the campaign and the higher education costs of these pupils.

The USPs of social marketing

There is no doubt that social marketing can be a very potent tool to induce healthier changes in society (for example see Kotler and Roberto, 1989; Lannon, 2008). This is perhaps due to the powerful interaction of its key characteristics.

Humanitarian interests override the commercial ones

The social marketing (SM) perspective to businesses is much broader than traditional commercial marketing since it focuses on long-term benefits primarily to the 'customer' and society in general. In the SM model, resources and 'bottom line', although very important, ultimately become subservient to the wider goal of achieving a social good rather than making a commercial profit or, even, saving a company. Clearly, this approach may be considered essential by a socially responsible marketer. However, in the current 'marketing environment' this may be seen as the exception rather than the rule. Note the recent debates on 'credit crunch' being 'caused' by unscrupulous marketers and marketing tactics. Ideally, and with much encouragement from marketing professional bodies, what is considered the exception can always become the rule. This is particularly reflected in the history of the quality assurance movement, which started as a separate movement that companies could follow or reject but now has become integrated into all serious companies' processes.

An effective multidisciplinary approach
By definition, social marketing is a multidisciplinary area that combines not only techniques borrowed from marketing, but all the other sciences that support its healthier aims which combine the strengths of both marketing and social practice. As an example, addiction counselling is traditionally tightly limited in its efficiency as it mostly applies to the one-to-one relationship between the client and the counsellor or therapist or, at best, may apply to a smaller counselling group. Social marketing, while making use of the intelligence and techniques of traditional counselling, can also reach large parts of local or international communities of thousands, or even millions.

Preventative effects
As well as the above advantage of 'reach' stated above, social marketing does not need to wait for a problem to arise before helping to address it, for preventative measures rather than curative may be adopted. In some cases this is the only effective option. As an example, the problem of domestic or other violence has led many policymakers to identify social marketing as one of the best available instruments to address the problem, since they discovered that the origins of the 'violent mentality' is in the early stages of development of individuals when they pick up damaging models from their surroundings (Donovan and Vlais, 2005).

'Collateral positive effects' on other practices
This advantage reflects the benefits of a mutually supporting or beneficial effect between the various fields of studies from which social marketing borrows.

Conclusion

For too long marketers have been accused of acting irresponsibly, as they were seen to promote a greedy and unhealthy society for the sake of financial profitability.

A year ago, I attended a Westminster debate about a motion that argued that marketing, as opposed to economics, offers a better potential for saving and protecting the environment. After about an hour of debate in which people argued for and against the motion, a vote was cast predominantly in favour of marketing. I had mixed feelings about this outcome. On one hand it was great to recognize the value that marketing can offer to help with social and environmental causes. On the other, it seemed to demonstrate another example of marketers flexing their muscles and mutually congratulating themselves, rather than highlighting the significance of their responsibility.

Having said this, there are many marketers who work tirelessly to help make the world a better place. Indeed, marketing, like any other tool, can be used for healthy or unhealthy goals. Social marketing has demonstrated its potential and should be adopted, or at least studied, by all managers of social initiatives.

Education is a social initiative and there have been countless arguments about how educationists could not only relate their work to real life issues, but find ways of making beneficial changes in the communities in which they live, for the solutions generated at the local level will need to be compatible with the broader global issues. No longer can a curriculum neglect global issues. If it does, it would not only be less relevant to our current and future world, but it would be irresponsible for educational managers to let it. SM can support the social educational agenda in at least five ways:

1. It contributes to the debate on what constitutes worthwhile educational aims.
2. It advises on how to relate local cultures to ethical and educational objectives.
3. It develops strategies that maximize effects and minimize costs.
4. It can reach and affect the behaviour of large sectors of the population.
5. It can adapt its practice according to existing best advice such as the latest occupational standards.

Point 4 above is particularly significant in a political climate that promotes mass education. Point 5 highlights the progressive nature of SM as it can be used to promote change, rather than reinforce existing obsolete practice.

As the list of issues presented above shows, SM has proven to be a versatile tool that could be used in several contexts. However, it does require expertise and commitment of resources as well as clarity of targets, rather than broad, ambiguous objectives. It also takes into consideration competing tendencies before estimating its level of success. Finally, it works with the target population by understanding it and communicating relevant or worthwhile messages. The complexity of the issues with which it deals requires in many cases multi-level commitment and support to ensure success of the initiatives.

Like most initiatives there are reservations about marketing in general, and social marketing in particular. These range from accusations about dishonest means of inducing changes, to focusing too much on profit issues at the expense of the bigger issues such as environment and social ills, to using means that are either too slow to take effect or inadequate (Crompton, 2008). In this respect David Norman from WWF UK stated: 'Environmental challenges will not be met while maintaining a narrow focus on the happy coincidence of economic self-interest and environmental prudence' (Crompton, 2008, p. 2).

However, most of its detractors have not managed to suggest alternative strategies. The irony of such an argument is that, if new effective ways of inducing changes are found, SM would be very keen to adopt them, too, for

SM is not restricted to a particular method or a specific target group. Many of its initiatives include persuading policymakers who can influence laws that override any economic benefit.

It is true that SM and its protagonists have their weaknesses. This does not mean that the concept is wrong; it just provides us with the opportunity to improve the methodology. Nevertheless, and despite any reservation, SM is a proven tool that is too effective to overlook, particularly when the issue at hand touches a large proportion of the population.

Notes

1 This paper draws upon several previous publications/presentations by the author on social marketing including:
   Developing world-class social marketing standards: A step in the right direction for a more socially responsible marketing profession. *Social Marketing Quarterly*, 15(2), pp. 14–24;
   With Great Powers come Great Responsibilities: A Social Marketing Perspective. Appeared in website: What's New in Marketing – 12 July 2008. www.wnim.com/archive/issue1207/index.htm
   National Conference on SM, Oxford University, June 2007; International Standards for Social Marketing, First International Conference on Social Marketing, Brighton 2008.
2 In the following chapter I will use the word 'product' also to cover services and ideas.
3 A standards-setting body is an organization in the UK that represents the interests of an occupational area. In this case the MSSSB represents the interests of the marketing and sales practitioners.
4 Note that the earlier identified article that announced the birth of social marketing in 1969 was by Kotler and Levy.

References

Andreasen, Alan R (2006), *Social Marketing in the 21st century*. Thousand Oaks, CA: Sage Publications.

Boutall, T. (2008), *Initial Report on Social Marketing Project*. Melbourne: MSSSB.

Cialdini, R. (2007), Presentation at the RSA. London, 25 January.

Crompton, T. (2008), *Weathercocks and Signposts: The Environment Movement at a Crossroads*. WWF – UK, http://wwf.org.uk/strategiesforchange (accessed 14 November 2009).

Degeorge, R. T. (1986), *Business Ethics*, 2nd edn. New York: Macmillan.

Donovan, R. J. and Vlais, R. (2005), Report to VicHealth by RJ D Consulting Pty Ltd: A review of communication components of anti-racism and prodiversity social marketing/public education campaigns. From www.vichealth.vic.gov.au/discrimattitudes

Fine, S. H. (1992), Marketing the Public Sector. New Brunswick, New Jersey: Library of Congress.

Fourali, C. (2008), 'Setting international standards of best practice in Marketing and Sales', GSSI International Conference. Clermont Ferrand, June.

—— (2009), 'Tackling conflict: a beyond opposites approach', *Counselling Psychology Quarterly*, 22(2), 147–69.

Hastings, G. (2007), *Social Marketing: Why Should the Devil Have All the Best Tunes?* Oxford, Butterworth Heinemann.

Kotler, P. and Lee, N. (2008), *Social Marketing: Influencing Behaviour for Good*. London, UK: Sage Publications.

Kotler and Roberto, E. (1989), *Social Marketing: Strategies for Changing Public Behaviour*. New York: Free Press.

—— and Zaltman, G. (July 1971), 'Social marketing: an approach to planned social change', *Journal of Marketing*, 35, 3–12.

Lannon, J. (2008), *How Public Service Advertising Works*. UK: WARK.

Mansfield, B. and Mitchell, L. (1996), *Towards a Competence Workforce*. London, UK: Gower.

MSSSB (2006), *NOS for Marketing*. Cookham, Berkshire: MSSSB. Available at www.msssb.org

MSSSB (2007), *Marketing Communications Standards Manual*. Cookham, Berkshire: MSSSB.

MSSSB (2008), *NOS for Social Marketing*. Cookham, Berkshire: MSSSB. Available at www.msssb.org

Prochaska, J. O., DiClemente, C. C. and Norcross, J. (1992), 'In search of how people change', *American Psychologist*, 47(9), 1101–14.

Rose, C., Dade, P. and Scott, J. (2007), *Research into Motivating Prospectors, Settlers and Pioneers to Change Behaviours that Affect Climate Emissions*. Available at www.campaignstrategy.org

Roth, A and Fonagy, P (2005), *What Works for Whom?* New York, NY: The Guilford Press.

Chapter 7

Basic education status of Afghan refugees in Iran

Maryam Danaye Tousi and Alireza Kiamanesh

This project was carried out with financial support of UNICEF, Tehran office

Introduction

The history of Afghan refugees and migrants dates back to the Soviet invasion of Afghanistan in December 1979 (Olszewska, 2007). The influx of Afghans into Iran continued to increase during the Soviet Union military attacks from 1980 until 1992. Nakanishi (2005) reports that the number of Afghans who came to Iran drastically increased in 2000, a year before September 2001. The influx of 1.4 million Afghan refugees to Iran during 2003 makes an in-depth study of their situation necessary. Among these refugees, some were officially registered and were entitled to work permission, basic government-subsidized services such as health care and education, and their children could enjoy equal education with Iranian students on all levels. The Literacy Movement Organization (LMO) programmes (2003) were also available to officially registered Afghan adults. However, there was almost the same number of Afghans who were living in Iran as undocumented workers. At the time of this study, there was no reliable data that shows the number of undocumented Afghans in Iran.

Undocumented Afghans were not legally allowed to stay in Iran, and the policy of the Iranian Government had been that the children had no right to receive formal education, while all documented refugee children had the right to free education. Clearly, the most seriously affected in terms of educational opportunity had been undocumented Afghan children, most of whom came to Iran after 1996 and could not attend government schools. There had been a growing demand from Afghans and international NGOs for undocumented Afghans to be allowed to enrol in government schools. A new approach, however, to support their children was made in 2002, where the Iranian Government decided to allow undocumented children to receive free primary education at schools run by the Literacy Movement Organization of Iran, a quasi non-governmental organization. Those who attended such schools were officially recognized as equivalent to students who went through government schools.

To provide primary health care and basic literacy to undocumented Afghan refugees, UNICEF started two health and education sub-projects in Iran that were funded by the Department for International Development (DFID). DFID is a UK Government department which tries to promote sustainable development and eliminate world poverty. The education sub-project of the DFID-funded project had been carried out at six provinces of high Afghan refugee concentration: Khorasan, Sistan and Baluchistan, Kerman, Hormozgan, Fars and Tehran.

The regular LMO curriculum was used for education, along with new components which UNICEF added to it. Usually, Iran's LMO is responsible for education of those who live in districts lacking the Ministry of Education's facilities or those who lack the conditions of acceptance in the formal education system. It covers the elementary school grades from 1 to 5. The education system of LMO set out what learners should be taught in Farsi, mathematics, Quran, social studies, science and health, and arts at two main levels of *basic* (containing four other sublevels: elementary, complementary, final and fifth grade – this level is equivalent with the fifth grade in the formal education system), and *continuous* education (taught in three different methods: by semi face-to-face education, by correspondence, and through media, i.e. newspapers and television programmes). It should be noted that new components were introduced by UNICEF to the regular LMO curriculum – life skills and learner-to-learner training – through participatory methods of teaching and learning in order to enrich the curriculum. In addition, LMO classes had been adequately resourced and the target households had obtained sufficient income to sustain basic needs (food, water, clothing and shelter) for the refugees during the project.

The LMO teacher-training programme has two modules of 'teaching skills' and 'special teaching skills'. 'Teaching skills' is taught during 232 hours and, besides that, there are 98 hours of instruction on 'special teaching skills' for the fifth and final grades. Usually, LMO teachers should pass the one-year course on educational skills during two semesters in order to be officially employed.

LMO non-officially employed teachers are selected from those who have got their diploma and are seeking jobs as teachers. Also, LMO non-officially employed teachers may be selected from among those young men who received their diploma and prefer to teach in remote areas as an alternative to serving in the army for about 21 months (for more information, see www.lmoiran.ir).

In order to use effectively participatory methods of teaching and learning for Afghan basic education, the LMO teachers should be able to allow the participants to practise and learn on their own terms, using their own language, concepts and understanding, and thereby build their confidence. By drawing on the participants' personal experiences and applying the knowledge and skills acquired in practical situations, full reinforcement is given to the learning process as a tool useful and relevant in all aspects of life (Boyden and Ryder, 1996). However, the principles of learner-centred education are totally unfamiliar to the teachers, who are more used to formal teaching and learning by rote. Also, these teachers are not trained on the correct use of textbooks and they are not instructed to prepare a daily lesson plan, in accordance with the special curriculum for Afghan refugees. Teacher training seldom includes skills useful in the context of refugee education, making it very difficult for them to assist the participants effectively.

The main objectives of the DFID education project were as follows (reported by Kiamanesh, 2003):

• to provide access to basic education services for Afghan refugees, especially children and women;
• to make basic education accessible and flexible to the needs of Afghan refugees;
• to reduce the non-enrolment of Afghan girls at schools; and
• to increase the completion rate of primary education of Afghan refugees.

The focus of this research was evaluation of basic education status of fifth-grade Afghan refugees who had already completed the elementary, complementary and final sublevels. Here we briefly explain the LMO basic education programme at these four sublevels.

The overall aim of basic education is to give students a good grasp of Farsi language, mathematics, Quran, social studies (including history, geography and citizenship), science and health, and arts (including calligraphy) during 1,648 hours of education (188 hours for elementary, 288 hours for complementary, 432 hours for final, and 740 hours for fifth-grade sublevel).

At each of the four sublevels, instruction is done at cognitive, affective and psychomotor domains, and educational objectives define what the students are expected to learn by the end of each sublevel. Also, their achievement is decided based upon the obligatory assessments – examinations – at the end of each sublevel.

Evaluation of the DFID project on education of undocumented Afghan refugees in Iran

The purpose of the DFID's evaluation programme is to examine rigorously the design, implementation and impact of selected policies, programmes and projects, and to record and share the lessons learnt from them so that these could be applied to current and future policies and operations (Al-Samarrai et al., 2002).

The main objective of DFID's evaluation programme in Iran was to assess the reading, spelling and mathematics ability of the participants at their highest level of education (primary fifth grade).

Methodology

In this study, the basic education status, consisting of the reading, spelling and mathematics ability of all 793 Afghan male and female fifth-grade refugees who benefited from the DFID project in different provinces of Iran at the end of the 2002–3 academic year, was evaluated (see Table 7.1).

Table 7.1 The sample size by age and gender

Age Group	Gender		
	Female	*Male*	*Total*
10-14	172	38	210
15–19	277	90	367
20 and over	186	30	216
Total	635	158	793

Instruments and procedures

A battery of tests with three domains – reading, spelling, and mathematics – was utilized. In the reading domain, appropriate reading passages were extracted, geared to the participants' highest level of education. For this purpose, five reading passages of 150–200 words were chosen from the Farsi textbook of the primary fifth grade. Then, the reading domain was divided into the following four subtests in order to ensure objective scoring: accuracy, fluency, intonation and punctuation marks, reading comprehension and meaning of words. Each reading comprehension passage was followed by two questions and nine new words. The reading comprehension passages were administered to the participants on a rotational basis and the total score for this domain equalled twenty, with five points allocated to each of the sub-tests.

For the spelling domain, a spelling test of 322 words was administered to the students, geared to the participants' highest level of education. The passage was extracted from the Farsi textbook of the primary fifth grade. It should be noted that the total score for this component equalled thirty.

For the mathematics domain, the content of the mathematics textbook of the primary fifth grade was analysed. After close scrutiny, the following seven main content areas were identified: 'Multi-Digit and Divisibility of Numbers';

'Common Fractions, Mixed Numbers'; 'Ratio, Proportionality, Percent'; 'Fractions and Decimals'; 'Geometry, Units'; 'Statistics: Mean, Examining Data'; and 'Complex Numbers'. The performance expectation levels in the mathematics domain were determined with regard to the mathematics framework for *Trends in International Mathematics and Science Study* (TIMSS).

Results

A two-way between-subjects analysis of variance (ANOVA) was conducted separately on the three main measures taken from the present study, consisting of reading, spelling and mathematics. The between-subjects factors were age, with three levels (10–14 years old, 15–19 years old, and 20 and over), and gender.

Reading test analysis
The descriptive data for reading and each of its sub-tests according to age and gender are represented in Table 7.2. Data showed that in the total reading test as well as in all sub-tests, male achievement was higher than female. There was no consistent pattern among the three age groups for total test and sub-tests.

Table 7.2 Descriptive data for scores on total reading and each of its sub-tests according to age and gender

Test	Test component	Age and Gender		10–14	15–19	20 and over	Total
Reading	Total (20)	Female	Mean	14.39	14.88	14.18	14.54
			SD	3.78	3.71	4.17	3.87
			N	171	275	182	628
		Male	Mean	15.26	15.31	16.33	15.49
			SD	3.25	3.07	3.16	3.14
			N	38	90	30	158
		Total	Mean	14.55	14.99	14.48	14.73
			SD	3.7	3.57	4.1	3.76
			N	209	365	212	786
	Accuracy (5)	Female	Mean	4.16	4.13	3.88	4.06
			SD	0.98	0.98	1.19	1.05
			N	171	276	183	630
		Male	Mean	4.19	4.23	4.3	4.24
			SD	1.04	0.92	0.86	0.93
			N	38	90	30	158
		Total	Mean	4.16	4.15	3.94	4.1

Test	Test component	Age and Gender		10–14	15–19	20 and over	Total
			SD	0.99	0.97	1.16	1.03
			N	209	366	213	788
	Fluency (5)	Female	Mean	4.1	4.15	3.85	4.05
			SD	1.01	0.95	1.22	1.05
			N	171	276	183	630
		Male	Mean	4.4	4.22	4.41	4.3
			SD	0.74	0.87	0.84	0.83
			N	38	90	30	158
		Total	Mean	4.16	4.17	3.93	4.1
			SD	0.97	0.93	1.19	1.02
			N	209	366	213	788
	Intonation and punctuation marks (5)	Female	Mean	3.86	3.93	3.76	3.86
			SD	1.16	1.16	1.3	1.2
			N	171	276	183	630
		Male	Mean	4.22	3.98	4.28	4.09
			SD	0.92	0.94	0.65	0.89
			N	38	90	30	158
		Total	Mean	3.92	3.94	3.83	3.91
			SD	1.13	1.11	1.24	1.15
			N	209	366	213	788
	Comprehension and Meaning of Words (5)	Female	Mean	2.33	2.71	2.56	2.57
			SD	1.57	1.48	1.38	1.49
			N	171	276	183	630
		Male	Mean	2.42	2.87	3.33	2.85
			SD	1.57	1.31	1.47	1.43
			N	38	90	30	158
		Total	Mean	2.35	2.75	2.67	2.62
			SD	1.57	1.44	1.42	1.48
			N	209	366	213	788

Results from ANOVA showed that the interaction of gender by age was not significant in all reading tests. The main effect for gender was significant at 0.05 level on total reading; reading fluency; intonation and punctuation marks; and on comprehension and meaning of words scores. In all of these tests, the male achievement scores were higher than the females' (see Table 7.2 for the mean scores of male and female in these tests). Also, there was a significant main effect for age just for 'comprehension and meaning of words'. The Tukey (HSD) test showed the significant difference between the mean scores of the 10–14 and 15–19 year groups. Finally, the participants' mean scores in the 'reading comprehension and meaning of words' was lowest, compared with mean scores of participants in accuracy; fluency and intonation and punctuation marks sub-tests.

Spelling test analysis

The descriptive data for total spelling scores in Table 7.3 showed that the females' achievement was higher than the males'. There was no consistent pattern among the three age groups for this test.

Table 7.3 Descriptive data for scores on spelling test according to age and gender

Test	Test component	Age and Gender		10–14	15–19	20 and over	Total
Spelling	Total	Female	Mean	22.65	22.95	20.62	22.19
			SD	5.79	5.91	6.95	6.27
			N	172	276	186	634
		Male	Mean	18.76	19.43	21.17	19.6
			SD	8.75	6.74	6.91	7.3
			N	38	89	30	157
		Total	Mean	21.95	22.09	20.69	21.67
			SD	6.58	6.3	6.93	6.57
			N	210	365	216	791

The results of the two-way ANOVA showed a significant interaction between gender and age factors. The gap between the performance of the males and females in the first two age groups was almost the same. In these two groups, performance of females was much higher than that of the males, but for the age group '20 years and over' the performance of females decreased and the males' increased: in this age group, the performance of males was higher than that of females.

Mathematics test analysis

The descriptive data for mathematics and each of its sub-tests, according to age and gender, are represented in Table 7.4.

Table 7.4 Descriptive data for scores on total mathematics and each of its sub-tests according to age and gender

Test	Test component	Age and Gender		10–14	15–19	20 and over	Total
Mathematics	Total	Female	Mean	6.12	6.26	6.45	6.28
			SD	3.82	3.71	4.09	3.85
			N	165	272	182	619
		Male	Mean	5.39	7.23	8.59	7.04
			D	3.55	3.73	4.23	3.91
			N	38	89	30	157
		Total	Mean	5.99	6.5	6.76	6.43
			SD	3.77	3.74	4.17	3.87
			N	203	361	212	776
	Multi-Digit and Divisibility of Numbers	Female	Mean	0.84	0.91	0.9	0.89
			SD	0.47	0.44	0.48	0.46
			N	171	275	185	631
		Male	Mean	0.95	1.06	1.06	1.04
			SD	0.48	0.44	0.44	0.45
			N	38	90	30	158
		Total	Mean	0.86	0.95	0.92	0.92
			SD	0.47	0.45	0.48	0.46
			N	209	365	215	789
	Common Fractions, Mixed Numbers	Female	Mean	1.6	1.63	1.64	1.63
			SD	1.09	1.04	1.17	1.09
			N	172	276	185	633
		Male	Mean	1.51	1.78	2.09	1.77
			SD	1.17	0.97	1.009	1.04
			N	38	90	30	158
		Total	Mean	1.59	1.67	1.71	1.66
			SD	1.1	1.03	1.16	1.08
			N	210	366	215	791
	Ratio, Proportionality, Percent, Fractions and Decimals	Female	Mean	1.16	1.24	1.3	1.24
			SD	1.07	1.05	1.08	1.07
			N	172	276	184	632

Test	Test component	Age and	Gender	10–14	15–19	20 and over	Total
		Male	Mean	0.75	1.34	1.48	1.22
			SD	0.76	1.06	1.35	1.09
			N	38	90	30	158
		Total	Mean	1.08	1.27	1.33	1.23
			SD	1.03	1.05	1.12	1.07
			N	210	366	214	790
		Female	Mean	0.51	0.5	0.5	0.5
			SD	0.57	0.55	0.53	0.55
			N	172	276	185	633
		Male	Mean	0.48	0.67	0.98	0.68
			SD	0.57	0.61	0.69	0.63
			N	38	90	30	158
		Total	Mean	0.51	0.54	0.56	0.54
			SD	0.57	0.57	0.57	0.57
			N	210	366	215	791
		Female	Mean	1.28	1.27	1.42	1.32
			SD	1.19	1.1	1.19	1.15
			N	167	276	183	626
	Geometry, Units	Male	Mean	0.87	1.32	1.64	1.27
			SD	1.04	1.04	1.01	1.06
			N	38	89	30	157
		Total	Mean	1.2	1.29	1.45	1.31
			SD	1.17	1.08	1.17	1.13
			N	205	365	213	783
	Statistics: Mean, Data Examination	Female	Mean	0.36	0.35	0.27	0.33
			SD	0.39	0.41	0.37	0.39
			N	172	276	185	633
		Male	Mean	0.35	0.4139	0.35	0.38
			SD	0.4	0.38	0.36	0.38
			N	38	90	30	158
		Total	Mean	0.36	0.37	0.28	0.34
			SD	0.39	0.4	0.37	0.39
			N	210	366	215	791
	Complex Numbers	Female	Mean	0.35	0.32	0.32	0.33
			SD	0.43	0.38	0.4	0.4

Test	Test component	Age and Gender		10–14	15–19	20 and over	Total
			N	172	274	185	631
		Male	Mean	0.37	0.56	0.89	0.58
			SD	0.37	0.56	0.69	0.57
			N	38	90	30	158
		Total	Mean	0.35	0.38	0.4	0.38
			SD	0.42	0.44	0.49	0.45
			N	210	364	215	789

Analysis of the data on participants' total mathematics scores and each of the sub-tests showed that the interaction of gender by age factors was significant for total mathematics; fractions and decimals; and complex numbers scores. For the first age group, the performance of the males and females in the total mathematics test as well as the two sub-tests fractions and decimals and complex numbers was almost the same. However, the gap between the performance of the males and females in the second two age groups becomes very significant. In these two age groups, performance of males was much higher than that of females in the total mathematics; fractions and decimals and complex numbers tests.

There was a significant main effect for gender on multi-digit and divisibility of numbers scores. The males performed better than females in this sub-test, and there was a significant effect for age on geometry and units scores.

Discussion

The main objective of this study is whether the DFID project has been successful in attaining its aims in educating Afghan refugees on reading, spelling and mathematics at primary fifth grade. In general, we could say that the DFID project has been successful in attaining its goals in providing its beneficiaries with basic education in reading and spelling, and not in mathematics. One reason for such a result could be the amount of time devoted to Farsi reading and writing instruction. As it was said earlier, Farsi reading and writing instruction was of first priority, and mathematics instruction had a secondary importance in the LMO curriculum.

With respect to the results of the tests, interesting observations could be made. First, in total reading tests and sub-tests, the males outperformed the females. In the spelling test, 10–19-year-old females outperformed their peer males, and by contrast, 20-year-old and older males outperformed their female peers. In the total mathematics tests, the 10–14-year-old females outperformed their peer males, but among the 15-year-olds and over the reverse was true. In general, 20-year-olds and older male participants outperformed their peer females on tests of all three domains. First of all, it should be noted this difference between males and females over 20 is not something restricted to Afghan refugees' education in Iran, as research has shown that in many areas of refugee population there are serious gender disparities in access to education, with girls consistently lagging behind boys. However, where gender inequity prevails, the causes appear to be largely cultural and the problem exists prior to such educational programmes (see, for example, Boyden and Ryder, 1996).

There was not a significant difference in participants' performance in reading sub-tests as their age increased, apart from 'comprehension and meaning of words'. In this sub-test, 15–19-year-olds outperformed both younger and older participants.

The participants' performance in the 'reading comprehension and meaning of words' sub-test was lower than their performance in the 'accuracy', 'fluency' and 'intonation and punctuation marks' sub-tests. Although DFID concentrated on providing participants with functional literacy knowledge and skills, the results showed that the participants simply acquired the decoding skills for reading aloud, showing weak performance in the 'reading comprehension and meaning of words' sub-test. This result indicates that, even in teaching reading, the low-level skill of visual word recognition (decoding) was emphasized, with little or no attention to reading comprehension, which is the main purpose of reading. Hence, more attention should be paid to promoting participants' reading comprehension ability. It should be noted that there is much evidence for pronounced effects of oral language proficiency on reading literacy (e.g. Droop and Verhoeven, 2003; Proctor et al., 2005; Geva, 2006), so instruction that provides substantial coverage in the key components of reading – identified by the National Reading Panel (NICHD, 2000) as phonemic awareness, phonics, fluency, vocabulary, and text comprehension – would help to increase the reading literacy of Afghan refugees in Iran.

The fact that the participants demonstrated rather good performance on reading and spelling and rather weak performances on mathematics suggests that here education has been conceptualized in terms of functional literacy, in line with UNESCO's original definition of literacy (reported from Grey, 1956, p. 19), which aims at equipping the illiterate with the skills and knowledge to function as workers and citizens in a print-dominated society. The functionality of such literacy is related directly to the economic functioning of the literate subject (Bhola, 1994). As the DFID project has not been successful in attaining its goals in providing its beneficiaries with basic education in mathematics, more attention should be paid to promoting participants' mathematics ability; because functional literacy without improved mathematics ability could fail to lead to change and development.

As mentioned above, the participants in this study performed weakly on reading comprehension and mathematics tests. Similar results were reported in other studies such as the Organisation for Economic Co-operation and Development's Programme for International Student Assessment (PISA) in 2000. One of the findings of PISA was that English-speaking immigrant students in Germany severely lag behind their native peers in reading, mathematics, and science (see Stanat, 2009).

Although the native language of Afghan refugees in Iran was also Farsi, there are many dialectal differences between the Farsi spoken in Iran and Afghanistan. So, the LMO could benefit from Stanat's findings for its future educational programmes for Afghan refugees. In particular, it should pay attention to incorporate extensive oral Farsi (i.e. Farsi spoken in Iran) into future literacy programmes for Afghan refugees.

One other reason for Afghan refugees' weak performance on reading comprehension and mathematics sub-tests could be attributed to a lack of required teaching skills among LMO teachers. The LMO teachers are not trained in the proper use of textbooks and teacher guides and on how to prepare a daily lesson plan for this special curriculum for Afghan refugee education. This highlights the importance of planning and developing a special teacher education system for those LMO teachers who are selected for teaching Afghan refugees. Besides that, more emphasis should be placed upon instructing teachers on how to teach reading comprehension and mathematics. In such a programme, the teachers should become familiar with refugees' ethnic and cultural background.

The main weakness of this approach was that by focusing so heavily on the supply side, insufficient attention was given to the social, economic and cultural factors that determine the demand for primary education of Afghan refugees in Iran. Furthermore, in this project, the focus was upon teachers as the main determinant of school quality, ignoring the importance of improving other key inputs (particularly management, classrooms, textbooks, curriculum and assessment) in order to achieve sustainable improvements in student competencies.

One of the objectives of this project was to replace ineffective 'chalk and talk', rote-learning teaching with active learning methodologies which had become the conventional wisdom in the primary education system in the UK and elsewhere. However, insufficient attention was devoted during the design phase to the acceptability of this major educational innovation to learners, teachers and education managers in drastically different socio-economic and cultural contexts. Evidence for this is that LMO teachers were asked to teach to the participants of this study without being trained and prepared for teaching literacy in such conditions. Another point is that active learning methodologies tend only to work well in education systems that are decentralized and democratic and where teachers are highly motivated 'autonomous professionals' rather than subordinate, low-status and poorly paid civil servants, as is the case in Iran and with LMO teachers (see www.lmoiran.ir). Also, it has to be recognized that the principles of learner-centred education are foreign to the participants and teachers, who are more used to formal teaching and learning by rote. Furthermore, wide-ranging reforms must be undertaken, at the same time, to provide other critically important complementary inputs, most notably the curriculum, textbooks, teacher guides and other learning materials and assessment systems. This highlights the importance of local input in the planning and development of a teacher education system and the need for adapting educational models and methods to local conditions and circumstances.

In this project, concerns about gender were mainly limited to research that focused on the reasons for low female attainment. The project was generally silent about how innovations such as active learning methods could affect male and female teachers and students differently. The project also failed to explore the effects of such changes on the affordability of primary education.

Finally, even if the project does not appear to have had much impact on reading comprehension and mathematics abilities of undocumented Afghan refugees in Iran, it might still play an important positive role in influencing education policy and general thinking about the future direction of basic education of Afghan refugees in Iran and other host countries.

References

Al-Samarrai, S., Bennell, P. and Colclough, C. (2002), *From Projects to Swaps: An Evaluation of British Aid to Primary Schooling 1988–2001*. Department for International Development, Evaluation Report, 639.

Bhola, H. S. (1994), *A Source Book for Literacy Work: Perspectives from the grassroots*. London: Jessica Kingsley/UNESCO.

Boyden, J. and Ryder, P. (1996), *Implementing the Right to Education in Areas of Armed Conflict*. Department of International Development, Queen Elizabeth House, University of Oxford.

Droop, M. and Verhoeven, L. (2003), 'Language proficiency and reading ability in first- and second-language learners', *Reading Research Quarterly*, 38, 78–103.

Geva, E. (2006), 'Second-language oral proficiency and second-language literacy', in D. August and T. Shanahan (eds), *Developing Literacy in Second-Language Learners: Report of the National Literacy Panel on Language Minority Children and Youth*. Mahwah: Lawrence Erlbaum Associates.

Grey, W. S. (1956), *The Teaching of Reading and Writing*. Paris: UNESCO.

Kiamanesh, A. (2003), *An Evaluation of Basic Education for Afghan Refugees in Iran*. A research report funded by UNICEF, Tehran office.

Literacy Movement Organization (2003), *A guide to LMO curriculum*. The Office for Research, Textbook Compilation and Educational Tehnology. Tehran; Iran.

Nakanishi, H. (2005), *Afghan Refugees and Migrants in Iran: Who is Responsible for Empowering Them?* A discussion paper for peace-building studies. Available at www.peacebuilding.org

National Institute of Child Health and Human Development (NICHD), (2000), 'Teaching children to read: An evidence-based assessment of the scientific research literature on reading and its implications for reading instruction' (Report of the National Reading Panel, NIH Publication No. 00-4754). Washington, DC: U.S. Government Printing Office.

Olszewska, Z. (2007), '"A desolate voice": poetry and identity among young Afghan refugees in Iran', *Iranian Studies*, 40(2), 203–24.

Proctor, C. P., Carlo, M., August, D. and Snow, C. E. (2005), 'Native Spanish-speaking children reading in English: toward a model of comprehension', *Journal of Educational Psychology*, 97, 246–56.

Stanat, P. (2009), 'Kultureller Hintergrund und Schulleistungen - ein nicht zu bestimmender Zusammenhang?' In: W. Melzer & R. Tippelt (Eds), Kulturen der Bildung. Opladen: Budrich, pp. 53–70.

Chapter 8

Respecting difference in early childhood centres in Northern Ireland

Siobhán Fitzpatrick

Background

Early Years – the Organization for Young Children (previously known as NIPPA) has been operating in Northern Ireland since 1965. Founded by local parents in response to the lack of pre-school places for young children, the development of the organization was influenced by the play movement in New Zealand and similar parent-led playgroup initiatives in the rest of the UK. Formed just a few years before the recent conflict, the history of the organization has been strongly influenced by the backdrop of a 40-year sectarian war. The main objective of the organization over the period has been to develop and support high-quality community-managed early childhood services, but as a result of the conflict, Early Years was also challenged to provide environments for young parents and children from across the religious, political and class divides to come together to create safe and equal spaces for children to play, learn and grow together.

Since its inception the work of the organization has been underpinned by a strong community development ethos, focused on helping communities to assess the need for, develop and manage, their own pre-school services.

During the1970s, 1980s and early 1990s early childhood groups, whether pre-school playgroups, parent and toddler groups or full day care groups, flourished across Northern Ireland. Currently there are 1,000 member groups affiliated to Early Years – the Organization for Young Children, servicing 30,000 pre-school children and their families on a daily basis. Each early childhood service in the community, voluntary and independent sectors is locally managed, in the main by local parents who are elected each year to oversee the management and development of the service. Each centre employs a staff team mainly qualified through a vocational system of professional development and training. Currently, however, there is a strategic policy focus to develop a graduate-led workforce within the sector over the next ten years.

Early education and care policy in Northern Ireland has been fragmented and up until recently (November 2007) early childhood services in the voluntary, community and private sectors were the responsibility of the Department of Health and Social Services and Public Safety, while Nursery Schools and Units were the responsibility of the Department of Education. Attempts were made as far back as 1978 to create greater synergy between the various sectors delivering early education and care, when under a short-lived direct rule Labour administration, Lord Melchett, the Minister responsible, introduced a policy statement on early childhood developments proposing a seamless delivery of early care and education. In 1994 a further policy statement on integrating care and education was published by the Department of Health and Social Services, but in reality up until the late 1990s the issue of early care and education was a low-level priority for both the Department of Health and the Department of Education. However, during the period the work of Early Years was increasingly recognized by government as an important contributor to early care and education, community development and the participation of parents in decision-making and democratic processes.

Early childhood services in Northern Ireland operate within a deeply divided society where most educational services are segregated across religious divisions. Figures from the Northern Ireland Council for Integrated Education suggest that as few as 5 per cent of children attend integrated formal education. Yet, in the main, groups in the informal early education system, affiliated to Early Years – the Organization for Young Children, have managed to maintain a cross-community, anti-sectarian focus and often provide the only opportunity for young parents and children from different backgrounds to get to know each other before entering a divided school system.

Early Years is the lead support organization for the early childhood sector in Northern Ireland. The organization employs a range of training and support staff who provide specialist help to the early childhood sector. This help ranges from curriculum assistance for centres, to business and community development planning for management committees, to developing innovative solutions to specific issues within the sector.

The main focus of the organization has been on developing the quality of experiences for young children, with staff supporting the sector towards internationally recognized quality assurance levels. In the mid-1990s, influenced by the High/Scope longitudinal research, the organization has assisted a number of member groups to implement the High/Scope approach. In a recently published government-led research 'Effective Pre-school Provision in Northern Ireland' (1997–2007), the quality of service for children in Early Years groups compares more favourably than similar pre-school groups in England and Wales. The rationale given for this is the quality of training and support given by specialist staff who provide five hours' mentoring, modelling and training to each member group each month.

In the past ten years the organization has increasingly focused on improving

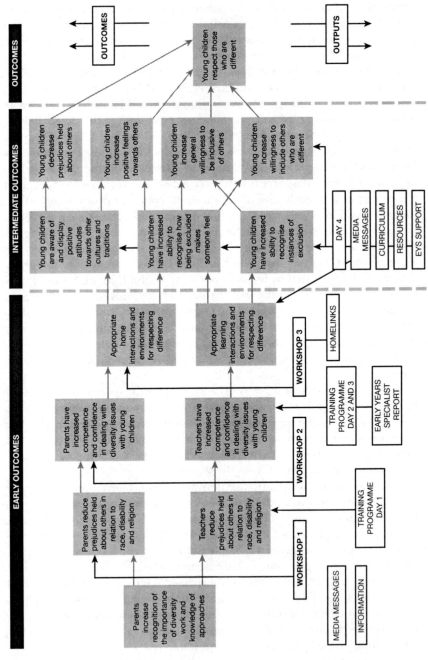

Figure 8.1 A logical framework approach to improving long-term outcomes

outcomes for young children. Influenced by the commitments to improve long-term outcomes for children articulated by the Northern Ireland 10 Year Strategy for Children and Young People, Early Years – the Organization for Young Children, has set strategic objectives to improve outcomes in three key domains: eagerness and ability to learn; emotional and physical well-being; and inclusion.

The Media Initiative for Children – a Respecting Difference Programme

By 1994 when the Irish Republican Army (IRA) and the Combined Loyalist Military Command (CLMC) ceasefires were announced, Early Years had developed into an organization well placed to make a significant contribution to peace building and inclusion. As a result of the history of cross-community, anti-sectarian work, Early Years was recognized by the European Union as a vital player in helping build the peace. The organization was granted Intermediary Funding status by the European Union and distributed £40 million (1996–2006) to support the early childhood sector take new opportunities created by the peace process and build services committed to reconciliation. It was recognized by the European Union, the UK Government and the local Northern Ireland Assembly that the early childhood sector could play a critical role in building a new society free from the sectarianism of the past.

Until the early 1990s Early Years had adopted a non-sectarian (not associated with a particular religious denomination) and non-political (not associated with any political party) approach but the emerging peace process created the opportunity to promote a more explicitly anti-sectarian approach that encouraged respect for, and celebration of, difference in a Northern Ireland context.

In 2001 new research conducted by Professor Paul Connolly, Queen's University, Belfast, entitled 'Too Young to Notice?' provoked the organization to reconsider and further develop its approach to dealing with sectarianism and its effects on young children. Connolly's research contradicted the popular myth in Northern Ireland at the time which suggested that three- to six-year-olds were not influenced by the conflict and sectarianism which surrounded them. Connolly's research highlighted that children as young as three years were developing ethnic preferences and by six years of age were developing ethnic prejudices. Connolly's research showed that at the age of three children were affected by the divisions that existed in Northern Ireland and were starting to internalize the cultural preferences and attitudes of their own communities. By the age of six one-third of young children were making sectarian remarks about others who they perceived to be different to themselves.

The early age at which children become aware of difference is supported by other international research. Derman-Sparks and Taus (1989) show that children between the age of two and five years are forming self-identities and building social interaction skills. At the same time they are becoming aware of, and curious about, gender, race, ethnicity and disability. Gradually young children begin to figure out how they are alike and how they are different from others and how they feel about those differences.

Early Years used this research to develop a new Respecting Difference Programme, which began to explore more explicitly issues of difference within a Northern Ireland context. Prior to this, issues of difference were usually set within a context of racial or ethnic distinctions, which at the time were external to Northern Ireland and were considered to be relatively safe for the early childhood sector to deal with.

At the same time as Early Years was exploring ways to deal more explicitly with issues of difference and exclusion, an American organization, Peace Initiatives Institute (PII), arrived in Northern Ireland wanting to support the process of peace building with a focus on children. They provided the catalyst for an advisory group of academics, early childhood professionals and media specialists to come together to develop a new programme of intervention, 'The Media Initiative for Children Respecting Difference Programme'.

The Media Initiative Respecting Difference Programme (MIFC) is an intervention programme aimed at improving long-term outcomes so that children, practitioners/teachers, parents and communities become more aware of diversity and positively change attitudes and behaviours to those who are different. It aims to make a respecting difference approach an integrated experience for children within the pre-school curriculum and is based on a meaningful partnership with parents. The anticipated outcome of the programme is that young children respect those who are different.

The programme is based on a number of key assumptions, which are supported by a growing body of national and international research. These are as follows: children are co-constructors of knowledge and identity; it is critical to have a skilled, competent and confident workforce to create and implement a respecting difference curriculum; parents are key partners in the process; a model of early childhood services based on community development principles and practices is important for social and educational change; the use of mass media can create a supportive environment for teachers to introduce a programme of respecting difference in conflict societies.

The Media Initiative for Children Respecting Difference Programme has a number of distinct components:

1. It is a comprehensive training programme for pre-school teachers, which helps adults working with young children to explore their own experiences of difference and develop strategies to represent differences in a positive manner. The training supports teachers' work in a

concrete way with young children around diversity issues, and helps teachers to weave activities around diversity and difference into the pre-school curriculum. The training programme is currently run over four full days.

2. It is a respecting difference service design and curriculum which uses a range of techniques and resources to help pre-school teachers present the issues of difference, whether physical, racial, sectarian or ethnic, in a meaningful and authentic manner. Puppets, jigsaws, feeling cubes representing Northern Ireland situations and characters have been developed to support the curriculum. Teachers use the resources to introduce the curriculum to parents in the home environment. Resources such as finger puppets and storybooks have been developed for parents to use at home and are employed by parents to complement the pre-school curriculum activities.

3. It is a media campaign that has developed five 60-second television messages which deal with physical, racial, ethnic and sectarian differences and highlight children's ability to resolve issues of difference in a positive and competent manner. These messages feature characters in a play park and their experiences around diversity issues. The messages are shown on national television in Northern Ireland/the Republic of Ireland three times per year for a period of three weeks at a time. The aim of using television as part of the programme is to reach a wide community of children, parents, grandparents and community activists so that there is support and recognition for the programme in the wider community.

Early Years Specialist support

The support of an Early Years Specialist is a critical aspect of the programme. Early Years provides ongoing assistance for practitioners and teachers implementing the MIFC programme through an Early Years support system. The Early Years Specialist is educated to at least early childhood degree level, with extensive experience in aiding curriculum planning and implementation, leadership and management. This aid takes the form of providing at least seven five hours' support visits to each pre-school setting implementing the programme. The purpose of the support visit is to provide practical assistance to Early Years teachers and concentrates on helping children develop autonomy and understanding around issues of difference and ability to grow a respecting difference culture.

The Early Years Specialist also provides three by three hours of clustered training sessions for pre-school settings implementing the programme. The purpose of these ongoing training sessions is to expand on the initial training and to address any implementation difficulties that teachers may be experiencing.

	Children will recognize feelings and emotions in themselves and each other	Children will recognize similarities and differences	Children will experience different cultural and social activities	Children will develop problem solving skills around differences, issues of inclusion/exclusion conflict	Children will develop confidence and positive attitudes about self and others
Learning Outcomes					
Activities	Small group activity – introducing the cartoon 'Tom Helps Out'	Small group activity – introducing the cartoon 'Kim Joins In'	Small group activity – introducing the cartoon 'Playing the Same Game'	Small group activity – introducing the cartoon 'We Can't Stop the Bullying'	Small group activity – introducing the cartoon 'Kathleen Makes New Friends'
Resources	Feeling cubes Freeling lottos Books (stories about feelings) Stickers Puppet play (Tom with sad face) Magnifying glasses Wheels/cogs	Puppets Dvd Discussion cards Songs Rhymes Books	Jigsaws Posters Discussion cards Sporting lottos Create a visual environment in which children/families are displayed Flags	Puppet play Sequencing cards Lotto game Helping Hands Tree/ Hurting Hands Tree Puppet Play Plaster Cast Hands Co-operative Collages Co-operative Games Sage Island Co-operation Board Express emotions to music movement and stories	Feeling cubes Dramatic play Role play Imaginative play Representation Dressing up Puppet Play Around Name calling Where we live Who we are Jobs people do Where we live Animals

Table 8.1 Towards resilience – an overview of programme activities

Engaging meaningfully with parents – building on the philosophy of parents as equal and active partners in the care and education of young children – means that parents are encouraged to attend initial information sessions to view the media messages and learn about the respecting difference curriculum. Parents will attend three further workshops throughout the year. As well as deepening parents' understanding of the programme, the workshops also give parents an opportunity to reflect on their own values, attitudes, prejudices and experiences of differences.

Community training for management committees and boards of governors

Research shows the importance of the local community in affecting attitudes to difference. Training for management committees and boards of governors has been designed to help them implement the principles of community development and develop inclusive policies and practices for children and families. The training helps committees reflect on their values and principles in relation to inclusion and how to put these values and principles into practice.

The importance of research and growing a culture of evidence-based practice around the programme has been important from the initial stages of programme implementation. A research programme which measures children's attitudes and behaviour to difference prior to, and on completion of, the programme, and compares these children's attitudes and behaviours to children who have not been exposed to the programme, has been developed. Also, as the programme has been developed and refined, ways have been developed to measure changes in the attitudes and behaviours of parents and pre-school teachers prior to and post programme implementation. Research findings have been used as a means of influencing government policy in relation to issues of inclusive education and professional development strategies for pre-school teachers.

The Respecting Difference Programme was initially introduced to the pre-school sector in 2003 on a pilot basis in 10 pre-school settings, then tested in 80 pre-school centres, and now is going to scale across the early childhood sector. To date 600 pre-school centres in Northern Ireland and 300 pre-school centres in the Republic of Ireland have been involved in the programme. Each phase of the implementation has been subject to random control testing, comparing the impact of the programme against children who have had no exposure to it.

The programme is showing promising results in terms of increasing children's socio-emotional development, changing their attitudes and behaviours towards, and understanding of, those whom they consider to be different from them. Young children exposed to the programme are showing an understanding of what being excluded feels like, are more willing to play with children

whom they consider are different, and are able to show positive understanding of, and identification with, cultural symbols which previously were seen
as divisive in a Northern Ireland context.

Pre-school teachers and parents have also reported changes in their attitudes and behaviour. Even in the most segregated Loyalist and Republican
neighbourhoods, parents and teachers have shown a very positive commitment to the programme.

The success of the programme has recently led the Department of
Education to fund the expansion of the training into the primary school

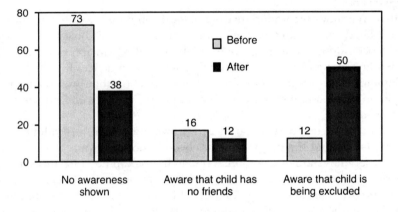

Figure 8.2 Ability to recognize instances of exclusion without prompting

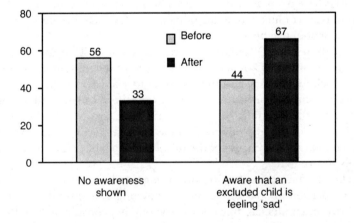

Figure 8.3 Ability to understand how being excluded makes someone feel

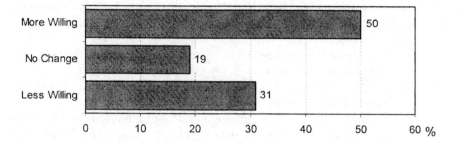

Figure 8.4 Willingness to play with others, including those who are different

sector, which means that an age-appropriate adaptation of the programme is now available for children between the ages of three and eight years old.

The programme has also received substantial investment from Atlantic Philanthropies, a major US-based foundation, and the International Fund for Ireland. This investment will allow Early Years to continue to implement the programme and track changes in the attitudes and behaviours of pre-school children, their teachers and parents over a longer period of time. The European Union continues to support the development and evolution of the approach. A recent investment by the European Union will allow Early Years to develop a Masters Programme on Peace Building and Advocacy with Young Children, a policy-influencing strategy which will ensure that the practice and research messages emanating from this project are used to shape the Cohesion and 'A Shared Future' policy currently being developed by the Northern Ireland Assembly. The European Union investment will also allow Early Years to work with early childhood professionals around the world in areas affected by conflict to adapt the programme in a culturally appropriate manner and apply it in a range of cultures and contexts.

International Developments

Early Years is currently leading an International Network on Peace Building with Young Children, which includes representation from countries such as Serbia, Palestine, Albania, Colombia, Nepal, Israel, Lebanon, Iraq, South Africa, USA, El Salvador, Turkey and Cyprus. The aim of the network is to explore the learning emerging from a Northern Ireland context and also to learn from developments in early childhood in other countries and regions affected by conflict. The aim of this work is to develop a common set of principles which would begin to underpin a framework for early childhood care and education practice in conflict and emergency situations.

The International Working Group has identified a number of key questions in relation to the work of the early childhood community in conflict and post conflict societies:

- What support is required by caregivers in helping them deal with the effects of violence in children's lives?
- How best can we listen to the voices of young children and help them explore in a safe environment their experience of conflict?
- In situations where there are high and intense levels of violence how do we go about meeting the needs of children when their families and communities are literally disintegrating?
- How can we work effectively with families and communities in many different contexts and cultures?
- How can we be effective advocates for children living in conflict-affected societies?
- What role can the early childhood professional play in terms of building peaceful communities?

Over the next three years the International Networking Group led by Early Years will develop a programmatic framework to provide dialogue around these questions. Central to the thinking and work of the group will be an attempt to establish a child's rights basis for programme development.

In defining a child's rights perspective to international programme development, the following child rights principles will underpin the work of the group:

- interdependence and indivisibility of rights;
- children as holders of rights and adults as both holders and duty-bearers;
- universality of rights and best interests;
- equity and non-discrimination;
- voice and opinion of the child;
- involving children, parents and community through participatory approaches;
- addressing unequal power structures such as class, ethnicity and gender;
- recognition of governments as duty-bearers accountable to their citizens and to the international community.

Programmatic approaches should consider all systems which impact on a child's development.

Structure of the child rights ecology will depend on the individual country, the child's socio-cultural environment within it, and how the child interacts with and is situated within each system.

Figure 8.5 Child rights ecology

Impact of programmatic approaches should also be at all levels: individual child/family/community/civil society/ government

In working at an international level it is important to understand the challenges and tensions of attempting to take a unified approach to programmatic development, in particular the risk of a global north-based thinking and approach predominating over those of the global south. In this respect the importance of reflexivity, cultural awareness and context is critical.

Developing a programmatic framework which has international relevance must also pay attention to the needs of children through the various stages of conflict and through all the development stages of childhood.

As well as using our own experiences to support the development of this international programme framework, Early Years will use the learning from

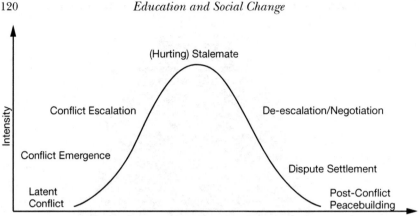

Figure 8.6 The five stages of conflict

this international partnership work to further develop its own approach to developing a culture of respecting difference in early childhood practice in Northern Ireland. The organization will also use this learning to influence policy development in terms of how young children's services are delivered and how those who work with young children are prepared for the critical role they play in educating young children in a post-conflict society.

Conclusions and reflections

Northern Ireland is in the middle of a period of significant change, as a new political settlement begins to take shape and a locally elected Assembly exercises responsibility for local governance. The role of education in a divided society has become a serious political issue, with major tensions between the main political parties on how education policy and practice should adapt and reflect the new socio-economic and post-conflict realities.

A new Cohesion and 'A Shared Future' Policy is about to be published by the Northern Ireland Assembly. We are in a position where we have the opportunity to create a range of policies that will help rebuild a society which has been torn apart by 40 years of recent conflict and 700 years of history. The early childhood community is in a gifted position to be part of that process. Evidence-based programmes such as the Media Initiative Respecting Difference Programme embracing a community-change model, working with young children, pre-school teachers, parents and community activists, has a significant role to play in developing the skills and confidence of the early childhood professionals. We believe that the approach being developed by the early education community can make an important contribution to creating and re-creating a new and shared future in Northern Ireland. We also believe that we are growing a body of practice and research that will have resonance internationally in areas of conflict. Our experience, practice and research in Northern Ireland have relevance for early childhood communities elsewhere which are committed to building approaches to inclusive education. The combination of a robust attitude to programmatic design, coupled with a rigorous approach to professional development and research showing improvements in inclusion outcomes for children, parents and pre-school teachers, is an advance which could have lessons for national and international replication.

References

Connolly, P. and Kelly, B. (2001), *Too Young to Notice?* Queen's University, Belfast: Community Relations Council, Northern Ireland.

Derman-Sparks, L. and Taus, K. (1989), *We're Different . . . and We're Friends.* London: Scholastic.

Effective Pre-school Provision in Northern Ireland Research Briefing (2006). Belfast: Northern Ireland Statistics and Research Agency.

Chapter 9

Elitism, inclusion and the specialist school

Carla Solvason

Introduction

'It's not about winning, but taking part, surely?' This was the reaction of the Chairman of the UK House of Commons Committee of Public Accounts to the information that £97 million of public money was to be bestowed upon elite athletes in training for the Beijing Olympics in 2008. He was unable to comprehend why Courbetin's original premise in developing the modern-day Olympics, with the emphasis on participation rather than winning, had become so distorted. Somewhat naively he asked, 'Why not just help sport generally?' (cited in House of Commons Committee of Public Accounts, 2006, p. Ev2). Since the UK Government's production of *A Sporting Future for All* in 2000 there has been a subtle but significant shift in emphasis away from inclusion and towards elitism within sports, which has run parallel to the marketization of education. This has not happened in the UK alone; Saltmarsh (2007, p. 336) describes how, in Australia, 'neoliberal reforms . . . promote the imposition of market models onto educational provision'. These changes have resulted in children no longer being viewed as future citizens but, instead, the child has become the 'cipher for future economic prosperity' (Lister, 2003, p. 433). Social justice now becomes the neglected stepchild to economic prosperity, in a system where employability has become the 'core mission' (Coffield, 2007, p. 6).

In the UK we continue to drive an educational system which focuses on academically talented children. Coffield (2007, p. 6) refers to the 'O level sheep and CSE goats'. Routes to traditional examination success continue to be those which are most generously resourced (in addition to being those that are the most uncomplicated for students to follow), while we fail to focus on those areas which would be of most benefit to those who find learning difficult. Coffield believes that this is a primary reason why the UK has a greater dropout rate of 16-year-olds from education than nineteen other countries, including USA and Australia. It seems somewhat ironic that, in a nation desperate for economic success, education decision-makers retain a myopic fascination with the academic as apposed to the vocational, as this appears to be a double-edged agenda. Not only are politicians bowing to the pressures of industry, with industry chiefs reluctant to loosen their grip on traditional industry markers of achievement (see Mansell, 2004), but they are also continuing to develop their concept of children as economically viable units of capital in a knowledge-centred economy.

One element of the development of the education marketplace in the UK has been the creation of specialist schools, whereby industry profits are injected into education in order to produce a more effective workforce. Newman (2001, p. 125) sees this inclusion of a wider range of stakeholders 'as a means of delivering public policy . . . enhancing the state's capacity to secure political objectives'. Peters (2001, p. 2) believes that this restructuring of the educational system has been 'guided by neoliberal theories of human capital, public choice and new public management'. But in this trade of human capital, and the emerging 'polarization of secondary school intakes' (Haydn, 2004, p. 417), what has happened to comprehensive ideals?

School specialisms emerged at around the same time that Britain began its drive towards a knowledge economy. During the 1990s education ceased to be about nurturing future citizens, and became a necessity for equipping a future workforce for success in the global economy (Department for Education and Skills (DfES), 2001). Equality of educational provision became overshadowed by a rather more selective drive towards excellence. My research into one English high school's approach towards ideas of inclusion and elitism took place between 2001 and 2005. I was concerned, as Coffield discussed in 2007, that 'In the QIA definition of excellence "equity" is not one of the criteria' (p. 23). The school (Green Acre[1]) had gained specialist status in 1998. Most secondary schools on adopting a specialism choose to refer to themselves as a 'college', a term historically reserved for those working within the further education sector. Green Acre, being no exception, had become Green Acre Specialist Sports College. A sports specialism has very specific anomalies which I will expand upon later in this chapter, but in general terms I believe that the very development of subject specialisms has added to Haydn's (2004) 'polarization' of schooling and bred further inequality and competition within the education sector. My fear was that within an already fiercely selective educational climate, introducing yet another level of elitism, in terms of expertise within one particular skill area, may have a negative effect on some students within schools.

The research adopted a case-study approach and asked how a school could possibly encourage all of its students to participate in physical activity for a healthy lifestyle at the same time as focusing on the production of elite sportsmen and women. I was also eager to discover whether the elevating of one particular area of expertise would make those with no talent in that area feel inadequate. But before I further explore the effects of this particular specialism, it is necessary to establish the context of specialist schools within the recent reformation of education in the UK.

The introduction of the specialist school

The adoption of the specialist school is just one aspect of what Taylor et al. (1997, p. 89) refer to as the blurring of 'clear-cut public–private divisions between state activities and those of the market'. Lister (2003) describes New Labour's shift towards 'partnership' between the state and individuals as the linchpin of their new agenda. She cites Newman (2001, p. 125) who says:

> Labour's emphasis on holistic and joined-up government, and its use of partnerships as a means of delivering public policy, can be viewed as enhancing the state's capacity to secure political objectives by sharing power with a range of actors, drawing them into the policy process.

Through the specialist schools system, business is being enticed in to become a key player in education policy development, regardless of the extent to which it is conversant with its processes.

The seeds for the specialist college were planted in 1994, with the introduction of the first City Technology Colleges. These introduced the concept of secondary schools receiving funding from the private sector under the assumption that the businesses providing the funding would, in return, receive a more thoroughly trained and capable workforce. The success of those first colleges prompted the expansion of the programme, and different specialisms such as languages were introduced. By its very nature this was a selective process that placed schools in competition for funding from prospective providers. Therefore some expected the specialist schools system to be abolished with the introduction of a Labour Government, traditional supporters of the comprehensive schooling system, in 1997. Those who worked in the education sector also 'hoped that there would be a lull in the avalanche of legislation, policy initiatives and reform' (Tomlinson, 2003, p. 195) with which they had been struggling. But, instead, New Labour readily adopted the specialist schools initiative and its expansion was pledged. In 2001 the Government White Paper, *Schools Achieving Success,* made explicit the link between education, 'economic health' and the need to succeed in a 'competitive global economy' (DfES, 2001, p. 5).

In 2001 the Labour Government announced their aim to reinvent 1,500 secondary schools as specialist schools by the year 2005 (DfES, 2001). By 2002 the future for non-specialist schools had already begun to look rather bleak; the DfES White Paper said:

> Every school will have incentives to develop a Specialism. New investment will create at least 33 Academies, 300 Advanced Schools and a further 1,000 Specialist schools by 2006, bringing the total to at least 2,000. Thereafter *we want all schools who are ready to be awarded specialist status.* Federations will

enable each school to play to its strength under specialist leadership. *Weaker schools will receive intensive support and be closed if they do not improve.*

(DfES, 2002, p. 17, my emphasis)

In 2003 the government made clear its intentions to 'create a new specialist system where every school has its own special ethos . . .' (DfES, 2003a, p. 5). Specialisms ceased to pertain specifically to industry, with the introduction of specialisms ranging from business, to arts, to music, to sport, and now there is also the option of combining specialisms. In 2008, a total of 2,886 schools had achieved specialist status (Specialist Schools and Academies Trust, 2008).

The specialist schools development, like so much policy production in England (the numeracy and literacy strategies spring to mind here) was fast and furious and completely 'out of sync with practitioners and researchers' (Coffield, 2007, p. 21). It is still unclear whether the improvement that has been seen in specialist schools' grades is due to the schools' attainment of vital funding,[2] or whether specialist status really does have *added benefits*. In 2003 the House of Commons Education and Skills Committee made this comment:

It is a matter of concern that the Government has made its decision to extend access to the Specialist schools programme, and associated funding to all schools, in the absence of clear evidence as to the alleged benefits of the specialism, balanced against those of other initiatives. Evaluation of this initiative is essential so that the public and policy makers alike can be assured that policy is developed on the basis of sound evidence rather than wishful thinking.

(House of Commons Education and Skills Committee (HCESC), 2003, p. 34)

Far too often policy is developed in isolation from its implementers and is based on suppositions. As Coffield (2007, p. 18) comments, there is no loop by which practitioners become involved in the development of policy, no systematic configuration 'whereby managers and tutors can report back to policy makers on the strengths and weaknesses of the reforms'. We see a pervading insistence on developing policy based on a satisfactory fiction. When discussing Olympic funding provision, with reference to the statements at the opening of this chapter, Green (2006, p. 233) comments how 'the storyline that Olympic success motivates the generality of the population to participate and compete' is used repeatedly to justify the significant amount of investment into elite athletes. Yet research has actually proven that there is no sustained participation as a result of the event.

What about equity?

The inequities within the specialist schools system are manifold, the most pertinent being the competition for funding between schools, rather than an equitable sharing of resources. And it would appear that it is inevitably the under-achieving schools that miss out on the additional funding that they are desperate for. Support is not offered to the 'failing corner shops', while it is lavished on the 'successful supermarkets' (Booth, 2000, p. 79). In the spirit of true Conservatism, those who have, get more. Perhaps the most poignant concern, from a social justice perspective, is what happens to 'the rest'? If specialist status is of such benefit to pupils, then how can the government be justified in preventing a large number of children from experiencing it? In addition, the HCESC (2003) pointed out that just as important as the improvements that were being seen within specialist schools were the detrimental effects that their success was having on their non-specialist neighbours. They questioned whether perhaps one was achieving at the expense of another. The government (DfES, 2003b) attempted to silence the cries of inequality by claiming that the ideal was that specialist schools *share* their skills with their (perhaps less fortunate) neighbours; but collaboration is difficult between schools in competition for funding (Aiston et al., 2002). Hargreaves (2003) cynically suggests that this 'caring–sharing' approach jars somewhat against the tenets of a market economy:

> In a highly competitive climate, the pressure on school staff is to keep successful innovations to themselves in order to maintain their competitive edge, that is, position in the league tables and popularity among parents. Why give away one's best ideas?
>
> (p. 52)

It appears that government policy has been developed upon the unfeasible ideal of a competitive education market that incorporates charitable support between schools.

Policy contradictions

In 2003 Tomlinson commented that New Labour's policies were 'At best contradictory, and at worst have sharpened divisions and insecurities' (p. 203). And the concept of the Specialist Sports College (SSC) has certainly caused some confusion. SSCs have a unique 'problem' not experienced by the other specialist schools, in what Penney and Houlihan (2001, p. 1) refer to as their 'dual policy' location. The Department for Education and Employment's (1997, p. 3) justification for the funding of a 'non-academic' subject area was that:

Sports colleges raise the standard of physical education and community sport, and promote sporting prowess in pupils of all abilities, helping them benefit from the enhanced self-esteem, interpersonal and problem-solving skills which sports foster.

So the development of skills, and the commitment, resilience and co-operation that comes from playing team sports in school will filter through to become a positive working ethos. But, as Parry (1988, p. 109) questions, 'Who would claim the McEnroes and the Bests to be among the moral giants of our time?'

The agendas of 'serious sport' and healthy physical activity are extremely diverse, and it is difficult to envisage the approach that SSCs would take in attempting to encompass them. The Mission Statement for SSCs asserts that:

Sports Colleges will raise standards of achievement in physical education and sports for all their students across the ability range. They will be regional focal points for excellence in PE and community sport . . . Sports Colleges will increase participation in physical education and sport for pre and post 16 year olds and develop the potential of talented performers.

(Department for Education and Employment (DfEE), 2000, p. 2)

There are dual requirements here: should SSCs be promoting sport as fun for all, or is it something to be taken seriously while focusing on a talented few? In addition, as Penney and Houlihan (2001) point out, it is very difficult to take any innovations within the PE and games curriculum in isolation, as they are watched closely by the national governing bodies and other sporting associations. For the Department of Culture, Media and Sport (DCMS), SSCs are not just educational establishments but potential venues for the production of the nation's future sportswomen and men. Even though research informs us that by the time that children reach 13 their founding in sports should already be established,[3] in *A Sporting Future for All*, SSCs were specifically mentioned within the new elite sports development infrastructure in the UK (DCMS, 2000, p. 15).

Immediately tensions are apparent and it is precisely these conflicts that were the focus of my research. Physical education and team sports are two very different agendas, as are the aims to 'increase participation' and 'develop the potential of talented performers' (DfEE, 2000, p. 2). Murdoch (1990) compared the agendas of PE and sports and came up with ten notable differences, including 'education' as apposed to 'recreation', 'teachers' compared to 'coaches' and 'learning' in contrast with 'performance'. PE and sport entail vastly different approaches. Is the aim of a SSC to promote an improved understanding of the benefits of exercise and to encourage mass participation, or is it to nurture elite performance? And is it possible for both agendas to coexist?

The two concepts, of inclusion and the development of talented performers, do not sit comfortably side by side. The term 'inclusion' is used in many and changing ways; in the PE curriculum guidelines it refers to:

> . . . boys and girls, pupils with special educational needs, pupils with disabilities, pupils from all social and cultural backgrounds, pupils from different ethnic groups including travellers, refugees and asylum seekers and those from diverse linguistic backgrounds.
>
> (DfEE, 1999, p. 29)

In my study school's application for SSC status inclusion refers to only one thing: providing for those with special educational needs, particularly in the form of physical disability. I prefer Slee's (2001) definition that states, '. . . inclusive education is not about special educational needs, it is about all students' (p. 116). Like Booth (2000) I was interested in inclusion in its oppositional role, when placed against the results-driven nature of the English educational system. In my research I aimed to discover whether the competitive nature of sport within the micro-setting, just like the macro educational marketplace that produces 'winners' or 'losers', was simply going to 'amplify already entrenched social inequalities experienced by marginalized groups' (Saltmarsh, 2007, p. 337).

What I found somewhat startling at the time, approaching this research from a position of naivety, was that the adopted sports status really had no impact on Green Acre at all. Two years into its functioning within its specialist status there was no apparent shared culture, no 'sporting' ethos. It appeared to be the same as any other high school, with a Director of Sports that did a great deal of work with middle schools and organized special events. The 'sense of grievance from other departments at the flow of additional resources to physical education' that Houlihan (2000, p. 186) found in his small-scale study was also in evidence at Green Acre, as staff from other departments commented that they felt 'second best'. Even staff within the PE department could see 'nothing special enough going on at the school' that justified them regaining their specialist status. Pupils struggled to see what was different about their school and quantitative data suggested an increasingly negative view towards physical activity when students had been at the school for a year. Their opinions of whether they felt that their form tutor enjoyed physical activity, whether their school taught them that physical activity was good for them, and their involvement in physically active extra-curricular activities had all become more negative.

Evidence from the DfEE (2001), the DfES (2001) and Jesson and Taylor (2002) suggests that the examination results of a school on achieving specialist school status would be markedly improved. In 2000 the DfEE said 'Sports Colleges will raise standards of achievement in physical education and sports for all their students across the ability range' (p. 2). Yet achievement at Green Acre had not shown a discernible improvement since its change in status.

In 2000 Yeomans et al. suggested that the government's reports of a rapid improvement in specialist schools overall 'masked considerable variations between the schools' and that in one-third of the schools that they looked at the percentage of pupils achieving five or more GCSEs at grades A*–C had actually declined (p. 2). The students at Green Acre were of well below average ability when they came into the school, and so standards of achievement remained low. But within PE the effect of the school specialism, and more importantly the additional funding, appeared to be negligible. In 1997, one year before the school gained its specialist status, Ofsted[4] reported that the teaching of PE was 'satisfactory or good' overall 'with a few shortcomings', similar to all of the other subjects. In 2002, after three years of additional funding for the specialism, the overall quality of provision in physical education was seen as 'satisfactory'.

In both 2001 and 2002 Green Acre did not meet the 'realistic' targets set in GCSE examinations. In 2002 the PE GCSE results were below average, although it was added that they were continuing to improve, and were above average for the rest of the school, so perhaps the additional funding into the area did have some effect. A subject specialism is endorsed as raising standards overall at the school, yet in 2002 Ofsted[4] commented that at Green Acre, 'The gap between the school's performance and the rate of improvement nationally is widening'. The additional funding which had been given to sport did not appear to have had any significant impact; on the contrary, Ofsted stated that, 'Teaching and learning are consistently good in design and technology, history and ICT and it is in these subjects that pupils are making the fastest progress'.

Because of the negligible effect that the sports specialism had had on Green Acre, my fears for those pupils without physical skills becoming marginalized were unfounded, but what is relevant to this discussion is a seeming reluctance within Green Acre's sports specialism to 'just help sport generally'. I used minutes from seven sports college management meetings to search for direct references to improving the quality of PE experience *for all pupils* at the study school, or to improving their health and fitness through physical activity. In all, 147 issues were discussed during those meetings. Other than improving facilities at the school, which was mentioned 10 times, the vast majority of issues tended to relate to activities involving a very small minority of pupils, and particularly those talented in sport. Millennium Volunteers (a 'coaching' role taken on by the more talented in sport), staff training and partnerships with feeder schools and organizations outside of the school were discussed regularly. Benefits for the majority of pupils at Green Acre, perhaps taken for granted, were rarely mentioned. There was one reference to the introduction of specialist classes, such as yoga, for a nominal charge (I was disappointed that the only remark about a 'non-sporting' fitness activity for the children was referred to as something for which they would need to be charged), but this was the closest that the discussions came to directly tackling the health and fitness of pupils at Green Acre. Not once was the 'average child' directly indicated during the management meetings, compared to gifted and talented children being mentioned eight times. We live in a market economy: those who have, get more.

Fink and Stoll (1998, p. 298) discuss how, despite intense pressure for reform, many schools actually remain 'remarkably untouched' by the policy deluge. At Green Acre I believe that much of this stemmed from the relatively small amount of staff involved in the bid for specialist status, and this is a view shared by others (Houlihan, 2000; Johns et al., 2001). The current pressures on the educational marketplace almost necessitate an elite group of staff making strides, whether through putting together funding applications or action plans, and their colleagues obediently following. Yet these strides continue to be encouraged on the basis of fiction, and the voice of logic muted. Green (2006, p. 223) comments that:

> . . . such is the currency of the narrative storyline around elite achievement at the highest political and institutional levels in the UK, that 'alternative voices' arguing for some perspective in respect of spending such large amounts of public money on the aspirational goal of a handful of Olympic medals, remain relatively suppressed.

If we support these athletes and they perform outstandingly, then all athletes will start to perform better. If we support this school and its results improve, then all schools will perform better. Only logic, and even, dare I mention it, qualitative research evidence, tells us that this is *not* the case. On the contrary, far from raising standards overall, favouring the few can cause bitterness, resentment and dissent.

Conclusions

Coffield (2007, p. 24) refers to 'The repeated cycle of unrealistic expectations and short-term punitive interventions' from the government as 'a recipe for long-term failure'. Here he is talking about the rapidity of education policy development in the UK, but he could just as easily be talking about our funding of elite athletes. If we continue to focus our time, efforts and, perhaps most importantly, finances on the few, in the hope of short-term rewards, we will, as Coffield comments, inevitably meet failure in the future. Within education we have, essentially, de-skilled our teaching workforce. Under the guise of supposedly encouraging schools to develop their own distinct character, and promoting choice by diversity, schooling is now so tightly audited and regulated that it has become, in Coffield's (2007, p. 16) words, 'professional proof'; it is virtually immune from the bothersome intervention of teachers.

Johns et al. (2001, p. 201) comment that 'when teachers engage in change they are often confused and threatened' and Coffield (2007, p. 19) describes our education system as a damaging one, based on fear. Learning for the joy of learning has gradually been eradicated, just as the concept of sport for enjoyment has been replaced by 'the active (child) citizen and elite performance' (Green, 2006, p. 232). Lister (2003, p. 434) remarks how 'in the target-filled world of the managerial state, education is reduced to a utilitarian achievement-oriented measurement culture of tests and exams, with little attention paid to the actual educational experience'. The same could be said of sport for sport's sake: Why should medals take such a high priority over fun, healthy physical activity?

This myopic focus on outcomes, which increasingly pervades the child's educational experience in the UK, pictures the child as a social unit of production. If we are to invest in that individual, then we must expect to see a tangible profit. Polakow (1993, p. 101) comments that there is no longer a place for 'expenditure which merely contributes to the well-being or enjoyment of children as children'. Health and happiness cannot easily be measured; certificates and medals can. Is there really any place for such nebulous concepts as the child experiencing a rewarding and fulfilling educational experience, or enjoying physical activity for fun, when we have the nation's future economic prosperity to worry about? It would seem not. In the UK at present our focus remains firmly set on winners, because our economy cannot be revitalized by us simply taking part.

Notes

1 The process of application requires a school to first choose a subject area that they deem to be a strength; it must be able to show an upward trend in its examination results in that subject (DfEE, 2000, p. 7). The school then needs to:
   - draw up a development plan;
   - commit itself to measurable performance indicators and quantified performance targets; and
   - build ongoing links with sponsors.

(DfEE, 1996, p. 5)

These plans, in addition to benefiting their own pupils, must also benefit other schools and their wider community. The most significant obstacle to applying is that the school must also attempt to raise funding of £50,000 (previously £100,000) through private sector sponsorship. If the school's application is successful then, in addition to the sponsorship that the school has raised, they will be awarded a one-off capital grant of £100,000 by the DfES. The school will also receive additional funding approximating to £129 per pupil per annum, dependent on pupil numbers. This funding lasts for four years before the school needs to apply for redesignation.

2 Ram (2004) explored studies in the United States which showed that, though modest, increased expenditure on schools did have an effect on achievement. Jenkins et al. (2006) studied schools in the UK and found associations between increased resources and examination results.

3 Kirk (2005) states that by the age of 13–15 children have already moved from the sampling stage to the second specializing phase in sport, moving from 'fun and enjoyment in itself to competitive success and enjoyment of winning' (p. 241).

4 In order to maintain confidentiality and with the agreement of the editors this reference is withheld by the author.

References

Aiston, S., Rudd, P. and O'Donnell, L. (2002), *School Partnerships in Action: A Case Study of West Sussex Specialist Schools*. Slough: NFER.

Booth, T. (2000), 'Inclusion and exclusion policy in England: who controls the agenda?', in . F. Armstrong, D. Armstrong and L. Barton (eds), *Inclusive Education: Policy, Contexts and Comparative Perspectives*. London: David Fulton Publishers, pp. 78–98.

Coffield, F. (2007), 'Running ever faster down the wrong road: an alternative future for education and skills', inaugural lecture at University of London, Institute of Education.

Department for Culture, Media and Sport (2000), *A Sporting Future for All*. London: DCMS.

Department for Education and Employment (1996), *Specialist Schools: Schools for the Future*. London: DfEE.

—— (1997), *Sports Colleges: A Guide for Schools*. London: DfEE.

—— (1999), *Draft Guidance, Social Inclusion, Pupil Support*. London: DfEE.

—— (2000), *Specialist Schools Programme: Sports Colleges Applications*. Guidance Paper ref: DfEE/0196/2000. London: DfEE.

—— (2001), *Schools Building on Success*. London: The Stationery Office.

Department for Education and Skills (2001), *Schools Achieving Success*. London: The Stationery Office.

—— (2002), *Education and Skills: Investment for Reform*. www.dfes.gov.uk (accessed 18 July 2003).

—— (2003a), *The Future of Higher Education*, www.dfes.gov.uk/highereducation/hestategy/ (accessed 4 July 2003).

—— (2003b), *A New Specialist System: Transforming Secondary Education*. London: The Stationery Office.

Fink, D. and Stoll, L. (1998), 'Educational change: easier said than done', in A. Hargreaves, A. Leiberman, M. Fullan and D. Hopkins (eds), *International Handbook of Educational Change*. London: Kluwer Academic, pp. 297–322.

Green, M. (2006), 'From "sport for all" to not about "sport" at all?: interrogating sport policy interventions in the United Kingdom', *European Sport Management Quarterly*, 6(3), 217–38.

Hargreaves, D. (2003), *Education Epidemic: Transforming Secondary Schools Through*

Innovation Networks. London: DEMOS. Available from www.demos.co.uk/ publications/everydaydemocracy.

Haydn, T. (2004), 'The strange death of the comprehensive school in England and Wales, 1965–2002', *Research Papers in Education*, 19(4), 415–32.

Houlihan, B. (2000), 'Sporting excellence, schools and sports development: the politics of crowded policy spaces', *European Physical Education Review*, 6(2), 171-193.

House of Commons Committee of Public Accounts (2006), *UK Sport: Supporting Elite Athletes*, 54th Report of Session 2005–2006. London: The Stationery Office.

House of Commons Education and Skills Committee (2003), *Secondary Education: Diversity of Provision*. London: The Stationery Office.

Jenkins, A., Levacic, R. and Vignoles, A. (2006), *Estimating the Relationship between School Resources and Pupil Attainment at GCSE*. London: DfES.

Jesson, D. and Taylor, C. (2002), *Value Added and the Benefits of Specialism*. London: Technology Colleges Trust.

Johns, D. P., Ha, S. C. and Macfarlane, D. J. (2001), 'Raising activity levels: a multidimensional analysis of curriculum change', *Sport, Education and Society*, 6(2), 199–210.

Kirk, D. (2005), 'Physical education, youth sport and lifelong participation: the importance of early learning experiences', *European Physical Education Review*, 11(3), 239-255.

Lister, R. (2003), 'Investing in the citizen-workers of the future: transformations in citizenship and the state under New Labour', *Social Policy & Administration*, 37(5), 427–43.

Mansell, M. (21 May 2004), 'Employers doubt diploma', *TES*, www.tes.co.uk/ article.aspx?storycode=395019 (accessed 24 September 2009).

Murdoch, E. B. (1990), 'Physical education and sport: the interface', in N. Armstrong (ed.), *New Directions in Physical Education, Vol 1*. Leeds: Human Kinetics, pp. 63–77.

Newman, J. (2001), *Modernising Governance*. London: Sage.

Parry, J. (1988), 'Physical education, justification and the National Curriculum', *Physical Education Review*, 11, 106–18.

Penney, D and Houlihan, B. (2001), 'Specialist sports colleges: a special case for policy research'. Paper presented at the British Educational Research Association Conference, Leeds, September.

Peters, M. (2001), 'National education policy constructions of the "knowledge economy": towards a critique', *Journal of Educational Enquiry*, 2(1), 1–22.

Polakow, V. (1993), *Lives on the Edge: Single Mothers and their Children in the Other America*. Chicago and London: University of Chicago Press.

Ram, R. (2004), 'School expenditures and student achievement: evidence for the United States', *Education Economics*, 12(2), 169–76.

Saltmarsh, S. (2007), 'Cultural complicities: elitism, heteronormativity and violence in the education marketplace', *International Journal of Qualitative Studies in Education*, 20(3), 335–54.

Slee, R. (2001), 'Inclusion in practice: does practice make perfect?', *Educational Review*, 53(2), 113–23.

Specialist Schools and Academies Trust (2008), *Specialist Schools Programme*, www.ssatrust.org.uk (accessed 7 January 2008).

Taylor, S., Rizvi, F., Lingard, B. and Henry, M. (1997), *Educational Policy and the Politics of Change*. London: Routledge.

TES (2004), 'Replacing GCSEs and A levels would be damaging, says CBI', www.tes.co.uk (accessed 22 March 2004).

Tomlinson, S. (2003), 'New Labour and education', *Children and Society*, 17(3), 195–204.

Yeomans, D., Higham, J. and Sharp, P. (2000), *The Impact of the Specialist Schools Programme: Case Studies*. Research Brief No. 197. London: DfEE.

Chapter 10

Higher education and civic and community engagement in the UK

John Annette

Civil/civic renewal and *active* citizenship

David Blunkett in his Edith Kahln Memorial Lecture and various publications and speeches called for a new *civic renewal*, or *civic engagement*, which emphasizes new forms and levels of community involvement in local and regional governance. This new democratic politics, which would include referendums, consultative activities, and deliberative participation, has found support from organizations as diverse as the Local Government Association and the prominent think tank Institute for Public Policy Reseach (IPPR, 2005). One outcome of this shift in thinking, which might be termed a switch from *government* to *governance*, is the obligation upon local authorities to establish Local Strategic Partnerships, a duty arising from the Local Government Act 2000. These partnerships seek to involve local communities in the development of community strategies. The Home Office established a Civil Renewal Unit, which has begun piloting an 'Active Learning for Active Citizenship' programme through which it is intended that adult learners will develop the capacity to engage in deliberative democracy at a local level. This unit is now the Community Empowerment Unit in the Department for Communities and Local Government and the 'Together We Can' cross-departmental strategy is being supported by the new 'Community Empowerment Strategy' (cf. Brannan et al., 2007).

In the USA this renewed civic renewal movement has led commentators to challenge the assumption of Robert Putnam and others that there has been a fundamental decline in social capital and civic participation. Carmen Sirianni and Lewis Friedland have mapped out the different dimensions of this movement and while recognizing the decline of more traditional forms of civic engagement and political participation, like membership of formal organizations, voting and membership of political parties. They argue that there is a new and changing form of civic renewal and call for greater and more creative forms of civic engagement (Sirianni and Friedland, 2001, 2005). Internationally, there is evidence of new global networks emerging

which promote these new forms of civic engagement and deliberative democracy (Fung and Olin Wright, 2003; Gastil and Levine, 2005).

This recent work on civic renewal also points out the limitations of social
capital theory as bonding and bridging social capital can correlate with civic
engagement but cannot explain why it takes place. It also highlights the need
to go beyond both bridging and bonding social capital and enable linking
social capital through political action. Without vertical political networking,
for example, poor communities do not necessarily gain access to new forms
of political influence (Field, 2003).

Citizenship education and the concepts of citizenship, everyday politics and civic engagement

It could be argued that the conception of citizenship underlying UK lifelong
learning should be a civic republican one which emphasizes democratic
political participation. This reflects the influence of Bernard Crick and the
Minister David Blunkett. One of the key challenges facing civil renewal and
the introduction of citizenship education in the UK is the question about
whether and in what respects citizenship is 'British'. Elizabeth Frazer has written about the 'British exceptionalism' towards discussing citizenship (Frazer,
1999a) and David Miller has written that:

> citizenship – except in the formal passport-holding sense – is not a widely
> understood idea in Britain. People do not have a clear idea of what it means
> to be a citizen . . . Citizenship is not a concept that has played a central role
> in our political tradition.
>
> (Miller, 2000, p. 26)

The question concerning to what extent British people are familiar or comfortable with the concept of citizenship raises questions about the extent
to which the political language of citizenship and civic republicanism can
increasingly be seen as a tradition of 'British' political thought that can provide the basis for a transformation of the more dominant liberal individualist
political traditions.

In the UK the current 'New Labour' government has espoused a programme of civil renewal that links the public, private and voluntary and
community sectors to work for the common good. This is informed by a set of
beliefs and values involving faith traditions, ethical socialism, communitarianism and more recently civic republicanism. According to David Blunkett when
he was the Home Secretary:

> The 'civic republican' tradition of democratic thought has always been

an important influence for me . . . This tradition offers us a substantive account of the importance of community, in which duty and civic virtues play a strong and formative role. As such, it is a tradition of thinking which rejects unfettered individualism and criticizes the elevation of individual entitlements above the common values needed to sustain worthwhile and purposeful lives. We do not enter life unencumbered by any community commitments, and we cannot live in isolation from others.

(Blunkett, 2003, p. 19)

It is this civic republican conception of politics which I would argue animates key aspects of New Labour's policies from citizenship education to its strategy towards revitalising local communities.

Richard Dagger in his influential study of civic education contends that a civic republican conception of citizenship can reconcile both liberal individuality and the cultivation of civic virtue and responsibility. He writes that, 'There is too much of value in the idea of rights – an idea rooted in firm and widespread convictions about human dignity and equality – to forsake it. The task, instead, is to find a way of strengthening the appeal of duty, community and related concepts while preserving the appeal of rights' (Dagger, 1997, p. 58; cf. Maynor, 2003).

The creation of a shared political identity underlying citizenship should also allow for multiple political identities based on gender, race, ethnicity, social exclusion, etc. It may be that the civic republican politics of contestability, as recently argued for by Philip Pettit (1997), may provide a more pluralist basis for citizenship in contemporary Britain than traditional republican politics. Equally, recent theorists of liberal democracy like Eamonn Callan also debate that an education for citizenship must hold fast to a constitutive ideal of liberal democracy while allowing for religious and cultural pluralism (Callan, 1997). A more differentiated but universal concept of citizenship (Lister, 1997), which encourages civic virtue and participation while maintaining individual liberty and allows for cultural difference, will create a way of understanding citizenship that is appropriate for an education for citizenship and democracy.

It could be argued that the recent establishment of an education for citizenship is based more on a communitarian concern for moral and political socialization than on promoting civic engagement. Following Elizabeth Frazer's distinction between a 'philosophical communitarianism' and a 'political communitarianism' (Frazer, 1999b; cf. Tam, 1998 and 2001), Adrian Little raises some important questions about the apolitical conception of community in communitarianism. He writes that:

As such, the sphere of community is one of contestation and conflict as much as it is one of agreement. Thus, essentially, it is deeply political. Where orthodox communitarians see politics as something to be overcome to the greatest possible extent, radicals argue that the downward devolution of power will entail more politics rather than less.

(Little, 2002, p. 154)

Both Little and Frazer in their studies of the political communitarianism consider the revival of civic republicanism as emerging from the debate between liberal and communitarian conceptions of the politics of community. In civic republicanism (cf. Pettit, 1997; Maynor, 2003) freedom consists of active self-government and liberty rests not simply in negative liberty but in active participation in a political community.

In the USA this debate is also reflected in the writings of Benjamin Barber, Michael Sandel and William Galston, which have been promoting a civic republican conception of citizenship (Barber, 1984; Sandel, 1996; Galston, 2001). According to Barber, the fundamental problem facing civil society is the challenge of providing citizens with 'the literacy required to live in a civil society, the competence to participate in democratic communities, the ability to think critically and act deliberately in a pluralist world, the empathy that permits us to hear and thus accommodate others, all involve skills that must be acquired' (Barber, 1992). Joseph Kahne and Joel Westheimer recommend a model of citizenship education based on the principles of social justice and Harry Boyte a model based on the concept of 'public work' (Kahne and Westheimer, 2003; Boyte, 2004). This debate about what is an appropriate model of citizenship for citizenship education raises questions about the need for students to move beyond an individualistic conception of citizenship and a consumer model of citizenship and develop a model of 'civic republican' democratic citizenship education.

This reconsideration of the concept of citizenship and citizenship education should also be informed by the recent work on the 'politics of everyday life', which can broaden our understanding of what 'the political' could mean in the lives of all citizens (Crick, 2005; Bentley, 2005; Boyte, 2004; Ginsborg, 2005; Stoker, 2006). We need to have more research into how people understand the 'political' as it relates to their everyday concerns in their communities as compared to the more formal political sphere of voting, political parties and holding public office. This broader conception of the political reflects the decline of formal political participation and lack of trust in formal politics at a time when there is evidence of continuing forms of civic engagement which may escape the radar of Robert Putnam's research into social capital (cf. Sirianni and Friedland, 2004 and Power Inquiry, 2006). This also reflects the important distinction that should be made between volunteering, which leads to active citizenship, and a more political form of civic engagement in community, which can lead to democratic citizenship.

An important feature of participatory politics which has recently been emphasized is that of the need to enable the capacity to participate in deliberative democratic engagement. From citizen juries to community visioning, the deliberative engagement of citizens has become an increasing feature of the new localism and also public service delivery (Lowndes et al., 1998; Fung and Olin Wright, 2003; Barnes, et al., 2007; Brannan et al., 2007; Smith, 2009). More recently there has been growing international interest in participatory budgeting from the more famous example of Porto Allegre in Brazil to developments in the UK like the experiment in Lewisham in London. The work of the Power Commission and think tanks like the IPPR, the New Economics Foundation, Involve, etc. now promote a more participatory and deliberative form of citizen engagement (cf. IPPR, 2004; Power Inquiry, 2006; Leighninger, 2008; Rosenberg, 2008). What has been lacking has been an analysis of what form of capacity building is necessary for citizens to participate in these activities and in what ways does participation in deliberative democratic engagement provide an education for democratic citizenship (Eslin et al., 2001; Gastil and Levine, 2005; Van der Veen et al., 2008). This involves a consideration of how deliberative democratic theory, like the emphasis on inclusion and voice in the work of Iris Marion Young, can influence educational practice. It also means that the analysis of the institutional practice of deliberative democratic engagement must develop an understanding of experiential learning and the means to analyse its learning outcomes. We need to know more about how citizens can develop the civic skills necessary for deliberative democratic engagement (Kirlin, 2003). A particular civic skill which is necessary is that of 'civic listening' and not just 'civic speaking'. This would include both levels of emotional literacy and intercultural understanding. We also need to learn more from the experience of 'participative governance' activities taking place abroad from participatory budgeting in Latin America, citizens' assemblies in Canada, and rural participatory action research in India, and so on (Cornwall, 2008).

Higher education and community engagement

There is an increasing interest in civic engagement and community involvement in the UK (cf. McIlrath and Mac Labhrainn, 2007; Watson, 2007). Recently the major research councils and higher education funding councils have established the Beacons for Public Engagement Programme (cf. www.publicengagement.ac.uk). This challenge to higher education in the UK – to provide opportunities for students to develop the values of social responsibility through volunteering, to develop accredited community-based learning and research in partnership with communities and to engage in Knowledge Exchange Partnerships which benefit the economic and social development of local and regional communities – should be seen in the context of the rethinking of higher education which has followed from the 'Dearing Commission' review of UK higher education. In 1997 a major Royal Commission under Lord Ron Dearing was established to examine the future of British higher education. One of the main aims of higher education, according to the Dearing Report (NCIHE 1997) on 'UK Higher Education in the Learning Society', is to contribute to a democratic, civilized and inclusive society. The emphasis on civic and community engagement highlights the need for the curriculum in higher education to prepare graduates to become active citizens and to participate not only in formal politics but also play a leadership role in civil society. This new commitment for higher education and civic/community engagement can be found in Australia with AUCEA, the Australian Universities Community Engagement Alliance (www.aucea. net.au); in Canada with the Canadian Association for Community Service Learning (www.communityservicelearning.ca); the Republic of Ireland with the Community Knowledge Initiative (www.nuigalwaycki.ie); in South Africa with the CHESP or Community Higher Education Service Partnership (www. chesp.org.za); and in many other countries internationally where community-based learning and research is developing (Annette, 2003a).

The Dearing Report (NCIHE 1997) follows on from an increasing range of work done since the 1970s, which has emphasized the importance in higher education of the development of what has been termed transferable, personal, core or key skills. The challenge for higher education, according to the Dearing Report, is to provide an academic framework that is based on the acquisition of critical knowledge, which is mostly structured upon the present framework established by the academic disciplines, and which provides students with the opportunity to develop essential key skills and capabilities. This emphasis on learning, not only for academic knowledge but also for key skills and capabilities, including student leadership and civic engagement, can also be found in the USA in the work of Ernest Boyer (1987) and the Carnegie Foundation and more recently in the writings of Thomas Ehrlich (Ehrlich, 2000, Ehrlich et al., 2003).

An important way in which students can develop key skills through work experience and experience an education for citizenship is through volunteering as well as service learning or community-based learning and research, as it is better known in the UK. Since the 1960s, student volunteering has been an exciting and valuable part of UK higher education, and today leadership is provided by Student Volunteer, England and also the new organization of professionals who support student volunteering, WiSCV. This has been assisted by the Higher Education Active Community Fund (HEACF), a fund that is assisting universities and colleges of higher education in England to promote volunteering and community partnerships and has now been rolled into the TQEF or Teaching and Quality Enhancement Fund (now TESS).

Community-based learning involves students working in partnership with local communities and studying through a structured programme of learning which includes reflection. While this development has resulted in the significant growth of exciting and challenging volunteer activities, there has also been an increase in the certification of volunteering and the development of an increasing number of academic programmes which accredit the learning involved. Throughout the UK we can find examples of universities recognizing the challenge of establishing partnership-working with local and regional communities. Increasingly we can also find evidence of the development of community-based learning and research programmes as a response to this challenge. The Higher Education Funding Council for England (HEFCE) has supported these developments through the Fund for the Development of Teaching and Learning (FDTL) programmes, the establishment of Centres for Excellence in Teaching and Learning (CETLs) in this area and the Higher Education Academy has encouraged this work through its subject centres.

At the core of community service learning is the pedagogy of experiential learning, which is based on the thought of John Dewey and more recently David Kolb and others. In the USA the National Society for Experiential Education (NSEE) has since 1971 been engaged in the development of, and research into, experiential education, and more recently, the American Association of Higher Education (AAHE), in partnership with the Corporation for National Service, has commissioned volumes by leading academic figures to examine the importance of service learning in higher education. What is impressive about the work of the NSEE and the AAHE is that there is research done on not only pedagogic practices but also going beyond anecdotal evidence, with research into the evaluation of the learning outcomes of service learning. More recently there have been the International Service Learning Research Conferences, which highlight the wide range of research being done internationally in this area. One of the leading research projects into the learning outcomes of service learning has been published as 'Where's the Learning in Service Learning?' by Janet Eyler and Dwight Giles (Eyler and Giles, 1999). What is important about community service learning is that it is multidisciplinary and can be integrated into a wide variety of academic disciplines and learning experiences. These could include environmental and global study and the opportunity for students to undertake community service learning while studying abroad, and the DEA is leading the way in promoting education for global citizenship and the skills to engage with global civil society.

The provision of the opportunity for students to participate in community service learning also requires partnerships with the university's local communities. This emphasis on partnership-working with local communities is especially true of those who advocate learning through community-based research (cf. Cruz and Giles, 2000; Gelmon et al., 2001; Strand et al., 2003, and Jacoby, 2003). The Higher Education Innovation Fund supported by HEFCE has provided key funding and strategic direction for universities to think creatively about establishing university-wide community partnerships and to create innovative knowledge transfer partnerships with local and regional communities. In 2002, Universities, UK published a series of research-based studies which examined the regional role of higher education institutions, and this has been supplemented by the work of HEFCE in promoting the achievements of HEF 1 and 2. An important new area of development in the UK has been how professional education (business, engineering, medical, teaching, etc.) has begun to address not only ethical issues but also civic professionalism, by providing community-based learning and research opportunities for its students in the UK and abroad to address issues of poverty, social justice and global citizenship.

In the UK the current 'New Labour' government has espoused a programme of civil renewal represented by its 'Together We Can' programme that links the public, private and voluntary and community sectors to work for the common good. Unlike the USA, most of the mission statements of universities and colleges of higher education in the UK do not use the rhetoric of civic engagement and do not talk about promoting citizenship or corporate citizenship and social responsibility. Despite the lack of a major movement for developing the civic role of higher education in the UK, there are an increasing number of academics who are now pushing for higher education to participate more fully in civil renewal. According to Bernard Crick, 'Universities are part of society and, in both senses of the word, a critical part which should be playing a major role in the wider objectives of creating a citizenship culture. I am now far from alone in arguing this' (Crick, 2000, p. 145).

One of the challenges in providing community-based learning and research which involves forms of civic engagement, is the evidence that increasingly young people are still interested in involvement in their communities but are alienated from the formal political process (cf. Annette, 2003b). Colby et al. argue that we need to analyse the motivations that encourage students to take advantage of these learning opportunities for active citizenship (Battistoni, 2002; Colby, et al., 2007). In the UK in a recent qualitative study, students at Anglia Polytechnic University and Cambridge University were analysed to consider how they learn both formally and informally for citizenship, to become what are called 'graduate citizens' (Ahier et al., 2003). While I believe this study has a somewhat limited understanding of contemporary citizenship and community, its life-course research reinforces the contradiction between students who want to become involved in their communities but are turned off politics. It also raises the issue that students are aware of the effects of globalization on themselves and their local communities and that an education for citizenship in higher education must take into account the role of global civil society.

It should be noted that one area in UK higher education where there is an increasing interest in learning for active citizenship is in Departments of Lifelong Learning and Continuing Education. This is important given the fact that increasingly students in higher education study part-time and are mature students. A number of universities have been part of the Active Learning for Active Citizenship programme for adult learning in the community, which was supported by the Community Empowerment Unit of what is now the Department for Communities and Local Government (Coare and Johnston, 2003; Mayo and Rooke, 2006; Annette and Mayo, forthcoming).

In the current funding crisis of higher education and the New Labour's 'higher ambitions' for higher education to contribute to economic growth, there seems to be little concern with civic responsibility. The major research councils and higher education funding councils across the UK have established the Beacons for Public Engagement Programme (cf. www.publicengagement. ac.uk). This is an excellent programme but it remains to be seen to what extent it will impact on higher education policy and practice in the UK. According to Chris Duke:

> What needs to happen to empower the student to feel part and to be an active part of his or her society? What need you learn and must you be able to do – and feel – to contribute to societal learning? What are the skills of civic and political participation, and where do they appear in the curriculum of higher education? It will be necessary to keep asking these questions to sustain a relevant and effective lifelong learning curriculum.
>
> (Dukes, 1997, p. 69)

To what extent will university graduates remain committed to volunteering beyond graduation? Will they go beyond volunteering and turn into more democratic citizens by becoming involved in civic engagement and political participation? Will they have the skills of democratic deliberation and civic listening necessary for a democratic political culture?

Throughout higher education there are academics, administrators and some senior managers who as part of their civic professionalism are committed to challenging the teaching and learning, the research and the student experience support activities, to enable students to become active in their local communities and to become democratic citizens. To what extent will they move from beyond the margins of higher education to the mainstream?

References

Ahier, J., Beck, J. and Moore, R. (2003), *Graduate Citizens? Issues of Citizenship Education and Higher Education.* London: Routledge Falmer.

Annette, J. (2003a), 'International service learning', *Frontiers: Journal of International Education*, 8, 83–93.

—— (2003b), 'Community and citizenship education', in A. Lockyer, B. Crick and
   J. Annette (eds), *Education for Democratic Citizenship*. Aldershot: Ashgate.
—— and Mayo, M. (eds), *Taking Part: Active Learning for Active Citizenship*. NIACE,
   forthcoming.
Barber, B. (1984), *Strong Democracy*. Berkeley and Los Angeles: University of
   California Press.
—— (1992), *An Aristocracy of Everyone*. Oxford: Oxford University Press.
Barnes, M., Newman, J. and Sullivan, H. (2007), *Power, Participation and Political
   Renewal*. Bristol: Policy Press.
Battistoni, R. (2002), *Civic Engagement across the Curriculum*. Providence, RI:
   Campus Compact.
Bentley, T. (2005), *Everyday Democracy*, Demos. Available from www.demos.co.uk/
   publications/everydaydemocracy
Blunkett, D. (2003), *Civil Renewal: A New Agenda*. Transcript of the CSV Edith
   Kahn Memorial Lecture, 11 June, www.communities.gov.uk/publications/
   communities/civilrenewal (accessed 17 January 2010).
Boyer, E. (1987), *Carnegie Commission Report on the Undergraduate Experience in
   America*. New York: Harper & Row.
Boyte, H. (2004), *Everyday Politics: Reconnecting Citizens and Public Life*. Philadephia,
   PA: University of Pennsylvania Press.
Brannan T., John, P. and Stoker, G., (eds) (2007), *Re-energising Citizenship: Strategies
   for Civil Renewal*. London:Palgrave
Callan, E. (1997), *Creating Citizens*. Oxford: Clarendon Press.
Coare, P. and Johnston, R. (2003), *Adult Learning, Citizenship and Community Voices*.
   Leicester: NIACE.
Colby, A., Beaumont, E., Ehrlich, T. and Corngold, J. (2007), *Educating for
   Democracy: Preparing Undergraduates for Responsible Political Engagement*. San
   Francisco: Carnegie/Jossey-Bass.
Cornwall, A. (2008), *Democratic Engagement: What the UK Can Learn From
   International Experience*. Demos. Available from www.demos.co.uk/ publications/
   everydaydemocracy
Crick, B. (2000), *Essays on Citizenship*. London and New York: Continuum.
—— (2005), *In Defence of Politics*, 5th edn. London and New York: Continuum.
Cruz, N. and Giles, D. Jr. (2000), 'Where's the community in service-learning
   research?', *Michigan Journal of Community Service Learning*, 7, 28–34.
Dagger, R. (1997), *Civic Virtues: Rights, Citizenship and Republican Liberalism*.
   Oxford: Oxford University Press.
Ehrlich, T. (ed.) (2000), *Civic Responsibility of Higher Education*. Phoenix, AZ:
   American Council on Education/Oryx Press.
—— , Colby, A., Beaumont, E. and Stephens, J. (2003), *Educating Citizens*. San
   Francisco: Jossey-Bass.
Eslin, P., Pendlebury, S. and Tjiattas, M. (2001), 'Deliberative Democracy, Diversity
   and the Challenges of Citizenship Education', *Journal of the Philosophy of
   Education*, 35,1.
Eyler, J. and Giles, D. Jr. (1999), *Where's the Learning in Service Learning?* San
   Francisco: Jossey-Bass.
Field, J. (2003), *Social Capital*. London: Routledge.

Frazer, E. (1999a), 'Introduction: the idea of political education', *Oxford Review of Education*, 25, 1–2.

—— (1999b), *The Problems of Communitarian Politics*. Oxford: Oxford University Press.

Fung, A. and Olin Wright, E. (eds) (2003), *Deepening Democracy*. London: Verso.

Galston, W. (2001), 'Political knowledge, political engagement and civic education', *Annual Review of Political Science*, 4, 217–34.

Gastil, J. and Levine, P. (2005), *The Deliberative Democracy Handbook*. San Francisco: Jossey-Bass.

Gelmon, S., Holland, B. A. and Driscoll, A. (2001), *Assessing Service-Learning and Civic Engagement*. Providence, RI: Campus Compact.

Ginsborg, P. (2005), *The Politics of Everyday Life*. Newhaven, Conn.: Yale University Press.

IPPR (2005), *The Lonely Citizen*. Available from www.ippr.org.uk

Jacoby, B. (ed.) (2003), *Building Partnerships for Service Learning*. San Francisco: Jossey-Bass.

Kahne, J. and Westheimer, J. (eds) (2003), 'Special section on education, democracy and civic engagement', *Phi Delta Kappen*, 85, 1.

Kirlin, M. (2003), 'The role of civic skills in fostering civic engagement', CIRCLE Research Paper.

Leighninger, M. (2008), *The Next Form of Democracy*. Nashville: Vanderbilt University Press.

Lister, R. (1997), *Citizenship: Feminist Perspectives*. Basingstoke: Macmillan.

Little, A. (2002), *The Politics of Community*. Edinburgh: Edinburgh University Press.

Lowndes, V., Pratchett, L. and Stoker, G. (1998), *Enhancing Public Participation in Local Government: A Research Report*. London: DETR.

Maynor, J. (2003), *Republicanism in the Modern World*. Cambridge: Polity Press.

Mayo, M. and Rooke, A. (2006), *Active Learning for Active Citizenship: An Evaluation Report*. London: Department for Communities and Local Government.

McIlrath, L. and Mac Labhrainn, I. (eds) (2007), *Higher Education and Civic Engagement*. Aldershot: Ashgate.

Miller, D. (2000), 'Citizenship: what does it mean and why is it important?', in N. Pearce and J. Hallgarten (eds), *Tomorrow's Citizens: Critical Debates in Citizenship and Education*. London: IPPR.

National Committee of Inquiry into Higher Education (NCIHE) (1997), *Dearing Report: Higher Education in the Learning Society*. Somerset: NCIHE Publications.

Petit, P. (1997), *Republicanism: A Theory of Freedom and Government*. Oxford: Oxford University Press.

Power Inquiry (2006), *An Independent Inquiry into Britain's Democracy*. York Publishing. Available from www.powerinquiry.org/report/index.php

Rosenberg, S. (2008), *Can the People Govern? Deliberation, Participation and Democracy*. London: Palgrave.

Sandel, M. (1996), *Democracy's Discontent*. Cambridge, Mass.: Harvard University Press.

Sirianni, C. and Friedland, L. (2001, 2004), *Civic Innovation in America: Community Empowerment, Public Policy, and the Movement for Civic Renewal*. Berkeley: University of California Press.

—— (2005), *The Civic Renewal Movement*, 2nd edn. Dayton, Ohio: Kettering
    Foundation.
Smith, G. (2009), *Democratic Innovations*. Cambridge, UK: Cambridge University
    Press.
Stoker, G. (2006), *Why Politics Matters: Making Democracy Work*. Basingstoke:
    Palgrave Macmillan.
Strand, K., Marullo, S., Cutforth, N., Stoecker, R. and Donohue, P. (2003),
    Community-based Research in Higher Education. San Francisco: Jossey-Bass.
Tam, H. (1998), *Communitarianism: A New Agenda for Politics and Citizenship*. New
    York: New York University Press.
Tam, H. (ed.) (2001), *Progressive Politics in the Global Age*. Cambridge: Polity Press.
Van der Veen, R., Wildemeersch, D., Youngblood, J. and Marsick, V. (eds) (2008),
    Democratic Practices as Learning Opportunities. Rotterdam: Sense Publishers.
Watson, D. (2007), *Managing Civic and Community Engagement*. Maidenhead:
    McGraw Hill/Open University Press.

PART III

Curriculum Reform

Overview

This section focuses upon specific reforms and approaches taken in different countries to help develop the curriculum to meet new challenges and the needs of the population it is designed to serve.

Elda Nikolou-Walker and Lynn Fee describe the impact of the knowledge economy on learning and in particular its increasing significance for both individual workplace learning and organizational learning, causing us to reassess what counts as knowledge in an organization, how this knowledge is transmitted and stored, who owns it and how it is shared. Focusing on the health sector, they argue that the contemporary atmosphere of nursing practice requires the creation of a learning culture which supports health practitioners in their practice, where the integration of education, practice, research, information technology and continued professional development is essential. They go on to locate work-based learning and research at the centre of this necessary integrated approach to professional development in health practice. From the starting point that work-based learning programmes are derived from the needs of the workplace as well as of the learner, therefore not controlled by the disciplinary curriculum, the authors explore how work-based learning has become one of the most essential tools for the reformation of the higher education curriculum in the contemporary context as a method of learning which is responsive to the needs of individuals, as well as society.

Kwame Akyeampong explores the impact of the evolution of government policy in basic education on teacher education in Ghana. The chapter analyses how education policies by design or default have influenced teacher education from the colonial era to the most recent reforms. The chapter also highlights the role that the World Bank played in the education reforms from 1987 and how this, more or less, shaped the landscape of education investment and growth, and challenges for teacher education, especially in addressing teacher supply and deployment to meet increasing demand in basic schools. Drawing from an analytic review of government policies, Akyeampong argues that teacher education has almost always been left out of strategic planning to expand educational access and improve its quality. He discusses some of the consequences that the restructuring of teacher education and qualification has had on matching teacher supply and demand in Ghana. Finally, he concludes by highlighting key lessons that Ghana's experience might have for other African countries, focusing especially on the need for policies that respond to challenges that threaten sustained access to quality basic education.

China's adult and continuing education has undergone dramatic changes in recent years following the rapid expansion of enrolment in universities. Ning examines strategies and approaches that adult and continuing education in China has taken to respond to the challenges and opportunities. He gives a critical review of neoliberal policies of marketization in higher education, and a historical perspective on adult and continuing education in China, giving a dual backdrop to the sector's strategies of responses. He explores how the restructuring has impacted on the adult higher education system and institutional structure, which in turn will decide whether educators in adult and continuing education can efficiently address the relevant needs in this changing economic and social environment and provide high-quality professional continuing education programmes. He concludes that the strategies adopted by adult and continuing education in China have been consistent with the global trend of marketization in higher education.

Francis Murphy's contribution takes the teacher-as-researcher idea as its starting point, from which he presents a model of curriculum development in which the teacher is at the centre, attempting to move away from a model in which experts developed new curricula centrally. With the 'essential attributes' approach it is the course teacher who analyses course documentation, wider debate literature and course stakeholder interviews. From the results of this analysis, the approach attempts to identify essential attributes that are necessary for graduates to function in their future profession, particularly targeting new essential attributes that may become necessary as the working environment changes. The author explores the contributions that the approach has made in terms of quality and excellence. How the model can be applied to include value systems is explained by referring to his own practice as a course leader for the Bachelor of Engineering (Honours) degree course in Mechanical Engineering at Cork Institute of Technology, Ireland.

Vocational Education and Training (VET) is considered today as an integral part of the lifelong learning ideal that plays a key role in human capital accumulation for the achievement of the European Union's social and economic objectives. However, although most European policies that target social cohesion advocate a distinct social role for VET, Zarifis argues that VET cannot and therefore must not be considered as the solution to combat all problems of social exclusion, or as the way through to social cohesion, unless we add to it and state that VET can only fulfil its role as an agent for strengthening or increasing social cohesion (defined in policy terms) if sufficient resources (human, social and monetary) are allocated. In light of this thesis, Zarifis seeks in this chapter to answer some principal questions: what kind of social benefits are more likely to be generated by VET in the EU, for which social groups, and through which mechanisms (funding, operational, policy, etc.)? Further, can these benefits guarantee social cohesion in the long run, and what sort of measures can be taken to sustain these benefits through VET?

Chapter 11

Beyond borders: expanding the uses of work-based learning

Elda Nikolou-Walker and Lynn Fee

Introduction

Education in the modern world has undergone massive changes. Globalization, the process by which the new industrial and financial transnational corporations dominate the international economic system, involves more than just the growth of large companies, the removal of restrictions on the movement of capital and investment, and the freedom of trade in all goods and services including intellectual property. The nature of work in the contemporary world is rapidly changing and globalization has resulted in the restructuring of the labour market, whereby there has been a high level of geographical and occupational mobility for skilled workers as well as the marginalization of the lower skilled. The increasing urgency of global warming, national and international conflicts, and the depletion of earth resources, have also contributed to an increase in awareness of the role of education in playing its part in helping resolve these issues. It is the impact of these immense shifts on higher-level learning about work that is the focus of this chapter, with particular reference to the case of work in the health sciences.

The changes that have been taking place in the world of work have also resulted in a new knowledge economy where the essential issues become what counts as knowledge in an organization, how this knowledge is transmitted and stored, who owns it, and how it is shared. Globalization affects economic, political, cultural, technical and social facets of all countries, which inevitably leads to uncertainty; for example, a changing labour market. The educational response to these uncertainties can be seen as a tool for combating social exclusion. Edwards et al.'s (1998) review of the literature on lifelong learning claims that the relationship between education, training and the performance of the economy is central to lifelong learning. They argue that lifelong learning has emerged as a response to the challenges of today and that lifelong learning is of key importance in the development of a workforce which is multi-skilled and competitive. All of these developments and challenges in education cause scholars and educationalists to assert that there should be a significant repositioning of the university and higher education to meet the needs of the age of 'super-complexity' (Barnett, 2000).

What is work-based learning?

The term work-based learning (WBL) has become increasingly popular within education and the workplace over the past decade. There are a number of terms in existence as well as a variety of subsequent definitions, which can contribute to some confusion when the question is posed as to what exactly is WBL. For learning to be classified as work based it would appear that the linking of the theoretical knowledge to the individual's workplace is central. The utility of WBL in the various sectors of higher education is indubitable and its relevance to university education may be perceived in the background of globalization and the post-industrial society where knowledge is perceived as a product (Armsby et al., 2008). It can be argued that the WBL approach is not a new phenomenon in education, as it is based on the theories of John Dewey, who had long emphasized the unique integration of life and learning (Dewey, 1916). Swail and Kampits (2004) also asserted that the best way to achieve optimum results in relation to education was to amalgamate education with the world of work.

From the perspective of the health sciences, WBL is an important tool in driving the higher education curriculum forward. Nixon et al. (2006) affirm that within higher education the tendency has been for the student to be based within higher education and engage in a work placement, with most of the higher education involvement being in the post-registration, post-graduate sphere. Therefore, there is capacity and scope within the higher education system in health sciences to extend the use of WBL. The rapid pace of change within the health sector poses the problem for formal higher education courses to keep apace of these changes, when curriculum reviews can take a significant period of time. The contemporary atmosphere of nursing practice requires the creation of a learning culture which supports health practitioners in their practice, where the integration of education, practice, research, information technology and continued professional development is essential. There are advantages of adopting a WBL approach in higher education as this method ensures opportunities for innovation and imagination, along with a sound evidence base. Neville (2008, p. 5) advocates the principles of 'student choice flexibility (and) a rigorous learning experience'. Neville also places the focus of learning firmly on contemporary, work-related issues that impact on clients and the service provided. Educators must continually assess the teaching strategies employed and create innovative approaches to enable staff to cope with the dynamic health care environment in which they practice (De Marco et al., 2002).

WBL is essential to facilitate the clinical competence of nursing students and is a vehicle for maintaining nurses' and midwives' competence once they have entered the profession. 'WBL values learning which takes place outside of an educational institution, integrates practice with theory, encourages reflection and contributes to the development of professional knowledge' (Morgan-Eason, 2009, p. 80). The significance of WBL in the practice and learning of nursing cannot be ignored and is valued as an approach which contributes to the development of the individual as well as society. Education in every field needs to meet the increasing demands of the period where globalization, as well as the knowledge industry, has changed the face of knowledge and learning. Mantzorou (2004) ultimately points to the relevance of WBL as a method of learning in nursing, in an environment where change is continuous and knowledge needs to be current.

The scope of work-based learning

Learning in the contemporary environment has been recognized as an important process, which involves experience with knowing. There is immense scope for WBL in every field of education. According to the UK's Campaign for Learning, people deliberately engage in learning in an attempt to make sense of the world, using their experiences, with the desired outcomes of increasing knowledge, skills and the ability to reflect. Subsequently (if the learning is effective), this will lead to an aim to further develop (www.campaign-for-learning.org.uk). This definition of learning highlights the importance of experience in the process of learning. 'WBL is essentially learner-centred, but has a range of additional dimensions when the student is a work-based learner rather than a student engaged in work placement or some other form of work related learning' (Armsby et al., 2008, p. 1). In an analysis of the various explanations and discussions of WBL, one recognizes that it is a theoretically sound approach to learning which ensures the most effective learning to the individual. 'WBL is much more than the familiar experiential learning, which consists of adding a layer of simulated experience to conceptual knowledge. In WBL, theory may be acquired in concert with practice' (Raelin, 2008, p. 64). The importance of learning through and from experience and the integration of theory and practice continue to be current debates regarding modernizing learning (Bass, 1985).

Traditional learning is regarded as academic and theoretical, leading to a qualification and knowledge; whereas WBL includes academic and theoretical learning, with the additionality of organizational application also leading to a qualification and knowledge. Additional outcomes such as the gaining of skills and competencies and the resultant performance improvement may also be achieved. According to Chapman (2004), WBL is a type of learning which is flexible and relevant to practice, helps practitioners to relate new knowledge directly to the work environment and enables them to focus on the realities of practice within a theoretical and reflective framework. 'WBL focuses on the learning process rather than the teaching process and the practitioner takes responsibility for their own learning and must be willing to look at their practice with fresh eyes' (Introduction and Guidelines to WBL, 2008, p. 5).

Garnett and Nikolou-Walker's (2005) definition of WBL does not make room for the recognition of WBL, if it is perceived as being below university level. This may be viewed as academic snobbery and exclusive to those who have not been able, for a variety of reasons, to access higher education through traditional routes. Some work has been done to 'map' vocational level awards to higher education levels, thus providing an access route to university education. This enables individuals to claim higher education level credit for WBL. Access will be further widened with the introduction of the new Qualifications Credit Framework (www.qcda.gov.uk/19674.aspx).

WBL acknowledges the value of experiential learning and in particular the development of an individual's ability to learn from experience (Walker and Dewar, 2000). WBL has the potential to meet the needs of nurses and midwives by promoting learning that is practice-driven, encouraging the practitioner to apply theoretical knowledge in their practice; the opportunity for the practitioner to develop reflective learning skills; and personalizing the process of education by placing reflection centrally (Dewar and Walker, 1999). Goodwyn's (1996) view would concur with that of Dewar and Walker, namely that any change process involves changes to attitude and behaviour. This would be in accord with elements of constructivist learning, as described by Merriam and Caffarella (1999), for example experiential learning, self-directed learning and reflective practice.

Hargreaves (1996) defines WBL as placing value on learning which takes place outside of an educational institution and integrates theory with practice. The definition assumes that the transfer of academic knowledge will occur in the higher education setting. However, as individuals and employers take more responsibility for their own learning and development, thus enhancing their ability to develop skills in lifelong learning (Peters, 2001), the transfer of knowledge may occur primarily in the workplace, with the university's role as an accreditation body. Connor's (2005, p. 2) definition fits well with the advantages of WBL for the employer in that it relates to performance improvement:

> Work-based learning is much more focused on learning in the workplace derived from work undertaken for, or by, an employer. It (WBL) involves the gaining of competencies and knowledge in the workplace (and) may include learning undertaken as part of workforce development.

This objective (WBL Network, 2006) supports Connor's perspective 'to promote learning for, in and through paid and unpaid work'. This focus then places learning in the workplace, and the motivation for learning relates to work. This may disregard the development of self that can, and some argue should, result from developing the skill of reflection. Boud and Solomon (2001) argue that learning which takes places within the work setting is consequently learner-centred and experience driven. Peyton (1998) suggests that adults are much more likely to engage in learning when they have a specific purpose in mind. WBL is centred on the individual's learning needs and therefore places control over the learning process within the work environment (Raelin, 1997). One of the goals of learning is performance, which can assist the individual in climbing from an unskilled present to a proficient future. The modern learner seeks to be more effective, to be able to act and produce the desired result through the process of learning. Therefore, WBL can enable learners in the achievement of their career interests. Additionally, Jordan (2000) claims that there is little empirical evidence that formal continuing professional education courses improve the care that is delivered to patients. The challenge now facing the profession is to refocus learning once more at the patients' bedside. According to Raux and College (2004), learning is not 'active' until it is transferred into the real workplace setting.

Informal learning (by its very name) implies that the learning is inferior to formal learning (i.e. that which is received through school or college). 'Informal', here, can be interpreted as 'unofficial' and therefore unendorsed and unsanctioned. It is time for educators to move away from these substandard connotations. Informal learning is mainly unrecognized and unvalued, as this is, either taken for granted or not even recognized as learning (Eraut, 1999). The resultant knowledge, then, tends to be regarded as the individual's innate capability rather than recognized and valued as something which has been learned (Eraut, 1999). Similarly, due to knowledge creation and the deployment of new knowledge in the workplace, the workplace itself is now recognized as a site of learning and knowledge production. Swanwick (2008) calls attention to the fact that, if WBL opportunities are not to be left to chance and identified as integral to the curriculum, it is essential that faculty development is such that supports the integration of WBL. In addition, educational infrastructure within the workplace needs to undergo development on a par with that within the higher education establishments.

WBL is developed within the work environment. Accreditation is of vital importance to professionals; therefore a partnership approach is desirable. Costley (2007) declares that a partnership approach to WBL between the higher education institution, the individual and the organization keeps academic requirements in touch with work requirements. This tripartite relationship is the way forward. Martin (1997) observes that partnerships between universities and employers appear to be the most effective model of WBL.

The sustainability of work-based learning

Dearing (NCIHE 1997) questioned the ability of formal education to bring about a change in practice that was sustainable. This would be in support of Chapman's (2004) view that WBL aids the practitioner to relate new knowledge directly to the work environment, as well as Connor's (2005) behaviourist perspective regarding linking WBL to performance improvement. Significantly, an aspect of WBL, namely to impact on performance in work, reflects the concept of work experience in the process of learning and is a practical approach to learning and experience. With the emphasis on high standards in the learning process of higher education, the question is now open about which approach educators may employ in order to achieve these standards. Even in high schools, educational reforms to help student development emphasize the incorporation of WBL, which integrates experiences outside of the school with classroom learning.

Over the last fifteen years, some education reformers have argued that integrating experiences outside of the school with classroom learning is an effective approach to engaging students in their studies and helping to prepare them for education and work after high school. Often these experiences involve work in private and public sector organizations. Reformers make a variety of claims about the educational benefits of this type of WBL, and in many cases these have struck a responsive chord (Bailey et al., 2004, p. 2).

WBL for higher education, according to Brennan and Little (2006), is a field of increasing interest and is recognized as a tool to develop those in work, both personally and professionally. WBL has become one of the most essential tools for the reformation of the higher education curriculum in the contemporary context and is a method of learning which is responsive to the needs of individuals, as well as society.

When budgets are tightened, usually the first fields to experience pain are education and development. If continued professional development is not invested in, how can government, for instance, expect nurses and midwives to meet the agenda for future healthcare delivery? This is where WBL, for example, becomes paramount – equipping healthcare professionals with the learning skills in order to learn and develop within the workplace. WBL is not designed to take over or replace formal education, but to be supportive of and complementary to formal education. Education policy and practice has always been developed within the context of the nation state; however, the interconnections made available by globalization, the entry of students from a variety of cultural backgrounds, media globalization and the availability of the internet, have prompted educationalists to review their practice in the light of international influences.

How work-based learning transforms the higher education curriculum

It is important to comprehend the distinctive features of WBL in order to realize its relevance in reforming the higher education curriculum. There are several advantages that support this system of learning. Learners are employees or have some contractual relationship with the external organization that negotiates learning plans approved by the educational institution and the organization (Armsby et al. 2008). The WBL programme is derived from the needs of the workplace as well as of the learner and is therefore not controlled by the disciplinary curriculum. In order to comprehend the relevance of WBL in higher education curricula it is essential to realize the strategic context of higher education. There is an important demand for higher-level skills in the contemporary context of the world where globalization and the knowledge industry dominate the scene. Thus it is obvious that WBL, in comparison to other forms of learning, is directly related to the needs of employers and employment needs of those in work or seeking work.

Gephart et al. (1996) argues that the provision of Continued Professional Development (CPD) short programmes increases both the knowledge of the individual practitioner and the collective knowledge of the organization. This increase in knowledge contributes to the organization becoming a learning organization. The move towards universities introducing a work-based component into formerly purely academic programmes demonstrates the acceptance of the need for employers to have staff who are not just knowledgeable, but who have the ability to relate this knowledge to their everyday practice. In the ever-changing work environment the skills of reflection and problem solving are essential for individuals in order to meet the demands of the contemporary workplace. Workplace learning, according to Gray et al. (2004, p. 5), 'is a process through which both individuals and organizations move towards desirable and sustainable outcomes'. However, within the reality of the work environment, these outcomes may not be one and the same. Individual objectives and organizational objectives may differ. Gray et al. argue that workplace learning can only achieve lasting development if there is concurrence between both personal and organizational desires. Therefore, the significance of WBL, which aids individual development, has been emphasized in the contemporary environment of the globalized world.

Significantly, learning in the workplace contributes to the progress in practitioners' practice through the recognition and valuing of one's own abilities (Swallow et al., 2001). Flanagan et al. (2000) take this further by outlining the potential of WBL in developing transferable work-based and professional skills such as critical understanding, professional attitudes, knowledge development and practical skills. This then has the potential to meet the academic, WBL and professional agendas. It is important, also, to note that WBL offers the attraction of combining individual, organizational and societal interests, which can develop individuals as well as societies. Therefore, the curriculum of higher education should aid the learner in this process. Several studies and conferences at the international level have suggested this significant need. However, Eraut's (1999) study found that most individuals still equated learning with formal education and learning and see working and learning as separate activities.

Evaluation of work-based learning

Usher and Solomon (1999) report that higher education institutions are frequently questioning the legitimacy of WBL and the subsequent tension between WBL and more conventional education programmes. Costley (2007) argues that because WBL is highly contextualized, this has raised issues relating to assessment and evaluation. Costley describes a variety of assessment processes, including utilizing work-place supervisors and the use of personal and professional development plans and portfolios. Peyton (1998) states that the closer the assessment is to reality (i.e. the workplace), the more valid it will be. However, Newble and Cannon (2001) question the reliability of 'real' workplace assessment, and specifically recommend that of direct 'observation'.

Adapting to theoretical approaches such as 'learning through', 'critical reading', and reflecting, as well as developing personal strategies, can be productive for both the individual and the workplace (Nikolou-Walker, 2008). Evidence-based evaluations of WBL are, however, still relatively uncommon, and much that is written supporting this mode of learning is at the level of theory and exhortation. However, in one as yet unpublished study (Fee, 2009) with students of nursing, medicine and allied health professions, both positive and negative consequences emerge .The clinical placements focus on work-based inter-professional learning, which is student-led and supported by clinical staff.

There was considerable consensus regarding the value of adding the WBL outcomes. The findings indicate that the majority had had some experience of attendance at inter-professional lectures, but no previous experience with inter-professional learning in the workplace. The WBL objectives were regarded as useful and that these should be expanded to include other areas and become an integral part of nursing, medical and allied health professional undergraduate clinical placements. Participants indicated that the added dimension of work-based inter-professional objectives encouraged (and promoted) communication between the students involved, as well as enhanced understanding of each other's respective roles.

Interestingly, all agreed (or 'strongly agreed'), that the work-based inter-professional learning promoted a sense of shared responsibility in patient care, as well as promoting the opportunity to learn from each other and enhancing understanding of other professionals' views regarding clinical matters.

Reported challenges, as evidenced by public inquiries in Northern Ireland (Regulation and Quality Improvement Authority (RQIA), 2005; Eastern Health and Social Services Board (EHSSB), 2006, 2007), criticize inter-professional working and communications. In this environment, where the lack of shared understanding between different professional groupings is frequently criticized, it is unrealistic to expect that, upon qualifying, different professionals will suddenly assume an ability to work together and communicate harmoniously. It is of vital importance that the professions are proactive in relation to developing these skills and the undergraduate stage is, perhaps, the obvious place to start.

One participant commented:

this was my first placement but it allowed me to experience a multidisciplinary team in action. I saw the working of each professional group to achieve their individual short-term goals and also their combined effort to achieve a common long-term goal. This [work-based inter-professional] placement also gave me the opportunity to see in detail the role of each discipline and their contribution to the patient journey. This maximised my learning experience.

Other comments included: 'I feel this [work-based inter-professional] programme is vital within the healthcare system', and 'work-based inter-professional education has benefited me with my understanding of each professional within the team. I feel it is vital to understand each role in order for the patient/client to get full benefits from the service we provide.'

WBL has been an essential tool for learning in nursing and other health-related areas for decades. WBL is an important way of approaching the needs of practitioners in matching the requirements of a rapidly changing health service and developing nursing practice. WBL approaches also promote learning which is practice driven and able to meet the demands of the contemporary context of professions.

We can conclude, therefore, that WBL is an effective driver of curriculum reform in higher education and social change, and is an invaluable tool to enable practitioners to answer the challenges raised in learning and education by the dominant practice of globalization in the contemporary world.

References

Armsby, P., Costley, C. and Garnett, J. (2008), 'The legitimisation of knowledge: a work-based learning perspective of APEL', *International Journal of Lifelong Education*, 25(4), 369–83.

Bailey, T. R., Hughes, K. L. and Moore, D. T. (2004), *Working Knowledge: WBL and Educational Reform.* New York: Routledge Falmer.

Barnett, R. (2000), *Realising the University in an Age of Supercomplexity.* Buckingham: SRHE and OU Press.

Bass, B. M. (1985), *Leadership and Performance beyond Expectations.* New York: Free Press.

Boud, D. and Solomon, N. (eds) (2001), *WBL: A New Higher Education.* Buckingham: SRHE.

Brennan, J. and Little, B. (2006), *Towards a Strategy for Workplace Learning: Report of a Study to Assist HEFCE in the Development of a Strategy for Workplace Learning.* London: Centre for Higher Education Research and Information.

Chapman, L. (2004), 'Practice development: advancing practice through WBL', *WBL in Primary Care,* 2, 90–6.

Connor, H. (2005), *WBL: A Consultation.* London: Council for Higher Education.

Costley, C. (2007), 'WBL: assessment and evaluation in higher education', *Assessment and Evaluation in Higher Education,* 32(1), 1–9.

De Marco, R., Haywood, L. and Lynch, M. (2002), 'Nursing students' experiences with and strategic approaches to case-bound instruction: a replication and comparison study between two disciplines', *Journal of Nurse Education,* 41(4), 165–74.

Dewar, B. J. and Walker, E. (1999), 'Experiential learning: issues for supervision', *Journal of Advanced Nursing,* 30(9), 1459–67.

Dewey, J. (1916), *Democracy and Education.* New York: Free Press.

Eastern Health and Social Services Board (2006), *Executive Summary and Recommendations from the Report of the Inquiry Panel (McCleery).* Belfast: EHSSB.

—— (2007), *Independent Review of Circumstances Surrounding the Death of Danny McCartan.* Belfast, EHSSB.

Edwards, R., Raggatt, P., Harrison, R., McCollum, A. and Calder, J. (1998), 'Recent thinking in lifelong learning: a review of the literature', *Research Brief RB80.* ISBN 0 85522 858 X, Department for Education and Employment.

Eraut, M. (1999), 'Typology of informal learning in the workplace', *University of Sussex Studies in Continuing Education,* 26(2), 247–73.

Fee, L. (2009), 'An evaluation to assess the efficacy of a work-based, interprofessional education initiative', unpublished paper.

Flanagan, J., Baldwin, S. and Clarke, D. (2000), 'WBL as a means of developing and assessing nursing competence', *Journal of Clinical Nursing,* 9, 360–8.

Garnett, J. and Nikolou-Walker, E. (2005), 'Work-based learning – a new imperative: developing reflective practice in professional life', *Reflective Practice,* 5(3), 297–312.

Gephart, M., Marsick, V., Van Buren, M., and Spiro, M. (1996), 'Learning organisations come alive', *Training and Development,* 50, 12, 34–45.

Goodwyn, L. (1996), 'The nurses' role as a change agent in the audit cycle', *Nursing Standard,* 22, 10, 43–6.

Gray, D., Cundell, S., Hay, D. and O'Neill, J. (2004), *Learning through the Workplace: A Guide to WBL.* Cheltenham: Nelson Thornes.

Hargreaves, J. (1996), 'Credit where credit's due – WBL in professional practice', *Journal of Clinical Nursing,* 5(3), 165–9.

Introduction and Guidelines to WBL (2008), *NHS Education for Scotland*, www.scot. nhs.uk (accessed 21 June 2009).

Jordan, S. (2000), 'Educational input and patient outcomes: exploring the gap', *Journal of Advanced Nursing*, 31(2), 461–71.

Mantzorou, M. (2004), *Preceptorship in Nursing Education: Is it a Viable Alternative Method for Clinical Teaching?*, www.nursing.gr/ protectarticle/preceptorship.pdf (accessed 17 June 2009).

Martin, E. (1997), *The Effectiveness of Different Models of Work-based University Education*. Department of Employment, Education, Training and Youth Affairs, 96/19. Canberra, Australia: Evaluations and Investigations Program, Higher Education Division.

Merriam, S. B. and Caffarella, R. S. (1999), *Learning in Adulthood: A Comprehensive Guide*, 2nd edn. San Francisco: Jossey-Bass.

Morgan-Eason, A. (2009), 'WBL in nursing education: the value of preceptorships', *WBL in Nursing Education*, www.lagcc.cuny.edu/ ctl/journal/ v3/pdf/MorganEasson.pdf (accessed 17 June 2009).

Neville, L. (2008), 'WBL: a different approach', *British Journal of Healthcare Assistants*, 2, 1, 34–6.

Newble, D. and Cannon, R. (2001), *A Handbook for Medical Teachers*, 4th edn. London: Kluwer Academic Publishers, Chapter 1.

Nikolou-Walker, E. (2008), *The Expanded University Work-based Learning and the Economy*. Harlow: Pearson.

Nixon, I., Smith, K., Stafford, R. and Camm, S. (2006), *WBL: Illuminating the Higher Education Landscape: Final Report*. The Higher Education Academy.

Peters, O. (2001), *Learning and Teaching in Distance Education*. London: Kogan Page.

Peyton, J. W. R. (1998), *Teaching and Learning in Medical Practice*. Guildford: Manticore Europe Limited.

Raelin, J. (1997), 'A model of WBL', *Organisation Science*, 8(6), 563–77.

—— (2008), *WBL: Bridging Knowledge and Action in the Workplace*. Hoboken, NJ: Wiley & Sons.

Raux, D. J. and College, S. (2004), 'Implementing active learning in college', *Explorations in Teaching and Learning*, 2(1), 2–4.

Regulation and Quality Improvement Authority (2005), *Review of the Lessons Arising from the Death of Mrs Janine Murtagh*. Belfast: RQIA.

Swail, W. S. and Kampits, E. (2004), *WBL and Higher Education: A Research Perspective*. Washington DC: Educational Policy Institute.

Swallow, V. M., Chalmers, H., Miller, J., Piercy, C. and Sen, B. (2001), 'Accredited WBL for new nursing roles: nurses' experiences of two pilot schemes', *Journal of Clinical Nursing*, 10, 820–1.

Swanwick, T. (2008), 'See one, do one, then what? Faculty development in postgraduate medical education', *Postgraduate Medical Journal*, 84, 339–43.

Usher, R. and Solomon, N. (1999), 'Experiential learning and the shaping of subjectivity in the work-place', *Studies in the Education of Adults*, 31, 155–63.

Walker, E. and Dewar, B. J. (2000), 'Moving on from interpretivism: an argument for constructivist evaluation', *Journal of Advanced Nursing*, 32(3), 713–20.

WBL Network (2006), www.uace.gcal.ac.uk/obj.html (accessed 23 April 2009).

Chapter 12

Government policy and teacher education in Ghana

Kwame Akyeampong

Introduction

Any interested observer of developments in Ghanaian education will have noticed how the evolution of government policies have impacted on the structures and delivery of education, most recently the impact that policy reforms in 1987 had on pre-tertiary education. In particular, the period from the 1970s to the mid-1980s witnessed several education review commissions by successive governments. These were intended to reform Ghana's education system to enhance its efficiency and effectiveness in producing a highly educated workforce capable of making significant contributions to economic development. Policy reforms in 1987 borrowed extensively from insights produced by these earlier education reviews, with most of them advocating strategies to universalize educational access and improve the management of education service delivery to ensure quality. During this period teacher education received sporadic attention. More recently, its strategic importance in meeting the demand for trained teachers, with the rapid increase in access, has led to teacher education receiving greater attention in government policy planning.

Developments in Ghanaian education present an opportunity to critically evaluate the implications for teacher education. In this chapter, we analyse some of these and also draw attention to the role that the World Bank played in influencing government policy in education through conditions it attached to basic education sector support financing. What it illustrates is the strategic influence of external assistance on education reform, and how this has often been used to direct investment to reform some sectors of the education system, particularly the primary education sector while leaving out others. One important conclusion that this chapter draws is the failure of post-independent governments in Ghana strategically to locate teacher education reform at the epicentre of basic education reforms, to ensure adequate supply and deployment of trained teachers as educational access improved.

To understand how teacher education has been affected by government policies on educational expansion, it is instructive to start with an historical overview. This is followed by a critique of the consequences of educational expansion on teacher education and recent responses that are attempting to address teacher supply and deployment to meet increasing demand. The chapter concludes with some key lessons for African governments moving rapidly to expand education provision for all without jeopardizing its quality.

Assessing policies on basic education in Ghana

The Guggisberg approach

The history of education reforms in Ghana can be categorized into three main eras. The first major period occurred under the colonial government of Governor Guggisberg in the early 1900s. What the Guggisberg plan proposed was an expansion of primary education linked to the supply of trained teachers to meet demand. In fact, as McWilliam and Kwamena-Poh (1975, p. 59) point out, 'during this time the government could have afforded to spend three times as much as it actually did on new school buildings (*increase supply*), but based new openings *firmly* on the number of trained teachers available' (emphasis added). With the goal to provide trained teachers of high quality, the government replaced the two-year post-primary (teacher education) programme with a three-year one, and shortly afterwards in 1927, introduced a four-year programme (McWilliam and Kwamena-Poh, 1975). The Guggisberg administration saw quality teacher education as an integral part of the strategy to achieve universal primary education (UPE) and ensured that the expansion of school places did not outstrip supply of well-qualified teachers. However, by extending the period of training, this effectively increased costs and slowed supply.

Post-Guggisberg to early years after independence

A second wave of major education expansion policies started in the 1940s. In 1945, a ten-year plan was proposed to achieve UPE in twenty-five years, that is, by 1970. This time, however, the plan based expansion on affordable costs for government, which ultimately slowed supply of educational infrastructure and growth in school places. Six years before independence, as the new political leadership emerged and looked forward to government, the urgency to rapidly increase the number of educated Ghanaians to drive aspirations of economic growth strengthened, and led to the formulation of the 'Accelerated Development Plan' (ADP) – to accelerate achievement of UPE and expand post-primary provision. The ADP plan produced the first major restructuring of pre-tertiary education, consisting of six years of primary education, four years of middle-school education (both terminal and continuous), five years of secondary schooling and two years of sixth-form education for entry into university. The ADP also abolished primary tuition fees. After independence in 1957, the new government under Dr Kwame Nkrumah introduced the 1961 Education Act which, among other objectives, aimed to shift the management of primary education to local authority level to improve the quality of its delivery. The Act required local authorities to fund about 40 per cent of teachers' salaries, with the remaining 60 per cent to come from central government. However, local authorities struggled to raise sufficient revenue to meet their obligations as enrolments and teacher demand increased (see McWilliam and Kwamena-Poh, 1975).

From 1957 to the mid-1980s there were nine attempts by successive governments to reform education, none of which altered the fundamental landscape and structure of education provision in Ghana (World Bank, 2004). It was not until the military government of Flt Lt Rawlings in the early 1980s that pre-tertiary education was restructured to support a vision of redistributing education financing to support rapid and equitable expansion of basic education. The plan was ambitious and the government sought financial assistance from the World Bank, agreeing to cost recovery measures targeting the secondary and tertiary education sectors, as well as wider policy reforms, as conditions for World Bank support to expand basic education (see World Bank, 2004, p. 20). Without this funding, as well as funding from bilateral donors, the scale of school infrastructure expansion would have been difficult to achieve. By 2003, over US $500 million of donor funding had been injected into Ghana's education system, mainly the basic education sector. From 1986 to 1994 the World Bank, acting as the principal donor, provided the bulk of funding to build new classrooms, supply head-teachers' accommodation, improve school infrastructure, supply teacher training instructional materials including the production of teacher materials and textbooks in primary and junior secondary schools. DFID, USAID, and the European Union also made important contributions to support education expansion and improve quality.

The 1987 education reforms
The third wave of major education reforms in Ghana started in 1987 and focused on the following:
- Expand and make access more equitable at all levels of education.
- Reduce pre-tertiary education from 17 to 12 years by introducing a restructured education system consisting of nine years' compulsory basic education made up of six years of primary and three years of junior secondary, and three years of senior secondary.
- Progress from primary to junior secondary school, made automatic by abolishing entrance examinations at the end of primary education, and by the introduction of a new pre-tertiary education curriculum, which combined general academic studies with practical skills training.

Although teacher education received some attention in the reforms, the scale of investment was small compared to what went to improve school level inputs. In the first allocation of resources for the reforms, teacher education received only about 8 per cent, compared to an allocation of 61 per cent to increase school places. In the second tranche of resource allocation, teacher education's share reduced further to just about 2 per cent, compared to 63 per cent which was allocated to build new school buildings and increase infrastructure (World Bank, 2004). Mainly, the World Bank investment went to improve supply of educational input, much of which had deteriorated rapidly due to poor investment in education following the near collapse of Ghana's economy in the 1970s.

In 1995, further measures were introduced under the framework of a new basic education policy known as 'Free Compulsory Universal Basic Education' (FCUBE). Its aim was to address weaknesses in the 1987 reforms thought to be undermining the achievement of UPE and quality education. FCUBE received further funding from the World Bank and set as its target the achievement of UPE by 2005, a target which it missed, although the new policy increased enrolments to the point where trained teacher demand considerably outstripped supply (Ministry of Education, Science and Sports (MOESS), 2006; Akyeampong, 2009). In a frank assessment, an implementation report concluded that continuing to expand access to basic education would not be productive unless it was accompanied by improvements in school quality, and that improving teacher supply needed more attention in policy planning (Ministry of Education (MOE), 1999). The World Bank's assessment of its contributions to the reforms was generally more positive. Following an impact evaluation, it concluded that the 1987 and FCUBE reforms had succeeded in reversing the deterioration of the educational system, increased the number of schools from 12,997 in 1980 to 18,374 in 2000, expanded enrolment rates by over 10 percentage points, and improved attendance rates in primary public schools (World Bank, 2004). Other assessments of impact, however, suggest a more uneven picture of progress and draw attention to the decline in teacher quality indicators and how this could potentially slow progress towards EFA by 2015 (see Rolleston, 2009, Akyeampong, 2009).

In 2004, the government went a step further in its quest to achieve universal basic education (UBE) by 2015, by introducing a capitation grant scheme (school operating budgets) for primary schools as part of a strategy to decentralize education provision and increase demand, particularly among poor households. But, not surprisingly, the surge in enrolments which resulted from this policy created a big deficit in classroom infrastructure – 'a deficit of 1,048 classrooms to be built every year for the past four years in public basic schools and which translates to one additional public basic school annually for each district' (MOESS, 2006). It also put pressure on the education system to increase supply of trained teachers.

Strategies to ensure equitable provision and deployment of trained teaching staff have remained elusive for a long time in Ghana. What Ghanaian policy planners have been searching for, but have yet to find, is a comprehensive policy plan on teacher supply and demand, accompanied by a forecasting model as a strategic and operational planning tool to project annual requirements for teachers as patterns of access changes.

In summary, government policies to improve access over the years have evolved from a focus on trained teacher supply as a condition for expansion, to expansion within limits of affordable costs, and more recently to fee-free education strategies, e.g. FCUBE and a capitation grant. Each policy has had some implications for the rate of education expansion – for example, in the early policies, the quality-imperative framed expansion strategies with the supply of trained teachers as the defining yardstick. Meeting the cost of expansion was central in the second wave of policies and led to setting a much longer timeframe for achieving UPE, although this was accelerated nearer to independence and the early years after. The 1987 education reforms highlight the significant contributions of external financing to further accelerate progress towards EFA but, as we shall see in the next section, this had implications for teacher education institutions, especially their capacity to produce enough teachers to meet a growing demand for teachers as access to basic education increased.

Educational expansion and teacher education: consequences and responses

One of the clear outcomes of education expansion polices in Ghana, particularly from the mid-1980s failure to make teacher education a key part of the expansion strategy, is the increasing gap between student intake in basic schools and supply of trained teachers. As Table 12.1 shows, within the timeframe of FCUBE the net student to trained teacher ratio actually widened, and the student trained teacher ratio increased from 43:1 in 1996 to 63:1 in 2005, while the number of untrained teachers doubled for both primary and junior secondary schools. Besides, the overall primary student teacher ratio increased by about 4 per cent between 1996 and 2005, with much of that the result of a high influx of untrained teachers (Akyeampong, 2009). What the data suggests is that effective planning and policy measures that would have ensured adequate production and utilization of trained teachers, as access increased, was either never pursued, or ineffectively planned. There are signs that recent reforms in teacher education may be laying the foundations for better responses to the challenges from recent large-scale expansion of basic education.

Table 12.1 Indicators for basic education supply in Ghana, 1996/7 and 2005/6

Attendance (All Ghana)	1996/7	2005/6
Number of students (primary)	2,333,347	3,122,903
Number of students (JSS)	738,057	1,041,002
Number of students in P6	326,003	402,253
Number of students in JSS3 (Grade 9 – end of basic)	212,563	279,683
Number of trained teachers (primary)	54,572	49,807
Number of trained teachers (JSS)	32,032	39,920
Number of untrained teachers (primary)	18,768	38,654
Number of untrained teachers (JSS)	8,385	16,565
Student to teacher ratio (primary)	31.8	35.3
Student to teacher ratio (JSS)	18.3	18.4
Student to trained teacher ratio (primary)	42.8	62.7
Student to trained teacher ratio (JSS)	23.0	26.1

Source: Data provided by EMIS Unit Ghana, MOESS

Restructuring teacher education and teacher qualification

Until 2004, teachers could obtain a basic teacher qualification (Certificate 'A') to teach in a primary or junior secondary school after completing three years' post-secondary teacher training in one of the thirty-eight government teacher training colleges (TTC). TTCs have now been upgraded to tertiary education level and designated colleges of education (COE), offering diploma-level qualification under a restructured programme in which trainees spend two years in residential training, and approximately one year in school-based training (the in–in–out model). Also, basic education teachers with Certificate 'A' qualification can obtain either a diploma or bachelor-level teacher qualification after completing two or four years respectively of university-level teacher education. Unqualified teachers, commonly called untrained teachers or non-professional teachers, can enrol on a four-year open and distance learning (ODL) teacher education programme to obtain either a Certificate 'A' or diploma qualification. Degree-level teaching qualification or the PGDE provides the qualification route for teaching in senior secondary schools. Table 12.2 provides an overview of changes in the teacher education programme and qualification structure.

Table 12.2 Teacher education in Ghana: programme and qualification status

Level	Duration of Course	Entry Level	Certificate Awarded	Level of Teaching after Certification	Remarks
Post-secondary level	3 years	Completion of senior secondary school	Post-secondary Certificate 'A'	Primary or junior secondary school	Discontinued in 2004 and replaced with in–in–out diploma programme
Higher education (non graduate level)	2 years total duration: from Certificate 'A' to diploma = 8 years	Completion of post-secondary + 3 years' teaching experience	Diploma	Primary, JSS or senior secondary	Teachers could attain this through distance learning
Higher education (under-graduate level)	3 years or 2 years for post-diploma	Teachers with diploma certificate or senior secondary graduates	BEd degree	Primary, JSS, senior secondary, or college of education	Graduates are less likely to opt for teaching at JSS level
Higher education (post-graduate level)	1 year	BSc and BA	Post-graduate diploma in education (PGDE)	Senior secondary or college of education	
Untrained teachers	4 years' distance learning programme	Middle-school leaving certificate, senior secondary, 'A' level, City & Guilds etc.	Certificate 'A' or diploma	Primary and JSS	Has current enrolment of about 20,000 unqualified teachers

Source: updated from Akyeampong (2003)

What the teacher qualification structure for basic education shows is that the length of time it previously took to become a trained teacher with a diploma or degree qualification has been reduced. A post-secondary student who entered TTCs prior to 2004 would have had to spend at least five years in full-time training to obtain a diploma qualification. If one added another three years of full-time teaching as the condition for a Certificate 'A' teacher to satisfy before becoming eligible to enrol for upgrading, this takes the time up to eight years. In effect, when the government upgraded TTCs to diploma-awarding institutions it cut the duration down to three years, with immediate benefits in terms of cost reduction and increased trained teacher turnout. A new-route diploma teacher who wishes to acquire the BEd qualification would now train for a total of five years, down from the old route, which would have taken somewhere between ten and eleven years. These reductions in years of training to obtain a diploma or degree-level qualification to teach in basic schools have been a direct response to the pressure on teachers to upgrade their lower qualification (i.e. Certificate 'A'), and which had contributed to the high primary teacher turnover in Ghana (Akyeampong, 2003).

Two teacher education programme models stand out as offering perhaps the best hope of increasing the supply of basic schoolteachers at reduced cost, while ensuring trainees have lengthy exposure to practical teaching through school-based training. The first is the in–in–out model. The move from a three-year residential teacher education programme to one in which approximately one year is spent learning teaching in real classrooms has the potential to produce teachers who are more accustomed to the realities of teaching and, therefore, are better prepared to make a success of it.

Trainees in the 'out' year could be deployed to fill teacher vacancies, which simultaneously offer colleges the opportunity to increase their overall intake by filling residential vacancies created by the 'out' students. However, there are no signs that this has been fully exploited, which may suggest that either the colleges have no incentive to do so, or the investment required to support increased intake has been lacking. In fact, the teacher education expenditure share of the education budget shows a downward trend in investments – it has almost halved from 4.5 per cent in 2002 to 2.6 per cent in 2008 (MOE, 2009).

The untrained teachers' diploma in basic education (UTDBE) programme is the other example of how an attempt has been made to retain teachers in the classroom while offering them the opportunity to obtain a professional qualification. Many of these untrained teachers, numbering about 24,000 in 2007, have several years of teaching experience, and many work in deprived rural areas where regular trained teachers often refuse to go. The UTDBE model ensures that teachers continue to do their jobs while receiving training, and therefore avoids creating vacancies that lead to teacher shortages as full-time residential training does. Questions have been raised about whether schools will suffer as a result of UTDBE teachers combining full-time teaching with part-time training. Evidence from a recent large-scale evaluation of the UTDBE programme suggests that this has not happened. In addition, teachers on the programme were found to be more effective in their teaching than their counterpart untrained teachers not enrolled on the programme (Ghana Education Service/Teacher Education Division (GES/TED), 2010).

Ghana operates a study leave with full pay policy for teachers to upgrade their qualification. This policy has been seen as a major source of attraction to the teaching profession. Unfortunately, it has also become a major contributor to teacher shortages, especially in primary schools where many teachers seize upon this opportunity to upgrade and move into secondary teaching or higher (Akyeampong, 2003). The government policy of upgrading TTCs to diploma-awarding institutions, and establishing the diploma certificate as the lowest qualification for teaching at the basic school level, has the potential to stem the flow of primary teachers using study leave to upgrade and move out of primary teaching.

Matching teacher supply and demand

Right up to the FCUBE reforms in 1995, government policy was to replace all untrained teachers with trained teachers produced by the TTCs. However, as knowledge of the limited capacity of TTCs developed, coupled with the high teacher turnover (MOEYS/GES, 2004), this policy was later abandoned. Studies in late 1990s revealed that even with significant investments, TTCs could not have doubled or tripled their enrolments because of their size, which on average accommodates only about 500 students (Akyeampong, 2003). In 2000/1, teacher vacancies in basic schools totalled around 19,000, but only about 6,000 places could be filled with trained teachers from the colleges. It was also estimated that to achieve UBE about an additional 33,000 teachers would have to be recruited (see Akyeampong, 2003).

Matching teacher supply and demand is a difficult business in low-income country contexts, particularly if one factors in the element of teacher deployment. In Ghana, the debate has been about whether indeed there is a teacher supply problem, or whether demand could be met simply by ensuring a more efficient and equitable deployment of teachers. There are two ways of looking at this issue. First, it is possible that teacher shortage is not as severe as some earlier analysis of teacher data predicted, especially when one takes into account the knowledge that many newly trained teachers refuse postings to rural areas, leave the profession in the early years of their career, or attempt to gain higher teaching qualifications via study leave, and enter other professions or into secondary school teaching (see Akyeampong, 2003). Because data on such teacher movement is rarely compiled, it is difficult to determine the true situation of teacher supply and demand.

The other issue has to do with the accuracy of projections or forecasts for future teacher demand across districts that have different teacher supply needs. A key element in projection calculations is the pupil–teacher ratio (PTR), which is usually based on a national norm. In reality, however, there are significant variations in PTRs within and across districts and regions. For example, Perry (2007) examined baseline PTRs in 2005 in Ghana and found that for primary education, 19 per cent of districts had PTRs greater than 45, while 12 per cent had figures lower than 30. For junior secondary, the majority of districts had very low PTRs with 59 per cent having a PTR less than 20 and only 6 per cent with PTRs higher than 30. Such wide variations signal inefficiencies in teacher deployment policy and practice, and gives some credibility to the view that resolving the deployment problem will effectively resolve the teacher shortage problem. Another suggestion is to raise the PTR norm to about 40:1 in order to reduce demand for new teachers as one way to improve teacher utilization (MOE, 2009). However, the counter-effect is that teacher–class ratios may rise considerably beyond a one-to-one ratio, which would make this solution not cost-effective.

The fact remains that schools in urban and district capitals have much higher enrolments and therefore higher PTRs than schools located in rural areas. Consequently, urban teachers tend to have heavier workloads compared to teachers in rural areas. Recent policy directive stipulates that where enrolment per class is below 30, classes should be combined but not exceed 35, and where three classes (e.g. Primary 2, 3 and 4) are combined enrolment should not exceed 25, to ensure that teachers are able to cope with the demands of teaching what would effectively be a wide-ability-range class. According to the Ministry of Education, by 2008/9, about one-eighth of primary schools in the country, mostly in rural areas, had 90 or less pupils with a complement of 6 teachers and a head teacher giving a PTR of about 15, and in general, nearly 40 per cent of primary schools have PTRs less than 30 (MOE, 2009). Government policy response to this problem has been to advocate multi-grade teaching in schools with enrolments of 90 or less on the basis of one teacher to 30 pupils; closure or a merger of very small schools with less than 30 enrolment; or to introduce mixed multi-grade and class teaching in larger schools (i.e. Grades 1–2 and 3–4 combined as multi-grade and grades 4 and 5 as 'normal' classes) (MOE, 2009). This rather complex set of arrangements would require an effective decentralized system of teacher management, which the country currently lacks. It is a familiar example of proposing strategies to education problems in low-income countries without much consideration as to whether the necessary implementation and management structures exist, or are strong enough to make them lasting solutions. In the case of Ghana, implementing these recommendations would require a much stronger decentralized system of education governance.

In urban schools with large class sizes a way forward could be to split up classes, but finding additional classroom space and trained teachers would be challenging in budget-constrained contexts. Double-shift schooling is another alternative for addressing the problem of large enrolments, but as Ghana's experience with double-shifting has shown, it increases teachers' instructional hours, and overall reduces the hours of instruction per pupil per year (MOE,

2002). Also, although it can reduce teacher costs per pupil, it puts enormous pressure on school infrastructure and resources, and creates conditions that could ultimately reduce teacher job satisfaction and increase attrition.

Conclusion: reflections and lessons

The analysis of Ghanaian government policy on education expansion and its consequences on teacher education presents a number of lessons for African governments moving rapidly towards improving access for all children. Countries such as Zambia and Uganda have vigorously pursued expansion policies through measures that have reduced the direct and indirect costs to schooling, and led to impressive student intake results (Deininger, 2003; de Kemp, 2008). Other countries striving to achieve EFA by 2015 are also introducing inclusive policies, hoping that this will improve access even further. However, 'the expected benefits of such policies are unlikely to materialize if expansion of school systems is not accompanied by improvement in the functioning of schools' (UNESCO, 2007, p. 24). As Lewin and Akyeampong (2009, p. 149) point out, 'improving physical access remains important but is hardly sufficient to meet conspicuous needs to enhance quality and relevance'. This is a problem, pointing to the importance of policy planning on teacher education to improve the supply of trained teachers. Adequate supply and effective deployment of trained teachers lies at the heart of enhancing quality, and Ghana's struggles and advances highlights the lessons and pitfalls for governments seeking solutions to this major challenge to education expansion in Africa.

The lesson is that teacher education reform should be closely aligned with policies to expand educational access or vice versa. In Ghana's case, serious teacher education reforms came much later and only in response to the problems generated by rapid expansion to basic education in the 1990s. Also, it is one thing to increase the supply of trained teachers, and yet another to ensure that an effective deployment policy is in place to ensure that trained teachers are where they are needed to cope with the growth of enrolments. Moving towards a decentralized system of teacher deployment and management would seem to be the way forward in addressing this issue.

The introduction of the UTDB programme shows that in systems where a large pool of untrained or contract teachers exist, retaining their services while offering them opportunities to obtain teacher qualification through ODL makes a lot of sense. Another important message relates to the changes that may be required in teacher education to shorten the length of time it takes to train a qualified teacher with school-based training as an important part of that training. In sum, strategies to improve educational provision should take sound lessons from the different histories and local conditions that have shaped each country's educational landscape and its teacher education system. Low-income countries should also explore methods of improving both the supply and deployment of teachers in ways that respond to local challenges that threaten sustained access to quality education.

References

Akyeampong, K. (2003), *Teacher Education in Ghana: Does it Count?* London: DFID.

—— (2009), 'Revisiting free compulsory universal basic education (FCUBE) in Ghana', *Comparative Education*, 45(2), 175–95.

—— , Djangmah, J., Oduro, A., Seidu, A. and Hunt, F. (2007), *Access to Basic Education in Ghana: The Evidence and the Issues*. CREATE Country Analytic Review. Winneba/Brighton: University of Education at Winneba/University of Sussex.

Bennell, P. and Akyeampong, K. (2007), *Teacher Motivation in Sub-Sahara Africa and South Asia*. London: DFID.

Deininger, K. (2003), 'Does cost of schooling affect enrolment by the poor? Universal primary education in Uganda', *Economics of Education Review*, 22, 291–305.

De Kemp, A. (2008), 'Analysing the effectiveness of sector support: primary education in Uganda and Zambia', *IDS Bulletin* 39(1), 36–50.

Ghana Education Service/Teacher Education Division (2010*), Report on the Evaluation of the Untrained Teacher Diploma in Basic Education (UTDBE) Programme In Ghana*. Accra, Ghana: Ghana Education Service.

Lewin K. M. and Akyeampong, K. (2009), 'Education in sub-Saharan Africa: researching access, transitions and equity', *Comparative Education*, 45(2), 143–50.

McWilliam, H. O. A. and Kwamena-Poh, M. A. (1975), *The Development of Education in Ghana*, new edn. London: Longman.

Ministry of Education (1999), *Background Paper for the National Education Forum*. Accra, Ghana: Ministry of Education.

Ministry of Education (2002), *Ghana EMIS Project: Policy Briefs*. Accra, Ghana: Ministry of Education.

Ministry of Education (2009), *Education Strategic Plan (ES): Policies, Strategies, Delivery and Finance*. Accra, Ghana: Ministry of Education.

Ministry of Education, Science and Sports (MOESS) (2006), *Education Sector Performance Report*. Accra, Ghana: MOESS.

Ministry of Education, Youth and Sports (MOEYS)/Ghana Education Service (GES) (2004), *National Framework for Teacher Accreditation and Programme for Untrained Teachers*. Accra, Ghana: MOEYS/GES.

Perry C. (2007), Ministry of Education, Science and Sports/Ghana Education Service, *Staff Supply/Demand Forecasting Model*. Accra, Ghana: Ministry of Education.

Rolleston C. (2009), 'The determination of exclusion: evidence from the Ghana Living Standards Surveys 1991–2006', *Comparative Education*, 45(2), 197–218.

UNESCO (2007), *Education for All by 2015: Will We Make It? Global Monitoring Report*. Paris: UNESCO.

World Bank (2004), *Books, Buildings and Learning Outcomes: An Impact Evaluation of World Bank Support to Basic Education in Ghana.* Washington DC: World Bank.

Chapter 13

Transforming China's adult and continuing education

Ning Rong Liu

Introduction

There were previously two parallel higher education systems existing side by side in China – regular higher education and adult higher education. While regular institutions of higher education admit secondary school graduates who pass the national college entrance examination, adult institutions of higher education enrol working adults to meet the huge demand for post-secondary studies. An important consideration in establishing adult institutions of higher education was to provide additional opportunities for adults to attain higher education, since the resources available in universities were scarce and thus could only admit a limited number of secondary school graduates.

In response to the demand for higher education, in 1998 the Chinese government decided to increase the enrolment numbers for the universities. As a result of the policy change, higher education expanded at an unprecedented speed. The total number of new students increased from 1.08 million in 1994 to 5.99 million in 2008, creating one of the largest higher education systems in the world. Thus, the restructuring of adult institutions of higher education in China has created a new emphasis on continuing professional education instead of providing academic degree programmes for working adults.

The new orientation has much broader implications that clearly shift the function and purposes of adult higher education. This emphasizes the assumption that adult education institutions must respond to market needs quickly and create more learning opportunities to upgrade the skills and knowledge of working professionals. In this context, adult higher education institutions are called upon to do more to meet the demands of social and economic development, and to do this it is argued that its operations need to be more market-oriented.

Higher education and the market

During the last two decades of the twentieth century, markets came progressively to be seen as the most desirable mechanism for regulating economies and reforming the public sector. The publicly funded provision of education has not been exempt from this trend. The reform agenda in education, therefore, is oriented to the market rather than to public ownership or to governmental planning and regulation. In order to improve their competitiveness and effectiveness, schools and universities are seen to need to restructure themselves and adopt marketization as their governance strategies. This trend is especially evident in higher education (Tiffin and Rajasingham, 1995). The impact of marketization on higher education has driven faculty members to become entrepreneurs (Slaughter and Leslie, 1997), and universities have increasingly adopted market-oriented principles and business-like criteria (Currie, 1998). Further, as Clark (1998) concludes, many universities, by means of entrepreneurial action, have transformed themselves.

   One visible change in such education reforms is the decline of professional dominance and the rise of consumerism – the belief that consumers have a right to express their views about services and that their knowledge and opinions have value and validity (Bridges, 1994). However, there is no clear evidence to confirm the claims that marketization can lead to a higher-achieving educational system (Green, 1997). Long before the global trend of marketization of education, Blaug raised a number of significant questions about the potential risk, stating that:

> we have too little experience with the market provision of education to predict the precise effect of enhanced choice backed up by purchasing power, and to argue that competition will necessarily improve education as it has improved the quality of automobiles is mere dogma.
>
> (Blaug, 1970, p. 314)

The reform of the education sector has also been driven and shaped by corporate management practices. As a result, corporate models have been increasingly implemented as governance in higher education institutions. Proponents argue that it is necessary to impose managerial methods more usually used in the private sector onto higher education institutions. These techniques include the use of internal cost centres, the fostering of competition between employees, the marketization of education services and the monitoring of efficiency and effectiveness through measurement of outcomes and individual staff performances (Deem, 1998). However, opponents argue that the trend of 'corporatization' of the university may ultimately lead to the ruin of the university as a cultural institution organized around the traditional humanistic disciplines as its core (Soley, 1995; Readings, 1996).

Adult education: the pioneer of higher education reforms

The Chinese higher education system has reacted to globalization and the knowledge economy in ways common to other countries (Postiglione, 2003). Facing the challenge of global economic integration and the knowledge economy, the Chinese government has adopted the two strategies of decentralization and marketization in restructuring higher education. These dual approaches have imposed a great impact on the governance of higher education in China (Yin and White, 1994). Higher education is increasingly seen as a channel for social mobility and personal development, and the government has begun to see higher education as consumption and a private good benefiting primarily the individual (Ngok and Kwong, 2003).

In the context of higher education reform, adult higher education in China was sometimes seen as an experimental field used to restructure the higher education sector. It can be said that adult higher education started the process of marketization and decentralization of higher education in China.

First, the development of adult higher education was the result of a timely response to the market need for higher education which arose after the era of the open-door policy. It could be divided into two different periods in term of its target students. Adult higher education mainly functioned to help those who lost educational opportunities during the Culture Revolution, when the majority of students were working adults before the mid-1980s. When the needs of this group of students were met, educators immediately turned to those secondary school graduates who could not enter the regular higher education institutions due to the limited number of enrolments set by the central government. Adult higher education offered them a second chance to pursue higher education. In other words, the development and rapid growth of adult higher education took advantage of the incapability of the higher education sector to meet market demands, and it challenged the constraints of highly centralized structures in regular higher education institutions.

Second, the reform of higher education financing originated in adult higher education. While higher education was seen as the government's responsibility to its citizens in the late 1970s, students who participated in adult higher education programmes either paid on their own or their working units reimbursed them for their studies. In 1985, two types of students were allowed to be enrolled in adult higher education programmes. One was contract students, selected by their company to study in colleges, and the other was self-financed students. Not until 1993 were thirty higher education institutions given the authority to carry out experiments with fee-paying schemes, which allowed students to enrol in universities with lower scores by paying tuition fees. By 1997, all students in higher education institutions would need to pay tuition fees. This departed from almost five decades of free higher education in China. It was the adult higher education system which first generated such funds for universities, because they were not allocated finances by the central government.

Third, adult higher education started full-scale development when universities and colleges were still closed to wider society. Since higher education developments prior to the reform era were decided and planned by the central government, universities were left no room to operate according to political, economic, and social developments. The development of adult higher education thus helped change the structure of higher education institutions in China, which in general did not emphasize the importance of linking what they taught in classrooms with needs in society. Since the majority of adult learners had some working experience, adult and continuing education was subject to external influences on its development. All in all, adult higher education helped Chinese universities to build much closer links with the economy and society.

Strategies of reforming adult higher education

For decades, the various forms of adult higher education in almost all universities took degree-level education as their main undertaking, often neglecting other types of in-service training in specific skills and continuing education. This phenomenon had two negative impacts. First, a potential problem of low quality in adult higher education was realized by the occurrence of high market demand for certificates. Second, adult education in the universities was not prepared to develop programmes of professional continuing education related to new disciplines, new techniques and new knowledge in which universities should have capacity.

After the rapid growth of enrolment in China's regular higher education institutions, the restructuring of adult higher education centred on changing the direction of adult higher education to provide professional training to upgrade the managerial ability and technical skills of professionals. Not only did this change afford a new opportunity to expand the sector, but this also had implications for, and impact on, the adult higher education system, institutional structure, business operation, and programme development.

Restructuring the adult higher education system
The first type of strategy of response adopted by Chinese universities was to restructure the adult higher education system. The massification of higher education provided an opportunity to revamp the adult higher education system, and it was developed into much broader areas to incorporate online education and include continuing professional education.

Adult higher education was traditionally considered as a university extension by offering degree programmes to working adults. Historically, this was the most important part of the adult higher education system. Most universities set up a school of adult education in the late 1980s and early 1990s to coordinate all award-bearing programmes for working adults. Although the main objectives of adult education were providing working adults with higher education opportunities part-time, many universities' adult education departments also enrolled secondary school graduates who had failed the national college entrance examination for full-time study. While the latter operation was terminated in seventy-six universities under the Ministry of Education in 2006, the adult education sector continues to offer part-time degree programmes to working adults.

Online education – once an independent unit in China's higher education system – was put under the umbrella of adult education, and the merger intended to strengthen its role to offer academic degree programmes off-campus. Since adult education institutions were allowed to only enrol part-time students, full-time online programmes could supplement the traditional adult education by providing a hybrid study mode. Started in 1999, when sixty-seven universities were given a green light to launch programmes online, online education enrols over one million students annually. The programmes offered by online education range from a higher diploma, a two-year top-up bachelor degree for those who already have a higher diploma, a four-year university degree, to postgraduate courses. Universities were given autonomy to admit students for online programmes based on their own criteria, set up the subjects without seeking an approval from the Ministry of Education, decide the tuition fees with more flexibility, grant awards which usually need to be authorized by the Ministry of Education, and allow students to accumulate their credits in a certain period. These factors are behind the high-speed development of online education, which has become one major area for further expansion of the university adult education sector.

However, the prime area for expansion and growth is continuing professional education, which became an engine for the further development of adult higher education. Continuing professional education did not start until the late 1980s when the development of the economy required more seasoned managers to run the growing business and professional operation for almost all specializations. Although China has made impressive gains in human resource development after more than two decades into the reform of market economy, the nation is still facing a critical shortage of well-trained managers and professionals.

Tsinghua University, one of the leading universities in China, provides the most prominent example in developing continuing professional education programmes. Tsinghua established China's first school of continuing education in 1986. In the five years since Tsinghua launched the reform in 2003 to focus on continuing professional and executive programmes as the core operation of adult education, more than half a million participants have attended various professional development programmes offered by the school, and its annual tuition income reached over US $60 million in 2008. Tsinghua's continuing education sector has also grown much larger in size since 2003, and the total number of staff members increased more than tenfold between 2003 and 2008. The development in this area also became a nationwide phenomenon and, with the rapid expansion of continuing professional education programmes, this sector generated additional tuition fees for universities. Thus, it was imperative to establish a business-oriented organization to meet this change, and the purpose of organizational restructuring was aimed at moving aggressively towards corporate management structures.

Establishing a business-oriented organization
The second type of strategy of responses adopted by Chinese universities was to establish a business-oriented organization to implement a corporate-style management. With the arrival of the 'Customer Century' in higher education, a university's adult and continuing education sector looked into its existing management and reengineered its structure to fit the changing environment.

A flat, centre-based structure was promoted and set up along the lines of professional business management to support its reformed operation. The centre-based operation was streamlined, according to the practice of the business community. Tsinghua University in Beijing started to offer professional development programmes in 2003, and by spring 2008 the school set up fifteen business centres. Zhejiang University in Hangzhou, just an hour away from Shanghai, restructured the School of Adult Education and established ten centres in 2007 to provide training courses, while traditional adult education and online education continue to offer academic degree programmes. Sun Yet-sen University in Guangzhou is two hours by train from Hong Kong, and also reorganized the School of Higher Adult Education and set up three centres to specialize in academic programmes for adult students, online education, and professional development programmes. Though different universities adopted various approaches, in general the operation tended to be more programme-based than department-based, and a programme leader was usually appointed to lead one or two programmes with a high degree of autonomy and flexibility. This eliminated unnecessary layers between the top management and front lines, allowing greater flexibility to react to changes in a timely and effective manner.

The adult higher education sector even established a training centre in partnership with private companies for the purpose of seeking financial back-up for the operation. The primary consideration for the collaboration was the lack of funding from the university. But this has broad implications, as this type of university–industry alliance would enable the adult education sector to link the educational service closely with the market and even help to introduce corporate governance into its operations. At Tsinghua

University, the Centre for Professional Training in the Science Park, finan-
cially supported by the Science Park adjacent to Tsinghua University, focused
on providing training in the areas of marketing and business management,
finance, and engineering management for all-level executives in the Park.
At Zhejiang University, the Centre for IT Training was set up with both the
technical and financial support from an IT company to provide training on
computer software. At Sun Yet-sen University, the programme on hotel and
hospitality management was launched, together with a multinational hotel
group for the purpose of internship and placement.

This newly established flat, centre-based structure provided flexibility and
accountability in order to maintain a balance between the transfer of authority
and responsibilities. Thus, the devolved budgeting system was implemented so
that programme teams could make sound decisions in the self-funding operation. Each business unit was a programme centre which provided different
kinds of professional development programmes for the specialized fields. It
also functioned as a budget unit responsible for its own financial outcome
and generating sufficient revenue to sustain its own growth.

However, the centre-based structure did accelerate bitter competition
among the different units. Despite bringing down the pyramid structure,
there was a need to enhance the horizontal and cross-functional structure
to promote co-operation between teams and help reduce the internal power
struggles and isolation, so that accountability could prevail. Lack of internal
integration has also taken a toll, with many programme teams fighting for
resources and territory in three universities. To resolve the internal competition, more trade- or industry-based centres, instead of discipline- or
specialization-based centres, have been formed to draw a much clearer
territory and reduce the possible inner conflict among the centres. The
centre-based structure had not only impeded horizontal integration, but
obstructed the flow of communications.

The introduction of market mechanisms, which was regarded as a major
theme of policy in the management of educational change, brought a fundamental transformation in the structures and management of China's adult
and continuing education institutions. The business-oriented operation
helped to secure the financial well-being of the sector but, more importantly, this transformation bred new values and cultures in China's adult and
continuing educational institutions. Thus, the reform and change of the
management style opened a new chapter for the organization, with market
demands and needs taking a more and more salient position in the outlook
of the significant decision-makers.

Designing market-driven programmes
The third strategy adopted by Chinese universities was to offer more flexible
and relevant curricula to meet the changing needs of students and society.

With the introduction of the centre-based structure and the underpinning of the entrepreneurial culture, programme teams in the adult higher education sector were empowered to look into the opportunity and work with academics and professionals to develop the most-needed courses. At the institutional level, the university's adult education sector was given more authority to launch both continuing professional education and online academic programmes. They were required to form an academic committee to be responsible for curriculum development, which functioned as an advisory board to make academic decisions.

With the fiercely competitive environment in China's adult higher education sector, universities were required to reverse the traditional way of developing courses, starting by feeding information about the learner needs back to the top management, then developing and adjusting programmes according to the identified needs and wants. Thus, the design of market-oriented and outcome-based curricula was crucial in the process of successfully launching the adult higher education programmes demanded by the market. While various channels of developing programmes were employed, three approaches were considered to be most important to capitalize on, following the three kinds of resources – academic staff in the university, experts in the professional bodies, and international co-operation.

The sector attempted to act proactively to the market needs and to link the university closely with the business community. Researchers for programme development kept abreast of the changing environment for professional training, and fed back information about market demands through periodic surveys. With the support from the university's academic staff in the programme and curriculum design, the adult and continuing education sector quickly introduced high quality programmes. By giving deep consideration to the requirements from the perspective of the business community, authoritative experts in their fields not only included the latest research results in China and abroad, but integrated theory and practice with a focus on practical application when designing the curricula of such programmes. The second, common approach used in launching the market-oriented programmes was to utilize the knowledge of experts in the field and the professional bodies, since they understood the trends in the field and the market needs. International partnership was the third approach to adult and continuing education programmes. Almost all collaborative programmes with overseas partners had one thing in common: the adult and continuing education sector was unable to locate experts in China to help it develop, or was not allowed to develop due to government regulation.

In developing continuing professional education programmes, it is clear that adult higher education institutions involved more experts in various professional bodies and associations than academics, and the content of programmes was strongly influenced by professional bodies and the job market

(Henkel and Kogan, 1988). As a result, there were better interrelations between theory and application in the programmes designed for professional adult students. Responsiveness to market needs, and better marketing and communicating with learners, were the key to the success of adult and continuing education. However, in the end only quality helped to establish an enduring reputation of an educational institution and attract more potential learners.

Developing customer-oriented quality assurance

Assuring high quality of professional programmes was the fourth strategy of response adopted by universities in China in restructuring the adult and continuing education sector. This is an important step in the process of market-driven programme development and management. It is, however, not an easy task to define quality. While people in educational organizations agree with the importance of academic quality, in practice it is always debatable how to define it and achieve it, since the school, teachers, and students may hold different criteria. However, it has been found to be particularly true that in continuing education organizations 'quality is meeting or exceeding student expectations' (Lumby, 2001, p. 70).

Quality assurance included two aspects. One was the academic aspect, including content and design. The other was the administrative aspect. The restructuring of continuing education in China has provided an unprecedented opportunity to change people's perceptions. At Tsinghua University, the School of Continuing Education has adopted the market-oriented approach in pursuit of quality assurance, which can be viewed as a new form of legitimizing continuing education. This drive towards quality assurance 'can be seen partly as a strategy to secure market share and partly as a means to elevate the status of and generate confidence in the sector' (Cheung and Pyvis, 2006).

On the academic side, the school set up a Department of Academic Management in order to systematize the procedure of launching new programmes, and supervised teaching quality and evaluation. Unlike the full-time on-campus academic programmes, the approach to quality in the school tended to centre on students or other customers. 'The market-led system will generate consumer oriented approaches to quality assessment' (Barnett, 1992, p. 3). The school considered feedback given by learners in evaluating programme quality as very important and valued comments given by industry professionals highly in evaluating programme quality.

Regarding the administrative aspect, three universities – Tsinghua, Zhejiang, and Sun Yat-sen – were quite exemplary, and particularly impressive in their efforts to provide administrative support and service to learners. The ways in which students were supported and served illustrated their intention to ensure that good teaching and learning environment were provided. In general, one administrative staff member in the programme team was assigned to take care of each cohort and was responsible for students' overall needs. By demonstrating high standards of quality for teaching and student support services that cut across the whole institution, these three universities were able to communicate effectively about their strengths with students, prospects, and other stakeholders.

In a sense, the adult and continuing education sector in China has adopted the measures of total quality management which have been advocated in private business for many years, and which have also recently been embraced in the public sector in the West to assure quality services. The importance of market orientation was integral to the programme development and management, from planning the programme and packaging, to student admission and teaching arrangements. Each programme team needed to respond proactively to market demand. This outcome-oriented culture reshaped the organizational fabric of China's adult and continuing education.

Discussion and conclusion

Traditionally, higher education in China can be seen as hindering social participation. Its priority was not to serve the community, but to maintain political control and loyalty, since the operation of universities was directed by government regulations and the policies of the Communist Party. The way of responding to challenges by Chinese universities has noticeably demonstrated that market forces have been introduced as the major influence in China's adult higher education. The introduction of market-like relationships to achieve institutional efficiency has been adopted in the process of revamping the system and structure. The adult higher education sector has been reshaped by the application of corporate governance in its internal management and the emphasis on market needs in launching professional development programmes. 'The idea of the university as a community of scholars, students or disciplines, and as a public agency to some extent yielded to the idea of the university as a corporate enterprise' (Bleiklie, 2002, p. 30). This transformation has had dual effects. First, it has helped the university's adult education to respond proactively to the needs of the market. Second, it has fundamentally changed the way that traditional universities functioned and 'performativity' has become the norm.

As in many other countries, China no longer considers that human capital development should be solely the responsibility of the government, and the market is replacing the state as the major driving force for the development of adult and continuing education. As a result, adult and continuing education has become a consumption item, and adult and continuing education institutions are the suppliers in the market, which aim to meet market demands for manpower training. This market-driven approach to adult education and training is concerned mainly with developing the economy (Walters, 2000). Therefore, the strategies adopted by a university's adult and continuing education in China in restructuring this sector have been consistent with the global trend of marketization in higher education.

However, the restructuring of China's continuing education should not solely consider the needs of executive and professional training. Apple (1999) strongly rejects any approach that reduces education to mere training or is not grounded in the personal lives and stories of real teachers, students, and community members. Human resource development and lifelong learning should also contribute to broader educational goals, to critical thinking and to human development more broadly. This may also help to foster the earning capacity of the poor and eventually reduce poverty and enhance welfare while spurring economic growth. The government's priorities should therefore include improvements to the general equity, efficiency, and quality of education (Hossain, 1997). Thus, adult and continuing education should not only respond to market demands, but devote its efforts to serving a wide array of social functions and values. The public has raised concerns that some educators may only care about dollar value and place too much emphasis on short-term market needs. Therefore, in the process of marketization of higher education, it may be important to strengthen the role of the government in higher education as the supervisory authority, the more so when it no longer functions as the monopoly education provider with direct command and control.

References

Apple, M. W. (1999), *Power, Meaning, and Identity*. New York: Peter Lang.

Barnett, R. (1992), *Improving Higher Education: Total Quality Care*. Berkshire, UK: SRHE and Open University Press.

Blaug, M. (1970), *Education Vouchers, Economics of Education*. Harmondsworth: Penguin.

Bleiklie, I. (2002), 'Explaining change in higher education policy', in P. R. Trowler (ed.), *Higher Education Policy and Institutional Change*. Buckingham: SRHE and Open University Press, pp. 24–45.

Bridges, D. (1994), 'Parents: customers or partners?', in D. Bridges and T. H. McLaughlin (eds), *Education and the Market Place*. London: Falmer Press, pp. 1–8.

Cheung, C. and Pyvis, D. (2006), 'How university-based adult continuing education organizations have responded to Hong Kong's changing educational needs since the 1997 transfer of sovereignty', *Research in Post-Compulsory Education*, 11(2), 153–73.

Clark, B. R. (1998), *Creating Entrepreneurial Universities: Organizational Pathways of Transformation*. Oxford: Pergamon.

Currie, J. (1998), 'Impact of globalization on Australian universities: competition, fragmentation and demoralization'. Paper presented at International Sociology Association World Congress.

Deem, R. (1998), 'New managerialism and higher education: the management of performances and cultures in universities in the United Kingdom', *International Studies of Sociology of Education*, 8(1), 47–70.

Green, A. (1997), *Education, Globalization and the Nation State*. London: Macmillan.

Henkel, M. and Kogan, M. (1988), 'Changes in curriculum and institutional structures: responses to outside influences in higher education institutions', in C. Gellert (ed.), *Innovation and Adaptation in Higher Education*. London: Jessica Kingsley, pp. 66–91.

Hossain, Shaikh I. (1997), *Making Education in China Equitable and Efficient*. World Bank Policy Research Paper Series, No. 1814.

Lumby, J. (2001), *Managing Further Education: Learning Enterprise*. London: Paul Chapman.

Ngok, K. L. and Kwong, J. (2003), 'Globalization and educational restructuring in China', in K. H. Mok and A. Welch (eds), *Globalization and Educational Restructuring in the Asia Pacific Region*. New York: Palgrave Macmillam, pp. 160–88.

Postiglione, G. (2003), 'Universities for knowledge economies: Hong Kong and the Chinese mainland within globalization and decentralization', in K. H. Mok (ed.), *Centralization and Decentralisation: Educational Reforms and Changing Governance in Chinese Societies*. Hong Kong: University of Hong Kong, pp. 157–72.

Readings, B. (1996), *The University in Ruins*. Cambridge, MA: Harvard University Press.

Slaughter, S. and Leslie, L. L. (1997), *Academic Capitalism*. Baltimore, MD: Johns Hopkins University Press.

Soley, L. C. (1995), *Lasting the Ivory Tower: The Corporate Takeover of Academic*. Boston, MA: South End Press.

Tiffin, J. and Rajasingham, L. (1995), *In Search of the Virtual Class Education in an Information Society*. London: Routledge.

Walters, S. (2000), 'Globalization, adult education, and development', in N. P. Stromquist and K. Monkman (eds), *Globalization and Education: Integration and Contestation across Cultures*. Lanham, MD: Rowman & Littlefield, pp. 197–218.

Yin, Q. and White, G. (1994), 'The marketisation of Chinese higher education: a critical assessment', *Comparative Education*, 30(3), 217–37.

Chapter 14

An 'essential attributes' approach to curriculum reform

Francis Murphy

Introduction

The chapter begins by describing the 'essential attributes' approach to course effectiveness evaluation. The application of this approach to a case study of a Bachelor of Engineering (Honours) degree course in Mechanical Engineering is discussed in order to illustrate the method. The recommendations emerging from the case study are then given, together with some of the subsequent changes to the course curriculum. Some of the recommended changes that were not carried out, mainly due to problems in implementing new systems, are also discussed. One of these changes was the application of improved *assessment practices*. These practices would assist in teaching the essential attribute of 'critical evaluation'. This essential attribute is considered crucial across all disciplines. Critical evaluation techniques, together with a feature of the essential attributes approach called 'a concept of excellence', should help the student address many of today's social problems. Recommendations involving a concept of excellence and assessment practices are proposed with a view to improving the critical evaluation techniques of students. Suggestions on how to implement the recommendations are provided. Application of the essential approach, taking into account value systems, is demonstrated. Finally, the use of the essential attributes approach for curriculum reform and ultimately social change is recommended for all courses.

Fundamentals of the approach

A course which is claiming to educate students to a professional level should attempt to instil in those students certain essential attributes that are necessary for successful employment in the profession. For professional engineers, some of these essential attributes could be a high level of mathematical ability, creativity, problem-solving ability, team-working ability, and so on. First described by Murphy (2005a, p. 227), the 'essential attributes' approach originated from the teacher as researcher concept. According to Hammersley (1993, p. 211), the teacher as researcher emerged in the 1970s, attempting to move away from a model in which experts developed new curricula centrally. With the 'essential attributes' approach it is a course teacher who analyses course documentation, wider debate literature and course stakeholder interviews. From the results of this analysis, the approach attempts to identify essential attributes that are necessary for graduates to function in their future profession, particularly targeting new essential attributes that may become necessary as the working environment changes.

The approach is based on the concepts of micro-quality and macro-quality, both described by Scott (1998, p. 104). Micro-quality asks the question; 'Are we doing the thing right?' Macro-quality asks the question: 'Are we doing the right thing?' Hence for micro-quality the approach compares the outcomes of the course, obtained from stakeholder interviews, with the course documentation. Micro-quality, or 'Are we doing the thing right?', gives an idea of the 'fitness for purpose' of the course. The approach then goes further and compares the outcomes of the course with some wider debate documentation, which is considered to be indicative of excellence. This is macro-quality, or 'Are we doing the right thing?' This gives us an idea of how the course is approaching some concept of excellence that we have set.

Conceptual map

There is considerable wider debate literature and internal course documentation available. Decisions concerning the most relevant literature must be made when time is limited and the researcher is working alone. Literature categories are therefore ranked, with what is considered to be the most important category placed first. The approach therefore starts by drawing a conceptual map of the influences on the course with a view to ranking the literature. The case study scrutinized in this research was a Bachelor of Engineering (Honours) degree course in Mechanical Engineering from Cork Institute of Technology, Ireland. This was chosen simply because the researcher is a teacher on the course and thus has a vested interest. In Figure 14.1 the conceptual map relating to this course is shown (Murphy, 2005a, p. 30).

At the centre of the conceptual map can be seen the 'BEng curriculum', the 'BEng essential attributes' and the 'delivery of the BEng essential attributes'. These are highlighted with circles or ellipses. Surrounding the circle and ellipses are boxes containing the influences on the course. Important among these would be the Higher Education and Training Awards Council (HETAC). This body has delegated the degree-awarding authority to Cork Institute of Technology (CIT). Other important influences on the course are the Institution of Engineers of Ireland (IEI – the accrediting body) and the Higher Education Authority (HEA – controlling funding to CIT). The BEng stakeholders are also an important influence on the course. Feedback from these is obtained by the analysis of interviews and, with a limited number of in-depth interviews, the analytical methods used are qualitative. All of these primary influences on the course are enclosed by a box labelled 'Micro-quality – Are we doing the thing right?' Outside of this micro-quality box, the wider debate on engineering higher education is shown enclosed by another box.

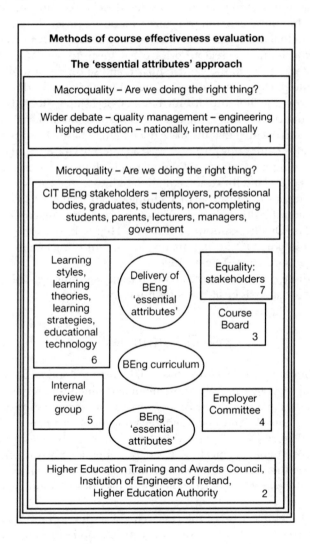

Figure 14.1 Conceptual map

There is a considerable amount of literature on this topic including international quality management literature. This wider debate box and the previous boxes are all now enclosed by a box labelled 'Macro-quality – Are we doing the right thing?' This then is the first stage of the essential attributes approach and we can therefore surround the diagram with a box labelled 'The "essential attributes" approach'. Because the approach is just one of many methods of course effectiveness evaluation, the final box is labelled 'Methods of course effectiveness evaluation'.

Placing numbers in what are considered to be the most important influences on the course can now prioritize a literature review. From Figure 14.1 it can be seen that the first priority was given to the wider debate on engineering higher education. The second priority was given to HETAC, IEI and HEA. The third was given to the Course Board, and so on down to number seven for stakeholder equality. Following the literature review, documents were selected from the literature for further analysis using QSR NUD*IST version 4 (N4) software. Remembering that the case study was undertaken from 2000 to 2004, it was decided that the main document to be analysed as representing micro-quality (fitness for purpose) was the internal CIT document: 'Bachelor of Engineering in Mechanical Engineering: submission to the Institution of Engineers of Ireland for re-accreditation of the degree course in Mechanical engineering at Cork Institute of Technology, April 2000' (CIT, 2000).

The following document was chosen to represent macro-quality (excellence): 'The Quality Assurance Agency for Higher Education (1998) Subject Overview Report QO 11/98: quality assessment of mechanical and manufacturing engineering, 1996 to 1998.'

Both these documents were analysed using N4 software. This software was also used for analysis of stakeholder interviews.

'Essential attributes' model

Theory building produced the 'essential attributes' model shown in Figure 14.2 (Murphy, 2005a, p. 239). Subsequent to the literature review, a concept of excellence was chosen for the BEng course. From the literature a 'Sustainable World' was considered to be a suitable concept of excellence. This was now added to Figure 14.2, thus providing the course with focus. This focus was not intended to be specifically defined by academics, but was left for students to interpret themselves. This would encourage them to be more proactive in realizing the social and environmental impact of the solutions they present to problems.

One of the objectives of the research was to develop the 'essential attributes' approach so that eventually it can be applied to any course. Some essential attributes are generic and will apply to many job situations and many professions. The only way to determine which essential attributes a course should deliver to students is to go through the 'essential attributes' approach procedure of analysis of course documentation, wider debate documentation and interviews with stakeholders. For the case study, engineering excellence has emerged as the concept of a sustainable world. This concept of excellence may not apply to other disciplines. Each discipline would require appropriate research to determine its own concept of excellence. Concepts of excellence

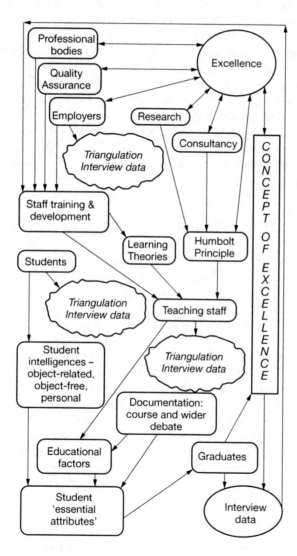

Figure 14.2 'Essential attributes' model

can differ with different courses, thus the results from the case study cannot be generalized, but the method (essential attributes approach) can be used for other courses.

Clark (1993, p. 3) explains the Humboldt principle (shown in Figure 14.2) as the link between research, study and teaching. Staufanbiel (1993, p. 33) points out that research offers numerous advantages for improving the quality of teaching, particularly by updating the curriculum from research. In the case study this link was considered to be a 'standard of excellence'.

It can be seen from Figure 14.2 that course feedback is obtained mainly from interviews with former graduates. It can also be seen that there is some triangulation feedback obtained from interviews with other course stakeholders (present students, teaching staff, non-completing students, employers). The case study indicated that quality feedback was obtained from former graduates who were working for engineering consultancy companies. This core stakeholder group of graduates had varied experience and were thus able to predict how industry was changing. They could therefore provide a strategy for the course. Thus the essential attributes approach can in itself be considered sustainable in that it can react to the workplace environment and change.

Data collection for the BEng case study

The data collection for the 'essential attributes' approach was undertaken in an iterative manner. Ten interviews were completed and then analysed. These interviews were with two former graduates, two present students, two non-completing students, two lecturers and two employer representatives. Respondent validation was undertaken following each interview; the transcript for each interview was returned to the interviewee for alteration. Once the transcript of the interview was validated, it could be imported into the N4 software for coding and analysis, and interview transcripts were coded ten at a time. Following coding, analysis and reflection, another ten interviews were completed. In theory this process should be continued indefinitely in order to obtain constant feedback on the course. For the case study four iterations (forty scheduled interviews) were completed. As the data collection progressed, it was found that the former graduates with varied industrial experience were enthusiastic about providing feedback. These were mainly graduates employed with engineering consultancy companies, hence the sample tended to skew towards this group at the third and fourth iteration.

The N4 software was used in the CIT research as a convenient method of managing the interview and documentation data. For former course graduates, interviews were completed at their workplace. Using the memo capacity within the software, workplace observations were stored against each past graduate, as well as the 'educational factors' to be stored against each 'essential attribute'. Thus all the data is stored within the software for future reference. The interview transcripts stored, as well as reports on each essential attribute, can be browsed within the software. It was this technique that highlighted the importance of 'safety, health and welfare of the public' and 'course strategy'.

Recommendations for the BEng case study

From the research, the following tangible recommendations were made (Murphy, 2005b, p. 169). There were five 'essential attributes' that needed to be developed in order to ensure that the BEng course reached 'fitness for purpose' standards. These were: personal attributes; written communication; safety, health, public welfare; reasoning and information research. Empirical 'educational factors', generated from N4 software analysis of interviews, relate to each of these essential attributes. Implementation of these educational factors has implications for the course curriculum and these are shown in Table 14.1. The interview feedback regarded these five 'essential attributes' as not being adequately addressed by the course.

Table 14.1 Course 'fitness for purpose'

Essential Attribute	Empirical Educational Factors
Personal attributes	Work placement in industry as part of the course; personal development course from the Irish Management Institute; confidence through chairing of large meetings; confidence building – presentations to the rest of the class.
Written communication	Use of multimedia/computers for writing reports; laboratory work and laboratory reports – more emphasis.
Safety, health and public welfare	Lectures on safety, health and welfare of the public.
Reasoning	Reduction of intense classes.
Information research	How to get information? – detailed instructions from project supervisor.

The essential attributes of management knowledge, problem-solving ability, self-directed learning ability, team-working ability and mathematical ability are mentioned in course documentation. Interview data indicates that their delivery could be improved by implementing educational factors and these are shown in Table 14.2.

Table 14.2 Course improvement

Essential Attribute	Empirical Educational Factors
Management knowledge	Role play (each member of the class playing a different team role); how to manage getting something done? (progress, costs, etc.); project management in first or second year (assisted by former graduates); modular approach.
Problem solving ability and teamwork ability	Small group tutorials; use of teamwork to solve problems; more problem solving.
Self-directed learning ability	More self-directed learning guidance from the academic staff.
Mathematical ability	Small group tutorials; practical examples and more examples.

As well as implementing the above recommendations, it is important that the course reaches international standards of excellence. These emerge from the wider debate literature, not from course literature or interviews. Views of relevant stakeholders in other countries are represented by this wider debate literature, thus the essential attributes of critical evaluation and time management were considered to be international standards of excellence. For critical evaluation there are no empirical educational factors emerging from interview data. However, educational factors derived from the literature indicate that for 'critical evaluation' consideration should be given to the educational factor of assessment practices.

A deep approach to learning needs to be developed. Internet-based assignment delivery and assessment systems with online tutors are some of the assessment practices that could be considered. There is some staff training now provided by the CIT Teaching and Learning Unit (TLU) with regard to these online systems.

With reference to the essential attribute of 'time management', the empirical educational factors recommended were:
- how to prioritize work;
- project management software.

The essential attributes that emerged from the wider debate documentation, but missing from the BEng, were defined as international standards of excellence. These were:
- personal attributes;
- written communication;
- reasoning;

- information research;
- time management; and
- critical evaluation.

To move towards these international standards of excellence, the following supporting standards of excellence needed to be given attention:
- course strategy;
- local/regional needs;
- national/international needs; and
- student/staff liaison.

These four supporting standards of excellence could be implemented through a system of regular interviews with former graduates and the subsequent analysis of the interview data. The 'standards of excellence' which have the greatest impact on the chosen concept of excellence (sustainable world) have originated from interviews with industrially experienced past graduates. This indicates that for the CIT BEng course, 'fitness for purpose' and 'excellence' are approaching each other. Thus, a further recommendation was that an overall concept of excellence should be established for each course and the Figure 14.2 'essential attributes' model be followed.

Curriculum implications for the BEng case study

Since completion of the case study in 2005 there have been considerable changes to the course. CIT courses are now semesterized and modularized. Most of the BEng subjects are now delivered in twelve-week modules. Most of the above recommendations have been addressed. For the future, the BEng course needs more work on delivering the essential attributes of 'reasoning', 'information research', 'self directed learning ability', 'mathematical ability', and 'critical evaluation'. More iterations of data collection need to be carried out to keep track of progress on these essential attributes. For students used to a traditional system, a new semesterized and modularized system is difficult to embrace and classes seem to be intense. For first-year students who enter the course under the new system this may not be a problem; however, it has been found that with many of the new modules there is too much assessment. The course board is planning to rectify this issue.

The essential attribute of 'critical review/thinking' emerged from the work of Waghid (2000). To develop this type of essential attribute, Johnston and Olekahns (2002, p. 103) describe an internet-based assignment delivery and assessment system (CALM) at the Faculty of Economics, University of Melbourne. Johnston and Olekahns (2002, p. 105) describe how the aim of CALM is to develop in students a deep approach to learning. Subjects that involve assignments can develop critical thinking in students. Entwistle et al. (2005, p. 12) also emphasize the importance for engineering students of a deep approach to learning and the necessity of a sophisticated assessment strategy.

With the modularized system and too much assessment students could take a surface approach to learning (Lawless, 2000, p. 97; Mann, 2001, p. 7; Reynolds and Trehan, 2000, p. 268). Also, with the advent of mass education and large classes, there will be many assessment scripts for teaching staff to correct. These scripts, together with the tight deadlines for submission of marks, could result in a surface approach to marking. The result is that capable students may not receive adequate credit for their work or, alternatively, weak students may obtain too much credit. Students should not be over assessed and reviews of assessment practices should be frequent.

Concept of excellence

Assessment practices will have a significant effect on the development of critical evaluation in students. Critical evaluation is a necessary essential attribute for students if their solutions to problems are to approach a chosen concept of excellence, such as a sustainable world. According to Wals and Jickling (2002, p. 224), higher education institutions (HEIs) should help develop in students the ability to critically evaluate, so that independently they can produce solutions to problems involving conflict of interests. Students should be capable of producing solutions which are ethical. Each essential attribute should contribute to moving towards the creation of a world which is environmentally caring and egalitarian. The student interpretation of a sustainable world could include sustainable growth, sustainable consumption, sustainable equality or sustainable peace. Some of these interpretations may involve human rights issues. Referring to human rights education and the UN Declaration, Todd (2007, p. 600) points to a proposal by some UN officials that human rights should be integrated into all aspects of education. It should not be treated as a separate topic in social studies. It is interesting to note that the Institution of Engineers of Ireland re-accreditation panel, when it examined the CIT BEng course in 2005, made a similar recommendation with regard to integrating ethical education into mainstream subjects.

Not all courses will have as their concept of excellence 'a sustainable world'. Another course could have as its concept of excellence 'successful globalization'. According to Little and Green (2009, p. 166), globalization can be defined as the accelerated movement of goods, services, capital, people and ideas across national borders. Successful globalization can be defined as development in the current global era. It can also be defined as growth with equality and peace (Little and Green, 2009, p. 172). The view of the concept

of excellence will vary slightly between individual students. It will be important that students critically evaluate their own solution to problems, weighing
up the effect of their solution on the various viewpoints available. According
to van den Anker (2007, p. 288), the UN, the EU and the Commonwealth
Secretariat consider that globalization requires education for multicultural
societies as well as for global citizenship. However, van den Anker (2007,
p. 299) considers that this should not be a top-down model of norm setting.
He argues that there should be local initiatives to implement the Durban
Agenda (World Conference against Racism, 2001) and other international
human rights laws. The 'essential attributes' approach, with its various concepts of excellence for different courses, could be one such local initiative.

It is interesting to note from the case study that the core stakeholder group,
graduates and students, are found to have provided standards of excellence
with the most impact on the engineering concept of excellence and course
sustainability. The wider debate documentation did not have as much impact
as originally thought. The core stakeholder group was demanding excellence
from the course and not just fitness for purpose. It will be interesting to see
if this is so for other disciplines. The core stakeholder group predominantly
consisted of past graduates with varied industrial experience and some present
students, also with some industrial experience. This group made the greatest
demands for excellence. Now that work placement is part of the course, it may
be possible for students, through their project work, to contribute to solutions
of problems such as global warming and depletion of world resources. Other
non-engineering courses may have successful globalization as a concept of
excellence. Students from these courses, with their work experience, may
be better equipped to solve problems relating to national and international
conflict or monetary issues. In the past, interviews with students have proved
to be productive. This mode of data collection looks more promising, as the
curriculum embraces global issues.

Future implementation

According to Bourn and Neal (2008, p. 3), HEIs should review engineering
courses in order to determine the extent to which the global dimension is
covered and consider partnerships with industry to move forward the global
agenda. Thus the 'essential attributes' approach should also be re-applied
to the BEng course in order to take account of issues such as sustainable
development, equality, access, globalization, poverty, and so on. The approach
begins again by producing another conceptual map similar to Figure 14.1,
which would include a box in the macro-quality section relating to these value
systems. This future conceptual map is shown in Figure 14.3.

Documents would have to be chosen for coding, possibly using an updated

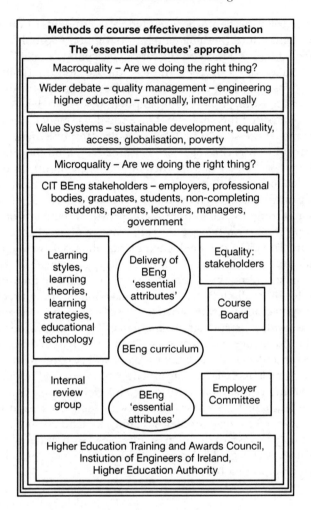

Figure 14.3 Future conceptual map

version of the software (QSR NVivo 8). From the internal course documentation (micro-quality), there is a newer edition of the 'Submission to the
Institution of Engineers of Ireland for Re-accreditation of the BEng Course',
produced in 2005. From the wider debate documentation (macro-quality), a
document representing value systems could be coded, as well as an updated
version of the QAA subject overview report. A suggested document to represent value systems could be: Bourn and Neal's (2008), *The Global Engineer
– Incorporating Global Skills Within UK Higher Education of Engineers.*

   Documents such as these are coded externally to the software, whereas
interview data is imported into the software for coding. With the external

documents, each page can be selected as a text unit. Each text unit can then be coded to a category, which the user chooses. For example, page 6 of a document might have information about 'mathematics' and 'teamwork'. The categories of 'mathematics' and 'teamwork' can then be created in the software and page 6 coded to these categories (called nodes in the software). Interview transcripts can be imported into the software, which automatically divides the transcript into text units. The text unit changes on each carriage return, and the user can change the text unit if necessary.

As in the case study, the aim should be to complete ten interviews before software coding. Of the thirty case-study interviews completed, two of the respondents were female (6.7 per cent), which is approximately the percentage of female students that complete the BEng course. Generally, the academic performance of female students is well above average. In recent years many female BEng students have won international prizes for their final year project.

An interview normally lasts thirty minutes, is semi-structured and field notes are taken. This is considered to be less obtrusive than a recording machine, which may inhibit the respondent. There is a provisional list of questions, but interviewees are encouraged to give their own opinions, frequently drifting off the set questions. An interview transcript is usually written up the same evening. Respondent validation then takes place, whereby the transcript of the interview is returned to the interviewee with a request for any additions or changes where necessary. Once the transcript is validated it can then be coded using the software.

Following the first iteration of ten interviews, reports can be produced whereby all of the information concerning each category or node can be pulled together, so every text unit concerning, say, 'mathematics' can be seen together. The empirical educational factors suggested by students and other stakeholders for mathematics can therefore be seen easily. These can then be compared with educational factors obtained from literature. A causal model can then be produced of the type shown in Figure 14.4 (Murphy, 2005b, p. 107). This shows the 'educational factors' obtained from the literature that could have an effect on the essential attributes. Following each iteration of ten interviews and subsequent analysis, the causal model can be further refined until ultimately it becomes an 'essential attributes' model similar to Figure 14.2. Once this stage is reached, the reports have enough data to highlight new essential attributes. In previous research one such essential attribute emerged from the category of 'safety'. This ultimately became the standard of excellence of 'safety, health and welfare of the public'.

With value systems now included in the conceptual map (Figure 14.3), literature on this topic will be reviewed and some documents on the topic will be coded using the software. Hence essential attributes relating to these value systems should emerge from the research. Educational factors that

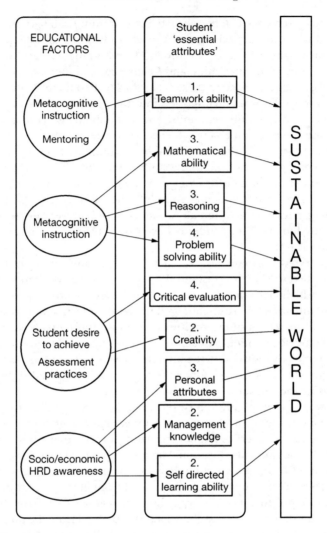

Figure 14.4 Causal model

develop these essential attributes in students should also emerge. These new educational factors and essential attributes should then augment Figure 14.4. Thus within Figure 14.4 it would be possible to see a link between educational factors (curriculum specification), essential attributes relating to value systems and a concept of excellence (sustainable world or other educational aim).

An individual teacher researching a course while undertaking a normal teaching workload could take up to three years to report on findings. It could take another three years to modify the course curriculum. Therefore contingency modifications to the curriculum are necessary. Enhancing student critical evaluation skills and linking with quality work placement to develop student value systems are an example of such contingency modifications.

Conclusion

The case study shows that the 'essential attributes' approach can produce tangible recommendations concerning curriculum reform and can be applied to any course. With the teacher as researcher and the subsequent qualitative analytical methods, the approach is an alternative to the methods of enhancing undergraduate course teaching demonstrated by Entwistle et al. (2005), which seem to require considerable resources. The case study also shows that the 'essential attributes' approach can point the way forward to social change. If a concept of excellence is established at the inception of each course, then the potential for educating students to a higher level is increased. As long as the concept of excellence is loosely defined, students will be able to provide solutions to problems such as the depletion of world resources or the elimination of racism associated with globalization. At CIT, interdepartmental liaison has already enabled business students to work on projects with engineering students. If each student group has a different concept of excellence on which to focus, the potential for innovative solutions to problems is even greater as synergy takes effect. The case study research has already shown that students with industrial experience can provide the basis for defining the standards of excellence of 'safety, health and public welfare' and 'course strategy'. These essential attributes did not emerge from the QAA subject overview report, which was expected to be indicative of excellence. All of the students entering the final year of the BEng course will now have industrial experience. With some guidance regarding critical evaluation, they could make an important contribution to the global agenda.

Critical evaluation skills are necessary for the higher-level solutions to be reached and assessment practices will have a great effect on this. Over-assessment of students will reduce their productive time, stopping them from taking a deep approach to learning. Orafi and Borg (2009, p. 10) point out the importance of altering an examination system to reflect proposed curriculum changes. With critical evaluation there could be a move away from formal examinations to assignments. These are becoming more prevalent for the assessment of critical evaluation skills, particularly as there is now anti-plagiarism software available (e.g. turnitin.com).

In the current economic climate, HEI management wishes to save money. Management may introduce more classes for lecturing staff, with increased student numbers. The danger is that this could result in lecturers not having the time to assess adequately the product of the student critical evaluation.

Training of lecturers in the evaluating of critical evaluation may be necessary, particularly if human rights and ethical issues are to be integrated into mainstream subjects. Techniques such as the 'essential attributes' approach can indicate the way towards curriculum and social change. Thus the approach should be continued with updated documents, some of which will relate to value systems. However, HEIs need to provide lecturers with the time and the resources to enable them to assist students in taking up today's social challenges.

References

Bachelor of Engineering in Mechanical Engineering (2000), *Submission to the Institution of Engineers of Ireland for Re-accreditation of the Degree Course in Mechanical Engineering at Cork Institute of Technology,* April.

Bourn, D. and Neal, I. (2008), *The Global Engineer – Incorporating Global Skills within UK Higher Education of Engineers.* London: IOE University of London, www.engineersagainstpoverty.org/_db/_documents/ WEBGlobalEngineer_Linked_Aug_08_Update.pdf (accessed June 2009).

Clark, B. R. (1993), *The Research Foundations of Graduate Education.* Oxford: University of California Press.

Entwistle, N., Nisbet, J. and Bromage, A. (2005), *Subject Overview Report: Electronic Engineering,* www.etl.tla.ed.ac.uk/publications.html (accessed June 2009).

Hammersley, M. (1993), 'On the teacher as researcher', in M. Hammersley (ed.), *Educational Research: Current Issues.* London: Paul Chapman Publishing.

Johnston, C. and Olekahns, N. (2002), 'Enriching the learning experience: a CALM approach', *Studies in Higher Education,* 27(1), 103–19.

Lawless, C. (2000), 'Using learning activities in mathematics: workload and study time', *Studies in Higher Education,* 25(1), 97–111.

Little, A. W. and Green, A. (2009), 'Successful globalisation, education and sustainable development', *International Journal of Educational Development,* 29, 166–74.

Mann, S. J. (2001), 'Alternative perspectives on the student experience: alienation and engagement', *Studies in Higher Education,* 26(1), 7–19.

Murphy, F. S. (2005a), 'Quality management: an "essential attributes" approach. A case study towards a sustainable model of course effectiveness evaluation', *Research in Post-compulsory Education,* 10(2), 227–44.

—— (2005b), 'Quality management: an "essential attributes" approach. A case study towards a sustainable model of course effectiveness evaluation', EdD thesis, Open University.

Orafi, S. M. S. and Borg, S. (2009), 'Intentions and realities in implementing communicative curriculum reform', *System (2009),* 243–253, available online at www.sciencedirect.com.

Quality Assurance Agency for Higher Education (1998), *Subject Overview Report QO 11/98 – Quality Assessment of Mechanical, Aeronautical and Manufacturing Engineering – 1996 to 1998.* www.qaa.ac.uk/revreps/subjrev/ overviews.asp (accessed March 2001).

Reynolds, M. and Trehan, K. (2000), 'Assessment: a critical perspective', *Studies in Higher Education*, 25(3): pp267-278

Scott, W. R. (1998), 'Organizational effectiveness', in A. Harris, N. Bennett. and M. Preedy (eds), *Organizational Effectiveness and Improvement in Education*. Buckingham: Open University Press.

Staufanbiel, R. W. (1993), 'German education in mechanical engineering from the perspective of the RWTH Aachen', *International Journal of Engineering Education*, 9(1), 29–42.

Todd, S. (2007), 'Promoting a just education: dilemmas of rights, freedom and justice', *Educational Philosophy and Theory*, 39(6), 592–603.

van den Anker, C. (2007), 'Global liberalism or multiculturism? The Durban agenda and the role of local human rights education in the implementation of global norms', *Globalisation, Societies and Education*, 5(3), 287–302.

Waghid, Y. (2000), 'Reconceptualising engineering education: creating spaces for outcomes and dialogical *agape*', *Higher Education*, 40, 259–76.

Wals, A. E. J. and Jickling, B. (2002), 'Sustainability in higher education: from doublethink and newspeak to critical thinking and meaningful learning', *International Journal of Sustainability in Higher Education*, 3(3), 221–32.

Chapter15

Reforming VET for social cohesion

George K. Zarifis

Introduction: the current trend

So far the European Union has shown an unambiguous preference in draw-ing Vocational Education and Training (VET) policies that intend to harness, so to speak, private and public investment in human capital for combating social exclusion. Undoubtedly education in general, but VET in particular, is considered today as an integral part of the lifelong learning ideal that plays a key role in human capital accumulation for the achievement of the European Union's social and economic objectives. True as it might be that social exclu-sion inhibits both social cohesion and economic growth, we should all bear in mind – as active EU citizens – that VET cannot and therefore must not be considered as the solution to combating all problems of social exclusion or as the way through to social cohesion, unless we add to it.

Nonetheless, most European policies that target social cohesion advoc-ate a distinct social role for VET. Some EU members have already launched many initiatives that ease the access of various socially vulnerable groups (unemployed, people with physical or mental disabilities, migrants) or people that are considered to be on the fringes of our society, to better and more appropriate education that subsequently is expected to lead to a more secure employment, and in the long run to a stable social situation. Improving access to education for all is a guiding principle highlighted in national laws and stra-tegic documents in many EU countries following the Lisbon and Copenhagen agendas. The idea is simple and straightforward. By raising the knowledge, skills and competences of EU citizens, VET contributes to the core elements of the EU strategy: sustainable growth, competitiveness, innovation and social inclusion. The overall aim should be to raise the employment rate to as close as possible to 70 per cent by 2010 and to increase the number of women in employment to more than 60 per cent by 2010. This vision is reflected in the period 2007–13, during which cohesion policy focuses investment on research and development, innovation, infrastructure, industrial competitive-ness, training, renewable energy sources and energy efficiency (European Commission, 2007a, p. iv).

Simple as it is in its conception, one can easily draw the conclusion that

VET can only fulfil its role as an agent for strengthening or increasing social cohesion (defined in policy terms) if sufficient resources – human, social and monetary – are allocated. This does not necessarily mean generating new financial resources, but certainly re-allocating existing ones to new types of VET programmes that are more attractive or perhaps more flexible in terms of their purpose and aims. Although this is reflected in the Helsinki Communiqué (European Commission, 2006) – which, among other relevant points, highlights the importance of investment in human capital[1] and calls for improving public and private investment in VET through the development of balanced and shared funding and investment mechanisms – little has been done so far to achieve social cohesion both within and among regions, and among member states.

The working purpose of this EU-ordered reform is to assist the Commission's argument that investment in VET, both initial and continuing, can support social cohesion. Allocation of more funds in VET may increase therefore learning outcomes in all areas that relate to VET, namely improving quality of provision, quality of qualifications achieved both by trainees, their teachers and trainers, quality of assessment and validation, professional guidance, organizing more attractive curricula, and aligning to the European Qualifications Framework (EQF; see Figure 15.1).

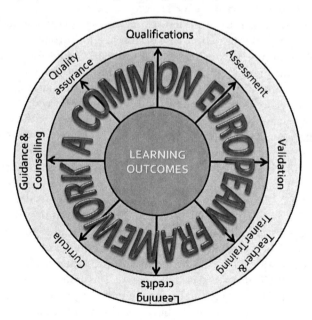

Figure 15.1 A common European framework for VET policies

Source and adaptation: CEDEFOP, 2008, p. 2

The shift to emphasizing the outcomes of learning is currently influencing the development of policies and practices in VET. The EU targets are to strengthen social cohesion and combat social exclusion, with the adoption of common VET policies on tools and principles that are considered vital for achieving the Lisbon set of goals. But are these policies enough? Even more so, are they pointing in the right direction?

As countries face difficulties in securing the necessary public resources, particularly after 2005 and the current economic downturn, greater emphasis is being placed on improving 'efficiency'[2] in redistributing existing resources by encouraging additional funds from the private sector. These investments in vocational education and training are indeed needed so that Europeans may acquire skills and competences relevant to the labour market, for employability and lifelong learning. Furthermore, investments are also necessary to improve the skills of those in working life. Shrinking as well as ageing workforces require measures to retain older workers and integrate inactive citizens into the labour force. This raises some principal questions: what kind of social benefits and for which social groups are more likely to be generated by VET in the EU, and furthermore through which mechanisms – funding, operational, policy, and so on? Even more so, can these benefits guarantee social cohesion in the long run, and what sort of measures can be taken to sustain these benefits through VET?

In 2008 one in six Europeans left school with a low educational attainment level. Almost 80 million people of working age in Europe are low qualified and need retraining, according to the European Commission (2009, p. 93). Although educational attainment levels continue to improve, 15 per cent of 18–24-year-olds in the EU are not in education or training, even though they have not completed a qualification beyond lower secondary schooling. Malta, Portugal and Spain have the highest proportion with 30 per cent or more of low-qualified young people who are no longer in the education or training system. Overall in the EU, young women (18–24) are less likely than young men to be among the low qualified, with an average of 13 per cent, compared to an average of 17 per cent of low-qualified young men in the EU. Designing effective and efficient VET policy interventions definitely cannot be the point of departure. These cannot be effective unless they guarantee secured employment, otherwise they might as well lead to the same result as no VET at all. Therefore a deeper analysis of the benefits of investment in VET for individuals and society is needed in order to better understand the relation between VET and social cohesion or VET as an agent for social change.

In the light of the above, and bearing in mind that social change is certainly not something that can be altogether prescribed and applied through policy measures, this chapter focuses on the contribution of VET to social cohesion, keeping in view that there are no perfect causal relations in real life; rather, many correlations. In order to correctly frame the subject of the analysis, I initially try to define social cohesion as an evolving social process more than a policy target, as the European Commission does, in order to highlight the contribution of VET. Then I question the benefits generated through investment in VET, especially in terms of promoting '*flexicurity*' through policy measures in the member states. I emphasize the potential means through which different VET orientations may generate social cohesion, especially in terms of reforming curricula in order to make VET more attractive, or not. Finally, I provide some references for VET orientation towards a broadened European learning exchange area that may operate as a comfort zone in a period of economic instability.

Defining social cohesion: the contribution of VET

If one considers social cohesion as a definitive concept that reflects the need of the old nation state to create a strong national identity to attain and retain social discipline and order, as well as to fortify the sense of social and cultural belonging through mechanisms that underline the differences with other nations, other societies, and other cultures, this would not be far from the truth. But social cohesion in today's globalized economies and supra-national formations such as the EU is that, and more. According to Green et al. (2003, p. 456), social cohesion is indeed:

> a fuzzy and politically freighted concept. It is widely used in both policy and scientific literature, but it has no clearly defined or common meanings. In different contexts its use may emphasize: (i) shared norms and values; (ii) a sense of shared identity or belonging to a common community; (iii) a sense of continuity and stability; (iv) a society with institutions for sharing risks and providing collective welfare; (v) equitable distribution of rights, opportunities, wealth and income; and (vi) a strong civil society and active citizenry.

These are only some aspects of social cohesion and not necessarily definitions. Equally important to the aspects described by Green et al. is to emphasize full and active participation, especially in economic life. This perspective, which is thoroughly analysed by the Council of Europe (2008), highlights the role of the market and the significance of economic inclusion (Council of Europe, 2008, p. 8). The political project that derives from this approach sees social cohesion as necessitating on the one hand redistribution towards those who are least advantaged and, on the other, the creation of institutions and processes that challenge the existing structures of power and distribution and mediate between sectors of the population with different interests and ambitions.

A further analysis on the above approach could also place emphasis on cultural factors. Especially in the context of multicultural societies and multi-national formations like the EU, social cohesion is seen to require tolerance and cultivation of diversity and respect for different cultures. Identity is central again here, as is recognition – people want to have their own beliefs and culture valorized, especially if these are different from those of the majority or the dominant culture. This view sees cohesion as being at risk if claims around different identities are not managed in a way that recognizes and accommodates diversity.

We could conclude that social cohesion comprises a sense of belonging – to a family, a social group, a neighbourhood, a workplace, a country or – why not? – to Europe. Yet this sense of belonging must not be exclusive; instead, multiple identities and multiple belonging must be encouraged. Social cohesion also implies the well-being of individuals and that of the community, founded on tenets such as the quality, health and permanence of society. In addition to social ties, cohesion must be built upon social justice. Social cohesion also constitutes a process of membership of and contribution to a blueprint for society. As active citizens, individuals must be able to feel responsible and to prosper both in terms of personal development and their income and living standards.

Considering the above general interpretation, when do we know that social cohesion has been achieved in a society? Even more so, how do we avoid the danger of looking at it in terms of an achieved level of homogenization, whether of cultures, of attitudes, of social and monetary policies, and so on? Is social cohesion a new approach to accommodate social and cultural diversity or is it just another 'model concept' in the European policy agenda? And in this indeed fuzzy context what is, or what could be, the contribution of VET?

Currently EU and member states' policies seem to focus largely on three interlocking areas as far as the contribution of VET in social cohesion is concerned: (i) investment in human capital; (ii) curricular reforms to make VET attractive; and (iii) direct links to the labour market. However, none of these areas has been thoroughly researched to the extent that a clear picture is formed in terms of what VET can offer European societies to accomplish and sustain social cohesion, as described above. What has been done, however, is to provide a generic yet useful description of quantified results based on a large variety of indicators such as levels of participation, levels of attainment, levels of income or levels of employability, that manifest only a fraction of the characteristics of social cohesion. The least contemplated area – as the other two relate more to the input and output of VET in contemporary European societies, namely financial investment and trained (as employable) human power – is raising attractiveness of VET, especially for those social groups to which VET, especially CVET, is less attractive: the unemployed, the low skilled and older workers.

One could easily argue that the contribution of VET largely depends on how the EU measures social cohesion, even more than the attributes to which it constantly relates. One of these attributes is certainly financial investment in VET; the EU needs to know how much is invested on VET and how much of this investment enters the labour market in the form of highly trained human resource. This is definitely and unarguably justifiable, but what seems to be missing here is the answer to a set of persistent questions, such as: how many well-trained Europeans are there for how many, and what kind of jobs – part-time, full-time, permanent or temporary? Who can provide these jobs? Do we have a clear picture of how the EU labour market operates? As a process, is VET capable of affecting the orientation and structure of this market, or is it the labour market that has the first and last word in this? Are there discrepancies in terms of labour input–output within and between member states? How do these discrepancies affect our social lives and the way we see each other? Will investment in attractive forms of VET lead to attractive jobs? Are the people who have been in VET and later been employed satisfied with their current employment? Can 'being satisfied with one's job' be an indicator of social cohesion if we consider that satisfaction with one's job affects performance, and therefore quality of provision to European society and economy?

The questions can go on and on for researchers and policymakers, and of course they cannot only relate to the role of VET in providing the labour market with highly trained workers. So what we need to consider at this stage is that investment in VET must not only be seen as an investment for what the EU calls '*flexicured*' employment. It must also be seen as an investment for attractive employment. Not necessarily one that pays, but one from which both the individual worker and society will equally be benefited and supported. This demands a different orientation for VET that essentially considers the needs and demands of the learners, and this could be the contribution of VET to social cohesion.

Investments and recipients in VET: how much, for how long?

According to the European Commission (2007c, p. 3), investment in VET has high returns. In addition, the social partners, individual employers and local communities have been involved both in actively assisting the social integration of disadvantaged groups and in providing appropriate support services. A high percentage of beneficiaries either (re)enter into employment after training or report better employment conditions and higher income. An understanding of the importance of human capital has led to the allocation of substantial amounts to increase the quality and availability of VET. An important role of cohesion policy is to support the adaptation of training and education systems to the new requirements of the labour market and to the needs of the knowledge-based society.[3] As noted in the Bordeaux Communiqué (European Commission, 2008a, pp. 5–6), VET constitutes an investment that should:

- take into account the objectives of social cohesion, equity and active citizenship;
- promote competitiveness and innovation; and
- make the concept of lifelong learning and mobility a reality.

Investment in VET has triggered the reform of education and training systems such as by adjusting curricula to labour market needs or improving the training of teachers in a number of member states; assisting in the development of new forms of training; and providing support for lifelong learning. It has also increased the access of individuals to education and training and supported counselling and career guidance activities. There remain, however, substantial disparities in the educational attainment levels of the workforce across the EU.[4] Furthermore, according to CEDEFOP (2009, pp. 55–6) companies' expenditure on Continuing Vocational Training (CVT) courses as a percentage of the total labour costs decreased from 2.3 per cent in 1999 to 1.6 per cent in 2005 on an EU average (Table 15.1).

Table 15.1 Expenditure on CVT 1993–2005 in selected member states (% of labour costs)

	EU27	BE	DK	DE	IE	EL	ES	FR	IT	LU	NL	PT	UK
1993	–	1.4	1.3	1.2	1.5	1.1	1.0	2.0	0.8	1.3	1.8	0.7	2.7
1999	2.3	1.6	3.0	1.5	2.4	0.9	1.5	2.4	1.7	1.9	2.8	1.2	3.6[1]
2005	1.6	1.6	2.7	1.3	–	0.6	1.2	2.3	1.3	2.0	2.0	1.1	1.3

Source: CEDEFOP, 2009, p. 56

Eventually this decrease in investments in VET (particularly from SMEs) was followed by a further decrease in public investments. Investments in VET indeed paid off for a short period after 1999, but immediately after the Copenhagen Declaration (see European Commission, 2002) and its revised version with the Maastricht Communiqué, the whole idea of 'investing', in terms of financing VET for achieving the Lisbon goals, was largely replaced by the idea of 'flexicurity'. This is a Danish model that, according to some policymakers, in many ways meets the challenges of combining labour market needs with personal protection. However, a study from CASA (2002) shows that parallel to a reduction in unemployment levels in the last half of the 1990s there has been a noticeable exclusion from the labour market that this particular 'Scandinavian welfare model' has not been able to solve.[5] Allegedly it became the means to reinforce the implementation of the Lisbon Strategy, create more and better jobs, modernize labour markets, and promote good work 'through new forms of flexibility and security to increase adaptability, employment and social cohesion' (European Commission, 2009, p. 102). It seems as if this significant period in terms of policy development between 1999 and 2005 witnessed some sort of a 'silent' economic downfall or crisis. This crisis that still continues has considerably changed the orientation of the EU policy agenda as well as the orientation of VET from investing in developing skills for job security to developing new skills for 'flexicurity'.

From 2005 onwards EU expenditures for VET have weakened. While the economic downturn put increasing pressure on public and private expenditure, the focus was turned on generating new skills in order to respond to the nature of the new '*flexicured*' jobs expected to be created, as well as to improve the adaptability and employability of adults already in the labour force, i.e. part-time, low-paid temporary employment, high degree of job mobility, a generous system of unemployment benefits and active labour market programmes, which also include job placement and on-the-job training schemes. Why this happened and what the consequences of 'flexicurity' will be for achieving social cohesion, are questions that remain to be answered.

Making VET more attractive: curricular reforms for individual and social change?

As 'flexicurity' was taken on board by European policies for VET, a new trend made an appearance. If financial investments in VET are not enough to achieve the Lisbon goals, the next best thing would be to raise the quality and attractiveness of VET by reforming its curricular base to more flexible modes of participating, learning and teaching.[6] Perhaps it is to be expected that improving the quality of VET on offer or by improving its transparency and accessibility will raise its attractiveness, as Leney (2004, p. 65) notes. But is this the case?

For EU policymakers, the concept of attractiveness implies that occasionally conflicting opinions and priorities of various stakeholders have been heard and adopted in VET policy and programme planning. Essentially, attractiveness should bridge the gap between learners' interests and those of society, including the crude interests of labour market players as Nieuwenhuis et al. (2004) put it. Attractiveness should therefore become visible in enrolment figures, in benchmarks and indicators and in opinion polls, but also in growing numbers of stakeholders involved in actual decision-making at system and programme level. The Helsinki Communiqué (2006) called for more attention to be given to the image, status and attractiveness of VET (Lasonen and Gordon, 2008), which was further emphasized by the Bordeaux Communiqué (2008). According to the Bordeaux Communiqué, attractiveness, accessibility and quality should allow VET to play a major role in lifelong learning strategies, with a twofold objective: (a) simultaneously promoting equity, business performance, competitiveness and innovation; and (b) enabling citizens to acquire the skills they need for career development, to take up training, be an active citizen and achieve personal fulfilment. VET should promote excellence and at the same time guarantee equal opportunities. The EU policy of VET attractiveness was therefore decided to be based on four pillars:

- *Individualization of VET pathways* and delivery to consider the various capacities and interests of individuals. Individualization of VET implies differentiation and flexibility. Internal differentiation relates to the teaching and learning process, whereas external differentiation refers to creation of new programmes/settings better to accommodate the needs and preferences of students. Flexibility induces possibilities for individuals and for the system itself to react rapidly in case of unforeseen developments or changes.

- Increasing attractiveness by *providing people with a growing range of opportunities* at the end of VET pathways. These opportunities can be of an educational nature (workplace learning or access to higher education), or related to employment (job opportunities, career development, opportunities resulting from policies of gender equality).

- Increasing the attractiveness of VET through *modernizing its governance*. The EU approach is based on the idea that modern governance implies streamlining and clarifying the educational offer, which may smooth and stimulate use of VET, thus favouring cumulative attractiveness. This view also recalls that modern governance means improving partnerships especially at local level to enhance the steering and development of the VET system.

- Action on image and status of VET includes *promoting its parity of esteem* with general and higher education, and encouraging excellence in skills, for example by applying world-class standards or through skills competitions.

Based on these four principles, most EU members introduced a series of measures to increase the attractiveness of VET for young people and adults. A rather popular measure aimed at young people was to make higher education more accessible for students on VET programmes, together with the creation of *occupational-oriented programmes at higher education level*. Even in those member states with a high participation rate in initial VET (i.e Germany and UK), increasing the access to tertiary education attracts policy attention. Also popular are *pedagogical reforms* in members such as Austria, Cyprus and Finland; *diversification* of routes and programmes in VET in countries like Bulgaria, France and Poland; the establishment of guidance and counselling systems; the integration of vocational subjects into general programmes and vice versa; or launching promotion campaigns (Leney, 2004, p. 77).

Besides these measures, however, there is still mixed evidence that the attractiveness of VET systems is growing. Limitations in data supply suggest that enrolment in VET programmes at upper secondary level is increasing in older member states, while participation in most new member states is declining. A wide range of countries report that VET is still regarded as second rate compared to general education pathways at upper secondary level. Data further shows that CVT participation is rising very slowly (Figure 15.2) and is biased by the high participation of higher skilled people, an outcome that challenges the effectiveness of some policy measures taken to date.[7]

According to 2005 data only 33 per cent of all employees participated in CVT courses organized by enterprises, measured by the number of participants in CVT courses as a percentage of all employees in all enterprises. Figure 15.2 shows that there is a large variation across the EU with respect to participation in training courses, ranging from almost 60 per cent in the Czech Republic to 14 per cent in Greece. Men are slightly more likely to participate, with 34 per cent compared to 31 per cent of women, a trend that is evident in 17 of the 27 countries for which data are available. The highest variation exists in the Czech Republic and Slovakia, where men are significantly more likely to follow training courses than women – 11 percentage points higher. By contrast, in Denmark and Slovenia significantly more women follow CVT courses than men. The comparison of participation in CVT courses in 2005 and 1999 reveals that newer member states are catching up, some by investing more in human resources. For example, in Slovenia and the Czech Republic participation rates in CVT courses have increased by

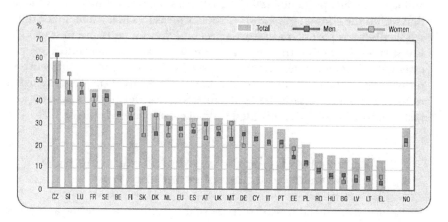

Figure 15.2 Employees (in all enterprises) participating in CVT courses by gender (% of all employees, 2005)

Source: CEDEFOP, 2009, p. 65

36 per cent and 28 per cent respectively. In the majority of newer member states, despite a significant increase, participation in CVT is still far below the EU average. However, participation rates decreased in some countries with a traditionally high participation of employees in continuing training such as Sweden, Finland and the UK. Despite this downward trend, these countries still belong to the best performing countries in this area.

The reasons for these variations of CVT participation need to be further analysed. Furthermore, the introduction of special – sometimes obligatory – programmes and facilities are popular policy measures in most EU member states in keeping those not otherwise in employment or training within the system. The introduction of such programmes is reported in 21 out of the 27 member states. In the majority of the cases, however, the strategy is not so much focused on making learning in VET more attractive, as on discouraging – or blocking, as Leney (2004) suggests – other pathways.

Overall, for strengthening links to the labour market, policymakers at large see flexibility of training institutions and systems as one of the priority issues in making VET more attractive. But what does flexibility mean in this context? In most member states in which such policy initiatives were introduced, 'flexible' directly relates to modular and active VET curricula. That means curricula that essentially appeal to the intrinsic motivation of people to learn; support individual learning paths and differentiation in modes of delivery; introduce guidance and counselling, credit accumulation and transfer; and validation of non-formal or even informal learning. These are considered to be key elements in realizing flexibility in VET. Although this gives a first indication of what flexibility might be, it also indicates that flexibility is a somewhat ambiguous concept. Leney (2004, p. 79) uses the word 'fluffy'. This means that within the context of '*flexicurity*', policy measures in most member states see flexibility as part of, or at least a precondition for, attractiveness of VET. But this should not be the case at all; flexibility and attractiveness are two essentially distinct concepts. That is to say, VET systems may be attractive in terms of the number of students they draw, or in terms of the status awarded to VET, without necessarily being flexible; whereas flexible VET systems and institutions may still be confronted with a lack of parity of esteem.

Epilogue: can VET be the answer for achieving social cohesion in a time of economic doubt?

VET policies should address all sections of the population, offering appealing and challenging pathways for those with high potential, while at the same time addressing those at risk of educational disadvantages and labour market exclusion. In short, VET should be equitable and efficient. To increase the attractiveness of VET, most EU countries – especially after 2005[8] – have put considerable emphasis and resources on: organizing new vocational training and retraining courses; developing national qualification frameworks, some in line with the European Qualification Framework (EQF); establishing well-equipped training centres, validation centres or external examination boards; introducing higher educational and post-secondary programmes to reduce dead-ends and increasing the level of qualifications; progressively developing counselling and career offices and organizing networks; training and re-training teaching and training staff; and reforming existing VET curricula, particularly in initial VET sectors. Has all this effort paid off? Has VET contributed so far to achieving social cohesion in the EU?

Policies to date seem to have put too much emphasis on drawing more resources to VET, basically investing more money and attracting stakeholders, and less emphasis on what Europeans really find inviting in VET, as a systematic evaluation of implemented attractiveness policies is lacking. This approach has essentially left out the most important factor in the equation, namely the learner-trainee.

The contribution of VET to social cohesion in Europe demands the creation of a broad learning exchange area in which all players, namely funding bodies, stakeholders and, most importantly, the learners themselves will participate, with constant networking, in order to make VET more attractive with curricula that basically respond to learners' requirements. VET reform must fit the learners' needs if VET is to become more appealing.

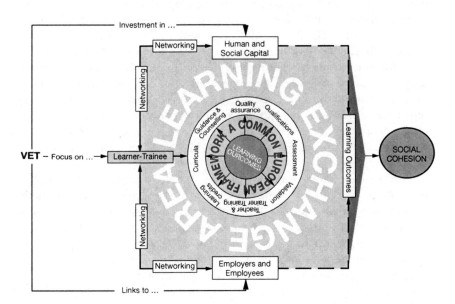

Figure 15.3 Learning exchange in a common European framework

If VET is to contribute to social cohesion, it must be attractive and accessible for all citizens, independent of age, educational attainment, employment or social status. Better coordination between different education and training sectors, institutional commitment, including sustainable models of funding, and partnership with all stakeholders, including the learners themselves, is required (European Commission, 2008b, p. 7). A consistent approach is needed since the simultaneity of initiatives taken at national or institutional levels in terms of vocationalism, academization or differentiation (Dunkel and Le Mouillour, 2008) might be counterproductive.

Having said that, there are three vital areas in which VET can contribute in order to achieve social cohesion in the EU (Figure 15.3). The first is investing in human and social capital. The second is creating links (direct and indirect) to the labour market (employers and employees), and the third and perhaps the most vital – as it has to relate more directly to the needs, whether individual, social, cultural, of the learner or trainee – is developing attractive, constantly updated curricula. Although this may not directly lead to social cohesion as a policy strategy, in practice it will initially strengthen the need for enhancing social and human capital, as well as develop different patterns of networking that in turn create a broadened, ever-growing framework for developing a European learning exchange area in which social cohesion will gradually develop.

The truth is that some work has been completed, but much remains to be done towards social cohesion, as wide-ranging measures to support investment tend to be indiscriminate having significant deadweight effects. Direct support measures should be carefully targeted and subject to rigorous testing of their likely effectiveness, such as through cost-benefit analysis. 'Soft' measures such as the provision of services, training and mentoring, and the support to networks and of training population clusters, can be effective as part of an overall strategy based on a clear analysis of needs and understanding of the demand. It is perhaps the right time as we go through an economic crisis to consider how to create those conditions of letting people choose in what type of training they wish to invest, instead of generating policies with diminishing returns.

Furthermore, coordination measures that are targeted, for example, at improving core skills and competencies, early school leaving and completion of upper-secondary education may help to increase access to jobs and social inclusion in some deprived European regions. Equally, EU programmes for enhancing co-operation in vocational education and training and adult education, under the so-called Copenhagen process, could contribute to strengthening regional competitiveness and increasing employment. In addition, policymakers need to consider supporting student exchange schemes, which are particularly important in disadvantaged regions, in order to increase the mobility of young people, strengthen networking and gradually reduce the disadvantage of living in regions with less developed educational facilities. Moreover, programmes encouraging transnational co-operation between universities can also contribute to reducing regional disparities in tertiary VET in terms of both teaching and research capacities. As part of the wider agenda on VET reforms under the Bologna Process, European universities must also be encouraged to play a more important role in the Lisbon strategy by mobilizing their potential for boosting job creation (European Commission, 2007c, p. 171). Last, but not least, more investment is needed in human capital, particularly in the new member states. Training is needed to reduce staff turnover and achieve the standards required to manage funding in the forthcoming 2010–13 period. This applies to all aspects of VET programme management as well as to those preparing projects for funding and those involved in monitoring VET programmes. It is therefore the human factor that will, no doubt, remain decisive in enabling the least-developed regions of the EU to catch up and bring about social cohesion and eventually actual social change.

Notes

1 Raising the quality of human capital explains more than half of the productivity gains in the last decade. European cohesion programmes co-finance the training of some nine million people annually, with more than half of them women. A high percentage of beneficiaries either (re)enter into employment after training or report better employment conditions and higher income (European Commission, 2007a, p. viii).

2 The term used by the Commission is 'flexicurity'. Flexicurity can be defined as an integrated strategy to enhance, at the same time, flexibility and security in the labour market. For more information on 'flexicurity', see European Commission (2007b, p. 10).

3 For more information see European Commission, (2007a, p. 114).

4 Among those aged 25–64, therefore, the proportion of women with tertiary education is slightly smaller than that of men in the EU as a whole (22.2 per cent as opposed to 22.6 per cent). Among those aged 55–64, however, the proportion of women with tertiary education is over 6 percentage points lower than for men. By contrast, 30 per cent of women aged 25–34 have tertiary qualifications as compared with under 25 per cent of men. The proportion of women who have completed tertiary education is, therefore, increasing at a much faster rate than for men (European Commission, 2007a, pp. 80–1).

5 For further information, see Leney (2004, p. 181).

6 According to the Helsinki Communiqué (European Commission, 2006), making VET systems more open, flexible and attractive is identified as an important part of the Copenhagen process of enhanced cooperation in VET as well as the European economic, employment and social agenda generally. The communication from the Commission *Modernising Education and Training: A Vital Contribution to Prosperity and Social Cohesion in Europe* (European Commission, 2005), stressed that improving the quality and attractiveness of VET continues to be a key challenge for the future.

7 For more information, see Leney (2004, pp. 77–8).

8 Specifically after the release of the joint progress report of the Council and the Commission on the implementation of the 'Education and training 2010 work programme: modernizing education and training: a vital contribution to prosperity and social cohesion in Europe' (see European Commission, 2005).

References

CEDEFOP (2008), *In the Finishing Straights: From Copenhagen to Bordeaux.* Thessaloniki: CEDEFOP.

—— (2009), *Continuity, Consolidation and Change towards a European Era of Vocational Education and Training.* Luxembourg: Office for Official Publications of the European Communities.

Council of Europe (2008), *Towards an Active, Fair and Socially Cohesive Europe – Report of High-level Task Force on Social Cohesion.* TFSC (2007) 31E. Strasbourg: Council of Europe.

Dunkel, T. and Le Mouillour, I. (2008), 'Qualifications frameworks and credit systems: a toolkit for education in Europe', *European Journal of Vocational Training,* 42/3, 184–202.

European Commission (2002), *Declaration of the European Ministers of Vocational Education and Training, and the European Commission.* Convened in Copenhagen on 29–30 November on enhanced European co-operation in vocational education and training. Brussels: Commission of the European Communities, http://libserver.cedefop.europa.eu/vetelib/eu/pub/ commission/ dgeac/2003_0026_en.pdf (accessed 26 January 2009).

—— (2005), *Communication from the Commission – Modernising Education and Training: A Vital Contribution to Prosperity and Social Cohesion in Europe.* Draft 2006 Joint Progress Report of the Council and the Commission on the Implementation of the Education and Training 2010 Work Programme. Brussels: Commission of the European Communities, COM (2005), 549 final/2, http://libserver.cedefop.europa.eu/vetelib/eu/leg/etvnl/ com_2005_0549_en.pdf (accessed 18 April 2009).

—— (2006), *The Helsinki Communiqué on Enhanced European Cooperation in Vocational Education and Training: Communiqué of the European Ministers of Vocational Education and Training, the European Social Partners and the European Commission.* Convened in Helsinki on 5 December to review the priorities and strategies of the Copenhagen process. Brussels: Commission of the European Communities, http://ec.europa.eu/education/ policies/2010/doc / helsinkicom_en.pdf (accessed 16 June 2009).

—— (2007a), *Growing Regions, Growing Europe: Fourth Report on Economic and Social Cohesion.* Brussels: European Commission.

—— (2007b), *Towards Common Principles of Flexicurity – More and Better Jobs through Flexibility and Security.* Brussels: Commission of the European Communities, COM (2007), 359 final, http://ec.europa.eu/ employment_social/news/2007/ jun/flexicurity_en.pdf (accessed 30 August 2009).

—— (2007c), *Fourth Progress Report on Economic and Social Cohesion: Commission Communication.* Brussels: Commission of the European Communities, COM (2007), 273 final.

——— (2008a), *The Bordeaux Communiqué on Enhanced European Cooperation in Vocational Education and Training. Communiqué of the European Ministers for Vocational Education and Training, the European Social Partners and the European Commission, Meeting in Bordeaux on 26 November to Review the Priorities and Strategies of the Copenhagen Process.* Brussels: Commission of the European Communities, http://ec.europa.eu/education/lifelong-learning-policy/doc/bordeaux_en.pdf (accessed 18 June 2009).

——— (2008b), *Communication from the Commission to the European Parliament, the Council, the European Economic and Social Committee and the Committee of the Regions. An Updated Strategic Framework for European Cooperation in Education and Training.* Brussels: Commission of the European Communities, COM (2008), 865 final, http://ec.europa.eu/education/lifelong-learning-policy/doc/com865_en.pdf (accessed 12 June 2009).

——— (2009), *The Social Situation in the European Union 2008: New Insights into Social Inclusion.* Brussels: Commission of the European Communities, http://epp.eurostat.ec.europa.eu/portal/page/ portal/product_ details/publication?p_product_code=KE-AG-09- (accessed 27 August 2009).

Green, A., Preston, J. and Sabates, R. (2003), 'Education, equality and social cohesion: a distributional approach', *Compare*, 33(4), 453–70.

Lasonen, J. and Gordon, J. (2008), 'Improving the attractiveness and image of VET', in CEDEFOP Background Report – Vol. 3, *Modernising Vocational Education and Training: Fourth Report on Vocational Education and Training Research in Europe.* Luxembourg: Office for Official Publications of the European Communities.

Leney, T. (2004), *Achieving the Lisbon Goal: The Contribution of VET.* Final report to the European Commission (1/11/04), The Lisbon-to-Copenhagen-to-Maastricht Consortium Partners. London: QCA.

Nieuwenhuis, L. F. M., Mulder, R. and van Berkel, H. (2004), 'Improving the quality of teaching–learning arrangements in VET', in W. J. Nijhof and W. van Esch (eds), *Unravelling Policy, Process and Performance.* Hertogenbosch: CINOP.

PART IV

Learning and Pedagogy

Overview

Our final section addresses convergent themes about educational theory and practice in different contexts. New ways of conceptualizing educational development are presented, together with recent experiments for enabling access to education by 'hard to reach' groups.

Doug Bourn and Sally Issler utilize a historical account to appraise the role of NGOs in Development Education as part of their transnational advocacy of human rights and social justice. With the support of the United Nations and national governments, NGOs' concern for the causes of and ways of overcoming under-development has infiltrated into formal and informal learning in many countries around the world. This chapter focuses on NGO partnerships with educational organizations in England, as an example of European practice. A number of key features have been identified, particularly the promotion of knowledge and values developed in the context of understanding of the importance of interconnectedness in a global world and the use of critical literacy to challenge injustice and stereotyping. It is understood that the young are the most affected by globalization, mainly as a result of consumerism and the use of the internet, but the introduction of the global dimension in education presents a considerable challenge to schools, including the need for strong leadership and well-qualified staff.

Education for global citizenship requires new pedagogic practices that enable young people to understand globalization, its effects and how to negotiate them. Such practices require teachers to understand the changing profiles and perceptions of learners responding to environments affected by globalization, and to devise methodologies that enable them to engage with complexity, embrace multiplicity and address inequalities by participating in dialogue and the application of critical analysis of their encounters with local or global issues. Vanessa Andreotti argues that this can be achieved by teachers who are equipped to raise standards by employing ideas related to knowledge construction, power relations and interrogations of the certainties of modernism. These ideas are emerging in the areas of postmodernist, post-structuralist and postcolonial traditions which stress the social construction of meaning, identities and cultures and which emphasize understandings of language that question assumptions of cultural supremacy. This 'discursive turn' in citizenship education can form the basis of pedagogic practices for teachers to shape change based on informed choices and their capacity to justify decisions in complex environments, and to negotiate with different variables and perspectives in order to provide learners with the ability to thrive in conditions of uncertainty.

Recent years have witnessed increasing policy activity in Europe on the identification, assessment and recognition of competences acquired through non-formal and informal learning. This has been anchored in the conception that validation of such learning can improve the efficiency of European labour markets by facilitating mobility and individual transitions (between countries, between economic sectors, between education and employment periods). Validation, however, is also seen to have an important social dimension as it can be used to recognize and value the knowledge, skills and competences of those who lack formal qualifications. Manuel Souto-Otero analyses the tension between new vocationalism and the social dimension of validation, and assesses how different types of validation methodologies affect the potential of validation to bring about social change. He shows that, in order to achieve social change, systems and methods adopted must be carefully designed to address political, social and institutional barriers which protect the interests of particular groups in society and perpetuate inequality.

Val Chapman describes the transnational co-operation within a European Union-funded project, QATRAIN2 (Quality Assurance and Accessible Training 2), led by the Centre for Inclusive Learning Support at the University of Worcester, UK, with partners in Bulgaria, Greece, Romania and Turkey. The methodological issues concerning transnational co-operation are discussed, including differences and similarities between the partner countries, the project's impact and the 'value added' by the partnerships. The major outcome of the project was the production of a web-based resource that helps teachers of VET to better meet the needs of disabled learners. Countering more traditional syllabus-centred approaches in some participating countries, the new web resource was built around the student-centred notion of 'learning outcomes', which was an extremely important element in the project's approach to meeting the individual needs of disabled learners.

In the early 1990s, the Australian federal government launched a series of reforms to the national vocational education and training (VET) system designed to increase the responsiveness of the VET system to the training needs of business, at the same time as encouraging employers to invest in the training of their staff. The reforms included both supply-side and demand-side measures. Supply-side measures include the establishment of a national VET system from the existing largely state-based systems, the establishment of a national system of VET qualifications based on competency standards developed with industry input, and the development of a competitive open market for training provision. On the demand side there have been a series of incentives for employers to utilize national VET qualifications in their training of workers. One of the avowed aims of training reform in Australia was to improve access to vocational qualifications for a broader range of learners. Erica Smith and Andy Smith examine some aspects of policies and practices designed to increase access to vocational qualifications in Australia. The chapter discusses and critiques the initiatives under two headings: qualification-related training in educational institutions and qualification-related training in workplaces. These are the two settings in which vocational qualifications are delivered and acquired. To assist in understanding the wider import of the arguments, the initiatives are related to developments in other countries.

Chapter 16

Transformative learning for a global society

Douglas Bourn and Sally Issler

Worldwide pollution, global warming and financial crisis resulting from accelerating globalization over the last thirty years have promoted a feeling of interconnectedness through a growing sense of a common fate of mankind (Held and McGrew, 2002). Coupled with this has been evidence of inequality arising from the deregulation of the financial activities of multinational corporations. These developments have given added impetus to the work of Non-Governmental Organizations (NGOs) who have been able to act as protagonists for human rights and social justice on a transnational basis, thereby forming a prototype for a global civil society. This method of advocacy has also influenced education agenda within nation states (Munday and Murphy, 2006) in both richer and more industrialized countries as well as lower-income countries. In this chapter, through the discourse of development education, the role of the NGO will be analysed in terms of its contribution to promoting concepts of social justice, human rights and global citizenship within the English education system and the implications for broader debates on education for social transformation.

Development education and NGOs

The term 'development education' first emerged in the UK during the 1970s, in part in response to the growth of development and aid organizations and the decolonization process, but also, as Harrison (2005) has commented, through the influence of UNESCO and the United Nations, who in 1975 defined it as follows:

> Development education is concerned with issues of human rights, dignity, self-reliance, and social justice in both developed and developing countries. It is concerned with the causes of underdevelopment and the promotion of an understanding of what is involved in development, of how different countries go about undertaking development, and of the reasons for and

ways of achieving a new international economic and social order.
(United Nations, 1975, quoted in Osler, 1994)

During the 1980s two broader influences began to have an impact on development education. The first was the thinking of Paulo Freire (1972) and his emphasis on participatory learning and the relationship between education and social change. Alongside this was the influence of what Harrison (2005) calls the 'globalist' approach through the World Studies Project led by Robin Richardson, and later Simon Fisher and Dave Hicks, and the work of David Selby and Graham Pike. (Pike and Selby, 1999; Hicks, 1990, 2003; Richardson, 1976, 1990).

These educational movements, however, suffered in the 1980s due to the growing influence of neo-liberal theories. Development and global education was perceived as political and it was left to NGOs to play the leading role (Arnold, 1987; McCollum 1996; Marshall, 2005; Hicks, 2008). The influence of these NGOs such as Oxfam, Christian Aid, UNICEF, Save the Children and ActionAid can be seen within the English education system from the 1980s until the present day. Examples include the development of the framework of education for global citizenship by Oxfam since 1997, Christian Aid's role-play games on fair trade and poverty, and the success of ActionAid's series of educational packs on an Indian rural community, Chembakooli (see www.globaldimension.org.uk), including a database of educational resources on global and development issues for schools.

The impact of these materials and approaches has been assisted in England by a network of local Development Education Centres, which have supplied teachers and other educational providers with access to quality support, professional development opportunities and resources. Central to the work of these organizations is the belief that, in promoting learning about global and international development issues, there is a need to promote the concept of living in an interdependent world and that a key feature of this practice is the challenging of stereotypes and the importance of education for a just and sustainable world.

Underpinning their practice is the promotion of the awareness of poverty and injustice in the world, recognition of the importance of human rights, and sustainable development. Within the context of the school curriculum, this means not only developing activities that deepen a pupil's knowledge and understanding of a topic such as poverty in a country like the Gambia, but developing the skills critically to assess from a range of views and perspectives the causes of this poverty. It also means ensuring that pupils have the skills to engage in the discussions on these issues that enable them to question the stereotypical assumptions that many may have of an African country, and to know where to go, and what to do if they wish to secure change.

This tradition of education practice is known as development or global education. An example of a definition of this practice is as follows:

> an active learning process, founded on values of solidarity, equality, induction and co-operation. It enables people to move from basic awareness of international development priorities and sustainable human development, through understanding of the causes and effects of global issues, to personal development and informed action.
>
> (Development Education Exchange in Europe Project
> (DEEEP, 2007, quoted in Bourn 2008b, p. 4).)

Development education and policymakers

During the Thatcher government period in the UK, this area of development education was seen as promoting an approach towards learning deemed to be too political (Bourn, 2008a). NGOs survived by relying on their internal resources and funding from the European Commission for promoting their materials and organizing of professional development activities. Teachers who were sympathetic to these principles welcomed these materials, but development education remained marginal to most schools (McCollum, 1996). This has, however, changed in the UK since 1997 with a Labour government commitment to building public support and engagement for international development within education and the inclusion of areas such as citizenship, sustainable development and cultural understanding as an integral component of the school curriculum.

In 1998 the Department for International Development (DFID) produced a major policy statement, *Building Support for Development*, that promoted as its central message the movement from a perception of development as charity, to its being social justice:

> If we are to achieve this (breakthrough in development awareness), it lies in going beyond attitudes to development based on compassion and charity, and establishing a real understanding of our interdependence and the relevance of development issues to people's everyday lives.
>
> (DFID 1998)

This commitment led to the expansion of funding and resources, mainly aimed at NGOs who could provide resources, professional development and quality support to teachers and other educators (Verulam, 2009).

Within the English education system the commitment to citizenship, sustainable development (Bourn, 2008a) and cultural understanding enabled linkages to be made between what could have been a series of parallel initiatives. Two examples are given here from Citizenship and Science at Key

Stage 3, both of which emphasize social justice and mutual understanding. In relation to the aims of citizenship education programmes:

> Learners develop understanding of the key concepts of democracy and justice as they question and reflect on what may be fair and reasonable in different situations, explore the likely impact of decisions, and consider how the rights and responsibilities of individuals and groups are affected. Through in-depth research and enquiry, learners develop analytical and evaluative skills to ensure that their arguments are informed, clear and coherent. Pupils demonstrate toleration of different views, including those with which they may not agree, and they develop understanding of how different views are formed and influenced.

Another example of emphasis on intercultural exchange comes from the Key Concepts in Science, in relation to a section on 'Cultural Understanding', identified as 'Recognising that modern science has its roots in many different societies and cultures, and draws on a variety of valid approaches to scientific practice (www.qcda.gov.uk , November, 2009).

While these initiatives may not have had as big an impact within state education in England as, say, commitment to literacy or numeracy or changes to structures of secondary schools, they have provided opportunities for an approach towards learning that recognizes concepts of critical pedagogy and transformative thinking and challenges dominant orthodoxies of learning. Gearon (2006), in reviewing human rights education, suggested that there is danger in the practice of a number of NGOs with a more doctrinaire approach. Marshall (2005) has suggested that many NGOs are more concerned with the 'how' than the 'what – and greater emphasis on the affective and participatory domains than the cognitive'. Cameron and Fairbrass (2004) suggest that the discourse has become de-politicized by its close engagement with government. While noting these comments, this chapter will suggest that by merely opening up spaces for different ways and forms of learning, development education has put on the agenda a potentially more transformatory approach.

A different approach towards education

The approach towards learning of these development education providers in England, particularly the local development education centres, make connections between critical thinking, social justice and educational change. The centre based in Birmingham, for example:

> refers to entitlement of learners to develop positive sense of self, respect

for others and wider sense of social responsibility – skills of enquiry and critical thinking – confidence to communicate and work as part of a team and ability to engage with different perspectives.

(www.tidec.org)

Underpinning these practices is a discourse concerned with the mechanics of poverty, the causes of inequality and social justice, but also a form of pedagogic praxis intended to drive social change. A key influence here is the work of Paulo Freire. Best known for *Pedagogy of the Oppressed*, first published in 1968, he advocated the use of education as a method of democratic practice through the creation of a dynamic mutual learning partnership between teacher and pupil. The influence of Freire on development education was more implicit than explicit, but it had an impact on Henry A. Giroux, the critical literacy theorist. Concerned with the effect of the hidden curriculum as a determinant of success and failure of children at school, he was anxious to provide educators with methodologies that would enable them to be more critical of implicit assumptions in order to address causes of discrimination. His purpose is to celebrate diversity by finding ways to create new democratic discourses that address inequality through furtherance of mutual understanding, dialogue and practice (Giroux, 1988, 2001). The work of Vanessa Andreotti is in this tradition. She has a contribution to this volume on global citizenship and, through her work on looking at recognizing different perspectives and approaches, developed a methodology that is having a major impact on development education practice not only in the UK but in Canada, Ireland and New Zealand (Andreotti, 2006; Andreotti and De Souza, 2008; Bourn, 2008a, 2008b).

Vanessa Andreotti investigates the challenges to educators who adopt critical literacy, often in response to a complex changing environment where the outcomes are unknown, and proposes a strategy to inform both teaching and learning. She played a central role in the creation of a methodology towards education and learning called 'open spaces for dialogue and enquiry' that has been taken forward by a number of development education providers in England through professional development programmes and resource development. This methodology supports the creation for 'open safe spaces for dialogue and enquiry' about global issues and perspectives 'focusing on interdependence'. The approach encourages the learner to engage critically 'with their own and with different perspectives, think independently and make informed and responsible decisions about how they want to think and what they want to do'. The key, it is suggested, is to create space where people 'gather together to listen and transform themselves – learning and unlearning together, re-inventing ways of relating to one another and imagining other possible futures' (www.osdemethodology.org.uk).

Andreotti's other initiative, 'Through Other Eyes', takes this thinking forward and links it more closely to critical literacy, indigenous knowledges and the understanding of the other (www.throughothereyes.org.uk).

These linkages to theory and critical pedagogy pose some wider questions about the purpose and role of education in relation to understanding different perspectives, voices, notions of power and inequality, and knowledge construction.

Construction of knowledge and perceptions of power

Hyland (2004) identified the convention in higher education, whereby a Primary Knower makes available to a novice various institutionally sanctioned values and practices. This introduction to a socio-cultural system will include learners who have various levels of experience and who exhibit different levels of involvement. In common with Bourdieu (1977), Hyland recognizes the study of academic disciplines as sites of power that use their cultural capital to define their position and exclude others, thereby socially reproducing themselves. In connection with this, Hyland quotes Bhatia's (1997) observation that, in order to create new forms of knowledge, there is a need to achieve a degree of visibility, which for the majority means a requirement to meet the expectations of a disciplinary culture. This raises political questions in relation to knowledge production in relation to who gets involved, under what circumstances, and to what extent the understandings generated can challenge the existing order.

Development education by its very nature is a challenge to conventional academic discourse in that it provides opportunities for intercultural research and learning based on equality of partnership between teachers and learners from the 'north', with perceptions based on Enlightenment and post-modernist ideals, and those from the 'south', using different educational principles and ethical precepts derived, for example, from Muslim, Buddhist, or Ghandian thought. This approach not only supports international understanding, but also investigation of indigenous cultures and provides a voice for minority and marginalized groups in any society.

An example of the tensions in these debates within the English education system is the recent growth of interest and support for linking with, and partnerships between, schools in the UK and schools in Africa, Asia and Latin America. This interest has been sponsored and resourced by DFID with the aim of providing transformatory experiences for both teachers and students by means of experiential learning. Aside from the organizational and administrative skills required, there is a need to ensure that all participants are assisted in their ability critically to appraise their experiences overseas. In relation to this Alison Leonard (2004, 2008) investigated school linking in connection with geography teaching as a means to improve understanding of ethnicity and multiculturalism in order to promote global citizenship. Her concern was to establish evidence of a relationship that could establish equality and reciprocity. Her findings identified a real value in direct contact and dialogue, but she also found evidence in some cases of reinforcement of pre-existing stereotypes due to an inability to situate learning within the development discourse. Measures needed to be taken to counter northern dominance in decision-making, which prompted unintended paternalism.

Son Gyoh (2008), a development education consultant based in Ireland, showed how difficult it was to realize education capacity-building objectives derived from notions of interconnectedness and social justice. One of his main concerns was that intercultural agendas were jeopardized by a lack of a clear conceptual framework on the part of 'host' (north) policymakers and the larger NGOs, which resulted in a lack of capacity building in the global south. This was caused by a fracture between educational objectives concerned with promotion of knowledge acquisition and intellectual enquiry as against the advocacy, awareness raising and campaigning objectives of NGOs. In relation to international educational projects, funding structures privileged the realization of 'host' government objectives in conjunction with those of the larger NGOs (related to such campaigns as those for Fair Trade or 'Making Poverty History'). For example, projects that support global citizenship fit the education agenda of countries of the north, and they require high levels of expertise from 'host' countries, which leaves little room for participation from representatives from the global south. In these circumstances there was a preference for informal ad hoc intercultural projects that facilitated local capacity building and contributed to participant career development.

Son Gyoh's work adds weight to Andreotti's (2006) observations concerning the need for critical analysis to understand how postcolonial attitudes in relation to the global dimension are addressed. At a conference in October 2009 at the National University of Ireland, Son Gyoh presented a research model designed to mainstream the southern perspective. True to the principles of development education he used a participatory action research model which did not privilege the 'expert' in order to challenge Western hegemony. His purpose was to examine how southern development education concepts were constructed to establish the existence of a universality of methodology. This kind of research could enhance local capacity building by providing the basis of establishing equality as a basic principle in the formation of global intercultural partnerships. It has the potential to create a new form of knowledge in relation to civil society as a result of an interchange between the perspectives of both north and south.

Identity, citizenship education and value of global perspectives

A related area of the contribution of development education to broader discourses is in the linkages between learning, identity formation, behaviour and motivation. Educational psychologists increasingly recognize that identity formation is a key determinant of consciousness and behaviour of young people and their motivation and engagement in education. While education programmes might be concerned with acquisition of subject-based knowledge and skills or an introduction to working life, many students fail to engage with this agenda and do not appreciate its relevance to their attempts at identity formation. Transformatory learning is more likely to take place if the school can establish pathways to adult life which provide youngsters with acceptable challenges that not only invite their active participation in learning but give them increasing control over the process. Interactive learning experiences and problem-solving project work are recognized means of developing personal characteristics, as well as the inculcation of subject-based information (Illeris, 2007).

The argument here is that the introduction of global perspectives into subject-based education provides an opportunity for learners to interrogate their social attitudes and the general cultural orientation which underpins much of their lives and approach to learning. One important element is the furthering, through the use of appropriate frameworks, of the expertise to debate controversial issues in society. Particularly effective is the selection of issues that connect the local to the global, such as the treatment of immigrants within the community or environmental pollution. Within this context teachers are encouraged to act as facilitators by encouraging learners to take increased responsibility for the formation of their opinions. The ultimate outcome for the student should be the development of both critical and political literacy, including an appreciation of the value of tolerant behaviour in a society where not all social attitudes are compatible (Holden, 2007).

Citizenship education in England has made an important contribution to enabling students to relate who they are to their role in society and the wider world. Exploitation of the educational opportunities through participation in NGO campaigns such as Fair Trade or Eco Warriors has been accepted by teachers as a means of encouraging personal agency. This is a response to student demand to feel that what they learn matters and that they can, as a result, make a contribution to society (Martin, 2007). The National Curriculum in England, in relation to citizenship education, developed in response to the Crick Report (1998) and it reflects a long tradition of citizenship education dating back to the Athenian city state, and to the Enlightenment idea of the social contract on which the challenges of achieving socially harmonious relationships through a sense of civic responsibility in a global society have been imposed.

This concern for approach has been given additional impetus as a result of the Ajegbo Report (2007), 'Diversity and Citizenship Curriculum Review', which argued the need for schools to address who we are and how we are to live together and deal with difference. Brown and Fairbrass (2009) noted the reference made to disaffected, white, working-class British youths whose sense of alienation was compounded by the attention given to every identity with the exception of their own. Exploring the global dimension here enables the learner to situate their identity within the context of a rapidly changing globalized world. What is not sufficiently recognized is that it is on young people that globalization is having its biggest impact. They are directly experiencing globalization on an everyday basis through employment patterns, the friendship groups they develop, their usage of the internet (particularly for social networking) and its wider cultural influences on their lifestyle (Burbules and Torres, 2000; Edwards and Usher, 2008; Kenway and Bullen, 2008). Young people are now trying to find their place in this world, moving across the physical and virtual terrain in ways we are only beginning to understand and appreciate, and are the main targets of global consumer cultures.

With reference to teenagers' citizenship, the importance of the interrelationship between local and global is of key importance to young people's making sense of their own identity and role within both their own community and the wider world. An important influence for young people is also the ever-growing influence of the internet and cyberspace. In relation to this, Kenway and Bullen (2008) note the importance of young people being not only observers, but also critical engagers in understanding the wider world. These observations therefore suggest that seeing 'young people as global citizens' could be misinterpreted if it does not recognize the complex and multilayered identities and forms of engagement young people have with their communities and societies.

Within the context of a classroom, therefore, the questions of learning and understanding about the wider world could possibly start from a discussion of identity, culture and the relative influences on young people's lifestyle. Exploring and understanding their own and others' identities, the Ajegbo report suggests:

> is fundamental to education for diversity, essential as pupils construct their own interpretations of the world around them and their place within that world. They above all need to feel engaged and part of a wider multiethnic society.
>
> (Ajegbo, 2007)

What is evident is that, compared to a decade ago, more and more young people, whether at primary or secondary level, are becoming involved in some form of activity that relates to global and development issues. This is due not only to the introduction of the citizenship curriculum, but because of the increased media profile and resulting responses from NGOs on issues such as poverty, fair trade, debt and climate change. As Davies (2006) has stated, there is a need for longitudinal studies to track 'individuals and groups during and after their school life', and to 'engage in "backwards mapping" to work out what caused people to act as global citizens, and what "percentage" was due to exposure to a global citizenship programme in a school'. (Davies 2006, p. 23)

Pedagogic and organizational challenges

The linkages between development education and broader pedagogical questions should not detract from the challenge that these different approaches towards learning can be seen as threatening to many education policymakers and practitioners. Critical therefore to any successful engagement with development education in a school is the need to see this involvement as more than just a bolt-on extra but as an integral component of the school. This view is endorsed by a research report conducted by the Institute of Education in London for the UK Government on 'Exploring the Global Dimension in Secondary Schools' (Edge et al., 2009). It recommended the creation of formal leadership posts and the identification of opportunities for student leadership and development. Planning activity across the school was particularly necessary when addressing issues such as: interconnectedness, poverty, human rights, and conflict resolution. In relation to this, time had to be found in the curriculum to organize conferences, including the booking of outside speakers and other special events such as global days and workshops and the involvement of children in fundraising or local campaigning and school-link programmes and other educational exchanges.

   Another important consideration in relation to school organization is the requirement to support staff training and professional development. In this respect support is available from NGOs, Development Education Centres, the British Council, INSET programmes and initiatives such as Global Gateway (school linking) and Education Action International (refugee education). Key areas for teachers are the expertise to engage in participatory pedagogy, the ability to manage the global dimension across the curriculum and how to extend global education outside the classroom.

   There is much evidence to suggest that schools are beginning to understand the global agenda. The recent Institute of Education Report (Edge et al., 2009) undertook research in ten schools in a variety of English locations and found that:

   The impact of the Global Dimension on students seems to be positively
   related to the degree of the students' involvement. The majority of students

exposed to the Global Dimension seem to have a greater awareness of the world and its interconnectedness than before. Based on our interactions with various groups of participating students, they appear to have a broad understanding of global issues and other cultures. They also demonstrate an awareness of the impact their actions have on other people and the environment in a world context.

(Edge et al., 2009, p. 4)

In common with Brown and Fairbrass (2009), in the context of citizenship education a number of factors were identified as barriers to future progress. One was the importance of continual public funding and another was the failure of awarding bodies to embrace the global agenda. This would help to integrate global dimension into the curriculum and assure teachers that it was not an added burden. Although the benefits to the individual are now recognized, in a school with multiple priorities there is a preference for higher-profile award schemes than those already in existence.

Conclusion

This chapter has addressed, through an analysis of the contribution of development education to formal education in England, the contribution NGOs can play in providing resources, opportunities and spaces for more creative forms of learning. It has also shown that government-driven initiatives do not always lead to a prescribed outcome. They can create spaces for more radical and transformatory approaches towards learning. Development education and its related areas of global citizenship, global learning and education for sustainable development, may not yet be centre stage in terms of educational practices in the UK, but the need for a society that is informed about and understands the global interconnectedness of communities is a theme that will not go away. What is not yet clear is what this learning is for and in a global society what this could mean for the purpose of education. However, what the story of development education in the UK suggests is that it opens up a discourse that brings together areas such as cultural identity, knowledge construction, partnerships and forms of learning in a potentially transformatory way, and there is no doubt that debates around globalization and power relations, differing cultural perspectives and interpretations will become more centre stage within education.

References
Ajegbo, K. (2007), *Diversity and Citizenship Curriculum Review*. London: DfES.
Andreotti, A. (2006), 'Soft versus critical global citizenship education', *Policy and Practice: A Development Education Review*, 2, 40–51.

Andreotti, V. and De Souza, L. M. (2008), 'Translating theory into practice and walking minefields', *International Journal of Development Education and Global Learning*, 1(1), 23–36.

Arnold, S. (1987), *Constrained Crusaders – NGOs and Development Education in the UK*, Occasional Paper, Institute of Education, University of London.

Bhatia, V. K. (1997), 'The power and politics of genre', *World Englishes*, 17(3), 359–71.

Bourdieu, P. (1977), *Outline of a Theory of Practice*. Cambridge: Cambridge University Press.

Bourn, D. (ed.) (2008a), *Development Education Debates and Dialogues*. London: Bedford Way Papers.

—— (2008b), 'Development education: towards re-conceptualisation', *International Journal of Development Education and Global Learning*, 1, 5.

Brown, K. and Fairbrass, S. (2009), *The Citizenship Teachers Handbook*. London: Continuum.

Burbules, N. and Torres, C. (eds) (2000), *Globalization and Education: Critical Perspectives*. New York: Routledge.

Cameron. J. and Fairbrass, S. (2004), 'From development awareness to enabling effective support: the changing profile of development education in England', *Journal of International Development*, 16, 729–40.

Crick, B. (1998), *Education for Citizenship and the Teaching of Democracy in Schools, Final Report of the Advisory Group on Citizenship*. London: Qualifications and Curriculum Authority.

Davies, L. (2006), 'Global citizenship: abstraction on framework for action?', *Educational Review*, 58(1), 5–25.

DFID (1998), *Building Support for International Development*. London: DFID.

Edge, K., Khamsi, K. and Bourn, D. (2009), *Exploring the Global Dimension in Secondary Schools, Final Report*. London: Institute of Education, University of London.

Edwards, R. and Usher, R. (2008), *Globalisation and Pedagogy*, 2nd edn. London: Routledge.

Fisher, S. and Hicks, D. (1985), *World Studies 8–13*. Edinburgh: Oliver and Boyd.

Freire, P. (1972), *Pedagogy of the Oppressed*. New York: Herder & Herder.

Gearon, L. (2006), 'NGOs and education: some tentative considerations', *Reflecting Education*, 2(2). Available online at http://reflectingeducation.net

Giroux, H. A. (1988), *Teachers as Intellectuals: Towards a Critical Pedagogy of Learning Series*. Westport. CT: Bergin & Garvey.

—— (2001), *Theory and Resistance in Education*. Westport CT: Bergin & Garvey.

Gyoh, S. (2008), 'Structural constraints to global south actor involvement in development education in Ireland', *Policy and Practice: A Development Education Review*, 8, 41–9. Belfast: Global Education.

Harrison, D. (2005). 'Post-its on history of development education', *Development Education Journal*, 13(1), 6–8.

Held, D. and McGrew, A. (2002), 'Reconstructing world order, towards cosmopolitan social democracy', in J. Timmons Roberts and A. Bellone Hite (eds), *The Globalization and Development Reader*. Malden, MA, Oxford and Victoria, Australia: Blackwell Publishing Ltd.

Hicks, D. (1990), 'World studies 8–13: a short history, 1980–89', *Westminster Studies in Education*, 13, 61–80.

—— (2003), 'Thirty years of global education', *Education Review*, 265–75.

—— (2008), 'The global dimension; a futures perspective, and education for sustainability', in S. Ward (ed.), *A Student Guide to Education Studies*. London: Routledge.

—— and Holden, C. (eds) (2007), *Teaching the Global Dimension*. London: Routledge.

Holden, C. (2007), 'Teaching controversial issues', in D. Hicks and C. Holden (eds), *Teaching the Global Dimension*. London: Routledge.

Hyland, K. (2004), *Disciplinary Discourses*. University of Michigan.

Illeris, K. (2007), *How We Learn*. London and New York: Routledge.

Kenway, J. and Bullen, E. (2008), 'The global corporate curriculum and the young cyberflaneur as global citizen', in N. Dolby and F. Rizvi, *Youth Moves: Identities and Education in Global Perspectives*. New York: Routledge.

Leonard, A. (2004), *Impact of School Linking on Teaching and Learning about Development Issues and Global Citizenship in Secondary Geography*. BPRS, previously accessible on: www.teachernet.gov.uk/professionaldevelopment/resourcesandresearch/ bprs/search/index.cfm?report=2167

Leonard, A. (2008), 'Global school relationship: school linking and modern challenges', in D. Bourn, *Development Education: Debates and Dialogues*. London: Bedford Way Papers.

Marshall, H. (2005), 'Developing the global gaze in citizenship education: exploring the perspectives of global education NGO workers in England', *International Journal of Citizenship and Teacher Education*, 1(2), 76–92.

Martin, F. (2007), 'School linking: a controversial issue', in H. Claire and C. Holden (eds), *The Challenge of Teaching Controversial Issues*. London: Trentham, pp. 147–60.

McCollum, A. (1996), 'On the margins? An analysis of theory and practice of development education, in the 1990s', unpublished PhD thesis, Open University.

Munday, K. and Murphy, L. (2006), 'Transnational advocacy, global civil society? Emerging evidence from the field of education', in H. Lauder, P. Brown, J. A. Dillabough and A. H. Halsey (eds), *Education Globalization and Social Change*. Oxford and New York: Oxford University Press.

Osler, A. (1994), *Development Education*. London: Cassels.

Pike, G. and Selby, D. (1999), *Global Teacher, Global Learner*. Sevenoaks: Hodder & Stoughton.

Richardson, R. (1976), *Learning for Change in World Society*. London: World Studies Report.

—— (1990), *Learning for Change*. Stoke-on-Trent: Trentham.

Verulam Associates Ltd (2009), *Building Support for Development Strategy Impact of Strategy Expenditure and Activities*. London: DFID.

Chapter 17

Postcolonial and post-critical 'global citizenship education'

Vanessa Andreotti

The relatively recent rise in the popularity of global citizenship education can be interpreted as a response to a major social crisis and the perceived failures of education to address the complexities of globalization, and to fulfil the project of human rights, freedom, democracy and global justice that could be a response to the crisis itself (Todd, 2009). On the other hand, if global citizenship education is shaped by the forces and ways of thinking that have framed traditional accounts of education in the first place, we are bound to have more of the same kind of failures. Therefore, in this chapter I argue that, in order to move beyond our current limitations and to fully engage with the complexities, diversities, uncertainties and inequalities of globalization, educators need other lenses and other ways of knowing, being and relating available to them.

Hence, this chapter offers a conceptual framework for thinking about pedagogy that is grounded on what has been called the 'discursive turn' in the social sciences, which gives rise to the traditions of the 'post-', namely postmodernism, postcolonialism and postructuralism. I do not propose that educators should *adopt* any of these lenses. What I do propose is that we raise our professional game: that we lift the profile of education by increasing the levels of intellectual engagement and autonomy in the profession. My argument is that, if we are serious about engaging with globalization or the social crisis we are embedded in, we need more lenses available to make better-informed choices of what to do in the complex and diverse settings in which we work.

In the introduction of this chapter, I provide my working definitions of concepts that are central to this text. I also situate my interpretations of these terms in relation to my own background. I then present a very brief account of the 'discursive turn' in the social sciences and the 'post-' traditions. It is important to highlight the fact that this brief account is written for a pedagogical purpose and to inspire educators to engage in this debate. In this sense, it will grossly oversimplify a complex discussion that has been happening for over forty years, and this requires a commitment from the readers to take that into account. Next, I offer a brief analysis of recent literature related to education in the 'twenty-first century' and the implications of two different interpretations of 'post-' (i.e. as 'after', or as 'questioning'). In the last part of this chapter, I analyse the implications of these discussions in my current thinking and practices in education. I offer a glimpse of what a postcolonial and post-critical global citizenship education could look like.

Introduction

My definition of 'global citizenship' is one that privileges 'reciprocal and transformative encounters with strangers' (Anderson, 1998, p. 269) beyond geographical, ideological, linguistic, or other representational boundaries. These encounters are framed around radical appeals to openness, to difference and to the negotiation of meaning, rather than around normative appeals to notions of impartial reasoning or ideas of democracy, freedom, rights and justice that are presented as universal (Todd, 2009). This kind of 'critical' global citizenship is highly sceptical of normative projects grounded on views of progress, humanity or knowledge that conveniently 'forget' that other people may have very different and perfectly logical interpretations of these concepts. My working understanding of global citizenship *education* is that it should equip people to live together in collaborative, but un-coercive ways, in contemporary societies. This requires an acknowledgement that contemporary societies are complex, diverse, changing, uncertain and deeply unequal. I believe the role of global citizenship education is one of decolonization: to provide analyses of how these inequalities came to exist, and tools to negotiate a future that could be 'otherwise'. Rather than providing a normative and universal vision for a more just world, I see my role as an educator as one that enables the emergence of ethical, responsible and responsive ways of seeing, knowing and relating to others 'in context', as an ongoing project of agonistic co-authorship and co-ownership.

These definitions are grounded in a discursive orientation that is directly related to my background and cultural positioning. This positioning is shaped by a number of factors related to my history and learning journey. Important factors in this history or journey include: my upbringing in the 1970s and 1980s in a mixed-heritage family of indigenous ancestry in a transition period from dictatorship to representational democracy in Brazil; my work as a teacher in schools in Brazil in the early 1990s; the challenges of north–south relations I faced when working for the British Council and the World Bank in the late 1990s; the search for my indigenous identity and work on social justice issues with the World Social Forum; my position as a non-white, female academic from the 'Third World' working in the 'First'; and, as well, my experience as a migrant and as a mother of migrant children in England and in New Zealand.

My teaching ethic in global education is profoundly committed to addressing north–south inequalities in terms of power relations and the distribution of wealth and labour in the global context. Given my background and the challenges I face every day in relation to how I am positioned, I am particularly interested in the impact of cultural beliefs in the worth attributed to social groups and individuals and in the role of colonialism in constructing assumptions of 'Western' cultural supremacy. In this sense, I have engaged with the literature around critical pedagogy, and Marxist and feminist theories. Such theories have been extremely useful in providing valuable tools of analysis that helped me understand some of the historical aspects that have shaped current inequalities. However, they have also failed to address some of the issues I face in my professional and personal experiences today. The attention to complexity, critique and emerging forms of identity construction and relationality in the traditions of the 'post-' have provided a very useful focus that has had a substantial impact in my thinking for the past ten years. This focus is explored in more detail in the next section of this chapter.

The discursive turn and the 'post-' traditions

The 'discursive turn' in philosophy and social sciences is characterized by an emphasis on the ideological nature of language and its role in social praxis, including the social–historical construction of social realities and identities. This focus on the creation of meaning highlights that 'the relationships between words and the world are not neutral, but deeply ideological' (Weatherall, 2002, p. 147). In other words, the discursive turn proposes that the correlation between language and reality is not one where language 'describes' reality, but one where languages construct (different) realities. The implication is that 'society is, or should be, constituted by a plurality of discourses, none of which can claim overriding legitimacy in the manner that the "grand narratives" of progress and emancipation did for modernity' (Angus, 1998, para. 4).

In order to illustrate this point, I will use an example from education. Consider the definition of the role of education that I presented in my introduction: 'education should equip learners to participate together in a globalized world'. Each word in this phrase can be interpreted differently in different contexts. These interpretations will depend on shared cultural assumptions of what counts as real or ideal and what counts as knowledge. As an illustration, I will provide a double interpretation of the words: 'globalized world', 'participate' and 'equip'.

From a perspective grounded in a universalist representation of modernism, the interpretation of the phrase 'globalized world' could be based on a metaphor of an engineered machine. This would evoke ideas of order, control, stability, and predictability, based on an understanding of progress associated with consensus around a universal ideal for a harmonious future. The word 'participate' could be based on a metaphor of compliance with this definition of order and progress associated with the reproduction of received knowledge and the acceptance of existing structures and 'normal' ways of being, knowing and seeing. Following this logic, 'equipping learners' could mean inculcating values, and transmitting content and skills that would enable learners to conform to the predetermined idea of society described above.

From a different logic that could be framed as postmodern, the phrase 'globalized world' could evoke the metaphor of an organic system or of a network where the world is complex and always changing with interdependent but also autonomous parts that negotiate interchanges. This system or network cannot be engineered or controlled in its totality as it 'learns as it goes' with its multiple meanings, interpretation and interchanges 'in context'. The word 'participate' could then be related to the idea of being able to perform in such system or network: to negotiate meaning or carry out interchanges within and between different parts or communities, to generate new knowledge, to 'learn as you go along', in context. The word 'equip' could be related to creating spaces to enable learners to become competent in engaging with the complexity, uncertainty and diversity of the system.

The discursive turn in the social sciences is not necessarily represented in the second perspective, but in the ability to trace different interpretations of words to socially and historically constructed and culturally located 'meta-narratives', or stories that offer grand explanations of history or knowledge. These meta-narratives serve as the basis for how we construct meaning and how we justify our actions. Therefore, my illustration of the different meanings of the words 'globalized world', 'participate' and 'equip' perform the understanding of language that characterizes the discursive turn: language as unstable, contingent, dynamic and socially negotiated. From this perspective, language does not describe reality, as is commonly thought; it creates or constructs reality.

The implication is that when we name something we are choosing one possible story rather than a 'universal truth'. This does not mean that reality does not exist, but that our experiences of it will always be mediated by language and that language is always unstable – it cannot be pinned down – as meaning is always attributed in context, depending on other meanings that have been attributed before. Therefore, our stories of reality, our knowledges, are always situated (they are culturally bound), partial (what one sees may not be what another sees), contingent (context-dependent) and provisional (they change).

This linguistic – or discursive – insight can be framed as a response to and coming from within the modern/Enlightenment meta-narrative itself. However, it can also be traced to many of the cultures that have been deemed inferior in the (neo)colonial order, especially oral and monist traditions. In academia, the discursive turn has given rise to many interesting discussions and new academic traditions known as the 'post-' traditions.

The 'post-' traditions

The 'post-' traditions are orientations that emerge in the application of the insights of the discursive turn in different contexts. There are numerous 'post-' orientations (e.g. post-positivism, postnativism, postfeminism, post-humanism, and so on), but in this chapter I will focus on the key traditions of postmodernism, postcolonialism and poststructuralism. The 'post-' in these conceptualizations is usually defined in terms of 'interrogations' of taken-for-granted assumptions in the areas they are applied; however, some people interpret the 'post-' as 'after'. I will return to this crucial difference of interpretation in the next section.

Different authors represent postmodernism, poststructuralism and post-colonialism differently. Prasad (2005) maps the origins and influences of these three orientations in terms of four broader traditions of critique that are located within the modernity/Enlightenment meta-narrative itself: artistic and literary modernism; anti-Enlightenment discourses; critiques of colonialism; semiotics and structuralism; and Marxism and critical theories. Prasad's conceptual map of the 'post-' traditions (2005, p. 214) may help us to place the orientations in context and to identify the influences they share in common (i.e. anti-Enlightenment discourses), their specific influences, and their specific practical focus.

Postmodernism, for example, is defined by Prasad as an orientation that emerges in the area of art, literature and architecture. Therefore, its main preoccupation can be represented in the interrogation of the artistic, aesthetic or literary canon. It proposes the use of collage, appropriation and *bricolage*, among other strategies, to subvert the universalizing tendencies of the modernity/Enlightenment meta-narrative, especially concepts related to artistic genius.

Poststructuralism emerges in the field of linguistics and focuses on interrogating the role of language, especially the relationship between 'signifiers' and 'the signified', and the power/knowledge connection in the construction of subjectivities/identities that are disciplined into a 'norm' that privileges one side of a binary at the expense of another. It proposes 'deconstruction' as a strategy of resistance to destabilize these normative hierarchies, such as: heteronormativity (the idea that man/woman relationships are the norm and that same-sex relationships are abnormal), ableism (the idea that able bodies are 'normal' and other bodies are 'abnormal') or anthropocentrism (the idea that humans should be considered the centre of reality at the expense of other forms of life).

Postcolonialism emerges in the field of anti-colonial struggles and literatures. Its main preoccupation is the epistemic violence of colonialism and the interrogation of European cultural supremacy in the subjugation of different peoples and knowledges in colonial and neocolonial contexts. It borrows the poststructuralist tool of deconstruction to destabilize Western/European/ White supremacy and it appropriates tools from Marxism and critical theory to make explicit the connection between assumptions of cultural supremacy and the unequal distribution of wealth and labour in the world. It highlights the flow of capital and resources from the 'Third' to the 'First' worlds, while the flow of expert knowledge, interventions packages and rights-dispensing initiatives (based on the interests of the donor countries) take the opposite direction. One strand of postcolonial theory proposes hyper-self-reflexivity as a strategy that acknowledges everyone's complicities and investments in coercive and repressive belief systems. It does so in order to imagine a way of relating to each other that can be 'otherwise'. Other strands focus on reviving and protecting voices that have historically been subjugated by colonial violence.

In the next section of this chapter, I will explore why the traditions of the 'post-' may offer renewed lenses and analytical tools for educators to engage with critically and negotiate reforms that call for more relevance and account-ability in 'twenty-first century' educational contexts.

Why is this important for education right now?

The new thinking that has emerged in recent educational literature related to 'education in the twenty-first century' emphasizes that globalization and information technology have had a profound impact on the way knowledge, learning and identities are conceptualized in recent times (see for example, Richard and Usher,1994; Cope and Kalantzis, 2000; OECD, 2000; Gee, 2003; Hargreaves, 2003; Lankshear and Knobel, 2003; UNESCO, 2005; Gilbert, 2005; Claxton, 2008; Andreotti and de Souza, 2008a). Three arguments are central to this literature. First, that the profile of learners has changed and that teaching twenty-first century students requires practitioners to perceive knowledge, learning and education in ways that are different from the ways knowledge, learning and education were perceived in the twentieth century, when most current practitioners were brought up and trained. Second, that for this change of perception of knowledge, learning and education to hap-pen it will not be enough for practitioners to shift the ways they behave or do things, or even the ways they think – they will need to shift the ways they 'know' (i.e. an 'epistemological shift') and the ways they 'see' (i.e. an 'ontological shift'). These will also prompt a shift of perceptions and relationships that has an impact on all other areas, including the ways practitioners perceive their disciplines, themselves and their students (Gilbert, 2005; Gee, 2003; Richard and Usher, 1994; Cope and Kalantzis, 2000). Third, that these epistemological and ontological shifts involve knowledge about knowledge construction itself and the conceptual or theoretical underpinnings of current knowledge and future possibilities. (Trilling and Hood, 2001; Gilbert, 2005; Andreotti and Souza, 2008a). In summary, these arguments present a conceptualization of knowledge, learning, reality and identities as socially constructed, fluid, open to negotiation and always provisional. This epistemological shift is often conceptualized in terms of a shift from 'twentieth' to 'twenty-first century' ways of seeing knowledge, learning and identities.

However, these conceptualizations and changes that apparently borrow from the traditions presented in the last section, if driven by an economic (neoliberal) argument present a very different picture from what is proposed in section two. The neoliberal argument is still based on a teleological and seamless understanding of progress that conceptualizes the twentieth century as modernity and the twenty-first century as postmodernity. However, the prefix 'post-' in this argument is conceptualized as 'after' rather than 'interrogation', as per the orientations in the last section. This understanding of postmodernity claims that education should change to produce the right subjectivities for a new universal economic order. In other words education, which is understood solely as subordinate to the economy, should change to adapt to a new economic order. Educators are called to leave their 'twentieth-century' way of being (subjectivity), knowing (epistemology) and teaching (pedagogy) behind, as these ways are based on the needs of industrial economies that operate through a logic of production and scale that is no longer relevant in post-industrialized nations. In order to contribute to the maintenance or improvement of their country's economic advantage, educators are called to adopt 'twenty-first century' subjectivities, pedagogies and epistemologies that are more malleable in the constant shifts and uncertainty of economies of service and scope, where the focus is on the production of new products, new markets, new identities and new patterns of consumption. The new 'global world order' central to this new meta-narrative is one where 'world class excellence' in education is about the production of cosmopolitan subjects that will respond to the authority of the global market (Soudien, 2009).

The 'post-' orientations described in section two, different from the neoliberal orientation that dominates the literature, emphasize the need and provide the conceptual tools for a reconceptualization of knowledge, learning, progress and identities away from traditional universalist ideas that tend to read difference as deficit. They have the potential to help educators pluralize epistemologies and possibilities for thinking and practice and to renegotiate power relations on non-coercive grounds. In this sense, it offers educators the opportunity to shape change rather than adapt to it. From this perspective, a transformative, rather than a reformative, agenda of teacher education is required. This agenda should be grounded on a profile of educators who are critical and independent thinkers, who have a high degree of professional autonomy and who are intellectually confident about engaging with complexity, uncertainty and multiple theoretical approaches. The rationale for this professional profile is that, in educating diverse learners in contemporary societies, practitioners need to be equipped to make informed choices, negotiate with others and justify their decisions in complex educational environments where a number of different variables and perspectives need to be considered.

What does this look like 'in practice' in terms of education?

In this last section I will present examples of the implications of a postcolonial orientation to education and specifically to global citizenship education that relates to the profile of autonomous and intellectually equipped educators described in section three. This orientation would place an understanding of globalization, its effects and how to negotiate them, at the centre of the curriculum for teacher education. This orientation is based on the argument that, without a deep understanding of the complexity, interdependence and inequalities in local or global processes and contexts today, educators in all areas are poorly equipped to design and implement educational interventions that will be relevant for contemporary societies and meaningful for their learners. On the other hand, this statement also underscores the fact that, for education to be effective in contemporary educational contexts, it also needs to take account of the shifts in the profile of learners and the understanding of knowledge, learning, culture and identity happening as a result of globalization. This means that, in terms of meeting the needs of 'twenty-first learners', education needs to be designed in ways that acknowledges complexity, contingency (context-dependency), multiple and partial perspectives and unequal power relations. One way of addressing this demand is through the incorporation of critical literacy within a discursive orientation in professional education for a 'postcolonial/post-critical global citizenship education'.

From this perspective, a postcolonial or post-critical global citizenship education would equip learners to engage in dialogue, to see difference as a source of learning and not as a threat and to engage critically with local or global issues. This implies a move away from education that promotes the message 'think as I do and do as I say, there is only one right answer that can be used in all contexts', towards the message 'answers are context dependent: you will need to decide for yourself in ethical and accountable ways and take responsibility for the effects of your actions'.

This postcolonial or post-critical global citizenship education should equip learners:

- to engage with complex local or global processes and diverse perspectives: to face humanity (warts and all) and not feel overwhelmed;
- to examine the origins and implications of their own and other people's assumptions;
- to negotiate change, to transform relationships, to dream different dreams, to confront fears and to make ethical choices about their own lives and how they affect the lives of others by analysing and using power and privilege in ethical and accountable ways;
- to live with and learn from difference and conflict and to know how to prevent conflict from escalating into aggression and violence;
- to cherish life's unsolved questions and to sit comfortably in the discomfort and uncertainty that it creates;
- to establish ethical relationships across linguistic, regional, ideological and representational boundaries (i.e. to be open to the Other) and to negotiate principles and values 'in context'; and
- to enjoy their open and uncertain individual and collective learning journeys.

If teachers and students who are engaging in this kind of global citizenship education have been cognitively shaped by Enlightenment ideals and have an emotional investment in universalism (i.e. the projection of their ideas as what everyone else should believe), stability (i.e. avoidance of conflict and complexity), consensus (i.e. the elimination of difference) and fixed identities organized in hierarchical ways (e.g. us, who know, versus 'them' who don't know), then a postcolonial orientation would also suggest four types of learning. These are: learning to unlearn, learning to listen, learning to learn and learning to reach out. The definition of each type of learning is reproduced below from the project 'Through Other Eyes' (2008).

Learning to unlearn is defined as learning to perceive that what we consider 'good and ideal' is only one perspective and this perspective is related to where we come from socially, historically and culturally. It also involves perceiving that we carry a 'cultural baggage' filled with ideas and concepts produced in our contexts and that this affects who we are and what we see and that although we are different from others in our own contexts, we share much in common with them. Thus, learning to unlearn is about making the connections between social–historical processes and encounters that have shaped our contexts and cultures and the construction of our knowledges and identities. It is also about becoming aware that all social groups contain internal differences and conflicts and that culture is a dynamic and conflictual production of meaning in a specific context.

Learning to listen is defined as learning to recognize the effects and limits of our perspective, and to be receptive to new understandings of the world. It involves learning to perceive how our ability to engage with and relate to difference is affected by our cultural 'baggage' – the ideas we learn from our social groups. Hence, learning to listen is about learning to keep our perceptions constantly under scrutiny, tracing the origins and implications of our assumptions, in order to open up to different possibilities of understanding and becoming aware that our interpretations of what we hear, or see, say more about ourselves than about what is actually being said or shown. This process also involves understanding how identities are constructed in the process of interaction between self and other. This interaction between self and other occurs not only in the communities in which we belong, but also between these communities and others.

Learning to learn is defined as learning to receive new perspectives, to rearrange and expand our own and to deepen our understanding – going into the uncomfortable space of 'what we do not know we do not know'. It involves creating different possibilities of reasoning, engaging with different 'logics', trying to see through other eyes by transforming our own eyes and avoiding the tendency to want to turn the other into the self or the self into the other. Therefore, learning to learn is about learning to feel comfortable about crossing the boundaries of the comfort zone within ourselves and engaging with new concepts to rearrange our 'cultural baggage', our understandings, relationships and desires in dialogue with 'others'. This process requires the understanding that conflict is a productive component of learning and that difference is what makes dialogue and learning relevant and necessary.

Learning to reach out is defined as learning to apply this learning to our own contexts and in our relationships with others continuing to reflect and explore new ways of being, thinking, doing, knowing and relating. It involves understanding that one needs to be open to the unpredictable outcomes of mutual uncoercive learning and perceiving that in making contact with others, one exposes oneself and exposes others to difference and newness, and this often results in mutual teaching and learning (although this learning may be different for each party involved). Learning to reach out is about learning to engage, to learn and to teach with respect and accountability in the complex and uncomfortable intercultural space where identities, power and ideas are negotiated, and that the process itself is cyclical: once one has learned to reach out in one context, one is ready to start a new cycle of unlearning, listening, learning and reaching out again at another level.

(Andreotti and Souza, 2008b)

However, these kinds of learning or the principles for postcolonial/post-critical global citizenship education described above cannot be transmitted as 'values'. They can only become possible in the repertoire of educators once they are experienced as lived and living theories – lived in the sense of embodied experience and living in its provisional and contested nature. Therefore, there is a need for teacher education to enable spaces for teachers and student teachers to *experience* and to *theorize* these possibilities, rather than teach them as given and static 'content'. If we conceptualize morality as universalizable principles of normative behaviour and ethics as an ideal of relationship, a way of defining ourselves in relation to others (Andreotti and Dowling, 2004), then a postcolonial/post-critical global citizenship education needs to focus on ongoing processes. It cannot seek to produce a universal outcome based on moral grounds (i.e. normative behaviours). Its goal can be framed as the negotiation of an 'uncoercive rearrangement of desires' (Spivak, 1994) towards an ethic that cannot be considered in isolation from knowledge and power and that relates directly to the broader conditions within which human life is situated (Sedgwick, 2001).

In conclusion I have argued that, if societies have indeed been affected by globalization and technology and if many young people, especially those considered 'at risk', are choosing to disengage from schooling and from life, it is our ethical responsibility as educators to do our homework, to consider our options and to do what we can to make education more relevant for the learners and communities we work with. We cannot continue to use only the old tools (languages or concepts) that have been helpful (or unhelpful) so far. We cannot throw them away either. We need to acquire more tools and more lenses to engage with the complexity of the problem and to try out different solutions – and hence make *different* mistakes. The idea is not to find the 'right' lens or tool, but the appropriate lens or tool for specific contexts. As educators, this means we need to 'raise our game' and, instead of talking about best practices or normative projects, we need to focus on engaging with the complexity of context, on applying multiple lenses and choosing a tool or *lens in response* to a context, rather than *a priori*. Our analyses of power relations and commitment to difference, to interrogating dominant assumptions and to non-coercive education will denote whether or not we will be working from within a modernist, neo-liberal or 'discursive' orientation.

References

Anderson, A. (1998), 'Cosmopolitanism, universalism, and the divided legacies of modernity', in P. Cheah and B. Robbins (eds), *Cosmopolitics: Thinking and Feeling beyond the Nation*. Minneapolis: University of Minnesota Press.

Andreotti, V. and Dowling, E. (2004). 'WSF, ethics and pedagogy', *International Social Science Journal*, 56(182), 605–13.

Andreotti, V. and Souza, L. (2008a), 'Global learning in the knowledge society: four tools for discussion', *Journal of International Educational Research and Development Education*, 31, 7–12.

—— and Souza, L. (2008b), *Learning to Read the World through Other Eyes*. Derby: Global Education.

Angus, I. (1998), 'The materiality of expression: Harold Innis' communication theory and the discursive turn in the human sciences', *Canadian Journal of Communication*, 23(*1*), www.cjc-online.ca/index.php/ journal/article/viewArticle/1020/926 (accessed 29 November 2009).

Claxton, G. (2008), *What's the Point of School? Rediscovering the Heart of Education*. Oxford: Oneworld Publications.

Cope, B. and Kalantzis, M. (2000), *Multiliteracies: Literacy and Learning and the Design of Social Futures*. London: Routledge.

Gee, P. (2003), *What Video Games Have to Teach Us about Learning and Literacy*. New York: Palgrave Macmillan.

Gilbert, J. (2005), *Catching the Knowledge Wave? The Knowledge Society and the Future of Education*. Wellington, NZ: NZCER.

Hargreaves, A. (2003), *Teaching in the Knowledge Society*. New York: Teachers College Press.

Lankshear, C. and Knobel, M. (2003), *New Literacies: Changing Knowledge and Classroom Learning*. Buckingham: Open University Press.

OECD (2000), *Knowledge Management in Information Societies: Education and Skills*. Paris: OECD.

Prasad, P. (2005), *Crafting Qualitative Research: Working in the Postpositivist Traditions*. New York: M. E. Sharpe.

Richard, E. and Usher, R. (1994), *Postmodernity and Education*. London: Routledge.

Sedgwick, P. (2001), *Descartes to Derrida: An Introduction to European Philosophy*. Oxford: Blackwell.

Soudien, C. (2009), 'Multicultural education in South Africa', in J. Banks (ed.), *The Routledge International Companion to Multicultural Education*. New York: Routledge.

Spivak, G. (1994), 'Bonding in difference', in A. Arteaga (ed.), *An Other Tongue: Nation and Ethnicity in the Linguistic Borderlands*. Durham: Duke University Press, pp. 273–85.

Todd, S. (2009), *Toward an Imperfect Education: Facing Humanity, Rethinking Cosmopolitanism*. London: Paradigm.

Trilling, B. and Hood, P. (2001), 'Learning, technology, and education reform in the knowledge age or "we're wired, webbed, and windowed, now what?" ', in Paechter, C., Edwards, R. Harrison, R. and Twining, P (Eds) *Learning, Space and Identity*. London: Paul Chapman.

UNESCO (2005), *UNESCO World Report: Towards Knowledge Societies.* Paris: UNESCO.

Weatherall, A. (2002), *Gender, Language and Discourse.* New York: Routledge.

Chapter 18

Validation of non-formal and informal learning in Europe

Manuel Souto-Otero

This chapter is partly based on previous work by the author and a larger team of researchers for two projects on the production of European inventories on validation of non-formal and informal learning, undertaken for the European Commission in 2005 and 2008, and background research undertaken for the preparation of the 2010 Joint Report on the implementation of the *Education and Training 2010 Work Programme*. The views presented here are solely the author's and should not be taken to represent those of the European Commission or any other organization.

Introduction: Validation, vocationalism and social change

The notion of lifelong learning is based on the idea that people learn throughout all stages of life and in a variety of contexts. This means that not only learning activities occurring within formal systems of education and training, but also within non-formal and informal activities have a crucial part to play. This notion has gained strong political momentum (Bjornavold, 2000). Whereas until fairly recently the predominant themes in discourses on education related to curriculum, teaching and control questions and the focus was on educational institutions and the school (Rasmussen, 2009), since the 1970s increasing acknowledgement has been made of the importance of learning and skills acquisition outside formal education settings. The analysis of education and its institutions it is now seen as one element, indeed a central element (Souto-Otero 2007), in learning, and not as its embodiment.

Validation of non-formal and informal learning is one of the most effective instruments available to promote lifelong learning (OECD 2007) and promoting lifelong-learning is the meta-reason why European countries have adopted validation initiatives (Souto-Otero et al., 2005a). It recognizes learning that happens outside the education system in professional and personal contexts. Whereas formal learning occurs within an organized and structured context, is designed as learning and links to a recognized qualification or award (OECD 2007), non-formal learning is embedded in planned activities not explicitly designed as learning but containing an important learning element. Informal learning results from daily life activities related to work, family or leisure. While formal and non-formal learning are intentional from the student's perspective, informal learning often is not (Colardyn and Bjornavold, 2004). Validation, on the other hand, refers to the process of identifying, assessing and recognizing a range of skills and competences which people develop through their lives and in different contexts (European Commission, 2001). It can take place in different contexts, including the public sector, but also the private and third sector (Souto-Otero et al., 2008a; Dyson and Keating, 2005).

Validation has been receiving increasing attention in the political agenda of European countries in recent years, as reflected in its important place within the so-called Lisbon Agenda that has driven much European policy since 2000, and the Education 2010 Work Programme of the European Commission (Souto-Otero et al., 2008b). Economically, new pressures from global competition and internal restructuring of European economies have resulted in more flexible labour markets and greater labour mobility. In this context, validation can help to promote staff development, ensure that companies are aware of the full set of competences of their employees and their training needs, and facilitate transitions between jobs and sectors. Such a need is accentuated in periods of strong technological change, as education systems can be slow in responding to them or may simply not take them into account in their provision. It also helps to address certain labour shortages, in particular in those jobs where compulsory qualifications are required to undertake certain tasks or roles, as so often happens, for instance, in the care and health sectors. For countries, validation can also be a cost-effective way to increase the formal qualifications of their population by recognizing the knowledge, skills and competences that are already developed (Fejes and Anderson, 2009). Although there are relatively few longitudinal studies on the effects of validation at the individual level, it has been suggested that it can lead to changes in job roles, improved chances of career progression (Duvekot et al., 2003), educational chances, and increased interest in further education and self-esteem (Smith and Clayton, 2009).

Validation is also seen as having an important social dimension, because of its potential to alleviate marginalization and promote equality (Souto-Oteroet al., 2008a; Misko et al., 2007; Victorian Qualifications Authority, 2004). It is expected to facilitate the re-integration in the labour market of disadvantaged groups such as immigrants whose academic credentials are not recognized in their country of destination, and unemployed people and older workers who have acquired many competences in the workplace, through training or personal activities, that they cannot certify or who simply may be unaware of the whole set of competences they have acquired. It is also used as a means to provide individuals, in particular school-leavers, with a 'second chance' to reach their full learning potential. As such, in an increasing number of countries and within the requirements set by the Bologna Process, validation is being employed to open up new routes of access to higher education, even though progress has been slower than desired (Rauhvargers et al., 2009). Validation can stimulate the creation of personalized study pathways and the take-up of educational opportunities by a wider range of non-traditional learners. It can do this by providing direct ways for them to gain formal qualifications or provide 'door openers' to courses which, while avoiding undue repetition, lead to the achievement of knowledge, skills and competences an individual already has, in order to progress to a further level of learning (Souto-Otero et al., 2008a). Harris (2006) thus contends that validation provides an opportunity to 'break down' often discriminatory barriers to access and routes to progress; to advantage the disadvantaged and the excluded; and to challenge the exclusive practices of formal institutions. In spite of this potential, there is also evidence that engagement with validation is often lower for those in disadvantaged groups (Bateman and Knight, 2003; Cameron, 2004). In the relationship between validation and social change there is the risk that those with higher qualification levels are also those who benefit more from validation, thus accentuating qualification inequalities. This issue has been addressed in a number of countries by setting up validation initiatives, targeting those with low levels of qualifications (Souto-Otero et al., 2005b; 2008a). Thus, Pouget and Osborne (2004) have argued that validation can be seen as undoubtedly entrenched in a Western culture preoccupied with individual choice and individual freedom. These conceptions can be considered as an ethnocentric phenomenon, encapsulated in a Western post-capitalist culture.

Economic factors have indeed often been taken as the primary driver for validation, in association with a wider move of education systems towards a 'new vocationalism' that conceives education as an engine for economic regeneration and advocates strong links between education and the world of work. This has led to an emphasis on the vocational relevance of education, which in turn has been an important factor in leading to the emergence of competence-based qualifications in several countries, including the UK. From this perspective, the emergence of the notion of competence is attributed to a general trend towards greater penetration of economic imperatives in education. Yet, as Williams and Raggatt (1998) highlight in their study of the UK, the emergent thinking about work-based learning, competence-based education and validation during the 1960s and 1970s was, in contrast to the above interpretation, chiefly influenced by the radical critique of the formal education system in liberal democracies led by Illich (1971) and Freire (1972), among others. They depicted education systems as serving Western capitalism through the propagation of practices that reproduced economic and labour market inequalities. 'Progressive' educationalists thereby became interested in the notions of work-based learning, experiential learning and the accreditation of prior learning rather than teaching and course curricula, since those put the individual and what they knew at their core, regardless of where and how they had acquired their knowledge, and sought to replace the educational bureaucracies of the 'establishment' that only reproduced inequality. Validation could thus be linked to a wider revolution within, or perhaps operating in the margins of, skills production systems.

The European Union itself has driven much of the process towards the establishment of validation systems (Souto-Otero et al., 2008b). Member states, on the other hand, have developed a wide range of validation initiatives: only in the last two years, at least twelve member states (Belgium, Czech Republic, Denmark, Estonia, Italy, Latvia, Lithuania, Malta, Portugal, Slovenia, Spain and Sweden) have approved new legislation or developed delivery structures in this area. Validation is embedded within and has supported the development of qualifications frameworks and learning outcomes-based approaches to education (Souto-Otero et al., 2008b, Bjornavold and Coles, 2007). What glues these developments together is the notion that knowledge, skills and competences are the crucial aspects, rather than the context in which they have been acquired.

Such an idea has important implications in terms of social change, because it goes to the core of an established conception of formal education systems as having a monopoly on legitimate generation and recognition of learning. Given the strong link, on the whole, between performance in the formal education system and social background (Breen, 2004) validation could be expected to contribute to changing the role of education in the relationship between social origins and destination by enabling alternative pathways to the achievement of educational qualifications. On the other hand, validation can also recognize learning that is socially important but has not found its place in the education system. Validation can use similar standards to those employed in formal education and training and lead to the award of a certificate or diploma, or to a part-award by waiving some credits; it can provide access to a course, but it can also be independent from the offer provided in formal education systems and use other standards. One of the dilemmas facing validation is that, while the practices using divergent assessment and focusing on individuals' knowledge, skills and competences in an unprejudiced manner, unrelated to predefined standards, are those with the greatest potential to induce social change – by playing outside the norms defined by the education system (Torrance and Pryor, 1998) – they may also be less beneficial for the integration of disadvantaged groups. This will be the case unless wider changes towards a greater acceptance of a plurality of legitimate forms, types and combinations of knowledge, skills and competences are accepted in society and the world of work. In any case, the bulk of methodologies developed at national levels during the last two decades in Europe have been closely integrated into formal education and training systems, making it possible to earn full or partial credit or access to courses through the recognition of informal and non-formal learning (Souto-Otero et al., 2005c).

To an important extent, although by no means exclusively, the effects of validation practices on disadvantaged groups depends on the appropriateness of the range of methodologies used for validation and the existence of national validation systems that they can access, and are recognized as legitimate by stakeholders in the labour market and educational institutions. Those are the topics covered in the remainder of this chapter. The next section provides an overview of validation methodologies, its types, features and usage. Section three presents my conclusions. Throughout, the chapter illustrates how alternative validation methodologies and system design affect the potential of validation to bring about social change.

Methodologies for the validation of non-formal and informal learning: types, features and usage

Non-formal and informal learning are much more diverse, less structured, and their outcomes much less defined, than those of formal learning. The diversity and complexity of informal and non-formal learning has to be appropriately reflected by the methodologies used to validate them. The technical complexities to ensure the reliability and validity of validation methods are many, and the highly context-, even person-specific character of validation makes 'one size fits all' approaches unsatisfactory. These challenges are aggravated by the scepticism of stakeholders such as educational institutions, which makes validation methods, sometimes unfairly, more subject to scrutiny and criticism than more established forms used to assess formally acquired knowledge, skills or competences. Although there is emerging evidence that when validation is used to provide access to or partial exemption from courses, students that have made use of validation seem to perform at least as well as those who do not (Van Kleef, 2007; Arscott et al., 2007; Aarts et al., 1999), the bottom line is that validation initiatives need to be technically sound for their outcomes to obtain a satisfactory 'currency' in the labour market and educational sectors.

The main methods to extract evidence for the validation of non-formal and informal learning identified by recent international research include tests and examinations, observations, evidence collected from work, simulations and declarative methods – all of which are covered in this section. Evidence extracted through these methods needs to be documented during the validation process. This documentation can take the form of a simple, written self-report on competences developed – say, in the context of the use of a declarative method, an examination paper, a recorded conversation, a photograph of a piece of sculpture, painting or other output produced, or a video recording of a simulation, for example. But documentation can also take more complex forms such as portfolios that include evidence extracted and documented through a variety of methods, and which I discuss in this section.

Extracting evidence

This section covers different methodologies to extract evidence for validation purposes, starting with tests and examinations, to which we devote greater attention than to other methodologies given their wide usage, observations, evidence collected from work, simulations and declarative methods.

The identification and validation of informal and non-formal learning through or with the help of examinations or tests is often linked to those offered in the formal system.

Examinations and tests can be either written or oral, for instance in the form of interviews or presentations. Tests and examinations are very often used for validation purposes. In Germany, Austria, Liechtenstein, Luxembourg and Lithuania, for instance, proof of several years' work experience in a particular occupation normally grants access to the final examination of the relevant occupation, even if the individual has not been formally enrolled in the relevant training programme. There are, however, variations on this system practised in other European countries. In Norway, for instance, adults have by law the right to have their knowledge and skills documented *at all levels* within the public education system, independently of how these competencies were acquired. This is in addition to the right to access to vocational training examinations based on work experience. A large number of higher education institutions in Europe have also set up systems for validating competences acquired through such methods (Leathwood, 2005).

Tests and examinations are generally accepted as reliable and objective methods to extract evidence for the validation of an individual's knowledge or competences. This is in spite of the existence of strong limitations in these approaches (Price, 2005) and well-documented difficulties in establishing discipline-based benchmarks at national level (Yorke, 2002) and the local level, as different markers often judge the same work differently unless efforts are made to seek shared subjectivity (Wright, 1996). This was achieved in the past through small and closed academic communities that were able to establish common standards (Holroyd, 2000), but the system is now under threat for a variety of reasons, including fragmentation of programmes of study, increased interdisciplinary work and larger staff workloads. The processes of assessing learning from experience and other non-formal and informal learning, moreover, tend to conform to other assessment processes than those that educational institutions have in place, that were originally devised for the assessment of learning gained through study in an educational context (Peters, 2005). For individuals accessing validation as a 'second chance', in particular in those cases when they have dropped out of formal education earlier in life, tests and examinations may represent a barrier to access as they are associated with previous negative experiences of education and training.

Observations consist of the extraction of evidence of competences from individuals while they are performing everyday tasks at work, which are judged by a third party. Examples of observations may often be found in the vocational education and training sector, which tends to use competence-based approaches for the development of standards that make it easier to apply observations. Observation is often a key element in the validation methods developed and applied in the private sector. In the wood-processing sector in Finland, for instance, it is possible to award nationally recognized qualifications to employees with no formal qualifications, on the basis of practical tests carried out at the workplace, which are assessed by an external assessor, employer and employee representatives (Souto-Otero et al., 2008a).

Evidences from work can also be used as a validation method, whereby a candidate collects physical or intellectual evidence of learning outcomes from work situations, voluntary activities, family or other settings (Colardyn and Bjornavold, 2004). This evidence then forms the basis of validation of competences by a third party. Evidences from work can also include written work, such as essays or transcript reviews.

In simulation methodologies, individuals are placed in a situation that fulfils all the criteria of a real-life scenario in order to have their competencies assessed. They are less used than most of the other methods described in this section (see Souto-Otero et al., 2005a), yet some examples are well known, for instance the assessment of the competences of aircraft pilots. Simulation requires a large amount of studies and job analysis to be prepared properly and often involves judgement by a third party. The major difficulty is to ensure that the job analyses needed before a simulation can actually be valid and reliable (Colardyn and Bjornavold, 2004).

Declarative methods are based on the individual's own identification and recording of competences against given criteria or none at all, normally signed by a third party, in order to verify the self-assessment. This method is often a simple recording process because the purpose is purely the *identification* of skills gained through non-formal and informal learning. It tends to be a bottom-up approach and formative in nature, as opposed to the top-down and summative character often predominating in tests and examinations, and is more accessible and less threatening to groups at a distance from formal education and training. Since this method is characterized by the individual's recording of experiences, though some external checks tend to be built into the methods, it is often considered less reliable than other systems described here. In reality, the validity and reliability of this method depends on clear guidelines or standards for the individual to use, on the provision of support or 'mentoring' during the preparation phase, and on the individual's ability to provide a realistic assessment of their own competences.

Documenting evidence

Portfolios are one of the most complex and used methods to document evidence for validation purposes. Portfolios aim to overcome the risk of subjectivity by introducing a mix of instruments to extract evidence on individuals' competences and can incorporate assessments by third parties. Moreover, they provide the audience with comprehensive insights into the achievements and successes of the learner (Kimeldorf, 1997). Portfolios have been widely taken up for validation in public service professions such as teachers and trainers, or more generally as in the French VAE (Validation des Acquis de l'Experience) system, but they are also intensively used in a bottom-up way by private and voluntary sector organizations (Souto-Otero et al., 2005a). Portfolios can be developed to help disadvantaged people into social inclusion or into employment by taking into account the specific characteristics of these groups. For instance, the learning portfolio developed by the Community Women's Education Initiative in Ireland that targets traveller women uses portfolios that combine non-written techniques such as collages and photography, as well as interviews with individual traveller women to explore the value of story-telling and learning in the traveller culture.

The portfolio method tends to be process-orientated. There is much evidence that the selection process included in portfolio building promotes self-assessment and focuses students' attention to quality criteria (Dysthe and Engelsen, 2004). Some countries that provide national guidelines for validation, rather than prescribe the methods, recommend a stage in the validation process which involves some form of assessment by a third party (e.g. the jury procedure in France) in order to ensure greater validity and reliability of portfolios. Still, the introduction of third party assessment does not solve all problems. It is important that quality assurance processes are in place to ensure the consistency and transparency of the third party assessment and secure equality and fairness in the validation process for all candidates. One recent trend is the use of digital portfolios. While interesting and essentially building on the tradition of paper-based portfolios (Davies and Willis, 2001), digital portfolios are still at risk of the technological novelty of the product overshadowing its purpose and that the learning to use the technology itself could subsume the learning opportunities of portfolio construction, therefore offsetting to some extent the advantages that such portfolios could offer. These include the possibility of combining text, audio, graphic and video-based representations of information, and the greater capacity to accumulate data (Woodward and Nanlohy, 2004; Piper, 2000). Technology should support, rather than drive, portfolio development.

However, the most serious risk in the preparation of portfolios is the lack of focus that can occur when applicants prepare them alone or with a little mediation from one tutor. One practice that counters this possible limitation is gathering of groups of claimants together specifically for the purposes of sharing experiences and learning from each other, thus enabling all participants to proceed with greater assurance in preparing their portfolio for validation (Webb, 2007). This is particularly important in the case of disadvantaged groups, which have little experience in the presentation of their skills and frequently lack confidence in their skills. Such sessions can then be complemented with individual tutorials.

Conclusions

This chapter has reviewed methodologies for the validation of non-formal and informal learning in Europe. Stakeholders around Europe are developing and applying a variety of methods to validate learning, following concerns with the needs of the knowledge society for a qualified workforce and inclusion into paid work. The chapter has also outlined arguments through which validation can be linked to social change, one of its stated purposes, in particular by contributing to breaking down some of the long-standing barriers built into formal education systems. The chapter has shown that different methods and system development and design have significant consequences on the effects that validation can be expected to have on disadvantaged groups. While validation can provide an important tool for social change, there is a risk that it can contribute to an accentuation of existing inequalities. The validation of informal and non-formal learning cannot be reduced to a question of methodological quality. There is also a political and institutional aspect, related to the support provided to validation by different stakeholders and how it is designed to favour particular groups in society, that will play a fundamental role in the contribution it has to make to social reform in the future.

References
Aarts, S., Blower, D., Burke, C. R., Howell, B., Howorth, C. E., Lamarre, G. H. and Van Kleeb, J. (1999), *A Slice of the Iceberg: Cross-Canada Study of Prior Learning Assessment and Recognition*. Canadian Associations for Prior Learning Assessment and Recognition. Belleville, ON.
Arscott, J., Crowther, I., Young, M. and Ungarian, L. (2007), *Producing Results in Prior Learning: A Report from the Gateways Project*, http://gateways.athabascau.ca/media/FINALreport.pdf (accessed 23 July 2009).

Bateman, A. and Knight, B. (2003), *Giving Credit: A Review of RPL and Credit Transfer in the Vocational Education and Training Sector, 1995 to 2001*. Adelaide: NCVER.

Bjornavold, J. (2000), *Making Learning Visible*. Luxembourg: CEDEFOP.

—— and Coles, M. (2007), 'Governing education and training; the case of qualifications frameworks', *European Journal of Vocational Training*, 42/3, 203–35.

Breen, R. (ed.) (2004), *Social Mobility in Europe*. Oxford: Oxford University Press.

Cameron, R. (2004), *Recognition of Prior Learning (RPL) in 2004: A Snapshot*, www.ala.asn.au/ research/2004-11-CameronRPL.pdf (accessed 31 August 2009).

Colardyn, D. and Bjornavold, J. (2004), 'Validation of formal, non-formal and informal learning: policy and practices in EU member states', *European Journal of Education*, 39(1), 69–89.

Davies, M. and Willis, E. (2001), 'Through the looking glass . . . preservice professional portfolios', *Teacher Educator*, 37(1), 7–31.

Duvekot, R., Kaemingk, E., Klarus, R. (2003), 'People learn anyway! The use of VPL on the Dutch labour market', *Opleiding & Ontwikkeling*, 11, 10–15.

Dyson, C. and Keating, J. (2005), *The Recognition of Prior Learning: Practices in the Workplace*. Report to the International Labour Office. Geneva: ILO.

Dysthe, Olga and Engelsen, K. S. (2004), 'Portfolios and assessment in teacher education in Norway: a theory-based discussion of different models in two sites', *Assessment & Evaluation in Higher Education*, 29(2), 239– 58.

European Commission (2001), *Making a European Area of Lifelong Learning a Reality*. Brussels: European Commission.

—— (2008), *Draft 2008 Joint Progress Report of the Council and the Commission on the Implementation of the 'Education & Training 2010 Work Programme'*. Brussels: European Commission.

Fejes, A. and Anderson, P. (2009), 'Recognising prior learning: understanding the relations amongst experience, learning and recognition from a constructivist perspective', *Vocations and Learning*, 2, 37–55.

Freire, P. (1972), *Pedagogy of the Oppressed*. London: Sheed & Wood.

Illich, I. (1971), *Deschooling Society*. London: Calder & Boyars.

Harris, J. (2006), 'Introduction and overview of chapters', in P. Andersson and J. Harris (eds), *Re-theorising the Recognition of Prior Learning*. Leicester: National Institute of Adult Continuing Education.

Holroyd, C. (2000), 'Are assessors professional? Student assessment and the professionalism of academics', *Active Learning in Higher Education*, 1(1), 28–44.

Kimeldorf, M. (1997), *Portfolio Power: The New Way to Showcase All Your Job Skills and Experience*. Princeton, NJ: Peterson's Publishing Group.

Leathwood, C. (2005), 'Assessment policy and practice in higher education: purpose, standards and equity', *Assessment and Evaluation in Higher Education*, 30(3), 307–24.

Misko, J., Beddie, F. and Smith, L. (2007), *The Recognition of Non-formal and Informal Learning in Australia: Country Background Report Prepared for the OECD Activity on Recognition of Non-formal and Informal Learning*. Canberra: Department of Education, Science and Training.

OECD (2007), *Education and Training Policy, Qualifications Systems: Bridges to Lifelong Learning*. Paris: OECD.

Peters, H. (2005), 'Contested discourses: assessing the outcomes of learning from experience for the award of credit in higher education', *Assessment and Evaluation in Higher Education*, 30(3), 273–85.

Piper, C. (2000), 'Electronic portfolios in teacher education reading methods courses', AACE SITE2000, www.chapman.edu/soe/faculty/ piper/aera.htm (accessed 5 March 2009).

Pouget, M. and Osborne, M. (2004), 'Accreditation or validation of prior experiental learning: knowledge and saviors in France – a different perspective', *Studies in Continuing Education*, 26, 45–65.

Price, M. (2005), 'Assessment standards: the role of communities of practice and the scholarship assessment', *Assessment and Evaluation in Higher Education*, 3(3), 215–30.

Rasmussen, P. (2009), 'Lifelong learning as a social need and policy discourse', in R. Dale and S. Robertson (eds), *Globalisation & Europeanisation in Education*. Oxford: Symposium Books, pp. 85–101.

Rauhvargers, A., Deane, C. and Pauwels, W. (2009), *Bologna Process Stocktaking Report*. Leuven: BFUG.

Smith, L. and Clayton, B. (2009), *Recognising Non-formal and Informal Learning: Participant Thoughts and Perspectives*. Adelaide: NCVER.

Souto-Otero, M. (2007), 'Access to post-compulsory education and training: lessons from economics, sociology and political science and remaining research gaps', *Comparative Education*, 43(4), 571–86.

——, McCoshan, A. and Junge, K. (2005a), *European Inventory on Validation of Non-formal and Informal Learning*. Final Report to the European Commission. Birmingham: ECOTEC Research and Consulting, pp. 13–24.

——, McCoshan, A., Junge, K. and Winter, J. (2005b), 'Overview of findings: needs and initiatives', in Souto-Otero et al., *European Inventory on Validation of Non-formal and Informal Learning*.

——, McCoshan, A. and Junge, K. (2005c), 'Conclusions: Validation approaches in Europe', in Souto-Otero et al., *European Inventory on Validation of Non-formal and Informal Learning*.

——, Nevala, A.M. and Hawley, J. (2008a), *European Inventory on Validation of Non-formal and Informal Learning: 2008 Update*. Birmingham: ECOTEC Research and Consulting.

——, Fleckenstein, T. and Dacombe, R. (2008b), 'Filling in the gaps: European governance, the open method of coordination and the European Commission', *Journal of Education Policy*, 23(3), 231–49.

Torrance, H. and Pryor, J. (1998), *Investigating Formative Assessment*. Buckingham: Open University Press.

Van Kleef, J. (2007), 'Strengthening PLAR: integrating theory and practice in post-secondary education', *Journal of Applied Research*, 1(2), 1–22.

Victorian Qualifications Authority (2004), *Report on the Recognition of Informal Learning*. Melbourne, AUS: Victorian Qualifications Authority.

Webb, E. (2007), 'Recognition and validation of non-formal and informal learning for VET teachers and trainers in the EU member states', CEDEFOP Panorama Series 147. Luxembourg: Office for Official Publications of the European Commission.

Williams, S. and Raggatt, P. (1998), 'Contextualising public policy in vocational education and training: the origins of competence-based vocational qualifications in the UK', *Journal of Education and Work*, 11(3), 275–92.

Woodward, H. and Nanlohy, P. (2004), 'Digital portfolios: fact or fashion?', *Assessment and Evaluation in Higher Education*, 29(2), 227–38.

Wright, P. (1996), 'Mass higher education and the search for standards: reflections on some issues emerging from the graduate standards programme', *Higher Education Quarterly*, 50(1), 75–81.

Yorke, M. (2002), 'Subject benchmarking and the assessment of student learning', *Quality Assurance in Education*, 10(3), 155–71.

Chapter 19

Transnational co-operation in learning support for disabled learners

Val Chapman

Introduction

This chapter describes the transnational co-operation within a European Union (EU)-funded project, QATRAIN2 (Quality Assurance and Accessible Training 2), led by the Centre for Inclusive Learning Support (CILS) at the University of Worcester, with partners in Bulgaria, Greece, Romania and Turkey. The methodological issues concerning transnational co-operation are discussed, including differences and similarities between the partner countries, the projects' impact and the value added from the partnerships.

Background

European policy explicitly recognizes the disadvantages faced by disabled people and, in particular, the discrimination they can experience in finding employment at a level commensurate with their abilities. The European Social Inclusion Report (2001) highlighted the fact that disabled people were more likely to be unemployed (including long-term unemployed), less likely to achieve medium or higher education qualifications, and more likely to be trapped in poverty.

With the passing of the Special Educational Needs and Disability Act (SENDA, 2001, also known as the Disability Discrimination Act Part IV), all education providers in the UK became liable for all aspects of their provision under the Act, including learning, teaching and assessment – a powerful catalyst for change. Both sets of legislation were strongly informed by the social model of disability, though there is variability both within the UK and across Europe in relation to the interpretation of this model. In the UK, there is a groundswell of support (particularly in HE) for use of the terminology 'disabled people' rather than 'people with disabilities' as this emphasizes the point that, while the 'ownership' of the impairment is located within the individual, the disabling factors are externally imposed. This text adopts the terminology, though recognizes that 'people with disabilities' may be the preferred terminology within other countries or local cultures.

QATRAIN2 was a Transfer of Innovation project building on the work of an earlier project, QATRAIN2 (Quality Assurance and Training), funded under the Life Long Learning (LLL) Leonardo da Vinci (LdV) programme, 2005/7. The project addressed one of the key aims of the LLL's Horizontal policy 'to help promote their [learners with special needs] integration into mainstream education and training to combat discrimination based on disability' (2007). This policy recognized the disadvantage experienced by disabled people in employment and vocational education and training (VET) in all European states, with higher unemployment, lower pay, lower participation in VET and lower qualifications (Weiler, 2004; Commission of the European Communities, 2005).

Full accessibility for disabled people to mainstream VET requires adjustments in teaching, learning and assessment. Teachers and trainers are best positioned to create and implement these; however, it was noted that developing strategies to teach disabled people in mainstream classes was not yet a feature of teacher training in the partner countries.

QATRAIN2 aimed to enable teachers and trainers to help the integration of disabled people into mainstream VET by removing unintentional barriers to their entry and successful participation. The project also aimed to inform and influence staff concerned with the development of curricula and the provision of VET programmes since, in effect, these individuals constitute the gatekeepers who control the access of disabled people to such programmes. It was anticipated that improvements resulting from engagement with the project's resource would open up a wider range of opportunities to disabled people and help them to gain qualifications that broadened their career options and reduce discrimination against them in employment.

More specifically, the QATRAIN2 project aimed to transfer a proven online resource, Strategies for Creating Inclusive Programmes of Study (SCIPS), from the UK to other EU partners; this included the modification of resources, originally developed for tertiary education, into a form appropriate for users in each of the partner countries. In meeting this aim, the project would contribute to the LLL targets of improving the participation rate of disabled people in VET and their integration into mainstream provision, so helping them achieve learning outcomes and gain qualifications that would enhance their ability to compete in the job market.

The SCIPS model, developed first in the UK (Chapman, 2006; Chapman and Carlisle, 2006), and extended to Poland, Greece, France and Bulgaria through the original QATRAIN2 project, enables mainstream teachers/trainers to make their programmes more accessible. Full accessibility for disabled people to mainstream VET requires adjustments in teaching, learning and assessment. Conventional methods often disadvantage or exclude disabled people; small changes to practice can create substantial opportunities for disabled people (without any threat to standards) and the EU Directive requires such adjustments wherever practical.

Ample evidence exists to show that the web-based resource has been highly successful in the sector, as indicated by its high usage. SCIPS, Google page ranked 6/10, averages over one million requests for pages per annum and is used 24/7 throughout the year. Of those who visit SCIPS via Google, 78 per cent bookmark the site. It is one of thirty equality and diversity resources featured in the Diversity Resources Project Report published by the Leadership Foundation for Higher Education (Bebbington, 2006, pp. 72–3), and was endorsed by Subject Centres in the Higher Education Academy (HEA) publication, *Embedding Success: Enhancing the Learning Experience for Disabled Students* (Dickinson, 2006, pp. 51–3). The site was further endorsed through the UK Department for Children, Schools and Families' (DCSF) further addition of forty pages from SCIPS to their Inclusion website (http://inclusion. ngfl.gov.uk), leading to the resource becoming more widely used by teachers in secondary education.

The SCIPS resource can be browsed using combinations of the key terms listed under 'subject', 'disability' or 'key skill'. Though targeted initially at academic staff involved in curriculum design, SCIPS has wider uses. The website can be accessed by staff wishing to discover potentially problematic aspects of their curricula, those wishing to understand how best to support students with particular impairments, and to help users to develop an understanding of the principles of inclusive teaching, learning and assessment.

Methodology

The project's partnership included universities, training providers, NGOs and Small/Medium Enterprises (SME). All of the partners had experience of engaging in EU projects, some had substantial expertise in working with disabled learners, and all shared a commitment to effect change and to create a more inclusive society.

During the lifetime of the project, the partners communicated using telephone, email, Skype, and face to face communication during transnational meetings. The language of communication between partners was English (though it quickly became apparent that using the same words did not necessarily mean sharing the same meaning). Although communicating face to face yielded the fewest opportunities for misunderstanding or confusion, limited resources and workload commitments of all partners meant that most communication took place through email. Access to the project's documentation and/ or work in progress was successfully provided through shared access to a dedicated site within the communications platform called ATutor (www.atutor.ca).

In order to enable effective communication within the partnership, and to ensure that the proposed resources met the needs of the local contexts, research was carried out in the initial stages of the project to establish the similarities and differences between the partner countries in terms of legislative drivers, and definitions of disability and of VET. Such information was vital in informing the cultural adaptation of the resource to best meet the needs of the local context as well as ensuring the maximum benefit to the targeted end users.

Research was also conducted into the most commonly used teaching approaches/ methodologies used in VET in each country, and respondents were also asked about any adaptations to practice which had been made to accommodate disabled students. A questionnaire (administered face –to face, online and by telephone) was designed centrally, and translated by all partners. The results were analysed using SPSS (Statistical Package for Social Sciences) and compiled in a report which was made available on the project website. The research results were subsequently used to create a conceptual framework underpinning the structure of the new web resource, and a glossary of terms was also compiled to ensure that the language used in each national version of the web resource was appropriate to local users. In addition, the partners identified resources for an online toolkit.

During the second year of the project, following the development of its technical infrastructure, all partners translated the documents for the web resource and toolkit, including information about different disabilities, learning categories, adaptations to teaching practices and case studies, as well as a hard copy promotional guide; these were also culturally adapted where necessary.

Following a period of testing and review by all partners with key stakeholders at national level (over 150 users across the partnership in each country), the web resource was modified and refined to make it more user-friendly and even more appropriate to the needs of the end users. Once the resource's complete content had been translated and uploaded to each national site, the materials were culturally adapted through, for example, the inclusion of local case studies of good practice, references and links to national legislation and to other resources unique to the individual country.

For the duration of the project the partnership maintained rigorous quality assurance procedures. The lead partner engaged in regular monitoring of other partners who reported on their project and dissemination activities and finances on a quarterly basis. This was supplemented by systematic internal and external evaluation. An external evaluator was appointed both as critical friend and independent observer. Each partner appointed a national advisory group, comprised of key stakeholders, end users, gatekeepers and disabled students, who met on five occasions during the project. In addition to the five international partnership (project team members) meetings held, one each in the UK, Bulgaria, Turkey and Greece, a bilateral meeting was held in Romania and a final joint project dissemination conference held in Brussels at the project's end.

Outcomes and discussion

The research revealed that substantial differences existed between the partners' contexts despite the apparent unifying demands of the EU legislation. In some partners' countries, disability was still highly stigmatized and some partners reported that, despite the legislation, in more rural communities families of disabled people still felt embarrassed or ashamed, often keeping the individual hidden at home out of sight. Generally, the definitions of disability were similar in each partner country. They described a disabled person as someone with a physical or mental impairment which has a considerable effect on their ability to conduct day-to-day activities. However, clear differences were also reported; for example, some partner countries continue to use the term 'handicapped', a term regarded as unacceptable in the UK but which, due to its English origins, holds no implicit associated negative connotation in those countries. In Turkey the definition of 'disability' includes people who are gifted (in sport, leadership, entrepreneurialism and music). According to the Greek partner, there did not appear to be a clear, unified definition of the term 'disability'; the educational system ascribes to the social model of disability, while other departments, such as the Social Affairs Department, adopt the medical model and describes disabled people as those with physical, psychological or mental impairments who are unable to undertake normal activities as ascertained by medical professionals. Such differences of taxonomy made accessing sensible comparative data very difficult.

While there was significant commonality between partner countries in defining VET, there were sufficient differences to require the partnership to adopt a clear definition specific to the needs of the project. For the purposes of the project, a definition for VET was agreed upon as 'any form of initial education or training and apprenticeship which contributes to the achievement of a vocational qualification recognized by the competent authorities in each partner country and that normally leads to employability'. VET students were regarded as those who had completed compulsory education and were under 25 years of age.

The major outcome of the project was the production of a web-based resource that helps teachers of VET to better meet the needs of disabled learners. The new national web resource was built around the notion of 'learning outcomes'. This was an extremely important element of the project's approach to meeting the requirements of disabled learners. Traditional approaches, which were still mainly the norm in Bulgaria, Romania, Turkey and Greece, are based upon syllabus content rather than being learner centred, and these standardized modes of delivery can inhibit the development of adaptations to practice for disabled students. If a VET programme is stated in terms of learning outcomes, it directly expresses those common results that all learners are expected to accomplish, whether they are disabled or not – the fixed, essential point is the achievement of the learning outcome. With such an approach it becomes easier to develop, and evaluate, alternative means that may enable disabled people to complete the essential elements of the programme, whatever their background, ethnicity, social status, nationality or disability.

In attempting to help teachers and trainers of VET make their curricula and teaching more accessible for disabled learners, the project team noted that these individuals play a dual role in any VET reform (European Training Foundation (ETF), 2006). It was key to acknowledge that teachers and trainers are professionals in their pedagogical roles, and that they are also stakeholders in the system itself, '. . . there is a growing recognition that failure to fully engage teachers and trainers as active participants in the reform process is one of the main reasons why many educational reforms the world over have gone wrong in the past' (ETF, op. cit., p. 13) All partners were committed to the close involvement of end users in the project's operation and development of outputs. Key stakeholders and end users were involved as members of National Advisory/Steering Groups and, as far as possible, in local project teams. The testing and review procedures provided regular user-input into the production and evaluation of the main project outputs. The provision of a template on each site that allows ongoing feedback from users through their uploading examples of good practice, tips for trainers, useful websites/resources, and additional case studies will ensure that the sites become increasingly tailored to the national contexts over time.

Results of the early testing and review of the resource indicated that users in all partner countries rated it as effective and helpful, allowing access to information on conditions/impairments which may cause a barrier for learning. Navigation was regarded as very straightforward, self-explanatory and easy to follow, and users appreciated the ability to search the site without the need for any prior specialist knowledge. In Romania, a representative of the Ministry of Education, recognizing the lack of knowledge, competences and skills of specialists who work with disabled people, promised to promote the completed QATRAIN2 resource; while at a project's second joint dissemination event in Turkey, 2008, a Ministry of Education representative declared that their web resource was the most accessible he had yet seen in his country.

At a later multi-EU project joint dissemination event held in Brussels, 2009, a special needs teacher from Bulgaria who works with children and young people with learning disabilities and speech/language impairments, formerly the headmistress of a school specifically for children and young people with learning disabilities, reported on her involvement within the project as a tester of the resource. She praised the web resource:

> which is extremely useful for anyone working in the field of special education. We are happy in the knowledge that we were probably among the first to whom the materials and information were presented. The material enabled us to better meet the children and young people's needs regarding their education and personal development. We now feel better prepared and effective when communicating and working with young, disabled people for a number of reasons:
> - The information on the website is a useful and adaptable tool for the teachers and trainers when going about their daily work.
> - The information itself is easily accessible and well structured.
> - It contains practical suggestions and strategies for organizing and planning courses.
> - The information describing the characteristics of different types of disabilities, as well as their impact on learning and teaching, helps teachers and trainers to effectively develop individual work plans for each student to suit their needs.
> - The case studies detailing the types of adjustments that have already been made for individuals are also a very valuable source of information, demonstrating the theory in practice.

She emphasized the importance of the project in contributing to the removal of barriers for disabled people. She also noted that, although many developments have taken place in Bulgaria relating to the inclusion of disabled children and adults in society in recent years, including the introduction of legislation to protect their rights, there is still much work to be done.

In managing the project it was easily observable that there were cultural differences between the partner countries. Acknowledging and accepting differences not only encouraged cultural adaptation of the project's information and resources to best suit the local requirements, but also highlighted the need for mutual sensitivity in relation to communication and management as revealed in the following examples.

In the UK over the last decade, in line with the Widening Participation agenda, most HEIs have attempted to demystify the process of studying for a degree. While students are still expected to read widely for their studies, the language used in teaching and in the literature is far less exclusionary than previously. The emphasis is on promoting understanding and learning. In some partners' countries, however, the use of plain language is seen as insufficiently academic, and the credibility of the project (and the partner organization itself) with key stakeholders (particularly with government Ministers and/or educational policymakers) seemed reliant on the sort of status conferred by 'scholarly language'. Some partners appeared hostage to the nationally held belief that use of technical/scientific academic language indicates a hallmark of quality. Not only was the nature of the language an issue, but also the wordage. While feedback from end users in the UK meant that text was pared down, succinctly expressed with a heavy use of bulleted lists, for reports or dissemination materials, some partners preferred presentational styles that were more ornate, with dense text and 'academic' language.

One of the benefits of participating in EU-funded projects is the opportunity to travel, to meet with, and learn from, colleagues in their home countries. Through these visits, all participants gained far more insight into the country and its people than the superficial view that a tourist might gain. These visits also allowed the partners to get to know each other as colleagues, develop as a team, and to become friends. Such bonds made outside meetings over breakfast, lunch, and dinner, helped form a cultural cushion. When back in their respective home country and confronted by, on the face of it, an abrupt email, the personal relationship already established with the sender made recipients far more likely to seek clarification rather than take offence.

Despite the differences described above, following the completion of the piloting phase and the collation and analysis of feedback from key stakeholders in all partner countries, the project partners took great pride in their collective achievement of developing a well-received web resource. They were fully agreed, based on the evidence that they had collected, that this will empower teachers and trainers of VET through enhancing their knowledge and understanding of how to teach disabled learners. They shared the conviction that effective use of the project's materials and resources will result in substantial local impact through the enhancement of disabled people's lifestyles and perspectives, and they noted that the information and guidance provided in the resource is also having a significant impact on the disabled learners' families and friends as evidenced, in part, by some of the cases studies included on each national website.

At the conclusion of the project, an evaluation of the partners' experiences was conducted using an Appreciative Inquiry approach (Cooperrider and Whitney, 1999). This methodology avoids the usual deficit model of evaluation and focuses instead on only positive experiences. The findings showed that despite some clear cultural differences between partners and the odd misunderstanding caused by language, partners regarded themselves as highly successful at:

- sharing experiences, ideas and learning from each other;
- engaging in open, honest dialogue in a courteous manner to overcome challenges and differences of opinion;
- maintaining a very positive working relationship that is based on trust and mutual respect; and

- capitalizing on the substantial professional expertise and experience of team members.

They felt most truly committed, enthusiastic and engaged when working together, face to face, at transnational meetings, and also when working collaboratively to solve problems in the development of the web-based resource. They felt most valued and valuable when their contributions to transnational meetings were appreciated, and when they received positive feedback about the web resource from key stakeholders.

As a direct result of engaging in the project, in addition to the achievement of the intended objectives, there were also a number of unanticipated benefits that were recorded. For example, the Turkish partners reported that:

> We became aware of the importance of involving people with disabilities in daily life. As a result of this we have started to incorporate concerns of disabled people in our consultancy work; for example, we advised one client (a company dealing with shopping centre management) to place signs in the car park for disabled parking. Through the contacts gained during this project, we were also able to direct them to suppliers of motorized wheelchairs to be used in the shopping centre. They were also advised to get certification to promote themselves as 'disability friendly'. We now recommend a focus on people with disabilities as a market niche since disabled people constitute 12 per cent of the Turkish population.

The business case for employing disabled people was well made and the power of the 'disability Euro' will continue to increase. The Turkish partners also noted that their friends and business partners became more open about their relatives who are disabled.

In Bulgaria, a new social enterprise for people with disabilities was established, a PR campaign having been launched to change attitudes and raise awareness about disabled people. The partners, an NGO, stated, 'The web resource has been used for improving the knowledge and competence of our staff about different disabilities such as dyslexia, dyspraxia and learning difficulties; and the knowledge and competencies obtained are used in daily practices.' Individuals from the Greek and Romanian partnerships observed that their own teaching practice had been modified to become more inclusive and enabling following their engagement with the project and its materials and resources; and, though the UK team had substantial knowledge and understanding of disability issues which has been disseminated through the new resource, they learned a great deal about the social, political, legal and educational contexts for disabled people in the partner countries.

EU legislation, coupled with the promotion of the social model of disability over recent years, has resulted in an increasingly shared transnational value system that is witnessing a move away from labelling people as unemployable or as dependent on others, towards an emphasis on people's ability, capability and employability. There is a growing focus on the entitlements of disabled people to adjustments to practice that promote their engagement in education, training and work. The Centre for Inclusive Learning Support at the University of Worcester will draw heavily on the lessons learnt from projects already completed to further promote social justice as they engage in the next, QATRAIN4Students (Q4S) LdV-funded project (1 October 2009 to 30 September 2011). This project, with partners in Greece, Turkey and Bulgaria, will see a further transformation of the original SCIPS model, this time to develop a resource that will be used by disabled learners themselves. The intention is to enable disabled learners to engage more effectively with VET so that they will gain qualifications that will allow them to become employed in the mainstream labour market, thus promoting social inclusion.

References

Bebbington, D. (2006), *Diversity Resources Project*. Leadership Foundation for Higher Education, August, pp. 72–3.

Chapman, V. (2006), 'Academic standards and benchmark descriptors: developing strategies for inclusivity', in Y. Dickinson (ed.), *Embedding Success: Enhancing the Learning Experience for Disabled Students*. York: Higher Education Academy, July, pp. 51–3.

—— and Carlisle, H. (2006), 'Academic standards and benchmark descriptors', in M. Adams and S. Brown (eds), *Towards Inclusive Learning in Higher Education: Developing Curricula for Disabled Students*. London: Routledge, pp. 44–5.

Commission of the European Communities (2005), 'Communication from the Commission to the Council, the European Parliament, the European Economic and Social Committee and the Committee of the Regions', Situation of Disabled People in the Enlarged European Union: the European Action Plan 2006–2007, COM (2005), 604 final. Brussels. Available from: http://eurlex.europa.eu/LexUriServ/LexUriServ.do?uri=SPLIT_COM:2005:0604(01):FIN:EN:PDF

Cooperrider, D. L. and Whitney, D. (1999), 'Appreciative inquiry: a positive revolution in change', in P. Holman and T. Devane (eds), *The Change Handbook*. San Francisco: Berrett-Koehler Publishers, Inc., pp. 245–63.

Dickinson Y. (2006), *Embedding Success: Enhancing the Learning Experience for Disabled Students*. Higher Education Academy, pp. 51–3.

European Social Inclusion Report (2001). Available from http://europa.eu.int/comm/employment_social/soc-prot/soc-incl/index_en.htm)

European Training Foundation (2006), *Live and Learn: the ETF Magazine*, 6, December, www.etf.europa.eu/web.nsf/%28RSS%29/11092B383BD65F36C125722E00587A60?OpenDocument&LAN=EN (accessed 10 October 2009).

SENDA (2001), Special Educational Needs and Disability Act. London: The Stationery Office Limited, www.opsi.gov.uk//acts/acts2001//20010010.htm (accessed 10 October 2009).

Weiler, A. (2004), 'Annual review of working conditions in the EU: 2003–2004', European Working Conditions Observatory (EWCO), available at www. eurofound.europa.eu/ewco/reports/EU0406AR01/EU0406AR01_8.htm. Accessed 10 October 2009.

Chapter 20

Vocational Education

Erica Smith and Andy Smith

Introduction

This chapter examines some aspects of policies and practices designed to increase access to vocational qualifications in Australia. In the early 1990s the Australian federal government launched a series of reforms to the national vocational education and training (VET) system. These were designed to increase the responsiveness of the VET system to the training needs of business, at the same time as encouraging employers to invest in the training of their staff (Smith, 2003). The reforms included both supply-side and demand-side measures. Supply-side measures include the establishment of a national VET system from the existing largely state-based systems, the establishment of a national system of VET qualifications based on competency standards developed with industry input, and the development of a competitive open market for training provision. On the demand side there have been a series of incentives for employers to utilize national VET qualifications in their training of workers.

One of the avowed aims of training reform in Australia was to improve access to vocational qualifications for a broader range of learners. The chapter discusses and critiques the initiatives under two headings: qualification-related training in educational institutions, and qualification-related training in workplaces. These are the two settings in which vocational qualifications are delivered and acquired. To assist in understanding the wider import of the arguments, the initiatives are related to developments in other countries.

Training in educational institutions

The nature of the institutions

In Australia as in many other countries, VET qualifications are offered through a range of educational institutions. Traditionally VET in Australia has been the province of the Technical and Further Education (TAFE) system, the network of publicly funded VET colleges which are present in most cities and towns of over 10,000 people. There have always been a small number of private VET training providers, traditionally secretarial, hospitality and beauty colleges, but since the mid-1980s the Australian Government has encouraged the growth of VET through measures designed to increase the number of private training providers, such as access to certain tranches of government funding (Smith and Keating, 2003). There are now around 4,000 non-TAFE private Registered Training Organizations (RTOs) in Australia (Smith and Smith, 2009). Local community colleges which traditionally provided hobby courses and the like now increasingly offer formal vocational training. While these developments have provided greater access to VET they have not been uncontested; arguments against the changes have ranged from the perceived depletion of support for TAFE, the supposed low quality of some private provision, and the change in community colleges' focus as a result of chasing VET funding.

The nature of the qualifications
At the same time as the expansion of the training market, suites of national VET qualifications based on competency standards for all occupations were developed progressively from the early 1980s for most occupations and industries in the economy. These competency standards and qualifications, together with guidelines for assessment, have over the past decade been gathered together into over eighty Training Packages, which cover almost all occupations and industries (Smith and Keating, 2003). Training Packages are publicly available and can be viewed at www.ntis.gov.au. Most VET now uses Training Package qualifications or units of competency; training providers are not normally allowed to offer qualifications outside Training Packages. This has been regarded by some commentators as unreasonably narrowing the range of VET available and removing providers' ability to cater to niche markets or to learners with various forms of disadvantage. But, generally, there are more fundamental objections to competency-based training; these include dissatisfaction with its perceived behaviourism, its undue reliance on industry demands, and the sidelining of liberal or more general education for students (Smith, forthcoming).

In Australia, as in other countries such as the UK, formal VET has been provided through both full-time and part-time courses. Full-time courses are common for school-leavers in areas such as business administration and also in higher-level qualifications such as youth work or accountancy. Part-time courses are divided into two types: those provided to apprentices and trainees (see below) who work full-time and study part-time; and those provided, usually in the evenings, for those looking to change careers or advance at work and wishing to upgrade their qualifications.

In Australia, the apprenticeship system involving three- or four-year contracts of training in the traditional trades has existed since the first settlement by Europeans. In 1985, shorter one- and two-year traineeships (Kirby, 1985) were introduced. These were often in newer industry areas or the service

industries (Robinson, 2001) and enabled more women to take part in contracts of training. Apprenticeship and traineeships are brought together
under the umbrella of the 'Australian Apprenticeship' system, although in
common usage they are usually referred to separately (Dumbrell and Smith,
2007). Since the 1990s, apprenticeships and traineeships alike have been
available to mature people and to part-time and sometimes casual workers;
this has been a considerable change, as previously apprenticeships were only
available to young people in full-time work.

All apprenticeships and traineeships carry with them a formal Training
Package qualification, usually at Certificate III level or higher. Apprentices
usually attend a TAFE college or a private RTO for one day a week, or in
block periods, for two or three years. Trainees may also attend college, but it
is becoming increasingly common for trainees to be trained 100 per cent 'on
the job'. Even in the latter case, an RTO must oversee the training and be
responsible for the assessment and the award of the qualification. There are
not usually any regulations associated with the 'on the job' training provided
by the employer; this differs from, for example, the German dual system,
where 'on the job' training in apprenticeship tends to be closely prescribed.

After a slow start, traineeships began to grow rapidly in numbers in the
mid-1990s so that of the 415,000 Australian Apprentices (apprentices and
trainees) in 2006 (National Centre for Vocational Education and Training
(NCVER), 2008), 245,000 were trainees with a smaller number of 170,000
traditional apprentices. The 'new' occupational areas, which are generally
covered by traineeships rather than apprenticeships, tend to be where
employment growth is occurring, for example in aged care and hospitality.
The development of Training Packages for these occupational areas also
stimulated growth of training.

VET in secondary schools
A major change in Australian VET policy, which again has also occurred in
the UK, has been the opportunity for students at secondary school to undertake formal VET qualifications. Formerly, vocational subjects were available
but did not attract formal qualifications (e.g. 'domestic science' as opposed
to 'commercial cookery Certificate III'). 'VET in schools' programmes were
introduced in the senior secondary years (Years 11 and 12) during the 1990s,
providing training in a vocational area that leads to a VET qualification or
Statement of Attainment (part-qualification), usually at Certificate II or III
level. The programmes also count towards the senior secondary school-
leaving certificate in each state. In VET in schools programmes, students
may be trained at school or may go to TAFE or to another RTO for their VET
in school classes. VET in schools programmes usually involve the students
undertaking vocational placements in workplaces, where students practise
skills learnt at school or at the RTO.

A number of writers such as Polesel and Teese (e.g. Polesel et al., 2004) have studied VET in schools programme in some depth. They note that VET programmes in schools have tended to be the province of lower-achieving students and those with lower socio-economic status. Thus the programmes have low status within schools, which is consistent with the low status of VET compared with general education in society as a whole. However, most schools now provide VET in schools programmes; originally they were most common in the public sector, but private high-status schools are now beginning to offer them, sometimes in occupational areas such as media studies, which carry less of a 'low status' connotation than others. While there is an indication that students at risk of leaving early may be more likely to complete secondary school if they undertake VET, there is some risk of closing the door to moving directly to university, because of the way in which some Australian states calculate university entrance requirements.

There is now an Australian trend for some students to commence VET qualifications in junior high school (at age 14 or 15, i.e. Years 9 or 10), particularly in schools with disaffected or disadvantaged youths who may be encouraged to stay on at school by the provision of VET programmes. Indigenous students in remote areas, for example, are often targeted for such programmes. In the UK, VET has been offered for quite some time to students at Key Stage 4 (14- to 16-year-olds) (Office for Standards in Education (OFSTED), 2001, 2006) and, while presenting some challenges, has been successful on the whole.

Internationally there are many countries that stream students into 'vocational' and 'general' streams at an early age. In the German system, for example, students are moved onto an academic or vocational track, aged approximately 10 years (Cohen and Besharov, 2002, p. 27). There are many arguments made internationally for and against such streaming, such as the advantage of grouping students with similar attributes together versus the disadvantage of removing future options for some students (Paryono, 2005, pp. 45–7). The Australian and UK systems provide vocational opportunities while avoiding streaming, which appears at first glance preferable but with perhaps a more complex reality.

Summary
Institution-based training can either reinforce or rectify inequalities of access to VET qualifications. We have seen that VET in secondary schools can assist disadvantaged students, but also has the potential to confine their potential. Butler and Ferrier identified in 2000 a number of factors that reduced access to VET for women, including the lack of prerequisite qualifications, difficulty in attending classes because of childcare needs, and a lack of self-confidence. Broadening the Australian apprenticeship system through the introduction of traineeships has provided formal VET for more women, as traineeships

are often in areas where women work; women have always had much lower participation in apprenticeships in Australia, as in the UK (e.g. Miller, 2005), because traditional apprenticeships have been mainly in 'men's jobs' such as manufacturing and construction. In some less-developed countries apprenticeships are being used to provide training for severely disadvantaged groups; for example in Egypt they are being used with ex-child labourers who have never attended school (Azzoni, 2009). In post-conflict countries, VET is essential to rebuild economies; however, it can have the effect not only of alleviating inequalities but also of reinforcing them (Johnson and Kane, 2009).

Training in the workplace

'Traditional' training practices

Traditionally, employer-provided training in the workplace has been informal, unaccredited and focused on developing skills required for the immediate job in hand (Bishop, 1996). This view of employer training has been guided by human capital theory (Becker, 1962), which suggests that employers will only provide training that results in immediate increases in worker productivity and is, therefore, specific to the job and the workplace. Workers benefit from more general training because they are able to use skills and knowledge gained in other contexts, including with other employers, and so, it is argued, employers would not want to pay for this training.

However, the growing body of empirical research on employer training has shown an increasing number of employers providing training to workers that is more transferable to other workplaces and designed to develop the overall skills level of the workforce rather than job-specific skills that will produce an immediate productive pay-off. In the UK and Australia, where critiques of employer training have been among the sharpest (Keep, 2006; Hall et al., 2002), there is considerable evidence that this broader approach to training is being increasingly taken by employers, including moves to provide accredited qualifications through work-based training (Smith and Smith, 2007).

The distribution of training opportunities has historically been skewed, with certain privileged groups of workers consistently receiving higher levels of employer training than others. This skewed distribution of training is so widespread among developed economies that it has assumed something of the status of an 'iron law' of employer training. There are four major groups of disadvantaged workers that consistently receive less employer training. These are workers with low levels of prior qualifications, casual workers, older workers and women.

McKenzie and Long (1995) found in their analysis of training participation data from the mid-1990s that the higher the level of educational attainment, the more likely a worker was to receive training from his or her employer.

Thus employer training statistics worldwide show a marked tendency for most training to be provided to managers and professionals in organizations rather than to lower-skilled workers, i.e. 'The more you have, the more you get.'

Access to employer training also varies significantly by employment status. VandenHeuvel and Wooden (1999) showed that Australian employers tended to provide more training for their full-time and permanent staff than their part-time and, particularly, to their casual staff. For example, in-house training was provided to 40.7 per cent of full-time staff and 38.5 per cent of part-timers, but to only 14.5 per cent of casual staff. External independent study was sometimes funded by an employer, but this rarely happened for casual staff. Thus, casual employees were at that time significantly disadvantaged in terms of employer training. This is not altogether surprising, as employers may view casual employees as more likely to leave the enterprise and therefore as less worthy of investment.

Older workers also tend to receive less employer-provided training than younger workers. This reflects the traditional skills formation model that has operated in Australian enterprises, relying on the recruitment and training of young people to fill positions left by retiring workers: a front-end model of skill formation. However, the increasing scarcity of young workers will compel employers to retain their older workers longer and provide them with the training to adapt to changing skill requirements of enterprises (Ferrier et al., 2008)

Finally, women have been less likely to receive training from their employers than men. In Australia as in other Western countries, the participation of women in the labour force has always been lower than that of men, although the gap between women and men is now closing. With this differential participation in work it is not surprising that historically women have under-participated in VET, which has work-related training as its primary purpose (DfES, 2005, p. 3). This is clearly linked to the nature of employment that women undertake, with women more likely to be working part-time or casually.

Changes due to VET system reforms
In Australia, the equalization of access to employer training has been hastened by the government policy changes in the past twenty years discussed above. The sweeping changes to national VET policies since the late 1980s have led to the development of a new approach to training by some Australian employers. As we have seen, many lower-skilled occupations that had not enjoyed the benefits of a qualifications structure are now able to access nationally recognized qualifications. As a corollary to the development of Training Packages, employers in Australia were also allowed to register as qualifications-awarding bodies in their own, so-called Enterprise Registered Training Organizations, of which there were around 500 in 2008 (Smith and Smith, 2009).

The dramatic expansion of the apprenticeship and traineeship system introduced nationally recognized (qualification-based) training into many industries, such as retailing and process manufacturing, which had hitherto not offered much formal training to their employees. It introduced many individual employers to formal training through their employment of apprentices and trainees. Employers have therefore become increasingly involved with nationally recognized training, both as the employers of apprentices and trainees and the site of these workers' on-the-job learning and, in some cases, as providers of qualifications in their own right.

In the UK a similar path of workplace-focused VET system reform can be traced (Smith and Smith, 2007). Indeed, both countries studied closely the reforms undertaken in the other with a view to building on the successes each had achieved. The development of National Vocational Qualifications (NVQs) in the UK was aimed, like Training Packages, at getting employers to embrace the delivery of qualifications-based training in the workplace (Raggatt and Williams, 1999). However, NVQs met with more resistance from British employers than Training Packages in Australia, as they were closely associated in the public mind with the failed Youth Training Scheme of the 1980s and thus regarded as low-grade qualifications (Smith and Smith, 2007). Similarly, the recognition of employers as qualification-awarding training providers has not progressed so far in the UK as it has in Australia (Smith and Smith, 2009).

The effects of workplace delivery of qualifications on different social groups

With the growth of numbers of apprenticeships and traineeships, and other incentives for using qualifications as the basis of employer training, there has been an increasing convergence between employer training and the formal VET system. This has served in Australia and also in the UK to broaden the availability of VET qualifications to groups in society that previously had limited access.

Recent Australian research into the impact of nationally recognized training (NRT) in the workplace, funded by the National Centre for Vocational Education Research, examined the way in which employers were using NRT and focused on the use of NRT for different groups of workers. The research involved a survey of 600 employers, including 195 firms that were registered as Enterprise RTOs, and a number of company case studies. The research covered organizations that did not use NRT (non-users), those that purchased NRT from external training providers (purchasers), and Enterprise RTOs who were the most engaged with the national VET system since they could award qualifications.

The impact of NRT was substantial. The use of NRT acted as a catalyst for employers to increase the total amount of training that they provided, not just NRT. Table 20.1 shows that among Enterprise RTOs, the organizations most engaged with NRT and with NRT purchasers, the majority of employers reported that the total amount of training that they provided had increased since they first started to use NRT. Enterprise RTOs stated that the total increase in training was a flow-on effect from their use of NRT.

Table 20.1 Changes in total training provided since the introduction of NRT

	Enterprise RTOs (%)	Purchasers (%)
Increased a lot	43.1	14.7
Increased somewhat	49.0	44.1
No change	5.9	38.2
Don't know	2.0	2.9
TOTAL	100	100

The use of NRT also reversed the long-standing skewing of employer training provision towards the more educated and higher-level groups of workers in the organization. Figure 20.1 shows the percentage of organizations offering structured training (including but not limited to NRT) to more than 50 per cent of their workers in each of five categories: professionals, managers, clerical and administrative workers, technical and trades workers, and operational and shop-floor workers. The graph shows that in those organizations not using NRT ('non-users'), the traditional 'iron law' distribution of training prevails. Here, more training is provided to professionals and managers than to trades or shop-floor workers. But in the Enterprise RTOs, the greatest users of NRT, this distribution pattern is reversed. Here, more training is provided for operational workers than for either professionals (who receive the least training) or for managers. The figure indicates that the effect of NRT adoption in organizations is to lift the participation of lower-level and less-educated workers.

The use of NRT may also reverse the distribution of training away from part-time and casual workers. The data showed that Enterprise RTOs and purchasers employed much larger proportions of part-time and casual staff, yet still provided large amounts of training. Thus it is likely that Enterprise RTOs and, to a lesser extent, purchasers of NRT, were providing training to large numbers of non-permanent and non-full-time staff. This finding also bodes well for the position of women. Over-represented in non-full-time and permanent positions and often in lower-level occupations in organizations, women workers may gain the most from the opening of access to employer training provided by the adoption of NRT in organizations. The new availability of qualifications in women's work areas such as aged care and retail may also help to lift the status of that type of work. The recognition of skill in such areas of women's work may thus be beginning to challenge the

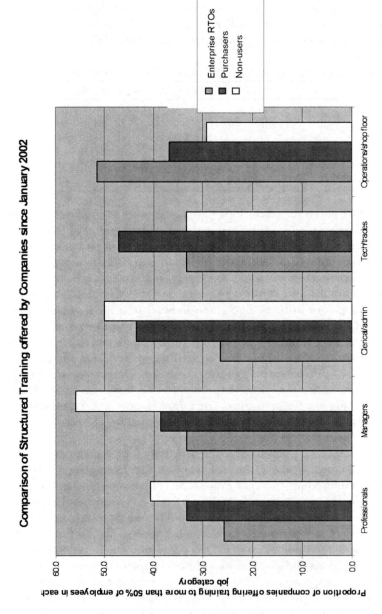

Figure 20.1 Companies offering structured training to more than 50 per cent of each of five different levels of employees in the years 2002 and 2003

Source: Smith et al. (NCVER: 2005, p. 42)

gendered nature of perceptions of skill, as described in social construction theory (Steinberg, 1990). The favourable findings concur with evidence from the UK where an evaluation of the Employer Training pilots, which were established 'to test the effectiveness of an offer of free or subsidized training to employees without a Level 2 qualification' (Hillage et al., 2006), found that women were generally more positive than men about their achievements in nationally recognized training at work.

As well as women and low-paid workers, other disadvantaged groups have been assisted by the availability of qualifications through work. A recent study of traineeships (Smith, Comyn, Brennan, Kemmis and Smith, 2009) has confirmed many other researchers' findings that traineeships have been valuable in providing qualifications to non-English-speaking migrant groups (for example in the meat processing industry), to long-term unemployed people (for example in cleaning) and to young remote indigenous people (in construction). These groups of people would have been unlikely to access institution-based training.

Conclusion and some challenges

This chapter has shown that policy changes in Australia mirroring those elsewhere, such as in the UK, have served to provide access to qualifications to groups in society traditionally less likely to attempt or complete formal qualifications. While some initiatives involve improving access by different groups to existing programmes or qualifications, these have had limited success. For example, Australian efforts to increase participation of women in apprenticeships have rarely succeeded except in relatively minor ways. The more successful efforts seem to have been those that have broadened the 'reach' of VET into a wider range of occupations. For example, these include providing qualifications in jobs previously regarded as 'unskilled', or a greater range of delivery settings such as workplaces. These processes do open up areas of vulnerability; for example, in Australia interest groups representing traditional male occupations have levelled a sustained attack on the availability of qualifications and government funding for training in occupations traditionally undertaken by women (Smith, 2006). In addition, as much of this 'newer VET' is in areas previously without qualifications, there have been many teething troubles in establishing an appropriate level of quality in training delivery, particularly in workplace-based programmes (Smith, 2006). Moreover, delivering qualifications through work inevitably rules out those people who cannot find work, the proportion of whom increases in times of economic recession. Access is limited also to people working for those companies who choose to participate in the delivery of qualifications through work. Disadvantaged people who find it hard to get work at all are less likely to be able to choose among employers on this basis than people who are more immediately attractive to employers. Such people need to be assisted with particular schemes, such as those mentioned above for long-term unemployed people or remote indigenous youths, where work-based training is accompanied by various forms of support and financial incentives for employers.

VET has the potential to be both enabling and disabling for disadvantaged groups. Sweet (2009) argues that traditional apprenticeship countries that use the dual system tend to narrow occupational choices for young people. This is because apprenticeship is part of a system of education which involves streaming during secondary school. In countries where schools are not divided into vocational or non-vocational streams, apprenticeships provide fewer barriers to social change. An early vocational orientation in secondary school may reinforce gender and ethnic stereotyping and reduce the chances of going on to post-school education. On the other hand, there are likely to be many positive outcomes such as lower dropout rates from school, better engagement in school studies and increased self-esteem that carries over into other areas of the young person's life, better employment outcomes, and so on. However, although the international literature provides useful insights, we need to be careful when reading across from other countries' experiences since national contexts differ so much.

The Australian system is not perfect, but it does allow access to VET qualifications for people in several different modes, and does not confine apprenticeships and traineeships to young, full-time workers. Australian school-leavers have an exceptionally good chance of being able to re-engage with the education system at any stage in their adult lives, including undertaking qualifications through work. The conclusion that might be drawn is that changes to VET systems to improve access to qualifications need to be drawn up in such a way that those participating in the programmes still have a set of available pathways.

References

Azzoni, L. (2009), 'Transforming a child labour scheme into a modern apprenticeship one: the role of NGOs and government. The apprenticeship component of the CCL project'. Proceedings of the Innovative Apprenticeships: promoting Successful School-to-Work Transitions conference, September 17–18, Turin, Italy, pp. 197–200.

Becker, G. (1962), 'Investment in human capital: a theoretical analysis', *Journal of Political Economy*, 70(2), 9–50.

Bishop, J. H. (1996), 'What we know about employer-provided training: a review of literature', CAHRS working paper. Ithaca: Cornell University.

Cohen, M. and Besharov, D. (2002), *The Role of Career and Technical Education: Implications for the Federal Government*. Washington, DC: Office of Vocational and Adult Education.

Department for Education and Skills (UK) (2005), *Skills: Getting on in Business, Getting on at Work*, Part 3 (White Paper). London: Her Majesty's Stationery Office.

Dumbrell, T. and Smith, E. (2007), *Pre-apprenticeships in Three Key Trades*. Adelaide: NCVER.

Ferrier, F., Burke, G. and Selby Smith, C. (2008), *Skills Development for a Diverse Older Workforce*. Adelaide: NCVER.

Hall, R., Buchanan, J. and Considine, G. (2002), 'You value what you pay for', Workplace Research Centre working paper. University of Sydney.

Hillage, J., Loukas, G., Newton, B. and Tamkin, P. (2006), *Employer Training Pilots: Final Evaluation Report*. London: Department for Education and Skills.

Johnson, D. and Kane, L. (2009), 'Learning for employment and citizenship in post-conflict countries', in R. Maclean and D. N. Wilson (eds), *International Handbook of Education for the Changing World of Work*, vol. 2. Dordrecht: Springer, pp. 765–74.

Keep, E. (2006), 'State control of the English VET system – playing with the biggest train set in the world', *Journal of Vocational Education and Training*, 58(1), 47–64.

Kirby, P. (1985), *Report of the Committee of Inquiry into Labour Market Programs*. Canberra: Australian Government Printing Service.

McKenzie, P. and Long, M. (1995), 'Educational attainment and participation in training', paper presented to the Efficiency and Equity in Education Policy Conference, Canberra, 6–7 September.

Miller, L. (2005), 'Addressing gender segregation in apprenticeships in England', *Education + Training*, 47 (4/5), 283–97.

National Centre for Vocational Education and Training (2008), *Australian VET Statistics: Apprentices and Trainees – 2007*. Adelaide: NCVER.

Ofsted (2001), 'Extending work-related learning at Key Stage 4'. London, UK: Ofsted. Available at www.ofsted.gov.uk .

Ofsted (2006), 'Evaluation of the Young Apprenticeships Programme'. London, UK: Ofsted. Available at www.ofsted.gov.uk

Paryono, P. (2005), 'A cross-national analysis of when and how vocational education is offered', *Journal for Vocational and Technical Education and Training*, 41–9.

Polesel, J., Helme, S., Davies, M., Teese, R., Nicholas, T. and Vickers, M. (2004), *VET in Schools: A Post-Compulsory Education Perspective*. Adelaide: NCVER.

Raggatt, P. and Williams, S. (1999), *Government, Markets and Vocational Qualifications: An Anatomy of Policy*. London: Falmer Press.

Robinson, C. (ed.) (2001), *Australian Apprenticeships: Facts, Fiction and Future*. Adelaide: NCVER.

Smith, A. (2003), 'Recent trends in Australian training and development', *Asia–Pacific Journal of Human Resources*, 41(2), 231–44.

Smith, A. and Smith, E. (2007), 'The development of training policies in England and Australia: a comparison', *London Review of Education*, 5(1), 51–67.

Smith, E. (2006), 'A woman's work is never certificated: how the implementation of nationally recognized training in workplaces helps women get qualifications', *Journal of Vocational Education and Training*, Special Edition, 58(4), 531–49.

—— (forthcoming), 'A review of twenty years of competency-based training in the Australian vocational education and training system', *International Journal of Training and Development*.

—— and Keating, J. (2003), *From Training Reform to Training Packages*. Tuggerah Lakes, NSW: Social Science Press.

—, Pickersgill, R., Smith, A. and Rushbrook, P. (2005), *Enterprise's Commitment to Nationally Recognized Training for Existing Workers*. Adelaide: NCVER.

Smith, E. and Smith, A. (2009), 'Making training core business: enterprise registered training organisations in Australia', *Journal of Vocational Education and Training*, 61(3), 287–306.

——, Comyn, P., Brennan Kemmis, R. and Smith, A. (2009), *High Quality Traineeships: Identifying What Works*. Adelaide: NCVER.

Steinberg, R. (1990), 'Social construction of skill: gender, power, and comparable worth', *Work and Occupations*, 17(4), 449–82.

Sweet, R. (2009), 'Apprenticeships, pathways, career guidance: a cautionary tale', *Proceedings: Innovative Apprenticeships: Promoting Successful School-to-Work Transitions*, September 17–18, Turin, Italy, pp. 17–33.

VandenHeuvel, A. and Wooden, M. (1999), *Casualisation and Outsourcing Trends and Implications for Work-related Training*. Adelaide: NCVER.

Conclusions and implications

Introduction

In the preparation of this book, twenty-eight researchers and reflective practitioners were invited to investigate the connection between education and social change in a postmodern, postcolonial world environment. A particular focus was the growing reality of social, economic and political interconnection as a result of globalization and policy initiatives to promote social cohesion and social justice. A glance at the contents page will reveal the worldwide variety of topics covered, ranging from Early Years education in Northern Ireland to primary education in Ghana and Tibet; vocational education and training across the European Union through to higher education in the UK to adult and continuing education in China.

In accordance with this diversity is a variety in the selection of research methodologies, embracing both qualitative and quantitative methods. The book opens with the use of story- telling to illustrate the dangers of uncritical imposition of Western-devised educational models in developing countries. A number of case studies are presented, one in the form of action research to improve provision in a college of further education, another using participant observation in a specialist college. There is an example of the use of quantitative analysis demanded by international policymakers for monitoring purposes. Many of the contributions utilize desk-based research, and some are highly speculative and suggestive of fruitful areas for further work.

Inevitably there are gaps in coverage. For example, only passing reference is made to the influence of education for sustainable development (with reference to climate change, migration and pollution) and the internet (in relation to cultural change). However, examples of the use of large-scale co-ordinated social techniques to change destructive cultural attitudes to promote sustainable social change are given by Fourali in relation to social marketing, and the use of similar principles to create a supportive cultural environment in the context of Early Years provision in Northern Ireland (Fitzpatrick). To balance loss, there are great gains. In spite of the geographical range and variety of subjects chosen there is a possibly surprising degree of consensus that has helped to identify major strands and themes of interest to educators, researchers and policymakers alike, and it is this which provides the basis for the discussion and conclusions reached in this final, summative chapter.

The organization of the book into four sections with an introduction and conclusion has helped to identify three key drivers of policy initiatives. These have prompted educational change as a consequence of the imposition of neo-liberalism at the end of the Second World War. This attempted to rebuild the international economic system as a result of the Bretton Woods Agreement (Eichengreen, 2008) and the 1945 United Nations Charter to promote social progress and better standards of life in greater freedom (United Nations Charter Preamble: www.un.org).

First, there are the accelerating effects of globalization as a result of deregulation. Second, there are the attempts by nation states and unions of nation states to resist these pressures, and finally there is influence this has on Non-Governmental Organizations (NGOs) and independent partnerships in education for development. Consequently, the conclusions reached are derived from two sets of considerations: the first is the result of investigations of national government and European investment in vocational education and training (VET) and citizenship education, and the second in the context of international development.

Any examination of the relationship between globalization and education policy has to include the impact of international organizations such as the World Bank which advocates, in an ever-changing international market-dominated environment, the fostering of entrepreneurial qualities in the individual, best delivered in a deregulated, competitive education environment.

A major counter-influence is the nation state, which is not a helpless recipient of international policymaking. Governments wish to maintain control over public services (Green, 1997). Furthermore, governments seek to maintain national integrity by promoting citizenship education programmes in response to the permeation of the influences of globalization.

Among a number of examples of economic and political transnational co-operation in various stages of advancement are the Union of South American Nations (UNASUR 2008) (www.unasur.org) and the Asia Pacific Economic Cooperation (APEC) (www.apec.org). By far the most developed is the European Union (http://europa.eu), which has served to inspire the others. It has a special role in the advocacy of transnational social democracy, especially in consideration of appropriate and accountable methods of governance (Held and McGrew, 2002). In the context of education policymaking and social change, examples of how these were applied and how they engaged the interest of contributors will be shown in the next section.

Finally, consideration was also given to the multifaceted encapsulation of the effects of global influences on the experiences of the indigenous populations used by Non-Governmental Organizations and other development partnerships to re-examine the significance of the relationship between global and local understandings of policy and politics in education, particularly in relation to human rights, social diversity, conflict resolution and social justice.

Vocational education and training: nation states and the European Union

With reference to the observation that European nation states are taking an increased interest in citizenship education (Green, 1997), Annette's critique of higher education and civic community engagement in the UK consists of a survey of the formative factors that have determined the role of higher learning in citizenship education and community action research. He points to similar programmes in Australia, Canada and South Africa, highlighting that the understanding of the global dimension is an important part of learning in this area. He ends with a comment on the efficacy of this approach, asking the critical question on the connection between investment in human capital and realized community action. This raises an important issue in relation to the purpose of human resource development policies: is it to serve the interest of the individual in a consumerist age, or for the common good?

An example of educational research to improve individual life chances is Murphy's use of teacher-led investigation in the context of a Bachelor of Engineering (Honours) degree course in Ireland. His identification of a 'special attributes' model as a means of recognizing and accrediting student capabilities supports individual needs and is sufficiently flexible to serve the learner in times of change. This case study, in common with the one below, shows the benefit of self-generated development in small, discrete environments that can equally meet individual and local requirements.

One of the effects of globalization has been the pressure on governments to invest in human capital development to improve economic performance and competitiveness. In addition to this, the demand to facilitate access to education and training has resulted in the increased corporatization of educational institutions, the 'commodification' of research, and the use of consultants and other educational experts to transfer methodologies from one nation to another (Ball, 1998). A number of examples are provided in this volume of transfer of expertise. Jones, Sallis and Hubert point to the borrowing of methodology from the UK by the domestically autonomous State of Jersey, with reference to the importation of quality assurance measures based on self-assessment that are contextually specific, but provide sufficient flexibility to change systems when used in the light of experience.

Erica Smith and Andy Smith show how the Australian Federal Government reform of the vocational education and qualification system reflected a number of influences including the UK use of competence-based qualifications. The intention was to make the VET system more flexible and responsive to employers' needs, and to encourage them to invest in their staff. The result was that, although increased flexibility provided access for a wider sector of the population and prevented early dropout from education and training, there were limited gains for those from disadvantaged groups.

An example of transnational sharing of expertise is the examination of the QATRAIN2 project (Quality Assurance and Accessible Training 2, a European Union-funded project led by the Chapman's Centre for Inclusive Learning Support at the University of Worcester, with partners in Bulgaria, Greece, Romania and Turkey). The programme was designed to meet European priorities in capacity building for social justice through increased access for students with disabilities. The major outcome was a web-based resource that helped VET teachers to meet the needs of disabled learners. The programme featured a learning outcomes approach to meeting the individual needs of learners.

Nikolou-Walker and Fee show how work-based learning in the UK has become a key influence in reforming the higher education curriculum as a method which supports the needs of the major stakeholders – the learner, the institution, and the employer – in the context of the profession and wider society. The influence of work-based learning globally is revealed in Liu's survey of change in adult and continuing education in China. Here, the need to compete economically on a worldwide basis promoted a demand for work-based learning in higher education in order to improve the skills base of the population. The resulting corporatization of higher education had profound effects on both the management and culture of advanced learning. Decentralization meant that universities were no longer under the control of the Communist Party, but were in a position to respond to the consumer demands of both learners and employers. Ning Rong Liu ends his contribution by questioning the wisdom of too great an emphasis on market-led education, arguing that other values in society should not be neglected and that the government should take some responsibility for the appropriate balance.

The effect of the introduction of the market ethos and increased managerialism in English secondary education is addressed in Solvason's case study, based on experience within a specialist sports college. She offers a critique of New Labour's part-privatization policies based on the aspiration that investment in excellence of achievement attained by the few will raise the standards of the many. She finds that the centralization of decision-making and the introduction of an ethos of vocationalism and competitiveness had little effect on achievement, and has failed to address deeply embedded inequality in education. Her contribution shows how the introduction of specialist academies is indicative of a shift in the balance from education for citizenship to preparation for work.

The barriers to the European Union's aim to become the most competitive economic area in the world, as set out in the Lisbon strategy, were examined in different ways by three contributors who come to similar conclusions. Zarifis

(vocational education and training policy), Souto-Otero (vocational qualifications) and Kirpal (teachers and vocational trainers) focus on the exact
connection between human resource development for competitive advantage, and social inclusion. All are in agreement that, if a connection is to be
made between the two, VET policies will have to be supported by comprehensive social reforms and better methods of economic planning and dealing with
market failure. In order to improve the situation, Zarifis suggests a number
of measures. These include the introduction of more democratic methods of
decision-making to include learners, using routes to learning and providing
qualifications that are socially valued, which ensures that VET policymaking
meets their requirements. As Souto-Otero commented, it was the privileged
who knew how to benefit from VET reform, not the disadvantaged.

Development and the global dimension

Three contributors provided insights into the policies of the United Nations
and the NGO-inspired Education for All and Millennium Development Goals
as major influences on government-driven education for social development
policies as drivers of social change. All examine the influence of access to
education for all, regardless of gender, on international policymaking. Two
of the contributions concentrate specifically on the influence of gender on
achievement rates beyond the first stages of basic education. The first example
looks at reasons for low achievement of girls in Ghana (Dunne), where equal
rights were embedded in the constitution, and educational development was
the result of a partnership between the government of Ghana and the World
Bank. The second (Kiamanesh and Danaye) focuses on both women and
girls in the Afghan refugee community in Iran. Both contributions concur in
concluding that, although the use of these programmes resulted in considerable gains, there is a need to gain greater understanding of the social and
cultural factors that create additional barriers especially against women and
girls. Without having to impose on other cultures what is right or wrong we
may consider, among possible reasons, the fact that some cultures may have
different priorities for different genders, even though education may still be a
high government priority. As Bainton and Crossley make clear in the opening
chapter of this volume, it would be arrogant to use a Western framework to
evaluate non-Western cultures.

Two significant points that are picked up by other contributors are made by
the Iranian researchers. The first is the danger of direct transfer of methodology from the First World to the Third, and the second is the importance of
having an adequate supply of teachers capable of providing basic education
programmes. The latter is the concern of Akyeampong's historical assessment
of Ghanaian government teacher education policy which shows how, in the

initial stages, World Bank-funded initiatives concentrated on school building and the provision of equipment to the detriment of teacher education, resulting in acute supply and demand failures which served to destabilize reform initiatives, particularly in rural areas. He suggests a number of management changes to improve the situation, which are of relevance to other sub-Saharan countries.

Evidence has been provided of gains as a result of government-driven education development policies based on the UN concept of human rights as a means of furthering human progress. There are, however, some unintentional and important losses in low-income countries, which is the focus of discussion by four contributors. Bainton and Crossley describe the early education experience of Tibetan nomads, who are given access to opportunity as a result of Western-based intervention programmes. With limited likelihood of progression and the danger of fracturing their traditional way of life in a fragile environment, questions are raised concerning the wisdom of uncritical transfer of educational models and ideas across cultures and contexts. To resolve this dilemma, the authors call for a reconceptualization of global education and in particular an ethic of respect for local experience and ways of knowing and doing. Bourn and Issler show that this desire is a well-recognized principle in education in their coverage of the history of development education, which originated in the practice of large NGOs in partnership with schools, supported by the UN, as part of their advocacy of human rights and social justice. In recent years the raising of the profile of southern NGOs has improved the capability to promote knowledge and values developed in the context of understanding the importance of interconnectedness in a global world, and the use of critical literacy to challenge injustice and give voice to the negated. Bourn and Issler indicate that the importance of this drive in education, to learn to live with one another in a globalized world, in common with many other countries, is part of mainstream education in the UK.

An example of a movement which articulates the needs of those from an indigenous culture is given by Stanfield in his account of private education for the poor. He draws a distinction between the human rights approach adopted by the UN and many major NGOs which results in a 'top-down' approach to development education and target setting, and a freedom-based approach which allows for partnership between parents, local education providers and international charities to enable local communities to take charge of their own education programmes. To support this process, governments needed to provide an enabling environment, and to interfere directly only in the event of market failure.

Andreotti's prescription for a new approach to global citizenship education within the development education tradition perhaps offers the beginnings of a solution. To meet the educational needs of students in a globalized environment, teachers need to 'up their game'. They need to grow the capability to develop the necessary tools for educating learners to confront cultural supremacy and inequalities, through comprehension of the complexities of interconnectedness in a fast-moving globalized environment. This understanding will enable them to interrogate the origins of their own prejudices, and know how to deal with them. An example of the implementation of a method of education and training based on similar principles is given in Fitzpatrick's account of the development of a culture of respecting difference in Early Years centres in Northern Ireland. The prominence of the need to promote a new shared futures policy recognized by the Northern Ireland Assembly has provided the opportunity for Early Years provision to have a key role in the promotion of social integration by crossing the sectarian divide. This was made possible because of an extensive capacity-building 'Respecting Difference' programme, which has used television to create a value base that supports respect for difference, backed by evidence-based research to ensure its 'fitness for purpose' for major stakeholders. The aim is to create and run safe learning environments for young children which establish human rights, address inequality and celebrate diversity. These learning centres are run on communitarian principles involving participation of parents, well-qualified teachers, governors and children. The programme is recognized by the European Union, which provides funding in partnership with the UK and Northern Ireland governments and an American charity. This level of support has enabled the creation of an international network in areas of social conflict, based on common principles, expecting governments to fulfil their duties and remain accountable.

Trends and Recommendations

Ample evidence has been provided of interconnectedness, mainly as a result of multinational organizations such as the World Bank and the United Nations education policymaking, and the campaigning and education support programmes on the part of NGOs and other partnerships. A number of trends have been identified:

1. The use of research by governmental organizations, communities and individuals to bring about change. The value of the Ghana study is that it provides an example of a country that had incorporated human rights values into its constitution and was in receipt of World Bank aid to achieve access to education for all. Even within this context, research revealed the need to address managerial problems associated with a 'top-down' approach and the requirement for funding bodies to use both quantitative analysis and qualitative research for monitoring purposes. Another important recommendation came from Northern Ireland, which showed the value of the use of research to initiate and

sustain an Early Years initiative, which was essentially a community-based project that had worldwide consequences. In addition, quite a number of case studies revealed the value of research where the government took a subsidiary role.

2. In relation to VET initiatives in Europe and Asia quoted here, most of the evidence concurs with Lingard and Ozga (2007) finding that the privileging of the business model allows governments to under-conceptualize the social and civil outcomes of education policymaking. The wider effects of globalization now becoming evident through migration, technical, social and cultural interchange are thus ignored. This was found to be particularly true of the lack of success in provision of access to training for disadvantaged groups in Europe. Here, a number of recommendations were made on the basis that VET policies on their own will not solve the problem; they need to be accompanied by a programme of social reform, including consultation with learners about the provision of qualifications they actually want and methods of funding and learning support that would provide access and give adequate status to their achievements.

3. Although nation states value citizenship education as a means of inculcating an idea of common cause, evidence has been provided here of the difficulty of creating the appropriate environment to ensure participation. The furthering of the ethos of the public good, as opposed to a constant emphasis on consumerism, was recommended and there was an identified need to improve citizenship education to provide learners with the capacities to deal with the complexities of a global age.

4. Northern global hegemony over the global south is a major theme. A variety of strategies have been suggested to articulate the voice of indigenous populations, including the encouragement of private enterprise schools for the poor and the growth of development education programmes providing a partnership between schools, and NGOs and other development organizations which engage learners in celebrations of diversity through an examination of their own prejudices and beliefs. Another model to achieve similar ends is the example of the 'Respecting Difference' programme in Northern Ireland.

There is the question of how far the combined policies of organizations such as the World Bank, the International Monetary Fund and UNESCO, or initiatives such as Education for All or the Millennium Development Goals, are creating the possibility of universal cosmopolitanism. Ample evidence has been presented here that, if this is to be realized at all, a great deal has to be done to overcome the gross inequalities created by the enactment of neoliberal policies in a globalized age.

Finally, this book started with the aim of making education more relevant to addressing today's inequalities and missed opportunities. Despite the diversity of the themes tackled by the contributors, it is clear that there might have been many other topics, close to the hearts of many readers, which you may feel have been overlooked. For instance, a simple issue alluded to above is that of determining tested methods for supporting the education of individuals who may have lost out in terms of access to education (e.g. because of geographical distance or the programme not being sensitive to local/family values/culture). It is clear that such a situation raises interesting challenges that need addressing urgently to ensure that individuals affected do not lose out. Indeed, there are many approaches already being adopted at family and community level which could be researched and reported on to learn from 'successful' initiatives and provide a wider array of choices for learning opportunities. We feel that this is a promising area for educational research partly supported by a movement for seeking alternatives to formal education (e.g. Stanfield, this volume).

This is just an example of urgent advice that is needed by individuals, families, educationists and policymakers, to mention just a few. There is no shortage of further advice associated with other problems. Indeed, some readers may even feel let down if they are, or have been, linked to one of the chronic world problems leading to humanitarian catastrophe, such as those observed in areas of conflict – for example in Rwanda, Sudan, Bosnia and the Middle East — racism (overt and covert), environmental issues, and so on. These readers may feel that, even by concentrating on certain geographical and substantive areas, while neglecting others, we have been oblivious to their plight and, worse, we have been Western/Eurocentric.

Although many improvements have resulted from the post-Second World War agreement and United Nation policies sixty years ago, it is clear that in the twenty-first century the failures as outlined here are all too frequent. One of the critical issues is the degree of Western centrism coupled with the use of top-down control systems resulting in gross inequality. As Stanfield, Fitzpatrick, Andreotti, Bourn and Issler (all in this volume) have pointed out, alternative methodologies need to be identified, researched and supported, particularly in the areas of the connection between expression of identity, community values, including celebration of diversity, and sustainable development in education. This is the challenge of multiculturalism in a global age. Education can make a considerable contribution to fostering the ability for us to live with one another, particularly if this value is embedded in the family and promoted in the local community. There is also, as Annette highlights, the difficulty of encouraging the use and development of political literacy to promote public participation in a democratic society, even at undergraduate level. Further research concerning these issues is a fundamental priority in an age when the importance of understanding the connection between the local and the global is all too evident. Without the skilled use of mutual co-operation it is unlikely that problems concerning the spread of disease, climate change, more equal distribution of the world's resources, environmental degradation, can be addressed. Without the ability to listen to and learn from one another, all our futures are placed in jeopardy.

In light of these concerns and priorities, we hold that people of all countries – north and south – are hugely affected by their lack of access to relevant education. This lack of access affects the students, who want to learn something relevant to their daily concerns but cannot find it. It affects the educators and teachers, who may despair of finding the advice and means of teaching something that improves society as a whole and minimizes disadvantage and discrimination. It affects current and future employers, who want to create companies that support their local community while creating sustainable businesses. It affects current and future politicians, who ought to be tutored to understand how education systems are critical to the maintenance of a just and sustainable society. This list could go on: parents, friends, counsellors, and so on. We recognize these problems and realize that there are no simple solutions. We also recognize that, by the very nature of this topic, one book cannot satisfactorily address the numerous and complex issues.

The idea of fairness (Stanfield, this volume) has gained a great deal of credence in recent years but, as Sen (2009) points out, this concept cannot conceal the hegemonic practices of the global north, which impose a model of government based on a form of democratic consensus which masks inequality. What is required is a notion of justice that embraces cultural conflict. It is our contention that this will provide the necessary environment for teachers to create spaces where students can expose inequality and diversity, and debate ways of living with it, thereby enriching the democratic process. We have here debated the challenges to policymakers and practitioners in order to achieve these ends, but there is yet a long way to go. We would like to see the aims of this book developed into future work in print that responds to world concerns and adopts a plan of action to help address inequalities and make the world a better place to live in for ourselves and our children.

References

Ball, S. J. (1998), 'Big policies/small world: an introduction to international perspectives in education policy', *Comparative Education*, 34 (2), 119–30.

Eichengreen, B. (2008), *Globalizing Capital: A History of the International Monetary System*. Princeton, NJ: Princeton University Press.

Green, A. (1997), *Education, Globalization and the Nation State*. Basingstoke: Macmillan.

Held, D. and McGrew, M. (2002), 'Reconstructing the world order: towards cosmopolitan social democracy', in J. Timmons Roberts and A. Bellone Hite (eds), *The Globalization and Development Reader*. Malden, MA; Oxford, UK; Carlton, Victoria, Australia: Blackwell Publishing.

Lingard, B. and Ozga, J. (2007), 'Globalisation, education policy and politics', in

B. Lingard and J. Ozga (eds), *The Routledge Falmer Reader in Education Policy and Politics*. London and New York: Routledge.

Sen, A. (2009), *The Idea of Justice*. London: Allen Lane, Penguin Books Ltd.

Selected Bibliography

Andreasen, A. (2006), *Social Marketing in the 21st Century*. Thousand Oaks, CA: Sage.

Apple, M., Au, W. and Gandin, L. A. (eds) (2009), *The Routledge International Companion to Critical Education*. Oxford, New York: Routledge.

Ashton, D. and Sung, J. (2002), *Supporting Workplace Learning for High Performance Working*. Geneva: International Labour Office. Available at www.ilo.org/public/english/employment/skills/workplace/index.htm

Ashton, D., Brown, P. and Lauder, H. (2003), *International Best Practice on Workforce Development. (Final Report)*, Education and Learning Wales. Available at www.elwa.org.uk/doc_bin/Research%20Reports/workforce_development_best_practice_211103.pdf (accessed 16 April 2010).

Bishop, D., Felstead, A., Fuller, A., Jewson, N., Lee, T. and Unwin, L. (2006), *Connecting Culture and Learning in Organisations: A Review of Current Themes*. Cardiff University School of Social Sciences, Learning as Work Research Paper No. 5. Available at http://learningaswork.cf.ac.uk/outputs/Connecting_Culture_and_Learning_Final.pdf

Brennan, J. and Little, B., with Connor, H, de Weert, E., Delve, S., Harris, J., Josselyn, B., Ratcliffe, N. and Scesa, A. (2006), *Towards a Strategy for Workplace Learning*. Bristol: Higher Education Funding Council for England. Available at www.hefce.ac.uk/pubs/rdreports/rd09_06 (accessed 16 April 2010).

Brennan, L. (2005), *Integrating Work-based Learning into Higher Education: A Guide to Good Practice*. Bolton: University Vocational Awards Council. Available at www.uvac.ac.uk/downloads/0401_publications/int_wbl.pdf (accessed 16 April 2010).

Bristol Papers in Education. Comparative and international studies book series. Available at www.symposium-books.co.uk/books/allbooks.asp?browse=2&sid=2.

Department for Education and Skills, Department for Trade and Industry, HM Treasury, Department for Work and Pensions (2003), *21st Century Skills – Realising our Potential – Individuals, Employers, Nation*. The Stationery Office. Available at www.dfes.gov.uk/skillsstrategy/uploads/documents/21st%20Century%20Skills.pdf

Department for Innovation, Universities and Skills (2008), *Higher Education at Work – High Skills: High Value*. HLSS 4/08. Sheffield: DIUS. Available at www.dius.gov.uk/consultations/documents/Higher_Education_at_Work.pdf

Dunne, M. (2008), *Gender, Sexuality and Development: Education and Society in Sub-Saharan Africa*. Rotterdam: Sense Publishers.

—— and Leach, F. (2005), *Gendered School Experiences: The Impacts on Retention and Achievement in Botswana and Ghana*. London: DFID.

—— , Humphreys, S. and Leach, F. (2006), 'Gender violence in schools in "developing" countries', *Gender and Education*, 18(1), 75–98.

—— and Leach, F. (2007), 'Gender conflict and schooling: identity, space and violence', in F. Leach and M. Dunne (eds), *Education, Conflict and Reconciliation: International Perspectives*. Bern/Oxford: Peter Lang, 2007, pp. 187–202.

Edwards, R., Raggatt, P., Harrison, R., McCollum, A. and Calder, J. (1998), *Recent Thinking in Lifelong Learning: A Review of the Literature*. Department for Education

and Employment: Research Report RR80. Sudbury: DfEE Publications. Available at
www.dfes.gov.uk/research/data/uploadfiles/RB80.doc

Elliott, G. (1996), *Crisis and Change in Vocational Education and Training*. Higher
Education Policy Series 36. London: Jessica Kingsley.

—— (1999), *Lifelong Learning: The Politics of the New Learning Environment*. Higher
Education Policy Series 44. London: Jessica Kingsley.

Eraut, M. and Hirsch, W. (2007), *The Significance of Workforce Learning for Individuals,
Groups and Organisations*. SKOPE report. Available at www.skope.ox.ac.uk/
WorkingPapers/Eraut-Hirshmonograph.pdf

Faithorn, B. (2005), *Learner Progression into Higher Education*. University Vocational
Awards Council. Available at www.uvac.ac.uk/downloads/0401_publications/
int_wbl.pdf (accessed 3 December 2006).

Fuller, A., Ashton, D., Felstead, A., Unwin, L., Walters, S. and Quinn, M. (2003), *The
Impact of Informal Learning at Work on Business Productivity*. Final Report to the DTI.
Leicester: Centre for Labour Market Studies and University of Leicester. Available at
www.berr.gov.uk/files/file11027.pdf

Garnet, J., Portwood, D. and Costley, C. (2004), *Bridging Rhetoric and Reality:
Accreditation of Prior Experiential Learning (APEL) in the UK*. Boston: UVAC. Available
at www.uvac.ac.uk/downloads/0401_publications/APEL%20report%20FINAL%20
18%20June.doc (accessed 16 April 2010).

Gray, D. (2001), *A Briefing on Work-based Learning*, Learning and Teaching Support
Network (LTSN). Generic Centre Assessment Series No. 11. York: Learning and
Teaching Support Network HEQE CHERI, A Review of Work Based Learning in
Higher Education. Available at www.ljmu.ac.uk/lid/ltweb/88718.htm

Gundara, J. S. (2000), *Intercultural Education and Inclusion*. London: Paul Chapman
Publishing Ltd.

Hasting, G. (2007), *Social Marketing*. Oxford: Butterworth-Heinemann.

Hicks, D. and Holden, C. (eds) (2007), *Teaching the Global Dimension*. London:
Routledge and Kegan Paul.

Jarvis, P. (2007), *Globalization, Lifelong Learning and the Learning Society: Sociological
Perspectives*, vol. 2. London and New York: Routledge.

J. M. Consulting Ltd (2003), *The Costs of Alternative Modes of Delivery*. Bristol: Higher
Education Funding Council for England. Available at www.hefce.ac.uk/pubs/
rdreports/2003/rd14_03/rd14_03main.pdf

Kerins, J. (2007), *Collaborative Initiatives and Work-based Learning Opportunities: A Case Study*.
A report for HEA. Available at www.ics.heacademy.ac.uk/italics/vol6iss1/kerins.pdf

King, M. (2007), *Workforce Development: How Much Engagement Do Employers Have with
Higher Education?* A report for Council for Industry and Higher Education (CIHE).
Available at www.cihe-uk.com/docs/PUBS/0702WFDEmployerEngagement.pdf

Kotler, P. and Roberto, E. (2008), *Social Marketing: Strategies for Changing Public Behavior*.
New York: Free Press, 1989, 2002 and 2008. (Latest title in Philip Kotler and Nancy
Lee, *Social Marketing: Influencing Behaviors for Good*. London: Sage.)

Lauder, H., Brown, P., Dillabough, J. and Halsey, A. (eds) (2006), *Globalisation and
Social Change*. Oxford: Oxford University Press.

Lee, T., Fuller, A., Ashton, D., Butler, P., Felstead, A., Unwin, S. and Walters, S. (2004),
Workplace Learning: Main Themes and Perspectives, Learning as Work. Research
Paper, No. 2, University of Leicester, Centre for Labour Market Studies.
Available at http://learningaswork.cardiff.ac.uk/outputs/Workplace_Learning_
Final.pdf

Little, B., Harvey, L., Moon, S., and Pierce, D. (2001), *Research Work: the Extent and
Variety of Forms of Work-related Learning*. Council for Industry and Higher Education,

Work-related Learning Report, pp. 23–4. London: CIHE. ISBN 1841856894. Available at www.qualityresearchinternational.com/ese/relatedpapers.htm

—— and HEFCE Enhancing Student Employability Co-ordination Team (ESECT) colleagues (2006), *Employability and Work-based Learning.* York: Higher Education Academy. Available at www.heacademy.ac.uk/resources/publications/learningandemployability

—— and Williams, R. (2008), *Interim Evaluation of Lifelong Learning Networks.* Report to HEFCE by Centre for Higher Education Research. The Open University. Available at www.hefce.ac.uk/pubs/rdreports/2008/rd05_08/rd05_08.pdf

Margesson, R. (2007), *Afghan Refugees: Current Status and Future Prospects.* CRS report for Congress.

McIntyre, J. (2000), *Working Knowledge and Work-based Learning: Research Implications.* Sydney: UTS Research Centre Vocational Education & Training. Available at http://eric.ed.gov/ERICDocs/data/ericdocs2sql/content_storage_01/0000019b/80/17/24/0c.pdf

Merrifield, J., McIntyre, D. and Osaigbovo, R. (2000), *Mapping APEL: Accreditation of Prior and Experiential Learning in English Higher Education.* London: Learning from Experience Trust.

Nikolou-Walker E. (2008), *The Expanded University: Work-based Learning and the Economy.* Harlowe: Pearson.

Nixon, I., Penn, D., Shewell, J. (2006), *Workplace Learning in the North East.* Report to HEFCE by the KSA Partnership. Wolsingham, County Durham: KSA Partnership. Available at www.hefce.ac.uk/Pubs/RDreports/2006/rd12_06/rd12_06.pdf

—— , Smith, K., Stafford, R. and Camm, S. (2006), *Work-based Learning: Illuminating the Higher Education Landscape.* York: Higher Education Academy. Available at www.heacademy.ac.uk/assets/York/documents/ourwork/research/wbl_illuminating

Park, C. (2007), *Redefining the Doctorate.* York: Higher Education Academy. Available at www.grad.ac.uk/downloads/documents/Reports/HEA/RedefiningTheDoctorate.pdf

Powell, S. and Long, E. (2005), *Professional Doctorate Awards in the UK.* Lichfield: UK Council for Graduate Education. Available at www.ukcge.ac.uk/OneStopCMS/Core/CrawlerResourceServer.aspx?resource=8793819F-95F4–4E23–96B0–7B12757BB1B6&mode=link&guid=a57997aa5a9f4450bb141144a86634e6

Samady, S. R. (2001), *Education and Afghan Society in the Twentieth Century.* Paris: United Nations Educational, Scientific and Cultural Organization Education Sector.

Sastry, T. and Bekhradnia, B. (2007), *Higher Education, Skills and Employer Engagement.* London: Higher Education Policy Unit. Available at www.hepi.ac.uk/pubdetail.asp?ID=232&DOC=Reports (HE skills).

Stromquist, N. P. and Monkman, K. (2000), *Globalization and Education: Integration and Contestation across Cultures.* Lanham, Boulder, New York, Toronto and Oxford: Rowman & Littlefield Publishers Inc.

Suarez-Orozco, M. (ed.) (2007), *Learning in the Global Era: International Perspectives on Globalization and Education.* Berkley and Los Angeles: University of California Press.

Tooley, J. (2006), *Educating Amaretch: Private Schools for the Poor and the New Frontier for Investors.* IFC and the Financial Times. Available at www.ifc.org/ifcext/ economics.nsf/AttachmentsByTitle/educating_amaretch_booklet.pdf/$FILE/educating_amaretch_booklet.pdf

—— (2009), *The Beautiful Tree: A Personal Journey into How the World's Poor are Educating Themselves.* Available at http://books.google.co.uk

—— and Dixon, P. (2005), *Private Education is Good for the Poor: A Study of Private Schools Serving the Poor in Low Income Countries.* Washington, DC: Cato Institute. Available at www.cato.org/pub_display.php?pub_id=5224

Visser, W. (2007), 'Corporate sustainability and the individual: a literature review', University of Cambridge Programme for Industry, Research Paper, Series 1. Available at www.cpi.cam.ac.uk/pdf/RP1%20Sustainability.pdf

Wedgwood, M. (2004), *Higher Education for the Workforce: Barriers and Facilitators to Employer Engagement.* Manchester: Manchester Metropolitan University (DIUS research Report). Available at www.dfes.gov.uk/research/data/uploadfiles/DIUS-RR-08-04.pdf

—— (2007), *Barriers and Facilitators to Employer Engagement.* Interim Report for DIUS. Available at www.universitiesuk.ac.uk/learningafterleitch/downloads/DfES%20Report.DOC

Journals

Comparative Education, www.tandf.co.uk/journals/titles/03050068.asp

Identity, Culture and Politics/Identité, culture et politique, www.codesria.org/Links/Publications/icp/issues.htm

International Journal of Development Education and Global Learning, www.trentham-books. co.uk/acatalog/ International_Journal_on_Development_Education_and_Global_Learning.htm

International Journal of Educational Development, www.ingentaconnect.com/content/els/07380593.

Jenda: A Journal of Culture and African Women Studies (JENDA), www.africaresource.com/jenda

Journal of Higher Education in Africa, www.codesria.org/Links/Publications/Journals/higher_education.htm

Research in Post-Compulsory Education, www.tandf.co.uk/journals/titles/13596748.asp

Social Marketing Quarterly, www.tandf.co.uk/journals/titles/15245004.asp

Selected Resources[1]

Theme	Resource	URL
The Global Policy Context	Action Aid	www.actionaid.org.uk/index.asp
	African Regional Sexuality Resource Centre (ARSRC), contains resources and networks on gender and sexuality in Africa	www.arsrc.org/publications/sia
	British Association for Comparative and international Education	www.baice.ac.uk
	Development Education Association	www.dea.org.uk
	DFID	www.dfid.gov.uk
	Education to Refugee Children	http://unesdoc.unesco.org/images/0013/001303/130372e.pdf
	E. G. West Centre	www.ncl.ac.uk/egwest
	European Union	http://europa.eu
	Learning Through Other Eyes	www.throughothereyes.org.uk
	OXFAM	www.oxfam.org.uk
	Pambazuka, an authoritative electronic weekly newsletter and platform for social justice in Africa	www.pambazuka.org
	Plan International	http://plan-international.org
	Plan UK	www.plan-uk.org/action/developmenteducation
	The Right to Education Project	www.right-to-education.org
	Royal Society of Arts, Manufactures and Commerce	www.thersa.org
	Save the Children	www.savethechildren.org.uk
	Small States	www.smallstates.net
	UNESCO	www.unesco.org
	UNITE	www.unitetheunion.com
	WEA	www.wea.org.uk
	World Bank	www.worldbank.org

Theme	*Resource*	*URL*
Community Integration and Inclusion	Active Learning for Active Citizenship programme for adult learning	www.communities.gov.uk
	Australian Universities Community Engagement Alliance	www.aucea.net.au
	Beacon for Public Engagement Programme	www.publicengagement.ac.uk
	Canadian Association for Community Service Learning	www.communityservicelearning.ca
	Community Higher Education Service Partnership	www.chesp.org.za
	Early Years – the organization for young children in Northern Ireland	www.early-years.org
	Marketing and Sales Standards Setting Body (MSSSB), 2008; National Occupational Standards for Social Marketing. MSSSB, London	www.msssb.org
	National Social Marketing Centre	www.nsmcentre.org.uk
	The Republic of Ireland with the Community Knowledge Initiative	www.nuigalwaycki.ie
Curriculum Reform	The Bordeaux Communiqué on enhanced European co-operation in vocational education and training	www.arqa-vet.at/fileadmin/download_files/Bordeaux_Communique_EN.pdf
	Campaign for Learning	www.campaign-for-learning.org.uk
	CEDEFOP/European Centre for the Development of Vocational Training	www.cedefop.eu.int
	The Copenhagen Declaration	www.bmbf.de/pub/copenhagen_declaration_eng_final.pdf
	European Commission: Education and Training 2010: Lisbon Strategy	http://ec.europa.eu/education/policies/2010/et_2010_en.html
	European Commission – Policy Areas – Vocational Training	http://ec.europa.eu/education/policies/training/training_en.html

Theme	Resource	URL
Curriculum Reform (*cont.*)	European Forum of Technical and Vocational Education and Training (EFVET)	www.efvet.org
	European Network on Quality Assurance in VET	www.enqavet.eu/welcome.html
	European Training Foundation (ETF)	www.etf.europa.eu
	Higher Education Academy	www.heacademy.ac.uk
	Institute for Work-based Learning, University of Middlesex	www.mdx.ac.uk/wbl/index.asp
	Leitch Review of Skills (2006), Prosperity for all in the global economy –World-class skills. Final report. Norwich: HMSO	www.dfes.gov.uk/ furthereducation/uploads/ documents/2006-12%20 LeitchReview1.pdf
	Maastricht Communiqué on the Future Priorities of Enhanced European Cooperation in Vocational Education and Training (VET)	http://ec.europa.eu/education/ news/ip/docs/maastricht_com_ en.pdf
	National Qualifications Authority (Ireland) (2006), Review of Professional Doctorates	http://escalate.ac.uk/4248
	Plagiarism prevention website	www.turnitin.com
	Qualifications and Credit Framework	www.qcda.gov.uk/19674.aspx
	Quality Assurance Agency for Higher Education (UK) website	www.qaa.ac.uk
	Universities Association for Lifelong Learning's Work-based Learning Network	http://homepage.ntlworld.com/ paul.ballard/james/UALL%20 learning%20network/about.html
	University Vocational Awards Council, Higher Learning by Doing	www.uvac.ac.uk/downloads/ practicallearning/newslet1
	Vocational and educational training – key for the future? Lisbon, Copenhagen, Maastricht: Mobilizing for 2010. CEDEFOP synthesis of the Maastricht study	http://ec.europa.eu/education/ policies/2010/studies/cedefop_ en.pdf
	Work-based Learning for Education Professionals	www.wlecentre.ac.uk/cms/index. php

Theme	Resource	URL
Learning and Pedagogy	BERA (British Educational Research Association)	www.bera.ac.uk
	CEDEFOP	www.cedefop.europa.eu
	Conducting impact assessments for equal opportunities in HE	www.hefce.ac.uk/pubs/ HEFCE/2004/04_37
	Development Education Association	www.dea.org.uk
	E-learning system website	www.blackboard.com
	FERA (Further Education Research Association)	www.fera.uk.net
	Global dimension – database of educational resources on global and development issues for schools	www.globaldimension.org.uk
	LearnHigher Centre of Excellence – resources to support students' learning	www.learnhigher.ac.uk
	Learning Through Other Eyes	www.throughothereyes.org.uk
	OECD	www.oecd.org
	QATRAIN disability projects (Quality Assurance and Accessible Training in Europe)	www.qatrain.eu www.qatrain2.eu
	Software for qualitative research	www.qsrinternational.com
	Strategies for Creating Inclusive Programmes of Study	www.scips.worc.ac.uk
	The Times Educational Supplement	www.tes.co.uk
	The Times Higher Education Supplement	www.timeshighereducation.co.uk
	UALL (Universities Association for Lifelong Learning)	www.uall.ac.uk
	Vocational education and training (VET) in Australia	www.ntis.gov.au www.training. com.au www.ncver.edu.au www.voced.edu.au

Note

1 Web links all accessed during December 2009.

Index

LIBRARY, UNIVERSITY OF CHESTER